Lecture Notes in Computer Science   14715

Founding Editors

Gerhard Goos
Juris Hartmanis

The series Lecture Notes in Computer Science (LNCS), including its subseries Lecture Notes in Artificial Intelligence (LNAI) and Lecture Notes in Bioinformatics (LNBI), has established itself as a medium for the publication of new developments in computer science and information technology research, teaching, and education.

LNCS enjoys close cooperation with the computer science R & D community, the series counts many renowned academics among its volume editors and paper authors, and collaborates with prestigious societies. Its mission is to serve this international community by providing an invaluable service, mainly focused on the publication of conference and workshop proceedings and postproceedings. LNCS commenced publication in 1973.

Aaron Marcus · Elizabeth Rosenzweig ·
Marcelo M. Soares

Editors

Design, User Experience, and Usability

13th International Conference, DUXU 2024
Held as Part of the 26th HCI International Conference, HCII 2024
Washington, DC, USA, June 29 – July 4, 2024
Proceedings, Part IV

Editors
Aaron Marcus
Principal
Aaron Marcus and Associates
Berkeley, CA, USA

Elizabeth Rosenzweig
World Usability Day and Bubble Mountain
Newton Center, MA, USA

Marcelo M. Soares
Federal University of Pernambuco
Recife, Pernambuco, Brazil

ISSN 0302-9743   ISSN 1611-3349 (electronic)
Lecture Notes in Computer Science
ISBN 978-3-031-61358-6   ISBN 978-3-031-61359-3 (eBook)
https://doi.org/10.1007/978-3-031-61359-3

This Springer imprint is published by the registered company Springer Nature Switzerland AG
The registered company address is: Gewerbestrasse 11, 6330 Cham, Switzerland

If disposing of this product, please recycle the paper.

Foreword

This year we celebrate 40 years since the establishment of the HCI International (HCII) Conference, which has been a hub for presenting groundbreaking research and novel ideas and collaboration for people from all over the world.

The HCII conference was founded in 1984 by Prof. Gavriel Salvendy (Purdue University, USA, Tsinghua University, P.R. China, and University of Central Florida, USA) and the first event of the series, "1st USA-Japan Conference on Human-Computer Interaction", was held in Honolulu, Hawaii, USA, 18–20 August. Since then, HCI International is held jointly with several Thematic Areas and Affiliated Conferences, with each one under the auspices of a distinguished international Program Board and under one management and one registration. Twenty-six HCI International Conferences have been organized so far (every two years until 2013, and annually thereafter).

Over the years, this conference has served as a platform for scholars, researchers, industry experts and students to exchange ideas, connect, and address challenges in the ever-evolving HCI field. Throughout these 40 years, the conference has evolved itself, adapting to new technologies and emerging trends, while staying committed to its core mission of advancing knowledge and driving change.

As we celebrate this milestone anniversary, we reflect on the contributions of its founding members and appreciate the commitment of its current and past Affiliated Conference Program Board Chairs and members. We are also thankful to all past conference attendees who have shaped this community into what it is today.

The 26th International Conference on Human-Computer Interaction, HCI International 2024 (HCII 2024), was held as a 'hybrid' event at the Washington Hilton Hotel, Washington, DC, USA, during 29 June – 4 July 2024. It incorporated the 21 thematic areas and affiliated conferences listed below.

A total of 5108 individuals from academia, research institutes, industry, and government agencies from 85 countries submitted contributions, and 1271 papers and 309 posters were included in the volumes of the proceedings that were published just before the start of the conference, these are listed below. The contributions thoroughly cover the entire field of human-computer interaction, addressing major advances in knowledge and effective use of computers in a variety of application areas. These papers provide academics, researchers, engineers, scientists, practitioners and students with state-of-the-art information on the most recent advances in HCI.

The HCI International (HCII) conference also offers the option of presenting 'Late Breaking Work', and this applies both for papers and posters, with corresponding volumes of proceedings that will be published after the conference. Full papers will be included in the 'HCII 2024 - Late Breaking Papers' volumes of the proceedings to be published in the Springer LNCS series, while 'Poster Extended Abstracts' will be included as short research papers in the 'HCII 2024 - Late Breaking Posters' volumes to be published in the Springer CCIS series.

I would like to thank the Program Board Chairs and the members of the Program Boards of all thematic areas and affiliated conferences for their contribution towards the high scientific quality and overall success of the HCI International 2024 conference. Their manifold support in terms of paper reviewing (single-blind review process, with a minimum of two reviews per submission), session organization and their willingness to act as goodwill ambassadors for the conference is most highly appreciated.

This conference would not have been possible without the continuous and unwavering support and advice of Gavriel Salvendy, founder, General Chair Emeritus, and Scientific Advisor. For his outstanding efforts, I would like to express my sincere appreciation to Abbas Moallem, Communications Chair and Editor of HCI International News.

July 2024   Constantine Stephanidis

HCI International 2024 Thematic Areas and Affiliated Conferences

- HCI: Human-Computer Interaction Thematic Area
- HIMI: Human Interface and the Management of Information Thematic Area
- EPCE: 21st International Conference on Engineering Psychology and Cognitive Ergonomics
- AC: 18th International Conference on Augmented Cognition
- UAHCI: 18th International Conference on Universal Access in Human-Computer Interaction
- CCD: 16th International Conference on Cross-Cultural Design
- SCSM: 16th International Conference on Social Computing and Social Media
- VAMR: 16th International Conference on Virtual, Augmented and Mixed Reality
- DHM: 15th International Conference on Digital Human Modeling & Applications in Health, Safety, Ergonomics & Risk Management
- DUXU: 13th International Conference on Design, User Experience and Usability
- C&C: 12th International Conference on Culture and Computing
- DAPI: 12th International Conference on Distributed, Ambient and Pervasive Interactions
- HCIBGO: 11th International Conference on HCI in Business, Government and Organizations
- LCT: 11th International Conference on Learning and Collaboration Technologies
- ITAP: 10th International Conference on Human Aspects of IT for the Aged Population
- AIS: 6th International Conference on Adaptive Instructional Systems
- HCI-CPT: 6th International Conference on HCI for Cybersecurity, Privacy and Trust
- HCI-Games: 6th International Conference on HCI in Games
- MobiTAS: 6th International Conference on HCI in Mobility, Transport and Automotive Systems
- AI-HCI: 5th International Conference on Artificial Intelligence in HCI
- MOBILE: 5th International Conference on Human-Centered Design, Operation and Evaluation of Mobile Communications

List of Conference Proceedings Volumes Appearing Before the Conference

1. LNCS 14684, Human-Computer Interaction: Part I, edited by Masaaki Kurosu and Ayako Hashizume
2. LNCS 14685, Human-Computer Interaction: Part II, edited by Masaaki Kurosu and Ayako Hashizume
3. LNCS 14686, Human-Computer Interaction: Part III, edited by Masaaki Kurosu and Ayako Hashizume
4. LNCS 14687, Human-Computer Interaction: Part IV, edited by Masaaki Kurosu and Ayako Hashizume
5. LNCS 14688, Human-Computer Interaction: Part V, edited by Masaaki Kurosu and Ayako Hashizume
6. LNCS 14689, Human Interface and the Management of Information: Part I, edited by Hirohiko Mori and Yumi Asahi
7. LNCS 14690, Human Interface and the Management of Information: Part II, edited by Hirohiko Mori and Yumi Asahi
8. LNCS 14691, Human Interface and the Management of Information: Part III, edited by Hirohiko Mori and Yumi Asahi
9. LNAI 14692, Engineering Psychology and Cognitive Ergonomics: Part I, edited by Don Harris and Wen-Chin Li
10. LNAI 14693, Engineering Psychology and Cognitive Ergonomics: Part II, edited by Don Harris and Wen-Chin Li
11. LNAI 14694, Augmented Cognition, Part I, edited by Dylan D. Schmorrow and Cali M. Fidopiastis
12. LNAI 14695, Augmented Cognition, Part II, edited by Dylan D. Schmorrow and Cali M. Fidopiastis
13. LNCS 14696, Universal Access in Human-Computer Interaction: Part I, edited by Margherita Antona and Constantine Stephanidis
14. LNCS 14697, Universal Access in Human-Computer Interaction: Part II, edited by Margherita Antona and Constantine Stephanidis
15. LNCS 14698, Universal Access in Human-Computer Interaction: Part III, edited by Margherita Antona and Constantine Stephanidis
16. LNCS 14699, Cross-Cultural Design: Part I, edited by Pei-Luen Patrick Rau
17. LNCS 14700, Cross-Cultural Design: Part II, edited by Pei-Luen Patrick Rau
18. LNCS 14701, Cross-Cultural Design: Part III, edited by Pei-Luen Patrick Rau
19. LNCS 14702, Cross-Cultural Design: Part IV, edited by Pei-Luen Patrick Rau
20. LNCS 14703, Social Computing and Social Media: Part I, edited by Adela Coman and Simona Vasilache
21. LNCS 14704, Social Computing and Social Media: Part II, edited by Adela Coman and Simona Vasilache
22. LNCS 14705, Social Computing and Social Media: Part III, edited by Adela Coman and Simona Vasilache

47. LNCS 14730, HCI in Games: Part I, edited by Xiaowen Fang
48. LNCS 14731, HCI in Games: Part II, edited by Xiaowen Fang
49. LNCS 14732, HCI in Mobility, Transport and Automotive Systems: Part I, edited by Heidi Krömker
50. LNCS 14733, HCI in Mobility, Transport and Automotive Systems: Part II, edited by Heidi Krömker
51. LNAI 14734, Artificial Intelligence in HCI: Part I, edited by Helmut Degen and Stavroula Ntoa
52. LNAI 14735, Artificial Intelligence in HCI: Part II, edited by Helmut Degen and Stavroula Ntoa
53. LNAI 14736, Artificial Intelligence in HCI: Part III, edited by Helmut Degen and Stavroula Ntoa
54. LNCS 14737, Design, Operation and Evaluation of Mobile Communications: Part I, edited by June Wei and George Margetis
55. LNCS 14738, Design, Operation and Evaluation of Mobile Communications: Part II, edited by June Wei and George Margetis
56. CCIS 2114, HCI International 2024 Posters - Part I, edited by Constantine Stephanidis, Margherita Antona, Stavroula Ntoa and Gavriel Salvendy
57. CCIS 2115, HCI International 2024 Posters - Part II, edited by Constantine Stephanidis, Margherita Antona, Stavroula Ntoa and Gavriel Salvendy
58. CCIS 2116, HCI International 2024 Posters - Part III, edited by Constantine Stephanidis, Margherita Antona, Stavroula Ntoa and Gavriel Salvendy
59. CCIS 2117, HCI International 2024 Posters - Part IV, edited by Constantine Stephanidis, Margherita Antona, Stavroula Ntoa and Gavriel Salvendy
60. CCIS 2118, HCI International 2024 Posters - Part V, edited by Constantine Stephanidis, Margherita Antona, Stavroula Ntoa and Gavriel Salvendy
61. CCIS 2119, HCI International 2024 Posters - Part VI, edited by Constantine Stephanidis, Margherita Antona, Stavroula Ntoa and Gavriel Salvendy
62. CCIS 2120, HCI International 2024 Posters - Part VII, edited by Constantine Stephanidis, Margherita Antona, Stavroula Ntoa and Gavriel Salvendy

https://2024.hci.international/proceedings

Preface

User experience (UX) refers to a person's thoughts, feelings, and behavior when using interactive systems. UX design becomes fundamentally important for new and emerging mobile, ubiquitous, and omnipresent computer-based contexts. The scope of design, user experience, and usability (DUXU) extends to all aspects of the user's interaction with a product or service, how it is perceived, learned, and used. DUXU also addresses design knowledge, methods, and practices, with a focus on deeply human-centered processes. Usability, usefulness, and appeal are fundamental requirements for effective user-experience design.

The 13th Design, User Experience, and Usability Conference (DUXU 2024), an affiliated conference of the HCI International conference, encouraged papers from professionals, academics, and researchers that report results and cover a broad range of research and development activities on a variety of related topics. Professionals include designers, software engineers, scientists, marketers, business leaders, and practitioners in fields such as AI, architecture, financial and wealth management, game design, graphic design, finance, healthcare, industrial design, mobile, psychology, travel, and vehicles.

This year's submissions covered a wide range of content across the spectrum of design, user-experience, and usability. The latest trends and technologies are represented, as well as contributions from professionals, academics, and researchers across the globe. The breadth of their work is indicated in the following topics covered in the proceedings, encompassing theoretical work, applied research across diverse application domains, UX studics, as well as discussions on contemporary technologies that reshape our interactions with computational products and services.

Five volumes of the HCII 2024 proceedings are dedicated to this year's edition of the DUXU Conference, covering topics related to:

- Information Visualization and Interaction Design, as well as Usability Testing and User Experience Evaluation;
- Designing Interactions for Intelligent Environments; Automotive Interactions and Smart Mobility Solutions; Speculative Design and Creativity;
- User Experience Design for Inclusion and Diversity; Human-Centered Design for Social Impact.
- Designing Immersive Experiences Across Contexts; Technology, Design, and Learner Engagement; User Experience in Tangible and Intangible Cultural Heritage;
- Innovative Design for Enhanced User Experience; Innovations in Product and Service Design.

The papers in these volumes were accepted for publication after a minimum of two single-blind reviews from the members of the DUXU Program Board or, in some cases, from Preface members of the Program Boards of other affiliated conferences. We would like to thank all of them for their invaluable contribution, support, and efforts.

July 2024

Aaron Marcus
Elizabeth Rosenzweig
Marcelo M. Soares

13th International Conference on Design, User Experience and Usability (DUXU 2024)

The full list with the Program Board Chairs and the members of the Program Boards of all thematic areas and affiliated conferences of HCII 2024 is available online at:

http://www.hci.international/board-members-2024.php

HCI International 2025 Conference

The 27th International Conference on Human-Computer Interaction, HCI International 2025, will be held jointly with the affiliated conferences at the Swedish Exhibition & Congress Centre and Gothia Towers Hotel, Gothenburg, Sweden, June 22–27, 2025. It will cover a broad spectrum of themes related to Human-Computer Interaction, including theoretical issues, methods, tools, processes, and case studies in HCI design, as well as novel interaction techniques, interfaces, and applications. The proceedings will be published by Springer. More information will become available on the conference website: https://2025.hci.international/.

General Chair
Prof. Constantine Stephanidis
University of Crete and ICS-FORTH
Heraklion, Crete, Greece
Email: general_chair@2025.hci.international

https://2025.hci.international/

Contents – Part IV

Technology, Design, and Learner Engagement

User Experience in Tangible and Intangible Cultural Heritage

Designing Immersive Experiences across Contexts

Exploring Student Attention in the Metaverse: A Systematic Literature Review from the Perspective of Design and Ergonomics

Layane Araújo[1,2]([⊠]) and Marcelo M. Soares[1]

[1] Federal University of Pernambuco, Recife, Brazil
layane.n.araujo@gmail.com
[2] Federal University of Alagoas, Maceió, Brazil

Abstract. This study aimed to provide a comprehensive overview of distance and immersive education's state of the art, specifically focusing on the metaverse in conjunction with ergonomics, design, educational environments, virtual reality, and attention. Conducted as a Systematic Literature Review (SLR) following the Preferred Reporting Items for Systematic Reviews and Meta-Analyses (PRISMA) method, the research targeted theoretical and methodological concepts, as well as methods and tools relevant to a thesis developed at the Federal University of Pernambuco. Searches were conducted across seven databases and additional sources, applying filters for peer-reviewed articles published in English, Portuguese, and Spanish in the last two decades (2003–2023). Exclusion criteria involved repeated works without focusing on key themes, research focusing on People with Disabilities (PwD), and studies exclusively addressing the metaverse. Sixteen keyword combinations were utilized, generating an initial pool of 6,161 papers. After a thorough screening, 45 studies were selected and classified into two groups. Group 1 focused on Metaverse and Virtual Reality in education. Group 2 highlighted Ergonomics in the Virtual Environment, and Metaverse applied to the social and educational context. However, the research identified a gap in scientific knowledge at the intersection of Metaverse, Attention, and Educational Environment from the perspectives of Ergonomics and Design Science Research.

Keywords: Metaverse · Immersive Education · Design · Ergonomics · Systematic Literature Review

1 Introduction

The study is based on the changes in educational paradigms, which occurred mainly after the Covid-2019 pandemic. According to Couto et al. (2020), teachers and students enrolled in previously "face-to-face" courses migrated to online educational activities after the pandemic.

According to Tori (2022), the new generations would not have the same psychological need to feel the physical proximity of their peers since young people usually meet virtually to study, talk, play video games, etc. In this way, the trend in teaching is moving towards hybrid learning, with the understanding that hybrid teaching students learn in both physical and virtual teaching environments.

Thus, this study focuses on inserting new technological resources to replace traditional teaching and provide a new approach to conventional physical classrooms. According to Tori (2022):

> In a metaverse environment, the avatar appears in the person's place, making them feel more at ease, without other colleagues feeling more distant, as they feel all together in the same environment. In addition, the gamified interface of these environments is enjoyable and easy to use for today's generations of students, even postgraduates (Tori 2022, p. 53).

Therefore, with the significant expansion of remote and online teaching practices, educational activities have been developed in metaverse environments, covering diverse areas such as military training (Siyaev and Jo 2021), health education (Koo 2021), educational science (Jovanović and Milosavljević 2022; Tori 2022), artistic expressions (Tasa and Görgülü 2010; Choi and Kim 2017), among others.

According to Tori (2022), Metaverses are multi-user online interactive digital spaces in which people interact with the environment and other users through avatars, which function as representations of themselves, controlled by themselves in these spaces.

According to the same author, the advantage of using metaverses is that they are particular cases of virtual reality, can be utilized as virtual learning environments, and have the characteristics of multi-user games.

The designer is the professional in charge of conceiving, developing, and configuring a variety of artifacts, environments, services, and elements in real and virtual realities. In its turn, Ergonomics is a discipline that optimizes user comfort, satisfaction, and safety and becomes essential in design activities. Ergonomics ensures that the product satisfactorily meets its purpose, resulting in greater acceptance by the user.

When applied in educational contexts, Ergonomics must consider various factors, including, among others, physical, cognitive, social, organizational, and environmental aspects (referring to the workspace). In addition, its applicability extends to the design of educational environments, covering both physical and virtual environments.

According to Attaianese and Duca (2012), environments influence people's daily lives. Thus, based on Ahmad, Osman and Halim (2013), students perform better when they like the teaching environment. In this framework, the design of the teaching environment can be improved from the perspective of human factors and design to meet the needs of education professionals and students.

As noted by Iida and Buarque (2016), ergonomics has shown a growing interest in teaching activities, helping to make them more efficient. Also, according to the authors, ergonomic proposals for educational environments must consider the following factors: the teaching process, the compatibility of the educational process, assessment methods, infrastructure, and the teaching environment, equipment, and teaching materials.

According to the Brazilian Association of Ergonomics (ABERGO 2023), the application of ergonomics in educational environments and the professional field adopts an interdisciplinary approach, playing a crucial role in assessing the environment and the impacts of the tasks performed. By integrating ergonomic elements into the design of educational environments, it becomes feasible to develop spaces that are more conducive to learning and, as a result, maintain students' attention.

Lima (2005) states that attention plays a crucial role in enabling individuals to interact effectively with their environment and providing support for the organization of mental processes. Through attention, it is possible to select which stimuli will be examined in detail to the detriment of others, thus guiding the behavior.

Kastrup (2004), Araújo (2020), Lima, Queiroz and Sant'anna (2018) call attention to the importance of the relationship between attention and learning and the teaching environment.

A Systematic Literature Review (SLR) was carried out in seven databases in the following languages: English, Portuguese, and Spanish. The SLR covered the last 20 years to scientifically support a doctoral thesis carried out at the Federal University of Pernambuco, Brazil.

The materials and methods used in this study are explained below.

2   Materials and Methods

The Systematic Literature Review aimed to synthesize the state of the art based on recent productions on the following themes: Design, Ergonomics, Educational Environment, Metaverse, Virtual Reality, and Attention.

A qualitative systematic review was carried out based on the PRISMA (Preferred Reporting Items for Systematic Reviews and Meta-Analyses) method. This method is based on a revised and updated method named QUOROM (Quality Of Reporting Of Meta-analyses). It was made due to the need to differentiate between Systematic Reviews and Meta-Analyses.

According to the Brazilian Ministry of Health (2012), PRISMA assists authors in improving the quality of their SR (Systematic Review) and Meta-analysis data reporting. It also helps critically evaluate a review and meta-analysis that has already been published.

The Systematic Review of this study was carried out by consulting seven databases: Scielo, Scopus, IEEE, Web of Science, Science Research, Pubmed, and Science Direct. The general aim of the search was to identify theoretical and methodological concepts, methods, and tools that could be used in the ergonomic analysis of learning spaces, analysis of the environment, perception of those involved in the study (students, education professionals, and specialists), and analysis of student attention in teaching spaces, especially in metaverses.

To this end, the terms were combined: Metaverse, Virtual Reality, Education, Educational Environment, Virtual Learning Environment, Attention, Design, Design Science Research, and Ergonomics.

The search occurred from August to October 2022 and again in September 2023. The inclusion criteria were articles and book chapters published in English, Portuguese, and/or Spanish in the last 20 years (2003/2023) filtered by peers.

The exclusion criteria were repeated works without focusing on the keywords, research that had feedback applied to the educational environment involving People with Disabilities (PwD), and studies that only addressed the metaverse.

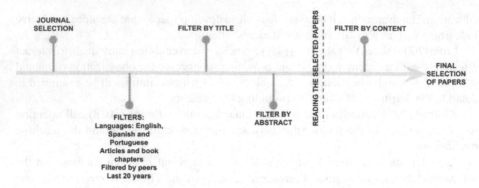

Fig. 1. Steps of the PRISMA method. Source: The authors (2023).

Figure 1 summarizes the steps taken in the search based on the PRISMA method.

A search was therefore carried out on the titles of the papers found. The first 100 titles in each group were checked to analyze and separate the most relevant articles. The first search by title returned a total of **6.161 papers,** having already established the filters

Table 1. Keyword combinations in Portuguese and English

Groups	Combinations
1	"Metaverso" AND "Realidade Virtual"
2	"Metaverse" AND "Virtual Reality"
3	"Metaverso" AND "Ambiente Educacional" NOT "Ambiente Virtual de Aprendizagem"
4	"Metaverse" AND "Educational Environment" NOT "Virtual Learning Environment"
5	"Metaverso"; "Ambiente Educacional" AND "Atenção"
6	"Metaverse" AND "Educational Environment" AND "Attention"
7	"Design" AND "Metaverso"
8	"Design" AND "Metaverse"
9	"Design Science Research" AND "Metaverso"
10	"Design Science Research" AND "Metaverse"
11	"Ergonomia" AND "Metaverso"
12	"Ergonomics"; "Human Factors" AND "Metaverse"
13	"Design"; "Ambiente Educacional" AND "Ergonomia"
14	"Design"; "Educational Environment" AND "Human Factors"; "Ergonomics"
15	"Metaverso"; "Educação" AND "Atenção"
16	"Metaverse"; "Education" AND "Attention"

Fonte: The authors (2023).

by peer, language, and publication period. **Sixteen different combinations** were using the keywords in Portuguese and English, as shown in Table 1.

The Booleans chosen for the searches were AND and NOT. Since using the OR Boolean meant that the search results were too broad, they were not directed towards the research itself. By title, a total of **115 papers** were returned.

The analysis showed that groups 5 and 6, 9 and 10, 11 and 12, and 15 and 16 did not obtain any results in any of the seven databases. This analysis shows a gap in scientific knowledge in the fields that unite Metaverse, Attention, and Educational Environment from the perspective of Ergonomics and Design Science Research.

Subsequently, a search was carried out in the abstracts of the papers previously selected by title to specify those that should be analyzed in full. This search returned a total of **76 relevant studies** to the research, analyzing theoretical and methodological concepts, methods, and tools that could be used to support the thesis mentioned above.

After reading the papers, **45 studies** consistent with the research were selected. The infographic in Fig. 2 illustrates the evolution of searches up to this point using the PRISMA method.

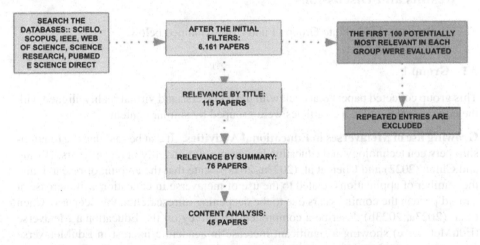

Fig. 2. Steps of the PRISMA method. Source: The authors (2023).

The papers selected by content were separated into two distinct groups: Group 1 and Group 2, as can be seen in Fig. 3. The first group focused on research that returned content relating to Metaverse and Virtual Reality applied to the context of education. In the second group, we highlight works that returned to Ergonomics in the Virtual Environment, and Metaverse applied to the social and educational context.

The other papers that did not pass this stage because they only dealt with Metaverse without any of the main focuses required for the study could be used as a theoretical contribution to the thesis. The results of the Systematic Review will be presented in the following section.

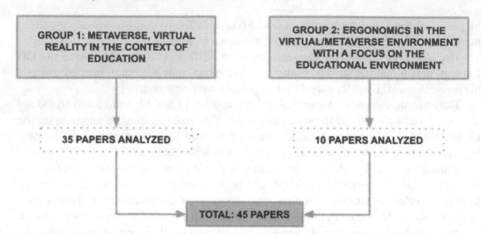

Fig. 3. Papers analyzed by content, separated by groups. Source: The authors (2023).

3   Results and Discussions

The results were divided into Groups 1 and 2, as explained below.

3.1   Group 1

This group collected papers that dealt with the metaverse and virtual reality aligned with the educational context. The articles were grouped by similar content.

Growing use of Metaverses in Educational Activities. It can be said that the relationship between technology and education has grown significantly in recent years. Hwang and Chien (2022) and Chen et al. (2023a, 2023b) state that the amount of research and the number of applications related to the use of metaverse in education will increase at a rapid pace in the coming years due to the deepening of research in this scenario. Chen et al. (2023a, 2023b) describe a comprehensive survey on the Educational Metaverse (EduMetaverse) showing a significant increase in academic interest in EduMetaverse from 2019 onwards.

Hao and Lailin (2022) corroborate with the above authors, arguing that a challenge to be overcome is building a high-quality and effective educational metaverse environment, sensibly taking advantage of the new technological features of the educational metaverse.

Furthermore, Dahan et al. (2022) warn that applications not running on the Metaverse will soon be abandoned, as the Metaverse is considered a significant transformation in the internet world.

Contributions to the Use of Metaverses in Education. Schlemmer and Backes (2015) believe that developing online education in the metaverse can raise the quality of education on the world educational stage through pedagogical proposals.

Kye et al. (2021) and Hines and Netland (2022), state that the metaverse is a helpful addition to teaching and is especially promising when used in a blended teaching approach. For example, in their study, Lee and Jo (2023) investigated students' experience in a problem-based learning (PBL) curriculum using Metaverse. The results showed that the participants were fascinated by the new features and functions of the metaverse in creating virtual spaces. Thus, to evaluate users' experiences in educational and practical activities in the metaverse, López-Belmonte et al. (2022) propose using evaluative questionnaires as valid and reliable instruments.

The studies by Till et al. (2022) have shown that implementing Metaverse can expand educational opportunities to explore historically inaccessible environments due to space, time, and cost barriers, thus solving real-world problems in virtual worlds.

Thus, in the research by Lee et al. (2022), using the metaverse platform in university education can enhance active participation in class, immersion, promotion of student interaction, greater personalization, increased creativity, high motivation, and engagement. In addition, it can extend traditional learning, offering experiences that would otherwise be very difficult. Based on this, Amemiya (2023), in his study, explains that the true potential of these metaverse platforms lies in proposing educational activities and training that can only be carried out in VR or that are primarily possible in the Metaverse.

Furthermore, Suh and Ahn (2022) revealed in their study in South Korea that, on average, 97.9% of elementary school students have had experiences with the metaverse, and 95.5% consider it closely related to their daily lives.

Guo and Gao (2022), based on their analysis of experimental data in three types of learning activities, showed that experiential situational English teaching with a metaverse could improve students' sense of interactivity, immersion, and cognition.

Virtual Reality and Metaverse. Jin et al. (2022) compared previous studies in educational VR and identified new empirical insights in the context of metaverse use, regardless of the course. They proposed classroom and subject configurations from a multistakeholder perspective, contributing to designing better VR technologies in higher education. Ortega-Rodríguez (2022), Till et al. (2022), and Dahan et al. (2022) stated that virtual reality offers a greater sense of immersion and presence than traditional teaching methodologies.

From the point of view of user perception in the metaverse, Liu (2022) and Hedrick et al. (2022) carried out a case study. They stated that VR offered students a completely different learning experience, composed of novelty, thus stimulating interest in learning. Students are visibly more involved in discussions in the virtual environment than in a live broadcast.

In addition, Lee and Hwang (2022) have shown in their studies that transformative experiences of realizing VR for instructional content are conducive to empowering teachers' technological readiness in training, thus promoting the implementation of the 4Cs (Critical Thinking, Creativity, Collaboration, and Communication).

Metaverse Applied to Math Teaching and Gamification. Enrique and Reyes (2020) and Mystakidis and Christopoulos (2022) demonstrated in their results that the incorporation of Augmented Reality facilitates not only the learning of mathematics but also allows students to go to teaching places motivated and taking active roles in the construction of knowledge. In addition, alternative instructional solutions can potentially increase cognitive benefits and learning outcomes.

Damaševičius and Sidekersniene (2023) applied the design and implementation of immersive and gamified experiences in the Metaverse as a means of enhancing student learning in mathematics, demonstrating how these principles can be effectively applied in a Metaverse environment to promote greater student engagement and motivation.

Also, based on gamified activities, Jin and Tiejun (2023) state that virtual game learning promotes teaching reform in colleges and universities. Such activities encourage learners to develop higher-order thinking skills such as creativity and criticism, solving the problems of traditional teaching and encouraging learners to move from "outside the teaching scene" to "inside the teaching scene" and from "outside knowledge" to "inside knowledge". This knowledge leads to a new direction for the future teaching mode.

Online Learning, E-Learning, and Metaverse. Vernaza et al. (2012) argue that implementing a virtual world to support e-learning systems provides exciting features such as flexibility, adaptation, and accessibility.

The studies by Jeong et al. (2022) demonstrate the importance of establishing an integrated digital learning platform in the metaverse context, as they help to minimize the distance between students by getting them much more involved with online courses. In this regard, Tamai et al. (2011) implemented an e-learning platform where students from abroad could learn the Japanese language and culture in a 3D metaverse environment developed in Second Life.

Lou and Xu (2022) state that combining learning theories related to online learning can contribute to the development of the PERMA model - Positive (P), Engagement (E), Relationship (R), Meaning (M), and Achievement (A), in positive education.

The research by Wagner et al. (2013) stood out for supporting technologies for distance learning and Massive Open Online Courses (MOOCs). Zahedi et al. (2023) presented a model of a virtual e-learning environment in Metaverse containing essential elements and infrastructures. Ryu et al. (2023) developed an online learning system based on Metaverse to evaluate its usability. The platform chosen was Gather.town.

Lee and Jo (2023) explored the potential of the metaverse for nursing students through online simulation learning methods. As a result, the authors concluded that the metaverse enables reflective learning based on experiential learning and strengthens awareness of different points of view.

Finally, Chen et al. (2023a, 2023b) highlight challenges, such as data security and privacy protection, and areas that need more attention, including preparing instructors for the Edu-Metaverse.

Design and Metaverse. Seiari et al. (2023) presented the design and implementation of a prototype metaverse classroom system that uses virtual and augmented reality technologies to enhance the educational experience. The prototype was developed using Unity 3D modeling software. The paper also discusses the benefits of the metaverse classroom system, such as increased student engagement and collaboration, as well as its limitations and potential improvements.

Böckle et al. (2023) and Chen et al. (2023a, 2023b) proposed a framework for metaverse. The first group of authors proposed a design framework including a three-phase model composed of the business opportunity, design, and construction stages; the framework developed was based on current metaverse literature, as well as an exploratory analysis of use cases, taking into account the Mechanics-Dynamics-Aesthetics (MDA) game design approach.

The second group proposed a five-layer framework for the Educational Metaverse, covering physical layers of computational data, interaction, and application. In addition, design criteria were presented for three key elements (virtual avatars, virtual learning resources, and virtual teaching scenarios) and modes of interaction.

Still considering the design and the metaverse, Rahman et al. (2023) developed a metaverse teaching space using the Mozilla Hubs platform. To this end, the authors listed design principles to propose a space with better academic performance.

Notably, the relationship between the Metaverse and the educational context is a topic of investigation in several studies that highlight the relevance of this growing scenario and its implications for the performance of activities and user interaction. In addition, such relationships meet the needs and demands that the conventional educational system often fails to deal with, to the detriment of developing more efficient and innovative structures. However, it is essential to say that Metaverse constantly evolves to improve its resources, strategies, and tools.

3.2 Group 2

In this group, we found papers that dealt with Ergonomics applied to the Virtual Environment and other Metaverse papers applied to education in theoretical contexts. The articles were grouped by similar content.

Immersive Virtual Environment and User Perception. When it comes to Immersive Virtual Environments (IVE) and their interrelationship with user perception, studies by Niu and Lo (2020), Mandolfo et al. (2022), Phillips et al. (2021), Tugtekin and Odabasi (2022) and Bale et al. (2022) showed that the sensations caused by Immersive Virtual Environments, such as the Metaverse, are characterized by peculiar experiences, since recording users' sensations and perceptions can reveal a space that has not yet been explored.

Niu and Lo (2020), Mandolfo et al. (2022), and Phillips et al. (2021) found that when there is quality in the scenarios, e.g., attention to the representation of the materials, elements, and configurations of the Immersive Virtual Environments, the results of the experiments proved to be very relevant thus ensuring greater user satisfaction and interest when compared to the same situation in the 2D field.

Considering the interaction of students in the metaverse field, Ge's (2022) studies show that due to the arrival of metaverses, various types of behavior in university students have been expanded since the effects caused by this technology have enriched such behaviors. These aspects go hand in hand with others existing, such as social networks, gaming platforms, etc. Such experiences are relative according to age, hobbies, and interests, among others.

In other words, Immersive Virtual Environments features can quickly engage users, which means that high-quality immersive interfaces, greater spatial vivacity, and the perception of control over the experience can be engaging elements during Immersive Virtual Environments navigation (Mandolfo et al. 2022).

Focusing on the educational scenario, Tugtekin and Odabasi (2022) explained that comparing experienced and inexperienced learners using interactive learning environments is necessary to understand the effect of instructional materials manipulated with multimedia principles on students' cognitive load and learning outcomes.

Ergonomics and Virtual Learning Environments. Ergonomics applied to virtual environments in the educational context is indispensable for developing strategies to improve the learning process. Thus, Dzakiria and Mohamad (2014) showed in their research that the interrelationship of the three fields of physical, mental, and organizational ergonomics are fundamentals for supporting and improving students' performance results and learning conditions in distance learning activities.

Focusing on this context, the tool called Pedagogical Ergonomic Tool for Educational Software Evaluation (PETESE), developed by Coomans and Lacerda (2015), has shown significant support for instructional designers and developers looking to improve the learning process, especially in the field of mathematics.

To this end, Stone's (2008) research corroborates the relationship between ergonomics and Immersive Virtual Environments, as he has shown that human factors and ergonomic knowledge can benefit the educational system. However, there is a need to constantly evaluate the benefits of new technologies in the classroom, in addition to the environmental design elements of the educational area.

However, regarding users' postures, research by Phillips et al. (2021) has shown that a sudden change in Immersive Virtual Environments at any speed can help induce postural instability and thus compromise the user's safety. For this reason, the authors emphasize care in the optic flow when the Immersive Virtual Environments hold different speeds and durations.

Finally, considering the relationship between the Metaverse and Universal Design, it can be said that Hutson's work (2022) demonstrated the need to implement accessibility resources for neurotypical people because it was seen in the author's studies, gaps concerning social interaction on the part of users with Autism Spectrum Disorder (ASD) and introverted people in online courses. The author mentioned above concluded that the preferences of introverted people include environments with low stimulation, while extroverts are described as energized by social interaction. However, given the right strategies, Immersive Virtual Environments can provide opportunities for socialization and collaboration between both audiences.

Therefore, it was concluded for Group 2 that ergonomics is an essential factor for Immersive Virtual Environments and Metaverse because the studies discussed showed guidelines and/or strategies aimed at improving the quality of these environments and thus promoting better experiences for the users of these spaces.

3.3   Other Searches

Other searches were also carried out on the Portals of Thesis and Dissertations on the Journal Portal of the Coordination for the Improvement of Higher Education Personnel (CAPES) journals database, on Google Scholar, and the database of the Federal University of Pernambuco, Brazil.

These searches found documents related to this study's subject because they dealt with education, the educational environment, and attention. However, they do not address the metaverse. These theses are: 'Conceptual Model of Learning Environment Suitable for Practices with Blended Learning for high schools', by Thaísa Sarmento, published in 2018, and the thesis 'The Role of the Built Environment on Education: the Influence on Attention and the Relationship with Learning', by Maiana Cunha Araújo, published in 2020.

The main focus of the first project was to develop a Conceptual Model of a Learning Environment suitable for blended learning practices for secondary schools, with innovations in interior design.

In this research, Sarmento (2018) studied the educational paradigm shift from traditional teaching, initially centered on the teacher, to a new approach - collaborative and user-centered - in which the learning environment welcomes users to contribute positively to their learning through technological resources, ergonomic suitability, and emotional satisfaction.

The research was conducted using the Design Science Research method (Dresch et al. 2015), in triangulation with ergonomic analysis and design methods - Ergonomic Methodology for the Built Environment (Villarouco 2009) and some steps of the Ergonomic Design Methodology (Attaianese and Duca 2012). In the end, four main products contributed to practical implications in new architectural and interior design projects, acting as a reference for sizing and specifying elements, furniture, and equipment for school environments.

In the second thesis, Araújo (2020) deals with the Ergonomics of the Built Environment applied to the analysis of teaching environments. The research aimed to identify the influence of the teaching environment on learning, and so, based on bibliographic surveys, the author verified the possibility of proving this relationship through the interference of the environment on students' attention.

The research took place in two public schools in Recife-Brazil, whose characteristics allowed for comparing their data. An ergonomic analysis of the classrooms was carried out using the Ergonomic Methodology for the Built Environment (Villarouco 2009), and the Psychological Battery for the Assessment of Attention (Rueda 2013) was employed to analyze attention. A relationship was thus established between the environment and attention, with students using classrooms that were better assessed in terms of ergonomic environmental aspects performing better in the test applied. It was also identified that specific environmental factors directly related to attention and the finding related to comfort indices and student perception.

From these works, we felt the need to explore the subject of attention and the educational environment and how attention depends on the educational environment. Given this, the environment can provide a restorative space that helps its users' behavior, conduct, and performance. Thus, the concept of restorative environment, an original term from environmental psychology, is used to describe the process of feelings aroused by the environment, which can have a positive influence on an individual's health and well-being (Kaplan and Kaplan 1982a, 1982b; Altman and Wohlwill 1983; Korpela 1989).

The idea of restorative environments has its roots in the theories developed by Rachel and Stephen Kaplan, as well as Roger Ulrich (R. Kaplan & Kaplan 1989; S. Kaplan 1995; Ulrich 1983, 1984).

The studies conducted by Kaplan and Kaplan (1989) investigate how the characteristics of environments, whether natural or built, can recover the fatigue and attention of their users. According to the authors, restorative environments are those that facilitate the renewal of focused attention, leading to a reduction in mental fatigue; in short, the space must establish conditions for this attention to reach a state of equilibrium.

According to Ulrich (1991), an environment is characterized as restorative when it does not impose stressful demands but instead favors the awakening of interest, pleasure, or calm in the user. Restoration, in this context, refers to recovering or renewing individuals' psychological and social resources, which can be affected by the demands imposed by contemporary environments. Ulrich (1983) also considered some aspects of nature, such as water and vegetation, capable of promoting psychophysiological recovery from stress.

Thus, taking into account the observations and research of Hartig et al. (2003), the two theories examined, both that of R. Kaplan and Kaplan (1989) and that of Ulrich (1983, 1984), show similarities in attributing restorative functions to natural environments.

Since metaverse teaching environments are virtual reality (VR) environments and do not provide natural landscapes, there are doubts about the applicability of Attention Restoration Theory (ART) in this context. However, a more comprehensive search of the literature revealed several studies that applied ART to digital environments, known as mediated restorative environments (De Kort and Ijsselsteijn 2006; Mayer, Frantz, Bruehlman-Senecal, & Dolliver 2009), as follows.

The studies by Laumann et al. (2001), in which the authors present videos of walks in the forest, in the park, on the beach, in the city, and in snowy mountains, to evaluate the restorative characteristics of the images presented and claim that the videos were able to predict users' preference for five different environments.

The research by Kahn Jr et al. (2008), with an experimental model in which the authors used a room with a plasma TV that projected scenes of nature, a room with a window to a park, and another room without windows, and concluded that although the window to the park was the best of the three options analyzed, the images seen on a plasma TV were a better option than no nature in the space.

And finally, Araújo's (2023) study investigated the environmental factors in teaching spaces with views of natural landscapes as restorers of student attention. To this end, the author carried out an experiment consisting of a teaching activity on a metaverse platform, in which 36 students were subjected to three types of environments: environment A - closed environment without windows, environment, B - semi-open environment with windows and views of landscapes, and environment C - open environment with views of landscapes. In the end, it was concluded that there are no right or wrong environments, but there are environments that are more suitable for certain types of activities. Therefore, the recommendations were: open or semi-open spaces are required for carrying out activities that require concentrated and/or divided attention, while closed spaces are recommended for educational activities that require the student to pay attention to one stimulus or another.

Therefore, according to Oliveira et al. (2019), a welcoming and restorative educational environment should improve students' health, representing relevant issues about public health, the environment, and social and institutional politics.

4 Final Considerations

The contributions of the Systematic Review were excellent, both in the theoretical and methodological fields of the study. Through the Systematic Review, methodologies and tools were identified that could be adapted to the situation of focus of the thesis developed:

- The Design Science Research methodology;
- Steps of the Ergonomic Methodology for the Built Environment (Villarouco 2009) and the importance of analyzing the user's perception of the teaching environment;
- Design principles (Rahman et al. 2023) that can help to develop comparative parameters for choosing the metaverse platform for the thesis experiment;
- The psychological tool for assessing student attention in the physical teaching environment, the Psychological Battery for the Assessment of Attention (Araújo 2020), as an option for evaluating students' attention before and during the metaverse experiment;
- Questionnaire tool to measure the results obtained from the experiment and the student's experience in the analyzed space;
- Gamification methods to propose more dynamic and immersive activities in the metaverse space, and;
- The Attention Restoration Theory (ART) helped analyze the environmental factors in the metaverse that may or may not influence the restoration of students' attention.

In addition, a survey of the articles in the databases searched revealed a variety of locations in the studies found.

Group 1 found articles from 13 countries, with South Korea, China, and the USA appearing most frequently. In addition, most of the studies are recent, with 12 studies from 2023, 17 from 2022, one from 2021, one from 2020, one from 2013, one from 2012, and one from 2011.

Group 2 found studies from seven countries, with the USA and China standing out. This group was more balanced in terms of the year of publication, with four studies from 2022, two from 2021, one from 2020, one from 2015, one from 2014, and one from 2008.

Thus, it can be said that the studies presented in Group 1 (Metaverse and Virtual Reality in the context of education) and Group 2 (Ergonomics in the Virtual Environment and Metaverse with a focus on the educational environment) of the Systematic Review were fundamental for the analytical construction of the concepts pointed out in the theoretical framework of the thesis, as well as for understanding the structures and strategies that supported the development of the research.

This statement comes from the results analyzed in Group 1, which corroborated the understanding that the development of online education in the metaverse can contribute to raising the quality of education in the global educational scenario through proposals encompassing Critical Thinking, Creativity, Collaboration, and Communication.

From the point of view of the works evaluated in Group 2, there was a reflection on the elements of the Immersive Virtual Environment that can influence users' environmental and postural perceptions. Furthermore, it was found that the interrelationship between the three fields of ergonomics (physical, mental, and organizational) contributes to the quality of learning conditions for students in distance learning activities.

References

ABERGO (Brazilian Association of Ergonomics). What is Ergonomics? https://www.abergo.org.br/o-que-%C3%A9-ergonomia/. Accessed Mar 2023

Che Ahmad, C.N., Osman, K., Halim, L.: Physical and psychosocial aspects of the learning environment in the science laboratory and their relationship to teacher satisfaction. Learn. Environ. Res. 16(3), 367–385 (2013). https://doi.org/10.1007/s10984-013-9136-8

Altman, I., Wohlwill, J.F.: Behavior and the Natural Environment, 6th edn. Plenum, New York and London (1983)

Amemiya, T.: The potential of the metaverse to transform education and training. Brain Nerve 75(10), 1107–1113 (2023)

Araújo, M.C.: O papel do ambiente construído sobre a educação: a influência sobre a atenção e a relação com o aprendizado. Thesis (Doctorate in Design) – Centro de Artes e Co-municação, Universidade Federal de Pernambuco, Recife (2020)

Araújo, L.N.: A atenção dos alunos no metaverso: um estudo sobre a concepção de ambien-tes de aprendizagem no metaverso, à luz do Design e da Ergonomia. Thesis (Doctorate in Design) – Centro de Artes e Comunicação, Universidade Federal de Pernambuco, Recife (2023)

Attaianese, E., Duca, G.: Human factors and ergonomic principles in building design for life and work activities: an applied methodology. Theor. Issues Ergon. Sci. 13(2), 187–202 (2012)

BRAZIL: Ministry of Health, Secretariat of Science, Technology and Strategic Inputs. Department of Science and Technology. S Me. [s.I: s.n.] (2012)

Bale, A., Ghorpade, N., Hashim, M., Vaishnav, J., Almaspoor, Z.: A comprehensive study on metaverse and its impacts on humans. Adv. Hum. Comput. Interact., 1–11 (2022). https://doi.org/10.1155/2022/3247060

Böckle, M., Booler-Stewart, F., Woolsey, K.: How to design for the metaverse: a strategic design perspective. In: IEEE International Conference on Metaverse Computing, Networking and Applications (MetaCom), Kyoto, pp. 99–103 (2023). https://doi.org/10.1109/MetaCom57706.2023.00029

Bürdek, B.E.: História, Teoria e Prática do Design de Produtos. Tradução Freddy Van Camp. Edgard Blücher, São Paulo (2010)

Chen, X., Zhong, Z., Wu, D.: Metaverse for education: technical framework and design criteria. IEEE Trans. Learn. Technol. (2023a). https://doi.org/10.1109/TLT.2023.3276760

Chen, X., Zou, D., Xie, H., Wang, F.L.: Metaverse in education: contributors, cooperations, and research themes. IEEE Trans. Learn. Technol., 1–18 (2023b). https://doi.org/10.1109/TLT.2023.3277952

Choi, H.S., Kim, S.H.: A content service deployment plan for metaverse museum exhibitions - centering on the combination of beacons and HMDs. Int. J. Inf. Manag. 37(1), 1519–1527 (2017)

Coomans, S., Lacerda, G.S.: PETESE, a pedagogical ergonomic tool for educational software evaluation. Procedia Manuf. 3, 5881–5888 (2015)

Couto, E.S., Couto, E.S., Cruz, I.d.M.P.: #Fiqueemcasa: Educação na Pandemia da Covid-19. Educação 8(3), 200–217 (2020). https://doi.org/10.17564/2316-3828.2020v8n3p200-217

Dahan, N.A., Al-Razgan, M., Al-Laith, A., Alsoufi, M.A., Al-Asaly, S.M., Alfakih, T.: Metaverse framework: a case study on e-learning environment (ELEM). Electronics **11**(10) (2022)

Damaševičius, R., Sidekersniene, T.: Designing immersive gamified experiences in the metaverse for enhanced student learning. In: International Conference on Intelligent Metaverse Technologies & Applications (iMETA), Tartu, Estonia, pp. 1–6 (2023). https://doi.org/10.1109/iMETA5 9369.2023.10294971

De Kort, Y.A.W., Ijsselsteijn, W.A.: Reality check: the role of realism in stress reduction using media technology. Cyberpsychol. Behav. **9**(2), 230–233 (2006). https://doi.org/10.1089/cpb. 2006.9.230

Dresch, A., Lacerda, D.P., Antunes Junior, J.A.V.: Design Science Research: Método de Pesquisa para Avanço da Ciência e Tecnologia. Bookman, Porto Alegre (2015). 181 p.

Dzakiria, H., Mohamad, B.: Communicating effectively the lifelong blue print and its demands to improve open distance learning (ODL) ergonomics. Procedia Soc. Behav. Sci. **155**, 539–546 (2014). https://doi.org/10.1016/j.sbspro.2014.10.336

Enrique, C., Reyes, G.: Percepción de estudiantes de bachillerato sobre el uso de Metaverse en experiencias de aprendizaje de realidad aumentada en matemáticas. Revista de Medios y Educación **58**, 143–159 (2020)

Ge, J.: Multiple influences of intelligent technology on network behavior of college students in the metaverse age. J. Environ. Public Health (2022). https://doi.org/10.1155/2022/2750712

Gil, A.C.: Como elaborar projetos de pesquisa. 6th edn. Atlas, São Paulo (2008)

Guo, H., Gao, W.: Metaverse-powered experiential situational English- teaching design: an emotion-based analysis method. Front. Psychol. **13** (2022). https://doi.org/10.3389/fpsyg.2022. 859159

Hartig, T., Evans, G.W., Jamner, L.D., Davis, D.S., Gärling, T.: Tracking restoration in natural and urban field settings. J. Environ. Psychol. **23**(2), 109–123 (2003)

Hao, T., Lailin, H.: Educational metaverse dilemmas and solutions: a stakeholderbased perspective. In: 12th International Conference on Information Technology in Medicine and Education (ITME), Xiamen, China, pp. 714–718 (2022). https://doi.org/10.1109/ITME56794.2022. 00150

Hedrick, E., Harper, M., Oliver, E., Hatch, D.: Teaching & learning in virtual reality: metaverse classroom exploration. In: Intermountain Engineering, Technology and Computing (IETC), OREM, UT, USA, pp. 1–5 (2022). https://doi.org/10.1109/IETC54973.2022.9796765

Hines, P., Netland, T.H.: Teaching a lean masterclass in the metaverse. Int. J. Lean Six Sigma (2022). https://doi.org/10.1108/IJLSS-02-2022-0035

Hutson, J.: Social virtual reality: neurodivergence and inclusivity in the metaverse. Societies MDPI **12**(4), 1–7 (2022)

Hwang, G.-J., Chien, S.-Y.: Definition, roles, and potential research issues of the metaverse in education: an artificial intelligence perspective. Comput. Educ. Artif. Intell. **3** (2022). https:// doi.org/10.1016/j.caeai.2022.100082

Iida, I., Buarque, L.: Ergonomia: Projeto e Produção/Itiro, I.; Guimarães, L. B. M. 3 edn. Edgard Blucher, São Paulo (2016)

Jeong, Y., Choi, S., Ryu, J.: Work-in-progress - design of LMS for the shared campus in metaverse learning environment. In: 8th International Conference of the Immersive Learning Research Network (iLRN), pp. 1–3 (2022). https://doi.org/10.23919/iLRN55037.2022.9815909

Jin, Q., Liu, Y., Yarosh, S., Han, B., Qian, F.: How will VR enter university classrooms? Multi-stakeholders investigation of VR in higher education. In: Proceedings of the 2022 CHI Conference on Human Factors in Computing Systems (CHI 2022), pp. 1–17. Association for Computing Machinery, New York (2022). https://doi.org/10.1145/3491102.351754

Jin, Y., Tiejun, Z.: The application of Metaverse XiRang game in the mixed teaching of art and Design in Colleges and Universities. Educ. Inf. Technol. (Dordr) **1**, 1–31 (2023)

Jovanovic, A., Milosavljevic, A.: VoRtex metaverse platform for gamified collaborative learning. Electronics 11(3), 317 (2022)

Kahn, P.H., Jr., et al.: A plasma display window? The shifting baseline problem in a technologically mediated natural world. J. Environ. Psychol. 28(2), 192–199 (2008). https://doi.org/10.1016/j.jenvp.2007.10.008

Kastrup, V.: A aprendizagem da atenção na cognição inventiva. Psicologia Sociedade 16(3), 7–16 (2004)

Kaplan, S., Kaplan, R.: Cognition and Environment: Functioning in an Uncertain World. Praeger, New York (1982a)

Kaplan, S., Kaplan, R.: Humanscape: Environments for People. Ulrich's Books, Ann Arbor (1982b)

Kaplan, R., Kaplan, S.: The Experience of Nature: A Psychological Perspective. Cambridge University Press, New York (1989)

Kaplan, S.: The restorative benefits of nature: toward an integrative framework. J. Environ. Psychol. 5(3), 169–182 (1995)

Koo, H.: Training in lung cancer surgery through the metaverse, including extended reality, in the smart operating room of Seoul National University Bundang Hospital, Korea. J. Educ. Eval. Health Prof. 18(33) (2021). https://doi.org/10.3352/jeehp.2021.18.33

Korpela, K.M.: Place-identity as a product of environmental self-regulation. J. Environ. Psychol. 9(3), 241–256 (1989)

Kye, B., Han, N., Kim, E., Park, Y., Jo, S.: Educational applications of metaverse: possibilities and limitations. J. Educ. Eval. Health Prof. 18(32) (2021). https://doi.org/10.3352/jeehp.2021.18.32

Laumann, K., Gärling, T., Stormark, K.M.: Rating scale measures of restorative components of environments. J. Environ. Psychol. 21(1), 31–44 (2001)

Lima, R.F.: Compreendendo os Mecanismos Atencionais. Ciências Cognição 6 (2005)

Lee, I., Sung, Y., Kim, T.: The expanding role of metaverse platform in college education. ICIC Express Lett. Part B Appl. 13 (2022)

Lee, H., Hwang, Y.: Technology-enhanced education through VR-making and metaverse-linking to foster teacher readiness and sustainable learning. Sustainability 14(8), 4786 (2022). https://doi.org/10.3390/su14084786

Lee, N., Jo, M.: Exploring problem-based learning curricula in the metaverse: the hospitality students' perspective. J. Hosp. Leisure Sport Tour. Educ. 32 (2023)

Lima, C.L., Queiroz, E.C.S.B., Sant'anna, G.J.: A relação entre concentração e aprendizagem: o uso de TIDC para a aprendizagem do aprender. Revista Científica Multidisciplinar Núcleo do Conhecimento 5(11), 161–186 (2018)

Liu, W.: A teaching design of ecological class based on immersive virtual reality spatial fusion. Front. Psychol. 13, 874101 (2022)

López-Belmonte, J., Pozo-Sánchez, S., Lampropoulos, G., Morenoguerrero, A.: Design and validation of a questionnaire for the evaluation of educational experiences in the metaverse in Spanish students (METAEDU). Heliyon 8(11) (2022)

Lou, J., Xu, Q.: The development of positive education combined with online learning: based on theories and practices. Front. Psychol. 13 (2022). https://doi.org/10.3389/fpsyg.2022.952784

Mandolfo, M., Baisi, F., Lamberti, L.: How did you feel during the navigation? Influence of emotions on browsing time and interaction frequency in immersive virtual environments. Behav. Inf. Technol. 42, 1216–1229 (2022). https://doi.org/10.1080/0144929X.2022.2066570

Mayer, F.S., Frantz, C.M., Bruehlman-Senecal, E., Dolliver, K.: Why is nature beneficial? The role of connectedness to nature. Environ. Behav. 41(5), 607–643 (2009)

Mystakidis, S., Christopoulos, A.: Teacher perceptions on virtual reality escape rooms for STEM education. Information 13(3), 136 (2022). https://doi.org/10.3390/info13030136

Niu, M., Lo, C.H.: An investigation of material perception in virtual environments. In: Ahram, T. (ed.) AHFE 2019. AISC, vol. 973, pp. 416–426. Springer, Cham (2020). https://doi.org/10. 1007/978-3-030-20476-1_42

Oliveira, R.A., Almeida, T.F., Suzart, N.S.: Psicologia Ambiental E A Subjetivação Do Espaço Acadêmico: Um Relato De Experiência. In: Seminário Nacional e Seminário Internacional Políticas Públicas, Gestão e Práxis Educacional, vol. 7, no. 7 (2019)

Ortega-Rodríguez, P.J.: De La Realidad Extendida al Metaverso: una Reflexión Crítica sobre las Aportaciones a La Educación. Teoría De La Educación. Revista Interuniversitaria **34**(2), 189–208 (2022). https://doi.org/10.14201/teri.27864

Phillips, D., Santos, F.V., Santoso, M.: Sudden visual perturbations induce postural responses in a virtual reality environment. J. Theor. Issues Ergon. Sci. **23**(1), 25–37 (2021)

Rahman, K.R., Shitol, S.K., Islam, M.S., Iftekhar, K.T., Saha, P.: Use of metaverse technology in education domain. J. Metaverse **3**(1) (2023)

Rueda, F.J.M.: Bateria Psicológica para Avaliação da Atenção – BPA. Vetor, São Paulo (2013)

Ryu, H., Lee, H., Yoo, H.J.: Development of a metaverse online learning system for undergraduate nursing students: a pilot study. Nurse Educ. (2023). https://doi.org/10.1097/NNE.000000000 0001509

Sarmento, T.F.C.S.: Modelo conceitual de ambiente de aprendizagem adequado a práticas com blended learning para escolas de ensino médio. Thesis (Doctorate in Design) – Centro de Artes e Comunicação, Universidade Federal de Pernambuco, Recife (2018)

Schlemmer, E., Backes, L.: Online Education in Metaverse: Novelty or Innovation? Learning in Metaverses: Co-Existing in Real Virtuality, pp. 183–214. IGI Global (2015). https://doi.org/ 10.4018/978-1-4666-6351-0.ch009

Seiari, S., Al Kaabi, H., Al-Karaki, J.N.: Exploring immersive learning in the metaverse: a prototype for interactive virtual classroom. In: International Conference on Intelligent Metaverse Technologies & Applications (iMETA), Tartu, Estonia, pp. 1–8 (2023). https://doi.org/10.1109/ iMETA59369.2023.10294515

Siyaev, A., Jo, G.S.: Neuro-symbolic speech understanding in aircraft maintenance metaverse. IEEE Access **9**, 154484–154499 (2021)

Stone, N.: Human factors and education: evolution and contributions. Hum. Factors **50**, 534–539 (2008). https://doi.org/10.1518/001872008X288466

Suh, W., Ahn, S.: Utilizing the metaverse for learner-centered constructivist education in the postpandemic era: an analysis of elementary school students. J. Intell **10**(1), 17 (2022). https://doi. org/10.3390/jintelligence10010017

Tamai, M., Inaba, M., Hosoi, K., Thawonmas, R., Uemura, M., Nakamura, A.: Constructing situated learning platform for Japanese language and culture in 3D metaverse. In: Second International Conference on Culture and Computing, Kyoto, Japan, pp. 189–190 (2011). https:// doi.org/10.1109/Culture-Computing.2011.59

Tasa, U.B., Gorgulu, T.: Meta-art: art of the 3-D user-created virtual worlds. Digit. Creat. **21**, 100–111 (2010)

Till, A., et al.: Is metaverse in education a blessing or a curse: a combined content and bibliometric analysis. Smart Learn. Environ. **9**(24) (2022)

Tori, R.: Educação sem distância: mídias e tecnologia na educação a distância, no ensino híbrido e na sala de aula. 3rd edn. Artesanato Educacional, São Paulo (2022)

Tugtekin, U., Odabasi, H.: Do interactive learning environments have an effect on learning outcomes, cognitive load and metacognitive judgments? Educ. Inf. Technol. **27**, 7019–7058 (2022). https://doi.org/10.1007/s10639-022-10912-0

Ulrich, R.S.: Aesthetic and affective response to natural environment. In: Altman, I., Wohlwill, J.F. (eds.) Behavior and the Natural Environment, 6th. edn., pp. 85–120. Plenum, Nova Iorque (1983)

Ulrich, R.S.: View through a window may influence recovery from surgery. Science **224**(4647), 420–421 (1984)

Ulrich, R.S., Simons, R.F., Losito, B.D., Fiorito, E., Miles, M.A., Zelson, M.: Stress recovery during exposure to natural and urban environments. J. Environ. Psychol. **11**(3) (1991)

Vernaza, A., Voinov, I., Ruiz, I.: Towards to an open and interoperable virtual learning environment using Metaverse at University of Panama. Technol. Appl. Electron. Teach. (TAEE), 320–325 (2012). https://doi.org/10.1109/TAEE.2012.6235458

Villarouco, V.: An ergonomic look at the work environment. In: Proceeding IEA 09: 17th World Congress on Ergonomics, Beijing, China (2009)

Wagner, R., Piovesan, S.D., Passerino, P.D.L.M., Lima, J.: Using 3D virtual learning environments in new perspective of education. In: 12th International Conference on Information Technology Based Higher Education and Training (ITHET), pp. 1–6 (2013). https://doi.org/10.1109/ITHET.2013.6671019

Zahedi, M.H., Farahani, E., Peymani, K.: A virtual e-learning environment model based on metaverse. In: 10th International and the 16th National 268 Conference on E-Learning and E-Teaching (ICeLeT), Tehran, Iran, pp. 1–7 (2023). https://doi.org/10.1109/ICeLeT58996.2023.10139894

A Neuroeducational Approach in the Integration of Virtual Reality Technologies in the Development of Serious Games: Case Study in the Field of Occupational Safety and Risk Prevention

Janaina Ferreira Cavalcanti[✉]

Universidade Politécnica de València, Camí de Vera, s/n, 46022 Valencia, Spain
cjanaina@gmail.com

Abstract. Accidents can generate significant social and economic losses with severe, harsh, and sometimes even irreparable consequences for individuals and companies. Each year the number of accidents with lost time injuries is increase. The leading causes of unsafe behaviors and, often, the resulting accidents at work are the lack of adequate knowledge and low-risk awareness. Safety signals are tools used to inform about a hazard when it cannot be eliminated. Still, even when they are present, they are often not visualized at the time of an accident. Another point to consider is the risk prevention courses which introduce individuals to existing hazards and the behavior to adopt when faced with them. However, these courses are deemed monotonous and ineffective by their audience. Technological evolution is making possible a series of improvements in the approach of these courses, which also do not imply too high economic cost. This paper approaches the use of new methodologies and technological advances as a tool to improve human behavior in risky situations. It presents a cocreation process to develop digital technologies solution for training using virtual reality and gamification to promote the correct behavior of the user in a critical condition. As main contributions, firstly, it should be noted that an immersive virtual environment has been developed to improve user behavior in a risk situation and evaluate the impacts that novel elements in signaling can have on human behavior. Also, this paper provides valorous insights for these which work with safety training.

Keywords: Virtual Reality · Gamification · Co-creation

1 Introduction

In recent decades, designers have moved closer and closer to the future users of what they design. This has given rise to co-creation, emerges, which has become an important process. Co-creation is an integrative, social process in which new ideas, products, and welcome solutions are developed together. Co-design is a human-centered design methodology used in research-action projects to design a product or service [1]. Thus,

A. Marcus et al. (Eds.): HCII 2024, LNCS 14715, pp. 21–31, 2024.
https://doi.org/10.1007/978-3-031-61359-3_2

in the co-design approach, end users (or potential users) participate in knowledge creation and idea generation together researchers and designers, for example. But it is also important to keep in mind that participatory research methods can be time-consuming, labor-intensive and costly. For this reason, some authors have sought to identify the specific challenges faced by system designers in applying co-design in charge of a general guide for the application of co-design frameworks and methods. So guidelines for a successful co-design process are creating. For mobile health, for example, Noorbergen et al. [2] proposed 7 guidelines, but during the interviews questions regarding the experience were absent. The guidelines consist of: understanding stakeholder vulnerability and diversity (1); planning for and assessing health behavior changes (2); identifying and involving co-design facilitators (3); immersion into the mHealth ecosystem (4); identifying and involving post-design advocates (5); applying health-specific evaluation criteria (6); collecting and analyzing usage data to understand impact (7). In the XRealities ambit, however there are still not have one guideline or methodological procedure validate for evaluate and redesign a product. This paper presents the redesign process of a Virtual Reality Immersive Serious Game (VRSG).

The original game, Sphere & Maze Shield Task (SSMT) presented a decontextualized maze where the user's main task was to get from the starting point to the exit in a maximum time of 3 min.

Incorporating gamification elements, our design introduced the presence of risks and a protective shield to confront them. The employed mechanics included challenges and rewards in the form of "karmas," represented as spherical entities distributed throughout the environment. These elements could exhibit static attributes, being fixed at specific points, or dynamic characteristics, moving along pre-established paths. Upon being interacted with (e.g., touched with one of the controllers), they emitted a sound. The player's secondary objective was to accumulate as many "karmas" as possible during their traversal.

The hazards were carefully selected to demonstrate varying levels of severity, categorized into three types: fires, cliffs, and wet ground. Contact with these hazards did not pose any tangible risk to the participant or their avatar, but it resulted in the loss of points ("karmas"), accompanied by a negative feedback response (horn sound and red light around the camera). The fire hazard was represented by a prominent flame spanning the width of a corridor, symbolizing the most imminent and severe danger. The cliff hazard was positioned in a corner, not projecting toward the avatar, classifying it as a less imminent danger compared to the fire. To progress through the labyrinth section containing the cliff hazard without point loss, it was unnecessary to use the shield; simply avoiding the corner of the precipice sufficed. However, if the player chose to approach the abyss, using the shield became imperative to prevent point loss. Lastly, the wet ground hazard, spanning the entire corridor width, portrayed a risk of lesser severity.

1.1 Ux Research

Ux Research is a process that aims at the optimization of a product or system. Usability tests are applied to the evaluation of the impact of user interface features and design choices on medical error [3], for example. Thus, Ux research aims to prevent usability problems in products. Since usability problems leads to reduce utilization, decrease user retention, and increased user frustration, this is an important and essential tool for product success.

When we think of usability, we must consider interactions that are usable, safe, effective, and comfortable interactions, easy to learn and with a low level of error occurrence. To this end, it is necessary to take into account the performance of users while interacting with the product (e.g., measuring the time to perform a task, the level of perception, and others). It is also necessary to take account the affective responses elicited by a product, which are classified according to the user's emotional state, which are dynamic and time-dependent.

Thus, taking into account the usability objectives mentioned above, it is important to proceed to key questions to address each objective. That is, when we think about:

- effectiveness - which says how good a system or product is at doing what it is supposed to do;
- efficiency - which refers to the way a system helps users to perform their tasks;
- safety – intended to protect the individual against dangerous conditions and undesirable situations;
- learning - which refers to the extent to which the system provides the right kind of functionality so that users can do what they need or want to do.

In this way, the usability inspection is a heuristic evaluation conducted by experts based on their skills, experiences, and practical knowledge [4].

2   Training Immersive Game: The Creative Process

Design jams consist of jointly discussing and solving design tasks during a given time interval. The people selected to participate in the sections must be active and knowledgeable about the topic and may or may not include potential future users. In the course of this project, two distinct sessions were conducted: a thematic exploration session (Session 1) and an ideation session (Session 2). The primary aim was to develop a serious immersive game designed to facilitate user learning and assess their behavior in a high-stress environment.

In Session 1, an in-depth analysis of the most pertinent and desirable project requirements was conducted, accompanied by a SWOT assessment of the current proposal's situation. Session 2 involved the generation of ideas through the formulation of challenges and the application of brainstorming techniques. Preceding both sessions, participants received an informational document outlining the context, objectives, and anticipated outcomes.

The primary challenges presented to the participants included:

- Assessing the appropriateness of the environment for evaluating users' responses to safety and danger signs.
- Proposing improvements to the environment to facilitate effective risk and stress training without causing harm to the user.
- Identifying optimal solutions to address cyber nuisance issues identified in the pilot test.

As for the participants, a specialized group was assembled, comprising experts in gamification, image and visualization, technology for education, occupational safety, 3D development, usability, and human-machine interaction. Each session, facilitated by a moderator, spanned three hours, with a seven-day interval between them. The composition of each session included six participants. The participants' ages ranged from 24 to 51 years, with a mean age (M) of 42 and a standard deviation (S.D) of 11.5.

2.1 Data Collected and Results

One of the pivotal considerations during the sessions was the imperative of maintaining environmental neutrality. Participants identified this characteristic as a hindrance to both the level of presence and the assessment of the impact of certain personal characteristics of subjects, such as previous accidents. Consequently, an analysis was undertaken to explore the feasibility of altering the environment to prioritize narrative elements, leading to the concept of re-creating the setting with characteristics resembling an office. This involved the addition of textures, elements, and lighting more in line with a workspace.

Another critical aspect taken into account was the environmental noises pertinent to the research, specifically the "karmas" and simulated walking sounds. The decision was made to eliminate the repetitive walking sounds as they proved more irksome than beneficial, given the monotony introduced. Sound was intentionally omitted to foster a sense of freedom for users to express their opinions and concerns while immersed in the environment.

Concerning characters, in alignment with the educational goals, emphasis was placed on maintaining a first-person experience. To enhance user control, the visualization of the user's hands was implemented. Additionally, for narrative reinforcement, the idea of equipping the hands with protection (gloves) was considered, given the context of navigating an office where an accident had occurred.

In crafting the experience, the focus shifted towards recognition. Among various scoring systems, the points-based system was selected for its visual and comparative efficiency. "Karmas" were replaced by elements granting players extra time, aligning with the strategy of personal conquest but providing a more functional reward.

Addressing the training room, participants underscored the importance of enhancing its connection with the main environment to foster a stronger sense of cohesion between the two. Consequently, the training room was designed to mirror the characteristics of the environment, including walls and floors. It was further determined that a direct connection should be established, effectively integrating the training room into the environment as a corridor-like extension.

The design team implemented a functional change by replacing the timer with a more seamlessly integrated element. This transformation materialized in the form of non-intrusive neon counters attached to the maze walls along the route, providing information in a visually integrated manner.

In light of the outcomes from the design jam, we pinpointed the following incremental requirements for the updated environment:

- Replicate the office level, incorporating textures, assets, and appropriate lighting.
- Rework the user's pathway to the objective.

- Introduce diverse types of traps.
- Equip the user with additional abilities, such as running and activating a fire extinguisher.
- Create warning signs with varied properties, including options for visibility only upon selection, blurred visibility, sharp visibility, and with or without flashing LED indicators.

3 The New Game

Building upon the requirements derived from the pilot study during the 'design jam' and subsequent analysis sessions, we undertook a redesign of the virtual environment. Recognizing gamification as a technique employed to stimulate specific behaviors through the application of game mechanics, our initial focus was to identify the processes or activities to be encouraged. In the context of this research, our aim was to assess user behavior in response to risk signals and varying levels of danger. Accordingly, our emphasis was on incentivizing natural behavior within an environment that presented elements of danger, risk, and potential loss. The targeted user demographic for the game comprised individuals within the working age population, ranging from 18 to 65 years old [5].

The subsequent step involved applying game mechanics conducive to enhancing the intrinsic motivation of our target audience. In our case, the emphasis lay on incorporating challenges, rewards, and feedback elements.

To implement the proposed changes, we migrated the environment to a new platform, considering various programming and updating considerations. Our primary objective was to recreate the previously developed environment, utilizing Unreal Engine 4 software, thereby improving its expansiveness and visual appeal to users. The chosen engine had been employed in prior research projects by the working group, leveraging previously configured user action setups [6–8].

In this way, an environment resembling an office was crafted, featuring partition-like walls (in purple with borders) and a floor adorned with vinyl marble tiles. Each section was distinguished by a unique color scheme, with purple, gray, and black assigned to different áreas (see Fig. 1). Furthermore, typical office elements such as a photocopier, bookshelf, coffee machine, and water dispenser were incorporated.

The scenario comprises two zones: a training corridor and a main room. Regarding the character's movement in response to player actions, linear speed was selected. This represents the simplest method and yields optimal results in mitigating motion sickness issues. Locomotion is initiated when the user presses the movement button, with a consistent speed, devoid of acceleration or inertia, as outlined by previous studies [9].

The virtual environment simulates an office setting where an accident has taken place. Textures resembling those of the partitions were applied to the walls. All selected hazards were designed to mimic real-life office scenarios, such as a short circuit resulting from water proximity to an electrical socket. The participant's objective was to identify and recognize the risks and hazards within the environment. Upon identification, the participant was required to activate the control, thereby earning bonuses or points. This gamified function was implemented to enhance user presence. Consequently, bonuses were awarded for successful identifications, while points were deducted for missed

Fig. 1. Maze image of the new game.

hazards. To communicate the reward duration to the player, the UE4 "cascade" particle effect was utilized to generate a green "+10" explosion.

The hazard signs incorporated three types: static signs utilizing the application of sign textures, dynamic signs featuring flashing LEDs, and intelligent signs that would only become visible when necessary. In their programming, we considered that these signs should remain invisible to the player until reaching a predefined threshold, at which point they would become visible.

Furthermore, certain plates were intentionally blurred to enhance the perception of danger, creating an atmosphere of an unhealthy environment with the smoke or fog resulting from the incident. This approach allowed for the evaluation of variables with and without the obscured reality. To provide contextualization, signage was strategically positioned in proximity to the identified hazards.

The corridor, situated at the outset of the stage as depicted (see Fig. 2), serves a dual purpose: to convey background narrative and to acquaint participants with the environment and its functionalities, including controls and keyboards. Composed of flooring, ceiling, and walls akin to the main room, the corridor features signage detailing an office incident, navigation commands, the participant's task of traversing the environment swiftly, and the opportunity to address an evident danger (extinguishing fire).

The signage within the corridor is programmatically enabled to facilitate user actions (e.g., picking up the time clock) and adaptable for use with remote controls or keypads. The signs are arranged as follows:

- Introduction: Provides context about the incident, aiming to enhance participant engagement by justifying the presence of imminent risks.
- Training: Describes the task, informing users about their objective in the game (crossing the corridor swiftly) without explicitly outlining the experiment's goal.

Fig. 2. Training saloon.

- Clock: Displays the stopwatch and indicates the maximum time allotted to complete the test.
- Time Clock: Introduces an element that grants additional time during the test, serving the dual purpose of informing about the time limit and observing the participant's response to risk.
- Speed: Instructs on how to move faster, facilitating evaluation of participant behavior in response to signals and imminent risks.
- Play Time: Indicates that contact with a hazard will reduce play time, simulating losses akin to those experienced in a real environment.
- Extinguisher: Notifies users of the option to select the appropriate extinguisher type for the fire using the trackpad.
- End: Signals the conclusion of familiarization and the commencement of evaluation.

Following command testing, participants proceed to the evaluation environment.

For the other side, the principal set is set up in a maze with three consecutive rooms of equal configuration and same hazards. To ensure that the subject passes through all the cues (experimental conditions), the maze is symmetrical, if they choose right or left they will pass through equal hazards and equal cues. In addition, it is equipped with programming that prevents the player from choosing the same section (walls appear that do not allow them to return to the same section and repeat the experimental objects).

The flooring and walls mirror those of the anteroom, with discrete alterations in color across sections. This change is implemented with careful consideration for maintaining environmental harmony while ensuring perceptibility, enabling the user to discern transitions between sections. Movement within the environment is facilitated through the remote control integrated into the headset.

4 The Usability Test

Considering the sample size endorsed by existing literature, which ranges from three to five specialists [10, 11], and mindful of the meticulousness required for the research project's efficacy, we engaged three usability specialists—each with expertise in games, architectural visualization, and virtual environments, respectively. The gender distribution comprised two female participants and one male participant, with ages of 40, 42, and 48 years, resulting in a mean age of 42 and a standard deviation of 4.1.

For our evaluation, we observed users' perception of and adherence to signs distributed along the route, employing the think-aloud technique wherein users verbalized their thoughts and actions without providing explanations for their behaviors [12]. The test took place at the IoTiCat at the Universitat La Salle - Ramón Llull. Subsequently, participants' dialogues were transcribed, followed by a two-phase extraction process to identify the main conclusions derived from this usability test.

5 Results and Discussion

The evaluated aspects, deemed important by the participants, were categorized into four distinct groups based on their respective driving forces:

- Category 1 (C.1) - Training Room: This category assessed the ability to achieve the room's objectives or functionalities, examining whether it facilitated participant familiarization with the technology and mechanisms in use. It also considered the reduction of initial noise that could impact experiments and whether the room featured elements enhancing the sense of continuity in the process.
- Category 2 (C.2) - Signage: This group reviewed various aspects, including the perceptibility and visibility of signage to users. It also considered whether the signage was comprehensible and reflected obedient behaviors.
- Category 3 (C.3) - System Usability: In this area, the user experience was analyzed in terms of cyber discomfort and the game's overall pleasantness. The interaction with game elements was assessed regarding ease of use, task performance, understanding of system commands, and system responsiveness.
- Category 4 (C.4) - Effectiveness as Virtual Reality Serious Game (VRSG): This category focused on evaluating the narrative's ability to induce emotional involvement, perception of different danger levels, presence, and verisimilitude of the virtual environment. Additionally, engagement levels were analyzed to determine the game's success in generating commitment and consistent behavioral responses.

Table 1 provides a summary of the categories, along with the points evaluated and selected excerpts from participants' comments.

Table 1. Usability inspection relevant comments in each category

Description	Expert 1	Expert 2	Experto 3
C.1 Training room			
Functionality	Allows to understand the metaphor of use of the game	Allows to become familiar with the actions to be performed	Is able to allow to train the commands before doing the tasks
Continuity	Very fluid	It is possible to identify similarities	Able to provide a spontaneous transition to the environment
C.2 Signaling			
Perception	Can help differentiate user profile types	Does not require user effort	Gamification may impair perception of the signal
Comprehensibility	Can be understood by different profile	Allows for agility of actions	Does not generate doubts
Obedience	Can help the user to a behavioral response	Is able to help the knowledge of the type of user profile	Is able to improve user knowledge
C.3 System Usability			
Cybersickness	Meets the requirements	I did not feel	I think people will not have
Interactions	Very good interaction	Intuitive	Allows executing commands without memory strain
Sensitivity/ Responsiveness of the system	Easy	Very agile	Is able to not produce discomfort
C.4 Validity as VESG			
Narrative	Participant will be more inclined to observe and obey s gnage	Improves participant involvement/empathy	Can help enhance safety cues
Presence	Can generate fear and similarity to a danger environment	Can make the participant feel in a moment of danger without causing harm	Eliminates noise or distractors
Engagement	Can be an efficient tool	Can provoke behavior in the participants	Can engage the participants

6   Conclusions

This paper presented the evaluation process encompassed the initial virtual environment (SSMT) and subsequent development of a serious immersive game (Game for Safety) aimed at addressing the deficiencies identified in the initial setting.

The SSMT, initially conceived as a versatile environment suitable for diverse research applications, proved inadequate for our specific focus on stress-induced emotion and high cognitive load. The lack of a robust narrative with elements stimulating such emotions led to a suboptimal acceptance of the SSMT among expert users who assessed the environment.

In contrast to the SSMT, the newly designed immersive formative game (Game for Safety) incorporates a more robust narrative and emotional engagement. Enhancements have been made to the overall aesthetics of the maze, hazards, and risks to foster a more natural experience and elicit spontaneous behaviors.

The new environment introduces additional tasks related to occupational hazards, enabling the assessment of user attention within an environment characterized by a dense cognitive state and emotional engagement.

A fundamental principle guiding the game's construction was flexibility and adaptability to user preferences, aligning with the learning-by-doing paradigm. Users are afforded autonomy to explore the environment and execute actions while being challenged to exit as promptly as possible. To ensure a successful experience, a delicate balance was struck between providing users with a sense of freedom and adhering to predetermined tasks.

Disclosure of Interests.   The authors have no competing interests to declare that are relevant to the content of this article.

References

1. Tremblay, M., Hamel, C., Viau-Guay, A., Giroux, D.: User experience of the co-design research approach in eHealth: activity analysis with the course-of-action framework. JMIR Hum. Factors **9**, 3 (2022)
2. Noorbergen, T.J., Adam, M.T.P., Teubner, T., Collins, C.E.: Using co-design in mobile health system development: a qualitative study with experts in co-design and mobile health system development. JMIR Mhealth Uhealth **9**, 11 (2021)
3. McColl-Kennedy, J.R., Vargo, S.L., Dagger, T.S., Sweeney, J.C., Kasteren, Y.V.: Health care customer value cocreation practice styles. J. Serv. Res. **15**, 370–389 (2012)
4. Nielsen, J.: Usability Inspection Methods, p. 448. Wiley, New Work (1994)
5. Instituto Nacional de Estadística: Mujeres y hombres en España. Empleo. Tasas de empelo según grupos de edad (2022). https://www.ine.es/ss/Satellite?L=es_ES&c=INESeccion_C&cid=1259925463013&p=%5C&pagename=ProductosYServicios%2FPYSLayout&param1=PYSDetalle&param3=1259924822888. Assessed 10 enero 2022
6. Fonseca, D., et al.: What is happening in the process of engaging architectural students and teachers for including virtual and interactive systems in the projects developments? In: Eighth International Conference on Technological Ecosystems for Enhancing Multiculturality (TEEM 2020), pp. 775–783. Association for Computing Machinery, New York (2021). https://doi.org/10.1145/3434780.3436540

7. Redondo, E., et al.: EDUGAME4CITY. A gamification for architecture students. Viability study applied to urban design. In: Zaphiris, P., Ioannou, A. (eds.) HCII 2020. LNCS, vol. 12206, pp. 296–314. Springer, Cham (2020). https://doi.org/10.1007/978-3-030-50506-6_22

8. Calvo, X., Fonseca, D., Sánchez-Sepúlveda, M., Amo, D., Llorca, J., Redondo, E.: Programming virtual interactions for gamified educational proposes of urban spaces. In: Zaphiris, P., Ioannou, A. (eds.) LCT 2018. LNCS, vol. 10925, pp. 128–140. Springer, Cham (2018). https://doi.org/10.1007/978-3-319-91152-6_10

9. Habgood, M.P.J., Moore, D., Wilson, D., Alapont, S.: Rapid, continuous movement between nodes as an accessible virtual reality locomotion technique. In: 2018 IEEE Conference on Virtual Reality and 3D User Interfaces (VR), Tuebingen/Reutlingen, Germany, pp. 371–378 (2018). https://doi.org/10.1109/VR.2018.8446130

10. Jeffries, R., Desurvire, H.: Usability testing vs. heuristic evaluation: was there a contest? ACM SIGCHI Bull. **24**(4), 39–41 (1992)

11. Nasir, M., Ikram, N., Jalil, Z.: Usability inspection: novice crowd inspectors versus expert. J. Syst. Softw. **183**, 111122 (2022). https://doi.org/10.1016/j.jss.2021.111122

12. Young, K.L., Salmon, P.M., Cornelissen, M.: Missing links? The effects of distraction on driver situation awareness. Saf. Sci. **56**, 36–43 (2013). https://doi.org/10.1016/j.ssci.2012.11.004

Does Virtual Reality Allow Essay Participants Better Conditions to Get Information Regarding the Perception of Architectural Contexts?

Mário Bruno Cruz[1,2]([envelope]) [iD], Francisco Rebelo[1,2] [iD], Jorge Cruz Pinto[1],
and Emerson Gomes[1,2] [iD]

[1] CIAUD, Research Centre for Architecture, Urbanism and Design, Lisbon School of
Architecture, Universidade de Lisboa, Lisbon, Portugal
mariobrunocruz@yahoo.com
[2] ITI/LARSyS, Universidade de Lisboa, Lisbon, Portugal

Abstract. This article integrates a research project that aims to understand the architectonic contexts' influence on meditation practice. One of the phases of the project refers to meditation practitioners' emotional reactions to a set of architectonic contexts using Kansei. Accordingly, we will use the Kansei inquiry method which allows the creation of predictive models that relate characteristics of architectonic contexts with the expected reactions of meditation practitioners. The more productive type of approach, real scale models, might be unpractical due to the high costs of implementation. The aim of this article is first to establish a conviction about which of the two ways of presenting models might be better for getting this information. Under these two conditions, 30 participants who practice meditation, 15 with PowerPoint (PP) and 15 with virtual reality (VR), classified 10 architectonic contexts on how they may be influencing their will to practice meditation. These 10 contexts vary in materiality and openings to the exterior. The Kansei word pairs (agitated-calm, distracted-aware, absent-present, uncomfortable-comfortable, numb-awake, unstable-stable, depressed-happy, and constrained-free) were used to evaluate the participant's perception. At the end, the volunteers were interviewed to collect information about their grade of Presence. The results showed higher punctuation attributed to VR in almost all questions of the Presence Evaluation Questionnaire (PEQ), this might suggest a higher immersion grade in VR than with the PP. Moreover, the Kansei results for mandala windows suggest that a glare effect is only clearly perceived in VR. Finally, we recommend further studies with larger samples.

Keywords: Artificial Intelligence · Architecture · Virtual Reality · Kansei · Meditation

1 Introduction

In the 21st Century, architecture might be facing tough challenges in meeting users' expectations more accurately. Building architectonic contexts underestimating their future users' effective needs might no longer be possible. To address their users' needs,

Architects might have to turn to other fields of knowledge such as neurology [1, 12, 19], biology, psychology [8], philosophy (namely phenomenology [17, 18, 20]), and others.

According to Zabala-Vargas, et al.: "The high volume of information produced by project management and its quality have (sic) become a challenge for organizations. Due to this, emerging technologies such as big data, data science and (sic) artificial intelligence (ETs) have become an alternative in the project life cycle." [23] Thus, we can see a growing proliferation of AI tools to improve Architects' efficiency in conceiving buildings and houses. Amongst such tools are BIM (Building Information Modelling) and CAD (Computer Aided Design). The efficiency of these AI tools depends significantly on the inputs stored in their databases. Inputs originating from investigation in Architecture might save Architects' research time when creating a building or a house.

This article is part of a research project that aims to understand the architectonic contexts' influence on meditation practice. One of the phases of the project refers to the meditation practitioners' emotional reactions to a set of architectonic contexts using Kansei. The Kansei engineering method is a survey method created in Japan, in 1970, by Mitsuo Nagamachi [14–16]. This inquiry method has been used in the Design industry to improve its products according to the way their customers feel. It has proved to give both a quite objective and true output when compared with traditional surveys.

We can use this method either in real scale models, virtual reality (VR) models, or computer screen images of the architectonic contexts that are being surveyed. The more productive type of approach, real scale models, might be unpractical due to the high costs of implementation and the necessity to have available facilities to build these models. However, we have these two other ways of presenting models of architectonic contexts to evaluate users' feelings through a Kansei inquiry. Accordingly, we have found it important first to establish a conviction about which of these two ways of presenting models might be better to ascertain users' feelings concerning architectonic contexts.

However, due to the impossibility of interacting with these contexts in a physical environment, as they are imaginary contexts, it is necessary to find an interface so that the persons can perceive these models and verbalize the experience they would have when they practice meditation in these same contexts.

We mean here by meditation, Buddhist Vajrayana such as Shamata, deity visualizations or mantras, Theravada Metta practice, only Shamata, and Zen. All these practices although using different techniques (breath, visualizations, sound, etc.) are meant to tame the mind, having its disturbances under control. We could embrace all these practices under the same Kansei word pairs and essay participants confirmed that this was possible by validating them through their comments at the end of their experience.

As stated above, we can have two types of digital interfaces, a screen with bidimensional visual information or VR. To provide the user with a tridimensional experience, the screen information can be presented with a sequence of various viewpoints. In VR, the contexts can be presented with the model inserted in a sphere with a 360-degree view. In this context, the problem is to choose the best interface to acquire the data. Following this problem, this article aims to research if there are differences between the results of the Kansei and Presence arising from the interaction with these two platforms.

Several previous studies address the theme of VR, amongst them systematic reviews. [11], we can see research on VR for Architecture [3, 4, 10, 13] and Design [7, 21], and some comparing computer screen images with VR in Human Behavior Studies [9]. This last one is a systematic scoping review referring that VR is a suitable platform for conducting experiences namely in Human Behavior Studies. Indicating that the VR worlds are more like the real world than computer screen images.

2 Methods

To apply the Kansei method is necessary to define a set of architectonic contexts that will be presented to the meditation practitioners.

2.1 Instruments

Contexts. We chose to use imaginary models that might not be possible to build as we were mainly interested in becoming aware of the reactions to the materials and openings to the exterior, wide or narrow, or from the ceiling, or even other more subtle ways of conceiving them. We were not interested in aesthetic taste appreciation. The entrance for the models was built into the walls, a door invisible to the meditation practitioners after they got inside the model.

There were 10 contexts, 5 in timber and 5 in granite, each five with a set of different openings to the exterior: 1 - mandala-inspired windows, 2 - yantra-inspired windows, 3 - frontal and lateral low cracks, 4 - lateral and ceiling front cracks, and 5 - usher circular windows.

On a computer screen, five sequential (frontal, left, right, upwards, and frontal) timed (one second each) PowerPoint (PP) images of each architectonic context were shown, with the fifth one lasting still. In the VR model experience, the participants put on a head-mounted display (HMD) and explored the first architectonic context shown (a model inserted in a 360-degree exterior sphere), and, 5 and a half seconds later, the first recorded Kansei question was played. After eight questions, we passed to the next model, leaving again 5 and half seconds for exploring it, and then we played the same set of eight questions, and so on, until the 10th VR model.

Questionnaires. We used 8 Kansei questions on a 1 to 7 scale, in each of the 10 contexts, and, in the end, participants filled out a Presence Evaluation Questionnaire. On arrival, some Demographic Information was collected, with meditation experience and preferences also included. In the end, there were collected comments participants delivered spontaneously and conducted by us.

As Kansei words, we selected a sequence of 8 word pairs: agitated-calm, distracted-aware, absent-present, uncomfortable-comfortable, numb-awake, unstable-stable, depressed-happy, and constrained-free.

Sample. We tested 30 meditation practitioners, from which 15 with the PP and 15 with the VR. Ages ranging between 36 and 74 years old, with a medium of the age of 52,36; for PP raging between 41 and 74 years old, with a medium of the age 55,13; for the VR raging between 36 and 66 years old, with a medium of the age of 49,6. The 30 volunteers were 56,66% women and 43,33% men; for the PP were 40% women and 60% men; for VR were 73,33% women and 26,66% men. Out of the 30 participants,

16,66% had a college education, and 83,33% had higher education; for the PP 20% had a college education, and 80% had higher education; for the VR 13,33% had a college education and 86,66% had higher education. Of the 24 Portuguese interviewees 2 were born in Africa, in Mozambique and Angola, the others were 3 Brazilian Portuguese, 1 German, 1 Spanish, and 1 Estonian. A percentage of 60% resided in Lisbon and 40% in the Lisbon region, the farthest in Palmela, Mafra, and Vila Franca do Xira. Concerning meditation experience it ranged from 5 to 50 years of practice, with a medium time of 18,76 years of practice; for the PP it ranged from 10 to 50 years, with a medium of 19,33 years of practice; for VR it ranged from 5 to 30 years, with a medium of 18,2 years of practice. The medium weekly meditation time ranged from 0 to 50 h, with a medium of 9:01 h per week; the PP participants ranged from 0 to 50 h with a medium of 10:09 h per week; the VR participants ranged from 0 to 40 h with a medium of 7:54 h per week. Almost all (29) the 30 participants normally practice at home except for one VR participant who practices everywhere. As for the ideal place to practice, for the PP volunteers, 7 mentioned their home, mostly (4) their room, 2 in a temple, 2 in nature, 2 with no preferences, 1 in retreats, and 1 in the Dojo; for the VR volunteers, 7 mentioned their home, mostly (4) their room, 2 in a temple, 2 in nature, 2 in retreats, 1 near Rinpoche, and 1 at work. Of the participants, 24 practice Vajrayana Buddhism, such as Shamata, deity visualizations or mantras, 3 practice Theravada Metta, 2 practice only Shamata, and 1 practice Zen; distributed by the PP, 11 practice Buddhist Vajrayana such as Shamata or deity visualizations, 2 practice Theravada Metta, 1 practice only Shamata, and 1 practice Zen; and VR, 13 practice Buddhist Vajrayana such as Shamata, deity visualizations or mantras, 1 practice Theravada Metta, and 1 practice only Shamata. Three of the participants of the VR experience had recently arrived from an enclosed Buddhist retreat of 6 and a half – 7 years in the South of France.

Protocol. Upon their arrival, they had to read and sign a Free and Informed Consent Form where they were informed about the experience's aims, dangers, and the possibility of freely leaving it. Next, they had to read on a computer screen, a previous statement about the experience: 'We ask you to relax and try to imagine yourself in the architectonic contexts that will be presented to you. We are interested in your emotional and intuitive answer, not in your critical judgment. Therefore, imagine being carried to the exhibited contexts in the next images (or virtual reality environments). Be only present in the situations and let the experience flow. Please, focus only on the images (or virtual reality environments)' adapted from (Bermudez, et al. 2017). Subsequently, the experience started. On a computer screen, five sequential (frontal, left, right, upwards, and frontal) timed (one second each) PP images of each architectonic context were shown, with the last one remaining still. Half a second later, started the first recorded Kansei question: 'Using a 1 to 7 scale, where 1 represents extremely agitated and 7 extremely calm, how would you classify how you feel to practice meditation in this place?' After the participant's answer, another similar Kansei question was played by the researcher: 'Using the same scale, 1 for extremely distracted and 7 for extremely aware, how would you classify how you feel to practice meditation in this place?', successively the same question was played for absent-present, uncomfortable-comfortable, numb-awake, unstable-stable, depressed-happy, and constrained-free. Then we repeated the nine PP models. In the VR models experience, participants put on an HMD and explored the first architectonic context shown, and, 5 and a half seconds later, the same first recorded Kansei question was played. After the first set of eight Kansei questions, we passed to the next model, also leaving 5 and half seconds for exploring it and then we played the same set of eight questions, repeating this process until the 10th VR model. In both experiences, with the PP and VR, we manually registered the answers in a chart and collected comments participants spontaneously made during these. For each volunteer, we changed the models' sequence to avoid vitiation. At the end of the experience, we registered all comments participants spontaneously produced. Then, participants answered a PEQ where were evaluated 1- Sensorial quality – immersion grade, 2- Interaction quality - control factors, 3- Sensorial quality – sensorial factors, 4 -Interaction quality – distraction factors, 5 - Sensorial quality – realism grade, 6 - Curiosity, and 7 - Augmented pleasure. The Sensorial quality – immersion grade question, evaluates the level of immersion in the computer screen or VR architectonic contexts; the Interaction quality - control factors question, evaluates the interaction with the architectonic context; the Interaction quality – distraction factors question, evaluates the level of concentration in the Kansei questionnaire task; the Sensorial quality – realism grade question, evaluates the level of design realism of the computer screen images or VR architectonic contexts; the Curiosity question evaluates the level of participants interest in Artificial Intelligence (AI); and finally Augmented pleasure question evaluates the level of pleasure participants withdraw from AI.

Data processing. The Kansei inquiry data was statistically processed through a TQ1 model, the same used in meteorologic previsions.

3   Results

3.1   Immersion Questionnaire

Chart 1 shows the results for Presence with the two conditions. The results showed higher punctuation attributed to VR in almost all questions of the PEQ, except for the questions related to 6 - Curiosity. The highest difference between PP and VR was found in the 1- Sensorial quality – immersion grade (Fig. 1).

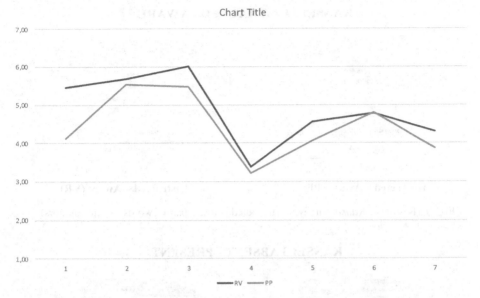

Fig. 1. The results for Presence for the PP and VR. (source authors)

3.2 Kansei Experience

The results of the Kansei experience showed more coherence in the materiality answers than in the 'Openings' answers. In some charts, for the same opening, we can see opposed results, for the PP and VR. The 'Openings 1' answers showed very opposed results in PP and VR for the first three pairs of Kansei words (Figs. 2, 3, 4, 5, 6, 7, 8 and 9).

Openings 1 - Mandala-inspired windows
Openings 2 - Yantra-inspired windows
Openings 3 - frontal and lateral low cracks
Openings 4 - lateral and ceiling front cracks
Openings 5 - usher circular windows

Material 1 – timber
Material 2 - granite

KANSEI 1 AGITATED - CALM

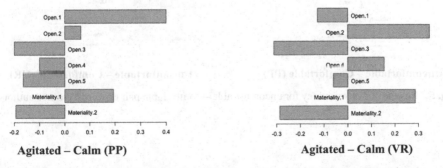

Agitated – Calm (PP)   Agitated – Calm (VR)

Fig. 2. Results of *Kansei* survey for agitated – calm pair of words. (source authors)

KANSEI 2 DISTRACTED - AWARE

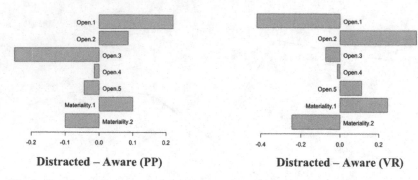

Distracted – Aware (PP)   **Distracted – Aware (VR)**

Fig. 3. Results of *Kansei* survey for distracted – aware pair of words. (source authors)

KANSEI 3 ABSENT - PRESENT

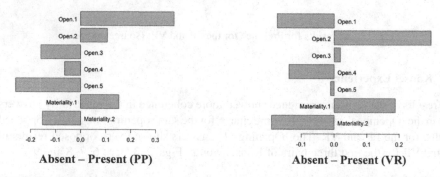

Absent – Present (PP)   **Absent – Present (VR)**

Fig. 4. Results of *Kansei* survey for absent – present pair of words. (source authors)

KANSEI 4 UNCOMFORTABLE - COMFORTABLE

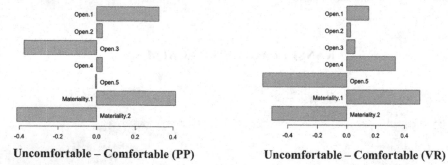

Uncomfortable – Comfortable (PP)   **Uncomfortable – Comfortable (VR)**

Fig. 5. Results of *Kansei* survey for uncomfortable – comfortable pair of words. (source authors)

KANSEI 5 NUMB - AWAKE

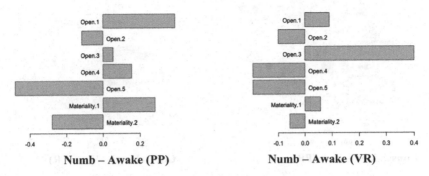

Fig. 6. Results of *Kansei* survey for numb – awake pair of words. (source authors)

KANSEI 6 UNSTABLE - STABLE

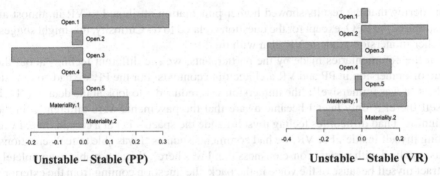

Fig. 7. Results of *Kansei* survey for unstable – stable pair of words. (source authors)

KANSEI 7 DEPRESSED – HAPPY

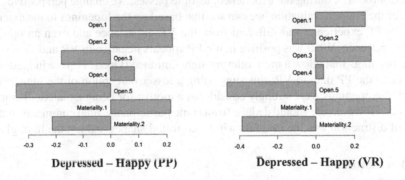

Fig. 8. Results of *Kansei* survey for depressed – happy pair of words. (source authors)

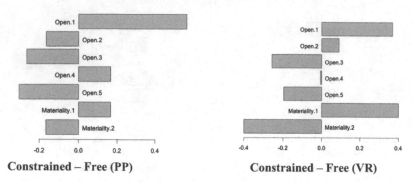

Fig. 9. Results of *Kansei* survey for constrained – free pair of words (source authors).

4 Discussion

Considering that the results showed higher punctuation attributed to VR in almost all questions of the PEQ, except for the questions related to 6 - Curiosity, this might suggest a higher immersion grade in VR than with the PP.

In the commentaries made by the participants, we see different feelings about the grade of immersion in PP and VR architectonic contexts. For the PP, we had comments such as 'it was immersive!'; 'the immersion was reduced – to look at the details'; 'I felt myself there!'; 'only later I became aware that the pavements were different'; 'in the beginning, I had difficulties feeling myself inside the space – but at a certain time, I was feeling myself inside'. For VR, we had comments such as 'I was able to feel sensations, I was involved with perfect consciousness that I was here'; 'I was not able to completely abstract myself because of the voice in the back, the question coming from the exterior'; 'at first, the stone remembered me the wine cellar of my infancy, then I understood that there was a spatiality and light control'; 'the glasses were very heavy, so I was very aware of it'; 'these places exist?', 'one gets really outside the place. One asks oneself, how was the exterior room?'; during the experience, as time passes, we change perspective'.

As for the Kansei evaluation, we can see that based on the 'openings to the exterior' results the PP experience was different from the VR experience and even an opposed kind of experience. What was positive in the PP appears negative in VR and vice versa.

The openings that allow a more relevant light entrance (Open. 1) were judged more favorably in the PP than in VR, this suggesting a lesser perception of the glare effect. In VR, these openings were strongly considered a motive for being agitated, distracted, and absent. However, we should deduce from some participants' final comments that the motive of distraction was the mandala windows' round shapes and not the light glare.

5 Conclusions

However, with a reduced sample of individuals we could detect some tendencies that might be more evident if we enlarge and diversify the sample. Concerning the aim of this study: to ascertain if VR allows a better perception of architectonic contexts, this experience suggested that it might be the case. There might be a higher level of immersion in VR than in PP, allowing a better perception of the contexts and a sharper detection of the problems with meditating, such as the frontal light glare effect. These findings allow better control of agitation, distraction, and absence through an improved conception of architecture and avoidance of unexpected problems in the final building. The grade of Presence has also been statistically proven to be higher in VR than in the PP. Finally, the practical possibility of showing the architectonic contexts was reduced to 5 images with the PP, while with VR the participants could be aware of all the space around them.

6 Recommendations

We recommend further studies with larger samples to have better Presence statistical data. And, to audio record and stimulate the comments of participants. Also, to video record, through mirroring, the interaction of participants with VR. Concerning the PP, as the participants tend to stay in a static position, the physical interaction is lessened. It might also be useful to evaluate the level of participants' anxiety before the experience, as it may vary from one individual to another which may influence the results.

Final Note and Acknowledgments. This work is financed by national funds through FCT - Fundação para a Ciência e a Tecnologia, I.P., under the Strategic Project with the references UIDB/04008/2020 and UIDP/04008/2020.

Disclosure of Interests.   The authors have no competing interests to declare that are relevant to the content of this article.

References

1. Assem, H.M., Khodeir, L.M., Fathy, F.: Designing for human wellbeing: the integration of neuroarchitecture in design – a systematic review. Ain Shams Eng. J. **14**(6), 2–9 (2023). https://doi.org/10.1016/j.asej.2022.102102
2. Bermudez, J., et al.: Externally-induced meditative states: an exploratory fMRI study of architects' responses to contemplative architecture. Front. Archit. Res. **6**(2), 123–136 (2017). https://doi.org/10.1016/j.foar.2017.02.002
3. Campbell, D., Wells, M.: A critique of virtual reality in the architectural design process (1994)
4. Chan, C.S.: Virtual reality in architectural design, Taiwan (1997)
5. Cruz, M.B., Rebelo, F., Cruz Pinto, J.: M-term architectonic context and meditation practitioners: a concept to be implemented in an informatic application to help architects. In: Marcus, A., Rosenzweig, E., Soares, M.M. (eds.) HCII 2023. LNCS, vol. 14031, pp. 413–425. Springer, Cham (2023). https://doi.org/10.1007/978-3-031-35696-4_30
6. Djebbara, Z., et al.: Contemplative neuroaesthetics and architecture: a sensorimotor exploration. Front. Archit. Res. **13**(1), 97–111 (2024). https://doi.org/10.1016/j.foar.2023.10.005
7. Dorta, T., Lalande, P.: The impact of virtual reality on the design process, Quebec, Canada, 138–163 (1998). https://doi.org/10.52842/conf.acadia.1998.138
8. Goldhagen, S.W.: Welcome to our World - How the Built Environment Shapes Our Lives, 1st edn. HarperCollins, New York (2017)

9. Hepperle, D., Wölfel, M.: Similarities and differences between immersive virtual reality, real world, and computer screens: a systematic scoping review in human behavior studies. Multimodal Technol. Interact. **7**(56), 1–25 (2023). https://doi.org/10.3390/mti7060056
10. Kalisperis, L.N., et al.: Evaluating relative impact of virtual reality system variables on architectural design comprehension and presence. In: Proceedings of eCAADe, vol. 24, pp. 66–73 (2006)
11. Korkut, E.H., Surer, E.: Visualization in virtual reality: a systematic review. Virtual Real. **27**, 1447–1480 (2023). https://doi.org/10.1007/s10055-023-00753-8
12. Metzger, C.: Neuroarchitecture. jovis Verlag GmbH, Berlin, 1st edn. (2018)
13. Milovanovic, J., Moreau, G., Siret, D., Miguet, F.: Virtual and augmented reality in architectural design and education an immersive multimodal platform to support architectural pedagogy. In: Proceedings of Future Trajectories of Computation in Design, 17th International Conference, CAAD Futures 2017, Istanbul, Turkey (2017)
14. Nagamachi, M. (ed.): Kansei/Affective Engineering. CRC Press, Taylor & Francis Group, Milton Park, Oxfordshire (2011)
15. Nagamachi, M.: Home applications of Kansei engineering in Japan: an overview. Gerontechnology **15**(4), 209–215 (2016). https://doi.org/10.4017/gt.2016.15.4.005.0
16. Nagamachi, M., Lokman, A.: Innovations of Kansei Engineering. CRC Press, Taylor & Francis Group, Milton Park, Oxfordshire (2011)
17. Pallasmaa, J., Holl, S., Pérez-Gómez, A.: Questions of Perception: Phenomenology of Architecture. A+U Publishing Co., Tokyo (2008)
18. Pinto, J.C.: A Caixa - Metáfora e Arquitectura, 1st edn. ACD Editores, Lisbon (2007)
19. Robinson, S., Pallasmaa, J.: Mind in Architecture - Neuroscience, Embodiment, and the Future of Design, 1st edn. MIT Press, Cambridge (2015)
20. Sharr, A.: La cabaña de Heidegger - un espacio para pensar, 2nd edn. Gustavo Gili, Barcelona (2015)
21. Wang, X.: Augmented reality in architecture and design: potentials and challenges for application. Int. J. Archit. Comput. **7**(2), 309–326 (2009). https://doi.org/10.1260/147807709788921985
22. Wheelan, T.J.: Social Presence in Multi-User Virtual Environments: A Review and Measurement Framework for Organizational Research. North Carolina State University, North Carolina (2008)
23. Zabala-Vargas, S., Jaimes-Quintanilla, M., Jimenez-Barrera, M.H.: Big data, data science, and artificial intelligence for project management in the architecture, engineering, and construction industry: a systematic review. Buildings **13**(2944), 1–19 (2023). https://doi.org/10.3390/buildings13122944

Panoramic 360 Image Versus 2D Video: What is the Best Inside Virtual Reality?

Bárbara Formiga[1]([✉]), Francisco Rebelo[1,2], Jorge Cruz Pinto[1], Emerson Gomes[1], and Ana Vasconcelos[1]

[1] CIAUD, Centro de Investigação em Arquitetura, Urbanismo e Design, Faculdade de Arquitetura, Universidade de Lisboa, Rua Sá Nogueira, Polo Universitário do Alto da Ajuda, 1349-063 Lisbon, Portugal
barbaranevesf@gmail.com

[2] ITI/LARSys, Universidade de Lisboa, Rua Sá Nogueira, Polo Universitário, Alto da Ajuda, 1349-055 Lisbon, Portugal

Abstract. The paper addresses the comparison between static 360 panoramic images and 2D videos, both in virtual reality (VR) to analyze the best option to the used in Kansei method.

This study uses a sample of 23 participants, who interacted with a virtual scenario using the OCULUS Quest 2, in two modalities, the 3D panorama, where it is possible to freely look around 360° and the 2D video, where participants could observe in virtual reality an animated image. Presence and the Kansei words were evaluated: agitated/calm, uncomfortable/comfortable, devitalized/revitalized, stressed/relaxed.

We verified that there are significant differences between the two modalities, and the 3D panorama has higher values on average than the 2D video, it appears that these differences did not affect the Kansei results, which are similar. We can therefore conclude that with the scenario used in this study, any of the modalities can be used, despite there being an advantage for the 3D panorama. Studies with more complex scenarios, where there is important information to the left and right of the participants, must be developed to assess whether in these cases there are more striking differences in the presence and results obtained by kansei.

Keywords: Virtual Reality · Kansei · 360 panoramic image · 2D video

1 Introduction

1.1 Context

This article aims to investigate and critically compare two types of content presentation within virtual reality (360° panoramic image and 2D video) to determine which one is more effective as an interface element applied to Kansei evaluation for architectural interior spaces.

We are increasingly aware of the importance of understanding the emotional reactions of individuals about architectural space, which has consequences for both the conception of architecture and design, in a continuous effort to promote built environments that meet functional needs and contribute to the emotional well-being of occupants.

The present study appears as part of a broader investigation that seeks to evaluate people's emotional reactions to architectural space to develop design practices more oriented toward occupants' emotional well-being and satisfaction with the designed environments.

Previously, we have carried out several studies with different methods, one of them using the Kansei with hand-drawn images of architectural environments [2], another using a 3D visualization model where participants could navigate the computer and virtually walk through the space [1]. However, none of them have been tested using virtual reality devices. This study compares 360° panoramic image and 2D video in Virtual Reality as an interface element applied to Kansei.

One of the central issues that arise in this context is the selection of the best method to capture and analyze emotional reactions within a virtual environment through Kansei questionnaires. With the advancement of technology, virtual reality (VR) has emerged as a powerful tool for simulating architectural environments and providing immersive experiences for participants. In this sense, the debate between 360° panoramic images (static image) versus 2D videos (dynamic image) within the virtual reality environment becomes relevant. Both approaches offer distinct advantages regarding immersion, narrative control, and conveying information about specific architectural features. However, we did not find studies comparing these two visualization modes to understand the most suitable one. One study [3] compared the user experience when touring a museum with 360 video technologies, using a laptop screen, versus a 360 virtual reality video experienced through a video device. The head-mounted display (HMD) reveals that the latter gives users better immersion and a sense of control. Another study [4] showed that teaching knot tying using 360° virtual reality videos was more effective than teaching conventional 2D video.

Although these studies do not directly compare observing 360° images versus presenting 2D video in VR, they address important technologies and methods that can influence the user experience and immersion in virtual reality environments.

It is understood that the use of both methods combined, that is, 360° video, would be the most desirable for this type of study. However, it requires much heavier computation and may not always be possible or justifiable.

Careful analysis of these approaches will help justify the methodology applied in future studies and inform other work that uses Virtual Reality to simulate architectural environments.

2   Methods

2.1   Instruments

Using a virtual 3D model, we designed a single architectural environment measuring 4x4 meters with concrete walls and wooden floors. This virtual scenario features a 4-m window open to the landscaped exterior, a reflecting pool next to the window and at the level of the wooden floor, and a skylight exactly above the reflecting pool with the same size. From this scenario, we developed the two visualization possibilities we wanted to study within Virtual Reality, as shown in Fig. 1 and Fig. 2, which correspond to the 360 panoramic image (static image) and the 2D video (dynamic image), respectively.

Fig. 1. Capture of 360 panoramic image.

Fig. 2. Capture of 2D video.

We used the Twinmotion program to generate the video and the Unity program to produce the immersive interactions. After, we did an APK file and installed it on the Oculus Quest 2 through the SideQuest 2 application. Participants used the Oculus Quest 2 to visualize the two hypotheses (panoramic image 360 and 2D video). In addition to the visual component, we explored the auditory component by introducing the sound of moving water.

Since this study aims to find the best visualization and presence option for carrying out Kansei tests, we chose to carry out a pilot test of this methodology. The Kansei method, or Kansei Engineering, is a systematic approach to developing products, services, or systems based on users' emotional and subjective responses. Originating from Japan, "Kansei" refers to emotional or aesthetic sensitivity.

The objective of applying this test was to understand how the designed architectural environment promotes people's relaxation and well-being, which is associated with positive emotional reactions. The Kansei words selected to evaluate this effect were agitated/calm, uncomfortable/comfortable, devitalized/revitalized, stressed/relaxed.

In addition to Kansei, a presence questionnaire was used to evaluate other important variables associated with the degree of immersion of the experience, control factors, distraction factors, and degree of realism, both for 360 panoramic images vs 2D video.

In the end, an open interview was carried out, where we sought to find out the participants' opinions about their experience while interacting with VR environments.

2.2 Sample

The sample was made up of twenty-three participants between 20 and 45 years old, 65% female and 35% male, nineteen university students, two architects, and two people from the area of communication.

2.3 Protocol

The tests were all carried out in person, and we explained the scope of the investigation and the study's objective.

The participants signed the data protection agreement, and we explained to each participant that their participation was voluntary, that they would not be identified, and that their personal data would not be disclosed. In this way, we proceed with the following protocol:

- 1st - Before putting on the VR Oculus, we asked the participant to sit in a chair and rate how they were feeling at that moment on a scale of 1 to 7, with 1 representing "extremely stressed" and 7 "extremely relaxed";
- 2nd - We wait for the participant to speak for 2 s;
- 3rd - The participant places the Oculus Quest 2 with the first environment (360 or video);
- 4th - For 5 s, participants explore the environment (looking from left to right and then up);
- 5th - In second 6 the first question arises: Using a scale from 1 to 7, where 1 represents "extremely agitated" and 7 "extremely calm", how do you classify how you feel in this space?
- 6th - We wait for the participant to speak for 2 s;
- 7th - the second question arises: using the same scale, from 1 for "extremely uncomfortable" and 7 for "extremely comfortable", how would you rate how you feel in this space?
- 8th - We wait for the participant to speak for 2 s;
- 9th - the third question arises: using the same scale, from 1 for "extremely devitalized" and 7 for "extremely revitalized", how would you classify how you feel in this space?

- 10th - We wait for the participant to speak for 2 s;
- 11th - the fourth question arises: using the same scale, from 1 for "extremely stressed" and 7 for "extremely relaxed", how would you classify how you feel in this space?
- 12th - We wait for the participant to speak for 2 s;
- 13th - We move to the second environment (if the first to appear was the 360° image, the video appears, and vice versa). For 5 s, participants explore the environment (looking from left to right and then up);
- 14th - In second 6, the first question appears, and the remaining three questions are repeated for this other scenario;
- 15th - After answering all the questions, the participant is asked to remove the VR Oculus and fill out an attendance questionnaire;
- 16th - The participant responds to the attendance questionnaire;
- 17th - The participant responds to an open interview with observations about the quality of the VR experience.

2.4 Results and Discussion

The graph in Fig. 3 presents the results of the 4 constructs that were used to evaluate presence, namely: sensorial quality (degree of immersion); quality of interaction (control factors); sensory quality (sensory factors); quality of interaction (distraction factors); sensorial quality (degree of realism); curiosity. We observed that the values of the 360 panoramic image present higher values than those of 2D video observation, except for distraction factors. Then, we did a second part in which we assessed whether there were differences between these four constructs.

For the degree of immersion, we started by carrying out a normality test using Shapiro-Wilk, and the following values were found: 0.946 for the 360 panoramic image and 0.915 for the 2D video. We concluded that the data followed normality, allowing the Student's t test to be used. We obtained a t-value of 2.98 and a p-value of 0.0069, verifying statistically significant differences between environment A (360 panoramic image) and B (2D video). Considering that the 360 panoramic image had an average value of 5.2 and the 2D video a value of 4.44, it is concluded that the 360 panoramic image was responsible for participants feeling inside the virtual environment, and feeling that they were completely involved in the environment, losing awareness of real space.

A statistical analysis to check whether there are significant differences between the constructs: control factors, sensory factors, distraction factors, realism factors and curiosity factors, in both conditions was carried out.

For the control factors, the Shapiro-Wilk test results for environment A (360 panoramic image) was 0.919 with a p-value of 0.062 and for environment B (2D video) the statistic value is 0.944 with a p-value of 0.218. We concluded that the data follows normality and that we can use the Student's t test. We obtained a t-value of 2.39 and a p-value of 0.026, indicating statistically significant differences between environments A and B. Considering that the 360 panoramic image had an average value of 6.03 and the 2D video a value of 5.59, we concluded that the 360 panoramic image was responsible for making it easier for participants to imagine themselves being in this environment, as well as greater naturalness in their gaze behavior and better adaptation to the experience.

For sensory factors, the results of the Shapiro-Wilk test for environment A (360 panoramic image) were 0.914 with a p-value of 0.049, and for environment B (2D

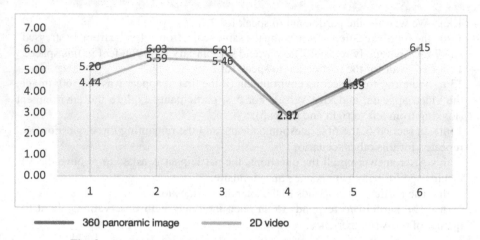

Fig. 3. Average results for the 360 panoramic image and the 2D video.

video) we obtained a value of 0.928 with a p-value of 0.101. In this case, environment A has a p-value slightly below 0.05, which suggests a marginal rejection of the null hypothesis of normality, indicating that the data may not follow a normal distribution. For environment B, the p-value is greater than 0.05, suggesting that the data can be considered normally distributed. Given the marginal normality of environment A, we used the Mann-Whitney U test, which is considered the most appropriate for this scenario. With this test, we obtained a value of 337.9 with a p-value of 0.113. This result suggests no significant difference between environments A and B. Although the average value of the 360 panoramic image is higher than that of the 2D video, there were no significant differences. Thus, we concluded that the quality of visual stimuli and the level of environmental exploration were similarly affected by the 360 panoramic image or the 2D video. We can explain this result by the fact that the environment has a strong point of attraction in front of the participant and only has side walls, without important visual elements.

For distraction factors, the results of the Shapiro-Wilk test for environment A (360 panoramic image) was 0.969 with a p-value of 0.662, and for environment B (2D video) we obtained a value of 0.911 with a p-value of 0.043. In this case, the values in environment A present a normal distribution, while the values in environment B do not present normality. We used a Mann-Whitney U test to assess whether there are significant differences between them and obtained a value of 282.5 with a p-value of 0.699. This means that there are no significant differences between the answers given for environments A and B. This result can be explained by the fact that the questions in this construct are more associated with the viewing device (Oculus) than with the environments experienced, namely the consciousness of the presence of viewing devices during the simulation and their level of distraction from the experience.

For the realism factor, the results of the Shapiro-Wilk test for environment A (360 panoramic image) was 0.960 with a p-value of 0.468, and for environment B (2D video), it was 0.923 with a p-value of 0.076, indicating the existence of normality for both variables. After performing the t-test, we obtained a t-value of 1.007 and a p-value of

0.325, meaning that there is no evidence of statistically significant differences between environments A and B. These results suggest that the perception of the degree of realism and involvement in the experience in virtual reality was the same in both interfaces, 360 panoramic image, and 3D video.

Finally, for the curiosity factors construct, the results of the Shapiro-Wilk test for environment A (360 panoramic image) and environment B (2D video) were 0.816 with a p-value of 0.000699. The values are the same for both environments; because they are very low, they show no normality. The result of the Mann-Whitney U test for environment A and B is 264.5 with a p-value of 1.0, which confirms once again that the responses do not present any significant difference.

At the end of the questionnaires, participants made some considerations, pointing out, for example, that despite the virtual environment being the same, the fact that the image of 2D video was shown further away gave them a feeling of greater openness and a larger scale than in the 360 panoramic image, in which some people reported feeling claustrophobic due to the apparently smaller scale. The way the image is projected in virtual reality alters certain architectural characteristics, such as scale, was one of the aspects that we could not control. This factor may have influenced the results of the experience. Participants indicated that this may have had a negative impact compared with the perception of the 360 panoramic image. Although, they noted that 360 panoramic image was the environment where they felt most involved and present during the experience, as in real life.

Regarding the sound component of the experience, in this case, the sound of water movement, we understood that some participants did not notice that the water was static in the 360 panoramic image, and the participants who noticed said that it did not bother them that the water was not moving and not following the sound.

Regarding the results obtained by the Kansei questionnaire, we found that there was only a small variation in the responses for both environments (360 panoramic image and 2D video). Regarding the state of agitation/calm, we obtained an average of 5.91 for the 360 panoramic image and 5.82 for the 2D video, compared to an initial average state of relaxation of 5.45. For the feeling of discomfort/comfort we obtained an average value of 5.77 for the 360 panoramic image and 6.00 for the 2D video. For the devitalized/revitalized state, we received an average of 4.77 for the 360 panoramic image and 4.95 for the 2D video. Finally, for the stressed/relaxed state, we got an average of 5.91 for the 360 panoramic image and 5.86 for the 2D video. We consider that these results could mean that the interfaces under study interfered in approximately the same way with the participants' perceptions and emotional reactions.

3   Conclusion and Final Considerations

The results obtained in this study provide important information about the comparative effectiveness of static 360 panoramic images and 2D videos in virtual reality (VR) about different aspects of perceived presence.

When analyzing the five constructs used to evaluate the presence, we consistently observed significant differences between the two modalities (360 panoramic image and 2D video). Participants reported greater immersion when viewing 360 panoramic images compared to 2D videos. Furthermore, control factors were perceived as more satisfactory in 360 panoramic images, indicating a greater sense of control over the virtual environment.

However, the results were less distinct when we looked at sensory factors and degree of realism. While participants perceived 360 panoramic images as more sensorial, there were no significant differences in terms of realism between the two modalities.

These findings highlight the importance of carefully considering the presentation modality of the environment when creating virtual reality experiences. While 360 panoramic images can provide greater immersion and control, 2D videos can be more effective at minimizing distractions. However, it is essential to highlight that the choice between the two modalities will depend on the specific objectives of the application and user preferences.

Regarding the results obtained through the Kansei method, we observed that, although both environments generated a general increase in the participants' state of relaxation, there were few distinct differences in emotional perceptions between the two, and we consider that these differences can be attributed to an altered perception of spatial scale in the two environments.

Furthermore, we think that the fact that values are very close is because both modalities aren't affecting the application of Kansei. Despite that, we would need more information, or several scenarios, to conclude that this proximity is due to the choice of Kansei words. We also think that using both modalities together would be the ideal that is, 360 panoramic videos in Virtual Reality. However, implementing this option for many scenarios would take hundreds of hours of computation, as producing a panoramic image with animation can take more than 24 h.

In short, this research contributed to understanding the best modality to use in Virtual Reality to apply the Kansei methodology, in this case, the 360° panoramic image., Although there are significant differences between the two modalities, and the 3D panorama has higher values on average than the 2D video, it appears that these differences did not affect the Kansei results, which are similar. We can therefore conclude that with the scenario used in this study, any of the modalities can be used, despite there being an advantage for the 3D panorama. Studies with more complex scenarios, where there is important information to the left and right of the participants, must be developed to assess whether in these cases there are more striking differences in the presence and results obtained by kansei.

Acknowledgments. National funds finance this work through FCT – Fundação para a Ciência e a Tecnologia, I.P., under the Strategic Project with the references UIDB/04008/2020 and UIDP/04008/2020 and ITI-LARSyS FCT Pluriannual fundings 2020–2023 (UIDB/50009/2020).

References

1. Formiga, B., Rebelo, F., Cruz Pinto, J., Gomes, E.: How architectural forms can influence emotional reactions: an exploratory study. In: Soares, M.M., Rosenzweig, E., Marcus, A. (eds.) HCII 2022. LNCS, vol. 13322, pp. 37–55. Springer, Cham (2022). https://doi.org/10.1007/978-3-031-05900-1_3

2. Formiga, B., Rebelo, F., da Cruz Pinto, J., Noriega, P.: Hospital lobby and user's perceptions architectural Kansei method. In: Rebelo, F. (ed.) AHFE 2021. LNNS, vol. 261, pp. 159–166. Springer, Cham (2021). https://doi.org/10.1007/978-3-030-79760-7_20
3. Kalving, M., Paananen, S., Seppälä, J., Colley, A., Häkkilä, J.: Comparing VR and desktop 360 video museum tours. In: Döring, T., Boll, S., Colley, A., Esteves, A., Guerreiro, J. (eds.) Proceedings of MUM 2022: the 21st International Conference on Mobile and Ubiquitous Multimedia, pp. 282–284 (2022)
4. Yoganathan, S., Finch, D.A., Parkin, E., Pollard, J.: 360° virtual reality video for the acquisition of knot tying skills: a randomised controlled trial. Int. J. Surg. **54**(Pt A), 24–27 (2018)

Kinesics Language Interaction in Virtual Reality

Ze Huang and Yancong Zhu[✉]

Faculty of Psychology, Beijing Normal University, Beijing 100875, China
202328061014@mail.bnu.edu.cn

Abstract. In the realm of virtual reality, the evolution and innovation of human-computer interaction are ongoing. Kinesics language interaction, which encompasses communication via gestures, facial expressions, body movements, and gaze, is being increasingly recognized as a vital strategy for interaction. This paper delves into the significance and current development of kinesics language interaction, enumerates the effects of kinesics language interaction on user experience in virtual environments, and explores the importance of kinesics language interaction from the perspectives of facial expressions, gaze, gestures, and postures. The paper proposes that future research and development should be centered on comprehensive kinesics language interaction to investigate the cognitive impact on users and potential adverse effects.

Keywords: Virtual Reality · Kinesics Language Interaction · Human-Computer Interaction

1 Introduction

Kinesics language, as a mode of conveying information through body movements, facial expressions, and other non-verbal cues, serves to supplement and reinforce communication. It, in conjunction with oral and written language, constitutes a diverse range of human communication paradigms and is considered an indispensable form of special language for humans [1]. Empirical findings by psychologists such as Aipal Merabian reveal that the communication occurring between words and sounds constitutes only a fraction of daily information exchange. Their research suggests a formula for the total effect of information communication: 7% of words +38% of voice tone +55% of facial expressions [2]. However, this notion is limited in its scope, as it overlooks other crucial aspects of non-verbal communication, such as gaze interaction and gesture interaction. Kinesics language, on the other hand, transmits non-verbal information and aids the listener in deciphering the intended meaning of the message maximizing the utilization of kinesics language can enhance the precision and efficacy of communication, thereby playing a pivotal role in daily interactions.

A. Marcus et al. (Eds.): HCII 2024, LNCS 14715, pp. 52–67, 2024.
https://doi.org/10.1007/978-3-031-61359-3_5

In recent years, virtual reality, an integrated perception and interaction technology, has garnered significant attention and rapidly evolved into an innovative technology across remote work, online education, entertainment, and other fields. The COVID-19 pandemic has accelerated the development of online education, which is beneficial for interdisciplinary teaching. Online teaching allows students and teachers from various disciplines to participate anytime and anywhere to achieve educational goals [3]. The increasing demand for remote learning will drive the need for more immersive and interactive educational experiences, and stimulate innovation and application of virtual reality technology in the field of education. The focus of recent research has been on the immersion, usability, and capability evaluation of virtual reality [4]. In virtual scenes, spoken language is replaced by voice interaction, written language by text interaction. Kinesics language plays a pivotal role in these scenarios, as it encompasses a multi-channel interaction mode and integrates the application of emotional language to provide users with a more robust experience and heighten their motivation to engage. This results in a more emotive user experience [5]. It is widely acknowledged that immersion, social presence, and increased interactivity are the primary characteristics of virtual reality [6], which align with the potential applications of kinesics language technology. By incorporating kinesics language such as gestures and facial expressions into the virtual environment's interactions, users can engage in a more natural manner, further enhancing immersion possibilities while fostering stronger social presence and overall user experience.

This comprehensive literature review was conducted through comprehensive searches of academic databases, including Google Scholar, utilizing keywords such as "virtual reality," "kinesics Language," and "non-verbal communication" to ensure in-depth coverage of the existing research. Initially, a total of 211 potentially relevant articles were screened based on the focus of kinesics Language interaction in both daily social and virtual environments. Subsequently, 42 papers were selected for further in-depth analysis, as they significantly impacted individual experiences within virtual reality contexts, pertaining to various methods of kinesics language interaction. This rigorous screening process aimed to accurately reflect the pivotal role of kinesics language in virtual environments. Drawing upon Wei X et al.'s (2022) classification framework analysis of ten major virtual reality platforms [7], this study meticulously examines facial expression interaction, gaze interaction, gesture interaction, and posture interaction within virtual reality, to unravel their practicality and potential in such environments. By delving into the significance of kinesics language in both real-life and virtual reality settings, as well as its implementation and application within VR scenarios and its impact on user experience, this research implies the necessity and inevitability of developing kinesics language interaction within virtual reality. Furthermore, this paper proposes potential avenues for future research. The findings from this investigation hold significant importance for enhancing interactivity within virtual reality and optimizing user satisfaction (Figs. 1 and 2).

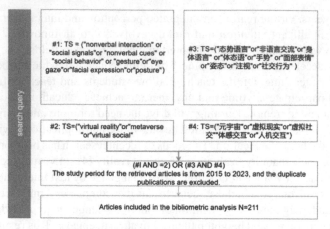

Fig. 1. The flowchart for data collection

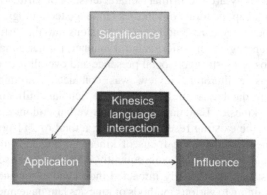

Fig. 2. Exploring Paths in kinesics language Interaction

2   Exploring Kinesics Language: Crafting a 'Mind Bridge' in Virtual Reality for Deeper Connection

Kinesics Language plays a vital role in interpersonal communication, serving as a crucial medium for the transmission of emotions, ideas, and information. In virtual reality user interaction, employing kinesics Language aligns with real-life communication norms and enhances users' immersion and satisfaction, while fortifying their sense of interaction and participation. Kinesics Language significantly contributes to directing others' attention, garnering recognition, fostering a friendly atmosphere, bolstering mutual trust, and amplifying social presence [7]. The utilization of kinesics language is crucial in daily communication and is considered the cornerstone of human-computer interaction, drawing on humans' inherent movement habits in virtual reality [8]. Facial expression interaction, gaze interaction, gesture interaction, and posture interaction all play essential roles in virtual reality. To construct a more realistic and immersive virtual social environment, research and application of kinesics language are indispensable components. With the aid of these interactive technologies, we can create a more immersive and interactive virtual social environment, better catering to users' needs and expectations.

2.1 Facial Expression Interaction

Precisely linked to individual emotions, facial expressions serve as the most perceptive nonverbal communication cue in interpersonal interactions, playing a crucial role in real-life scenarios. For instance, facial expressions can offer a wealth of user information, including emotions, mood, attitude, and personality [9]. In virtual reality environments, facial expressions perform analogous functions to their physical world counterparts. Several studies have demonstrated that functional magnetic resonance imaging (fMRI) activates the amygdala when observing subjects' brain states in response to both real human and virtual characters' expressions [10], indicating that facial expressions in virtual settings can also influence users' emotions.

Amplified facial expressions in virtual reality environments can significantly influence user experience, as demonstrated by Soo Youn Oh et al. (2016) in their study involving 158 participants [11]. By manipulating features such as the angle of the mouth, researchers found that participants experienced increased positive emotions and heightened social presence. These findings suggest that in high-social-presence environments, individuals are more likely to share ideas and information, thereby fostering innovation and creativity. The precision of adjusting facial expressions in virtual reality is daunting when compared to face-to-face communication settings. Additionally, virtual characters exhibit a broader range of facial expressions compared to their real-life counterparts. The design of various intensities of smiles, eyebrow movements, confusion or questioning expressions allows virtual characters to display a wealth of emotional expression abilities. When users engage with these expressive virtual characters during conversations, it enhances their sense of trust and intimacy towards them [12]. In essence, individuals may perceive a stronger connection with one another in the virtual world compared to reality. This heightened sense of intimacy not only promotes healthier social relationships but also strengthens connections between users by facilitating more effective teamwork and transactional behavior while curbing undesirable behaviors like conflict and harassment.

In summary, the integration of facial expressions in virtual scenes significantly enhances users' perception of social presence, intimacy, and trust. Moreover, it fosters efficient teamwork and cultivates a more optimistic social environment. Compared to face-to-face communication, facial expressions possess a broader application in virtual social interactions. Users can not only map natural expressions into the virtual realm to convey additional emotional or intentional information as social signals, thereby enhancing the ambiance of social events, but also flexibly control the facial expressions of virtual characters through a multitude of interaction methods, thereby enhancing the personalization and diversity of these characters. A comprehensive understanding and innovative approach to the utilization of facial expressions is crucial for human-computer interaction, as it not only enriches user experience but also ensures that authentic emotions are not replaced by virtual expressions.

2.2 Gaze Based Interaction

The act of gaze refers to the behavior of users focusing their visual attention on specific areas or objects. As a crucial component in social interactions, a comprehensive understanding of gaze plays a significant role in adaptive functions [13]. Gaze serves a dual purpose; it not only facilitates the extraction of information from others' eyes and the identification of their emotions, but also enables the expression of one's own emotions and intentions through gaze [14]. In virtual environments, gaze can not only recognize user emotions and enhance communication but also serve as an efficient, accurate, and low-cognitive-load interaction method.

In virtual environments, various eye-related behaviors, such as movement, fixation position, pupil diameter, and eye deviation, can be employed to infer emotions. For instance, a direct gaze may signify happiness or anger, while squinting could indicate sadness or fear [15]. Although eye contact with virtual characters can elicit similar attention effects and emotion-related psychophysiological responses as in real life, the physiological effects in virtual reality scenarios are generally weaker [16]. Some studies suggest that this discrepancy is due to the anonymity of virtual social interactions. Individuals can mask their true identities and personal information, engaging in virtual social activities under an anonymous or disguised persona. However, for those with social avoidance tendencies who avoid eye contact in real-life situations, the anonymity provided by virtual social interaction enables them to communicate through gaze [17]. Compared to real-life scenarios, the anonymity in virtual social settings can mitigate social pressure and discomfort, while enhancing emotional connections between individuals through gaze communication and improving communication efficiency.

Gaze plays a crucial role not only in interpersonal communication but also as an interactive operation. Eye movement interaction, also known as gaze interaction in virtual reality, is a complex phenomenon influenced by various factors. Kim M (2017) et al. designed and implemented a user interface based on the gaze pointer, which infers users' intentions by detecting the direction of their eye gaze [18]. They also modified the visual field range and incorporated three-dimensional elements into the interface, while establishing correlations between background color and emotions or other virtual scenes. This approach enhances user immersion and satisfaction, influences their emotions, and stimulates interest. In contrast to real life, emotional expression and eye movement interaction through eyes in virtual reality utilize visual channels; thus, it is imperative to analyze eye movement patterns and record fixation duration to ascertain whether users are engaged in communication or interaction at any given time. David-John B (2021) successfully predicted the initiation of interactive behavior by utilizing 15 participants who performed item selection tasks in virtual reality while collecting eye tracking data. The analysis encompassed parameters such as eye movement speed, distribution of attention focus, and visual eye movements during observation processes [19]. This research paves the way for achieving and refining immersive natural interaction in virtual reality.

Gaze, as a low-cognitive-load interaction modality, enables researchers to assess users' cognitive load and muscle fatigue through indicators such as blink rate and gaze retention time [20]. Compared to speech recognition and gesture interaction, gaze inter-action imposes less cognitive processing burden and mitigates user fatigue. Additionally, gaze interaction can reduce tracking errors and improve recognition accuracy [21].

In summary, gaze constitutes an indispensable mode of interaction in virtual reality. Consequently, the development of realistic eye models and eye movements remains a long-term research priority for fully exploiting the potential of gaze [22]. Within virtual reality environments, individuals can manipulate various conditions to influence and control the user experience; however, numerous challenges exist in providing seamless gaze interaction. Future research is required to enhance the precision and fidelity of gaze interaction while integrating diverse interaction methods to offer users an increasingly immersive and personalized experience.

2.3 Gesture Based Interaction

McNeill (1992) posits that gestures are of equal importance to verbal language, as they not only articulate intentions and convey information but also supplement and enhance verbal communication [23, 24]. Analogous to gaze, gestures in virtual reality serve a dual function of communication and interactive operation. In the virtual reality environment, gesture recognition exhibits innate and intuitive characteristics, rendering it suitable for diverse application domains.

In virtual environments, gesture language can convey a broader range of emotions and intentions, enhancing users' social presence in collaborative and communicative interactions. This can compensate for the absence of social presence induced by remote communication [25]. Although gestures can sometimes be more vivid and direct than verbal language, they may also lead to misinterpretations. Gestures are inherently social and may differ across cultures [7] (Wei X, 2022). For instance, Chinese individuals often gesture towards their face to indicate themselves, whereas individuals in the United Kingdom and the United States are more likely to point their thumbs towards their chest [26]. In virtual social settings, addressing this issue involves recognizing the significance of gestures within diverse cultural contexts.

On the application front, devices such as depth cameras, inertial sensors, and virtual gloves are extensively employed to acquire hand-related information. Generally, there are two approaches to processing gesture data. The first is marked data acquisition, which involves recording gesture data via sensor devices and assigning annotations to each gesture to signify their meaning. Although this method enhances gesture recognition accuracy, it compromises the naturalness of interaction. The second is unmarked data acquisition, which permits more natural interaction by refraining from assigning labels to gestures and employing gestures that closely emulate real-life interactions. However, this approach necessitates higher accuracy in data acquisition and subsequent algorithm processing [27].

Gesture recognition is extensively utilized in various virtual reality technology sce-narios. For instance, in the medical field, gesture recognition offers a therapeutic avenue for Alzheimer's patients with limited mobility. These patients can interact with virtual animals in an immersive virtual environment and receive treatment at a pre-constructed virtual zoo. This form of therapy can boost patients' positive emotions and enhance their motor coordination [28]. Gesture recognition also plays a pivotal role in the educational sector, enabling students to manipulate virtual objects and solve complex mathematical geometry problems via virtual hand operations. This teaching method not only spurs students' interest in learning but also enhances teaching quality [29]. For students with hearing impairments, utilizing gesture-based interactions with teachers in the classroom can not only reduce social barriers and enhance the frequency of communication with teachers, thereby improving classroom efficiency, but it can also boost the self-esteem of students with hearing disabilities [30].

From a technical standpoint, gesture recognition confronts challenges pertaining to diversity and complexity, necessitating real-time precision, resistance to environmental interference, and the management of substantial datasets concerning gestures. In terms of user experience, gesture recognition currently grapples with high learning costs [31]. How can we mitigate these learning costs, minimize sensations of fatigue and discomfort, and design gesture interactions that are more akin to real-life experiences? These topics warrant exploration for future research.

2.4 Posture Based Interaction

In virtual reality, the manifestation and interpretation of body language activate a broad range of human physical movements, significantly enhancing sociability. Body language encompasses static postures such as standing upright, arms-crossed and chest-raised, among others, which articulate an individual's stance and current state. It also includes dynamic contact movements like nodding, hugging, backslapping, and so forth, employed to signify intimacy, support, or friendliness towards the communicative partner. In virtual reality, posture language performs analogous functions to real life by supplementing verbal expressions and divulging users' emotions, moods, and attitudes. For instance, in Second Life, a user-generated virtual world developed by Linden Lab, individuals can interact with other virtual characters by donning motion-capture jackets, thereby conveying messages of encouragement and reassurance while amplifying the interactive experience through physical sensory feedback induced by actions like hugging and slapping [32]. Compared to conventional audio-visual telecommunication methods, posture language expands the interactive perceptual channel, thereby escalating user immersion and engagement, and establishing a unique presence within the virtual scene.

Nodding is a crucial expression in posture language, typically employed to convey agreement and support. Studies reveal that nodding occurs most frequently during brainstorming in virtual meetings, surpassing other physical behaviors [25]. Posture interaction preserves the significance of "nodding" as a vital social posture. In comparison to traditional audio and video conferencing, virtual reality conferencing enhances participants' sense of immersion and engagement, facilitating a better understanding of each other's attitudes through posture communication. In psychological research, postural communication is indispensable for conducting follow-up interviews as a research method. Follow-up interviews allow researchers to gain a deeper understanding of subjects' behaviors and feelings in specific situations. However, conducting face-to-face real-time follow-ups poses challenges for researchers. Virtual reality overcomes this issue by facilitating virtual reality scenes for follow-up interviews with subjects [33]. The study demonstrated that when participants witnessed researchers provide feedback on their nodding motion within the virtual scene, they experienced recognition and maintained continuity in the interview process. In real life, follow-up interviews center on capturing subjects' responses in their natural state; yet, face-to-face interaction comes at a higher cost. In virtual reality, posture interaction closely emulates human interaction in the real world, offering the potential to obtain more natural and realistic data. Researchers can interact with subjects anytime and anywhere while observing and analyzing their body postures in real time. This flexibility significantly enhances the feasibility of conducting studies.

Posture expression in virtual reality constitutes a vital method for identifying users' emotions. For instance, employing Laban's Movement Analysis framework enables the quantification of posture-related indicators from five dimensions: body part involvement, effort (considering time, space, weight, and fluidity of movement), space (the path of movement), shape (the contour and shape of the body during movement), and morphology (the transition of each movement). By analyzing the user's movement pattern and associating it with their current emotion, the machine can provide more accurate interactive feedback [34]. Detailed information on movements and postures facilitates the creation of a personalized user model for enhanced emotion identification. Posture expressions contribute to a more comprehensive and multidimensional analysis of emotions in virtual reality. In the medical field, postural interaction is primarily utilized in sports rehabilitation. For example, upper limb sports rehabilitation training can integrate postural interaction to stimulate patients' interest and boost motivation through rehabilitation games [35]. Compared to real-life scenarios, machine feedback on user interactions in virtual reality is more timely while maintaining standardized training processes. Patients experience a greater sense of autonomy and freedom when interacting with machines in virtual reality, which ultimately improves exercise rehabilitation outcomes.

Postural expression, typically an unconscious behavior, is among the most reliable cues in social interactions and is crucial for virtual social interaction [36]. From the perspective of human language development, postural expression and gesture communication precede spoken language and gradually evolve into written language. As society and culture advance, the directness and efficiency of written and spoken language receive increasing attention. Consequently, posture expression may have fewer application scenarios in virtual environments, potentially leading to a significant reduction in social intimacy. Thus, it is imperative for researchers to investigate methods of integrating postures into human-computer interaction and motion design for non-real virtual characters.

3 Discussion

3.1 The Implementation and Application of Kinesics Language Interaction: A Critical Analysis of Its Deficiencies and Developments

In the current study on interaction in virtual reality scenes, the methods of interaction related to kinesics language are not sufficiently perfect. The earlier system to use multi-channel interaction is the "Put that there" system proposed by Bolt in 1980, which generates graphics through gestures and speech [37]. In 2012, people used HMD and

CAVE immersive systems while actors dressed in full motion capture costumes rehearsed short plays. The system played a positive role in rehearsal and other aspects, but a major drawback was the inability to see actors' facial expressions [38]. Roth (2019) proposes a new architecture for social augmentation systems in virtual reality scenes that can track eye gaze, body movement, facial expressions in real-time along with gesture interactions to enhance social behaviors [39]. The existing studies have incomplete interaction methods leading to the absence of kinesics language in the virtual environment and affecting information transmission accuracy. On the other hand, Li Shujie (2019) analyzed the role of virtual reality in education and believed it would bring more immersive, interactive, and imaginative educational modes but pointed out unsatisfactory effects due to low-precision motion acquisition technology for virtual characters [40]. Coordinating interactive input/output display problems and establishing reasonable system architecture are directions that need improvement for future development. The imperfect mode of kinesics language interaction is not only limited by technical constraints but also hindered by high research equipment costs as well as marketing and popularization deficiencies. This limits diversity within virtual reality applications and ecosystem establishment which subsequently affects user attraction towards VR usage motivation. The utilization of rich visual and auditory channels in applications is prevalent; however, the development of haptic feedback in virtual reality remains underwhelming, primarily due to the limitations of current haptic feedback devices, such as their bulkiness and low fidelity [41].

With the ongoing instrumentalization of artificial intelligence, the Widespread adoption of advanced mobile communication technologies like 5G and 6G, the continuous enhancement of chip computing power, and the emergence of stable and reliable energy technologies, virtual reality is poised for further advancement. User interaction methods are expected to progressively improve and evolve. For instance, body-sensing gloves are anticipated to enhance touch sensitivity, enabling individuals to genuinely perceive the texture, temperature, and form of virtual objects. This advancement will help bridge the gap between virtual objects and real-life sensations. Future research should prioritize understanding the impact of multi-channel kinesics language on users in multi-modal interaction scenarios.

3.2 The Constraints of Kinesics Language Interaction Research

The existing literature predominantly emphasizes on enhancing user experience by augmenting or refining human-computer interaction strategies that incorporate kinesics language. However, it overlooks the potential negative consequences of its absence in virtual reality environments. There still exists a discrepancy between the current mode of human-computer interaction and the desired natural and efficient interaction. In virtual reality scenarios, input cues are filtered, resulting in the restriction of real-life social interactions such as sounds, images, expressions, and gestures. This constraint impedes the utilization of kinesics language, affects the efficiency of interpersonal communication, and may even give rise to user misunderstandings [42]. The absence of certain kinesics language in e-learning, attributable to cost-effectiveness and other factors, also impinges on the learning encoding and decoding process [43]. In virtual reality environments devoid of kinesics language, it becomes challenging for individuals to comprehend certain social cues, particularly during one-on-one interactions. Moreover, studies have indicated that users tend to adapt to the absence of kinesics language over time [44], which could potentially prejudice users. Considering the increasing popularity of virtual reality technology, its highly immersive experience might have a profound impact on cognition.

Based on the integration of embodied cognition theory and sensorimotor simulation metaphor theory, research has discovered that specific physical experiences play a crucial role in shaping individuals' construction of subjective social reality [45]. Virtual reality applications have the potential to predispose users to transpose behaviors and experiences from the virtual realm to the physical world, thereby altering attitudes and behavior patterns in daily life. Moreover, in a virtual reality environment, greeting may not solely involve waving, but rather, employing a finger movement to create a communicative expression through gesture recognition. Could this same gesture be employed in real-life greetings in the future? In terms of real-world social interaction, virtual reality may act as an "offline mode," where gesture recognition, eye tracking, and other interaction methods also influence the form and meaning of kinesics language in actual life. The implications of these factors on human behavior are worthy of further exploration.

3.3 The Influence of Factors on Users' Kinesics Language Interaction

In the pre-Internet era, interactions were primarily text-based, voice-based, and graphical interface-based. However, the widespread adoption of virtual reality technology has ushered in a revolutionary transformation in interaction. It now encompasses visual, gestural, postural, facial, and other multi-channel elements. This transition has rendered human-computer interaction more user-centric and efficient [46].

When examining the impact of virtual reality technology on human-computer interaction, it is crucial to consider not only how the new technology shapes individuals but also how users themselves are being shaped in the process of interaction [47]. With the widespread adoption of gestural language interactions, users' brain neurons will form stronger and faster connections, leading to the emergence of new habitual behaviors. It is crucial to promptly recognize and understand these habitual behaviors and their significance in order to better comprehend user actions. This understanding is essential in the study of interaction quality. There are substantial differences between kinesics language interaction and contemporary natural interaction. These disparities will continue to have an escalating influence as virtual reality technology gains popularity and progressively alters user behavior and characteristics.

The design concept of 'natural interaction' will gain increasing prominence, with a keen focus on narrowing the gap between virtual reality and natural interactions. In the future, multi-modal interactions in virtual reality are anticipated to introduce more complex interactive information. To enhance immersion, it is imperative to broaden information channels and increase kinesics language interactions. Consequently, this paper proposes a DCF model that elucidates the influence (I: Impact) in which kinesics language interactions affect users, the impact of this not only involves user satisfaction, user engagement, or learning outcomes, but may also affect users' social skills, cultural awareness, and even their way of thinking. The DCF model takes into account three primary factors:

1. D: The degree of disparity between kinesics language interactions in virtual environments and those in natural settings (D: Differences), including variations in interaction modes and discrepancies between the interactive environment and reality.
2. C: The complexity of information conveyed through kinesics language interactions primarily depends on both the quantity of information and its ease of comprehension for users (C: Complexity). For instance, intricate gesture interactions can heighten learning challenges and cognitive burden [26] (Yang LI, 2019).
3. F: Frequency refers to the frequency of kinesics language interactions (F: Frequency), encompassing factors such as the number of occurrences, duration, and speed at which users provide feedback. These aspects reflect users' cognitive load as well as muscle fatigue.

The DCF model is manifested through facial expressions interaction (fei), eye gaze interaction (egi), gestures interaction (gi), posture interaction (pi), and other interactive modes (oi). The influence of these interaction variations on users is amplified or mitigated by both the frequency of interaction and the complexity of the information exchanged. The logical representation of the DCF model is as follows.

$$I = D(fei) \cdot C(fei) \cdot F(fei) + D(egi) \cdot C(egi) \cdot F(egi) + D(gi) \cdot C(gi) \cdot F(gi)$$
$$+ D(pi) \cdot C(pi \cdot F(pi) + D(oi) \cdot C(oi) \cdot F(oi)$$
$$D \in (1, 10)\, C \in [0, 10]\, F \in [0.10] \tag{1}$$

This model reflects the impact of kinesics interaction on users, primarily in terms of interactive distinctiveness, information complexity, and interaction frequency. It operates through different interaction channels. A value of D approaching 0 indicates almost no difference compared to natural interaction, while a value approaching 10 signifies almost no correlation with natural interaction. A value of C at 0 represents information complexity that users can handle unconsciously, while a value of 10 represents information complexity at the limit of user capacity. F with a value of 0 denotes no interaction, and a value of 10 represents the limit of interaction frequency that users can tolerate (Fig. 3).

In the future, a concrete study can be conducted on the specific components included in each part of the model, how to quantify them, and a tangible investigation into their impact on users. Moreover, the impacts of various interactions may not be mutually independent, but rather interactive. Considering individual differences may also influence the outcome. By incorporating these factors, the model can be more comprehensive and accurate in predicting and explaining the impact of kinesics interaction on users, and applicable in a broader range of human-computer interaction scenarios.

Refining the classification of diverse influencing factors under various interaction modes can enhance our comprehension of the implications of Kinesics language interaction on users in virtual reality technology. As a fundamental framework for interaction design principles, this approach can aid researchers in conducting more effective classification research, emphasizing multiple influencing factors, and offering valuable references for future human-computer interaction designers. Additionally, it may contribute to the development of criteria for consideration in interaction design. In terms of user experience, this method can optimize the virtual social experience, facilitate user adaptation to the product, and provide deeper insights into the factors shaping user behavior

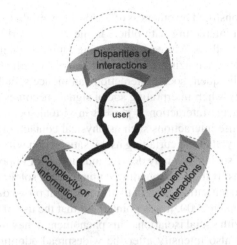

Fig. 3. The three aspects of user impact in kinesics language interaction.

and characteristics in virtual environments. This model can aid in proposing targeted solutions to mitigate any adverse effects resulting from alterations in interaction styles on users.

3.4 The Impact of Kinesics Language Interaction on Social Behavior

With the progression of technology, human-computer interaction within virtual environments has the potential to enhance users' memory, perception, cognition, and problem-solving abilities [48]. The integration of kinesics language interaction diversifies the expression and experience of virtual social interaction, enhances communication effectiveness, fosters emotional exchange, and strengthens individual identity expression. However, it is essential to recognize the distinct differences between the interaction mode in a virtual environment and daily interpersonal communication modes. Prior to the advent of the Internet, individuals primarily relied on direct face-to-face communication, observation, and imitation to establish personal social cognition and form an understanding and interpretation of contemporary society. Nevertheless, the application of kinesics language in a virtual setting holds significant value as it serves as a vital communication strategy for interpreting others' kinesics language information. Facial expressions, gestures, or dances can be employed to maintain social contact when voice and text channels are limited. Moreover, gestures and body language can aid in reducing users' social anxiety [49]. As our capabilities in kinesics language interaction continue to improve, the significance of virtual socializing in interpersonal communication will incrementally increase. However, kinesics language interaction can also engender negative impacts on users' social behaviors. For instance, the application of kinesics language in both virtual and real worlds can result in the adoption of distinct social norms, potentially giving rise to miscommunication. Certain behaviors may be interpreted as provocative or offensive, leading to increased misunderstandings and conflicts. If a user employs social behaviors in the virtual world that they deem normal in the real world but are misconstrued by others as offensive, they might experience discomfort and opt to refrain from interacting with others in the virtual world to avoid provoking misunderstandings or conflicts. Moreover, achieving multi-channel interaction is more straightforward in virtual socializing, exacerbating users' cognitive load and leading to information overload. Frequent social interaction can induce social fatigue and impair decision-making quality when interpreting social signals becomes challenging. Lastly, although kinesics language interaction is present in virtual social interaction, it lacks certain aspects of real-life interactions such as physical contact, olfactory authenticity, and auditory authenticity; thereby curtailing users' satisfaction with their online interactions. However, virtual socializing may deprive individuals of opportunities for normal face-to-face interactions. If their surrounding community is solely immersed in virtual socializing, fulfilling social satisfaction in the future might prove difficult.

In a study by Sanders in 2000, it was pointed out that the use of the Internet by adolescents is associated with social isolation. This phenomenon may not only occur during adolescence but might also intensify after the widespread adoption of virtual reality [50]. The adverse consequences generate a divisive pattern in users' social interactions, leading to a polarization of user engagement. A portion of users become profoundly ensconced in virtual social networking, fostering an escalation of their social reliance. Conversely, another group of users exhibit a decline in social activity, corresponding to an increase in their social alienation (Fig. 4).

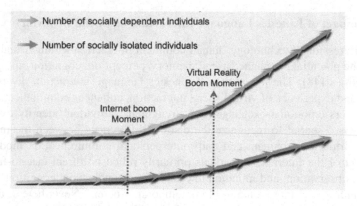

Fig. 4. Trends in Social Dependence and Isolation.

3.5   Kinesics Language Interaction and Data Privacy

With the growing popularity of virtual reality applications, ethical concerns related to data security and privacy are being exacerbated. In addition to collecting personal data such as location, social connections, verbal communication, search queries, and product preferences, technology companies also possess the capability to gather kinesics language, including a user's posture, gaze, gestures, facial expressions, and interpersonal distance. According to a 2018 study (Bailenson), nearly 2 million records related to posture language were generated within just 20 min of being in a virtual reality scene -

a phenomenon that is unprecedented since the advent of information technology [51]. Consequently, further exploration is required to design human-computer interaction effectively and implement appropriate measures for safeguarding users' privacy.

4 Conclusion

To summarize, despite existing shortcomings in kinesics language interaction within virtual reality, its development is increasingly recognized as crucial. It is anticipated that advancements in virtual reality technology will facilitate a more diversified human-computer interaction. Kinesics language, which leverages natural language processing and emotion recognition technologies, enables users to interact with virtual environments in a more natural and intuitive manner. Future research should accordingly concentrate on refining the human-computer interaction mode associated with kinesics language in virtual reality, while simultaneously considering the adverse consequences of its absence, as well as the potential influence of virtual reality on cognitive and behavioral patterns. Moreover, the manner in which designers safeguard user data security and privacy during commercial activities represents another focal point for future research.

Acknowledgments. We are grateful to the UX Program of MAP in the Faculty of Psychology at Beijing Normal University for their valuable support and assistance in the completion of this paper.

References

1. Li, J.: The status of body language. Seeker **02**, 102–105 (2001)
2. Mehrabian, A.: Silent Messages. Wadsworth, Belmont (1971)
3. Huang, J., Pan, W., Liu, Y., Wang, X., Liu, W.: Engineering design thinking and making: online transdisciplinary teaching and learning in a covid-19 context, 159–166 (2020). https://doi.org/10.1007/978-3-030-51626-0_19
4. Boletsis, C., Cedergren, J.E.: VR locomotion in the new era of virtual reality: an empirical comparison of prevalent techniques. Adv. Hum. Comput. Interact. **2019** (2019)
5. Rogers, K., Funke, J., Frommel, J., et al.: Exploring interaction fidelity in virtual reality: object manipulation and whole-body movements. In: Proceedings of the 2019 CHI Conference on Human Factors in Computing Systems, pp. 1–14 (2019)
6. Cipresso, P., Giglioli, I.A.C., Raya, M.A., et al.: The past, present, and future of virtual and augmented reality research: a network and cluster analysis of the literature. Front. Psychol., 2086 (2018)
7. Wei, X., Jin, X., Fan, M.: Communication in immersive social virtual reality: a systematic review of 10 years' studies. arXiv preprint arXiv:2210.01365 (2022)
8. Zhang, F., Dai, G., Peng, X.: A review of human-computer interaction in virtual reality. Sci. Sinica **46**(12), 1711–17361 (2016)
9. Lei, J., Ding, Y.: Facial expressions: some controversies. Adv. Psychol. Sci. **21**(10), 1749–1754 (2013)
10. Moser, E., Derntl, B., Robinson, S., et al.: Amygdala activation at 3T in response to human and avatar facial expressions of emotions. J. Neurosci. Methods **161**(1), 126–133 (2007)

11. Oh, S.Y., Bailenson, J., Krämer, N., Li, B.: Let the avatar brighten your smile: effects of enhancing facial expressions in virtual environments. PLOS ONE **11**, 9, 1–18 (2016). https://doi.org/10.1371/journal.pone.0161794
12. Potdevin, D., Clavel, C., Sabouret, N.: Virtual intimacy in human-embodied conversational agent interactions: the influence of multimodality on its perception. J. Multimodal User Interfaces **15**, 25–43 (2021)
13. Lin, Z.: Eye gaze: unique or not? Adv. Psychol. Sci. **13**(4), 398–405 (2005)
14. Çakır, M., Huckauf, A.: Reviewing the social function of eye gaze in social interaction. In: Proceedings of the 2023 Symposium on Eye Tracking Research and Applications, pp. 1–3 (2023)
15. Huo, P., Feng, C., Chen, T.: The influence of observers and observers on gaze perception. Adv. Psychol. Sci. **29**(02), 238–251 (2021)
16. Syrjämäki, A.H., Isokoski, P., Surakka, V., et al.: Eye contact in virtual reality–a psychophysiological study. Comput. Hum. Behav. **112**, 106454 (2020)
17. Baker, S., Waycott, J., Carrasco, R., et al.: Avatar-mediated communication in social VR: an in-depth exploration of older adult interaction in an emerging communication platform. In: Proceedings of the 2021 CHI Conference on Human Factors in Computing Systems, pp. 1–13 (2021)
18. Kim, M., Lee, J., Jeon, C., et al.: A study on interaction of gaze pointer-based user interface in mobile virtual reality environment. Symmetry **9**(9), 189 (2017)
19. David-John, B., Peacock, C., Zhang, T., et al.: Towards gaze-based prediction of the intent to interact in virtual reality. In: ACM Symposium on Eye Tracking Research and Applications, pp. 1–7 (2021)
20. Souchet, A.D., Philippe, S., Lourdeaux, D., et al.: Measuring visual fatigue and cognitive load via eye tracking while learning with virtual reality head-mounted displays: a review. Int. J. Hum. Comput. Interact. **38**(9), 801–824 (2022)
21. Hou, S., Jia, C., Zhang, M.: Review of eye movement-based interaction techniques for virtual reality systems. J. Comput. Appl. **42**(11), 3534–3543 (2022)
22. Zeng, D.: Research on virtual human eye model and its motion and expression. University of Science and Technology of China (2008)
23. McNeill, D.: Hand and Mind: What Gestures Reveal About Thought. University of Chicago Press (1992)
24. Kleinke, C.L.: Gaze and eye contact: a research review. Psychol. Bull. **100**(1), 78 (1986)
25. Ide, M., Oshima, S., Mori, S., et al.: Effects of avatar's symbolic gesture in virtual reality brainstorming. In: Proceedings of the 32nd Australian Conference on Human-Computer Interaction, pp. 170–177 (2020)
26. Brosnahan, L.: Chinese and English gestures: contrastive non-verbal communication (1991)
27. Yang, L.I., Huang, J., Feng, T., et al.: Gesture interaction in virtual reality. Virtual Real. Intell. Hardw. **1**(1), 84–112 (2019)
28. Ben Abdessalem, H., Ai, Y., Marulasidda Swamy, K.S., Frasson, C.: Virtual reality zoo therapy for Alzheimer's disease using real-time gesture recognition. In: Vlamos, P. (eds.) GeNeDis 2020. Advances in Experimental Medicine and Biology, vol. 1338, pp. 97–105. Springer, Cham (2021). https://doi.org/10.1007/978-3-030-78775-2_12
29. Moustakas, K., Nikolakis, G., Tzovaras, D., et al.: A geometry education haptic VR application based on a new virtual hand representation. In: IEEE Proceedings. VR 2005. Virtual Reality, 2005, pp. 249–252. IEEE (2005)
30. Zhu, Y., Zhang, J., Zhang, Z., et al.: Designing an interactive communication assistance system for hearing-impaired college students based on gesture recognition and representation. Future Internet **14**(7), 198 (2022)
31. Sagayam, K.M., Hemanth, D.J.: Hand posture and gesture recognition techniques for virtual reality applications: a survey. Virtual Real. **21**, 91–107 (2017)

32. Hossain, S.K.A., Rahman, A.S.M.M., El Saddik, A.: Interpersonal haptic communication in second life. In: 2010 IEEE International Symposium on Haptic Audio Visual Environments and Games, pp. 1–4. IEEE (2010)

33. Vindenes, J., Wasson, B.: Show, don't tell: using go-along interviews in immersive virtual reality. In: Designing Interactive Systems Conference 2021, pp. 190–204 (2021)

34. Tanenbaum, T.J., Hartoonian, N., Bryan, J.: How do i make this thing smile? An inventory of expressive nonverbal communication in commercial social virtual reality platforms. In: Proceedings of the 2020 CHI Conference on Human Factors in Computing Systems, pp. 1–13 (2020)

35. Sucar, L.E., Orihuela-Espina, F., Velazquez, R.L., et al.: Gesture therapy: an upper limb virtual reality-based motor rehabilitation platform. IEEE Trans. Neural Syst. Rehabil. Eng. **22**(3), 634–643 (2013)

36. Vinciarelli, A., Pantic, M., Bourlard, H., et al.: Social signals, their function, and automatic analysis: a survey. In: Proceedings of the 10th International Conference on Multimodal Interfaces, pp. 61–68 (2008)

37. Bolt, R.A.: "Put-that-there" voice and gesture at the graphics interface. In: Proceedings of the 7th Annual Conference on Computer Graphics and Interactive Techniques, pp. 262–270 (1980)

38. Anthony, S., William, S., Wole, O., et al.: Beaming: an asymmetric telepresence system. IEEE Comput. Graph. Appl. **32**(6) (2012)

39. Roth, D., Bente, G., Kullmann, P., et al.: Technologies for social augmentations in user-embodied virtual reality. In: Proceedings of the 25th ACM Symposium on Virtual Reality Software and Technology, pp. 1–12 (2019)

40. Li, S., Zheng, L., Xie, W., et al.: Problems and reflections on virtual reality (VR) education. Comput. Educ. **2019**(2), 41–44 (2019)

41. Bosman, I.D.V.: Using binaural audio for inducing intersensory illusions to create illusory tactile feedback in virtual reality. University of Pretoria (2018)

42. Ke, Z., Song, X.: From "mirror me" to "fog me": distortion and theoretical crisis of social interaction in virtual reality. News Writ. **2021**(8), 75–83 (2021)

43. Ahmed, R.: Effects of online education on encoding and decoding process of students and teachers. Int. Assoc. Dev. Inf. Soc. (2018)

44. Moustafa, F., Steed, A.: A longitudinal study of small group interaction in social virtual reality. In: Proceedings of the 24th ACM Symposium on Virtual Reality Software and Technology, pp. 1–10 (2018)

45. Frith, E., Miller, S., Loprinzi, P.D.: A review of experimental research on embodied creativity: revisiting the mind–body connection. J. Creat. Behav. **54**(4), 767–798 (2020)

46. Zhao, Q., Zhou, B., Li, J., et al.: Research progress of virtual reality technology. Sci. Technol. Rev. **34**(14), 71–75 (2016)

47. Frauenberger, C.: Entanglement HCI the next wave? ACM Trans. Comput. Hum. Interact. (TOCHI) **27**(1), 1–27 (2019)

48. Stephanidis, C., Salvendy, G., Antona, M., et al.: Seven HCI grand challenges. Int. J. Hum. Comput. Interact. **35**(14), 1229–1269 (2019)

49. Maloney, D., Freeman, G., Wohn, D.Y.: "Talking without a voice" understanding non-verbal communication in social virtual reality. In: Proceedings of the ACM on Human-Computer Interaction, 4(CSCW2), pp. 1–25 (2020)

50. Sanders, C.E., Field, T.M., Diego, M., et al.: The relationship of internet use to depression and social isolation among adolescents. Adolescence **35** (2000)

51. Bailenson, J.: Protecting nonverbal data tracked in virtual reality. JAMA Pediatr.Pediatr. **172**(10), 905–906 (2018)

Comparing the Therapeutic Effects of Using Traditional Methods and Virtual Reality Headset in the Treatment of Depression and Anxiety

Shuo Liu[✉]

Beijing City University, No. 269 Bei Si Huan Zhong Lu, Hai Dian District, Beijing, China
liushuo20182018@163.com

Abstract. As virtual technology continues to receive rising popularity particularly in the gaming industry, scholars have argued for its potential use in other fields including education, engineering and medicine. Over years, researchers have examined evidence and proposed the application of virtual reality in treatment of mental health conditions. However, even though there is growing evidence on the use of VR to treat mental illnesses such as depression, it is not clear yet how the VR incorporated therapies compared with traditional approaches to managing the conditions as far as benefits are concerned. This report undertook an evaluation of the current evidence with the aim of comparing the efficacy of VR therapies over conventional therapies. The findings show that there is strong evidence supporting the use of VR in mental health care especially in managing mental illness such as depression, anxiety and PSTD. However, the findings on their efficacy over conventional approaches in terms of cost effectiveness are mixed. This also few studies examining the cost effectiveness of VR. As such, more research is required to validate the benefits of VR in the management of mental conditions.

Keywords: Virtual Reality (VR) · Mental Health Care · Efficacy

1 Introduction

In the past 10 years, virtual reality innovations and technologies have been discussed as potential supplements for psychotherapy. Virtual realities do allow users to have interactions within computer generated contexts in three dimensions (Eichenberg & Wolters 2012). The fact that VR technologies trigger anxiety and simulate real experiences including physiological symptoms like nausea or sweating, has increased emphasis on their potential to replace the traditional exposure therapy (Krijn et al. 2004). In the era of evidence based practice, Dollaghan (2007) postulates that it is essential to establish the strengths and weaknesses of specific interventions in terms of cost-effectiveness and improving patient outcomes. However, Zeng et al. (2018) show that while there is evidence supporting the use of virtual reality in the management and treatment of mental health disorders such as depression, it is not quite clear whether the exercise of VR will

A. Marcus et al. (Eds.): HCII 2024, LNCS 14715, pp. 68–77, 2024.
https://doi.org/10.1007/978-3-031-61359-3_6

have benefits to mental health. Consequently, there is need for research in this area to support investment and implementation of this intervention in mental health care settings. Based on this, this journal reviews secondary data from different databases with an aim of establishing the benefits of VR compared to conventional therapies in the treatment of anxiety and depression.

2 Definition and History of Virtual Reality

Virtual reality has evolved to have a defining effect on the contemporary society. Earnshaw (2014) highlights that virtual reality has its origins in times which preceded the period in which the idea was both coined and formalized. Before considering how virtual reality has developed overtime, it is essential to consider technologies or acts that are viewed as virtual terms. In simple terms, Schroeder (2008) defined VR are an attempt to tricking the mind to belief as real, that which is not. In contemporary literature, however, virtual reality has been defined as computer-generated simulation of environments and images in a three-dimensional manner, which viewers can interact with in a way that seems physical and real through the use of electronic equipment like helmets with embedded screens or sensitive gloves (Dixon 2006). Burdea & Coiffet (2003) considered virtual reality as a compelling and powerful computer applications through which humans can interact and interface with computer generated contexts in a manner mimicking real life experiences and engaging with human senses. The understanding and definition of the VR concept emphasizes the idea of interaction and that the hardware and the imagery to be designed in a manner, which is completely immersive. From a historical point of view thereby, whatever is viewed as VR needs to be broadened.

The development of the concept of virtual technology can be dated back to the 19th century. Charles Wheatstone's research, which was conducted in 1838, indicated that the human brain processes two- dimensional pictures using every eye to form a single three-dimensional image (Dixon 2006). Consequently, viewing two stereoscopic images adjacent to each other provided the audience a sense of reality, depth and immersion. The design principles which were employed in the development of the stereoscope are employed in the low budget VR headsets for mobile phones as well as the popular Google Cardboard. Over time, the human race has been developing richer approaches to sensory stimulation. In the 20th century, with the advent of computer technology and other electronics, VR took on a new direction. Edward Link developed the "Link Trainer" in 1929, which was probably the first line of simulators for commercial planes that was fully electromechanical. This eventually played a very important role in the training of pilots. The science fiction theory by Stanley Weinbaum predicted the development of VR technologies. The Pygmalion's Spectacles, which were at the center of the story entailed goggles which made the wearer to experience a fictional world. Reflectively, the experience that Stanley referred to is uncannily similar to the contemporary virtual reality experiences (Mazuryk, & Gervautz 1996). The sensorama, developed in 1950s cinematography, by Morton Heilig revolutionized the VR concept. This was theater cabinet styled in an arcade manner, which would stimulate all the senses of the viewer to make them fully immersed in the film. The first head-mounted display of VR was developed in 1960 by the same cinematographer, Morton Heilig. This, however, lacked an interactive film medium with motion trackers. The first motion tracking headset was then developed in 1961. From this, advances have been continually made to establish a more realistic and interactive virtual experience in film and even video games. By 2019, mixed systems of reality and sophisticated technologies had already become standalone VR realities (Boeldt & McMohan 2019). Currently, the cost of VR technology has also significantly dropped and the hardware which is employed to turn virtual realities has considerably become mainstream.

3   Traditional Methods for Treating and Managing Depression and Anxiety

In the context of this research, traditional methods are any other methods used in nursing and clinical practice to manage the symptoms of anxiety and depression other than virtual reality based measures. Over the years, psychological and pharmacological effects have been largely employed in the management and treatment of both anxiety and depression. Some of the known pharmacological interventions include the use of benzodiazepines. Traditionally, this have been considered to be effective and affordable, hence most commonly employed (Brown & Dennis 2017). However, Bandelow et al. (2014) posits that this medication is not recommended for routine usage as it has strong side effects. Currently, other pharmacological therapies for anxiety include some medications for depression such as selective reuptake of serotonin inhibitors as well as the serotonin-norepinephrine reuptake inhibitors. The SNRIs and SSRIs have indicated to be effective in generalized disorders and symptoms linked to anxiety such as social phobia. These interventions do not have the same overdose and sedative risks as experienced in benzodiazepines (Baldwin et al. 2014). Tetracyclic antidepressants which are noradrenergic as well as particular serotonergic antidepressants like remeron have also shown some effectiveness in the management of anxiety and depression. Even though it has not been technically categorized as medication by FDA, deplin, which is also referred to as l-methylfolate has also been effectively employed in treating both depression and anxiety. This medication helps to control the neurotransmitters which regulate moods (Martin 2019). Merrell (2008) also examines and outlines guidelines to assist students to overcome both depression and anxiety. He posits that coverage of medication for psychiatric conditions has been revised extensively with most recent developments often updated to enhance clinical utility. Currently, there is a general focus on prevention-oriented emotional and social learning curriculum for classrooms. More controlled environments are employed to expose learners to stressful and fearful emotions and provide guidelines on how they can deal with the situations. While the effectiveness of the interventions has been debatable, they have been reliably employed the managed of this disorders. In some cases, these interventions have been linked with a number of side-effects, which vary depending on the type of medication.

In the context of holistic care, however, pharmacological interventions are not considered exhaustive, hence the need for psychological therapies as well as physiological interventions. Therapies are essential to help patients enhance their coping skills and change thinking patterns to be well-equipped to deal with the conflicts and stresses associated with the illness. Research also shows that psychological therapies can enhance recovery through helping patients to identify and change negative behavior and thoughts. According to Hollon & Beck (2013), cognitive behavioral therapies coupled with medication have proved to produce more positive outcomes on both patients with depression and anxiety disorders. The CBT is a structured approach, which holds the view that the manner in which people behave and think has an impact on the way they feel. Apparently, the CBT has been found to be the most effective interventions for depression and shown positive outcomes across a range of ages, including adults, adolescents, older people and children (Carvalho et al. 2010). This approach includes involving therapists to identify behaviors and thoughts that can likely hinder recovery and address. Interpersonal therapy is another intervention that focuses on issues embedded in personal relationships as well as skills which are needed to dress them (Lipsitz et al. 2008). Based on this model, the issue of relationships can significantly impact on people are experiencing anxiety and depression. It helps to identify patterns within relationships that make patients more vulnerable and eliminate them (Lipsitz et al. 2008). Based on these traditional interventions, patients with anxiety and depression have a range of challenges, which need to be addressed from different perspectives hence the conception of the potential benefits of virtual reality therapies.

4   Virtual Reality Therapies in Management of Anxiety and Depression

While there were some concerns that virtual reality experiences could actually be damaging to the brain, evidence points to the potential of virtual realities helping the gray matter in the brain (Shah et al. 2015). There has been a new wave of research in psychology pioneering the benefits of virtual realities in the diagnosis and treatment of clinical conditions such as anxiety, Alzheimer's disease and chronic pain. However, there have not been any conclusive evidence on the same hitherto. Some researchers have investigated the benefits of virtual reality in the management of common social fears, which in medical terms and standards may not be defined as mental health conditions. However, such studies provide important insights into the potential benefits and promise of this technology in the health care industry. Harris et al. (2002) for instance, examined the benefits of VR therapies in management of public speaking anxiety. The findings based on psychological measures and self-reporting appeared to show that four sessions of virtual reality treatment effectively reduced public speaking anxiety among college students, hence validating earlier studies on the effectiveness of VRT as psychotherapeutic approach. The findings offered knowledge on the potential of incorporating VR therapies in the management of even more complex mental health illnesses such as schizophrenia and depression. However, given the fact that the sample was limited on a younger population and only on public speaking anxiety, there is need for more research on VR to validate its findings and enhance its applicability.

Burden & Coiffet (2003) argued that while there has been strong fascination of the concept of virtual reality in the field of entertainment, its real promise is in the field of engineering and medicine. The employment of virtual reality to tweak and test the brain is a relatively new concept and with the current excitement around entertainment and gaming with virtual realities, it makes sense to launch inquiry into the potential of this technology in different fields including interventions and care for people with mental conditions. Riding in the growing interest in mental health technology, organizations which are creating VR content for therapeutic effects are receiving a surge in attention as well as funding, but the impact or rather benefits of these solutions compared to traditional approaches and interventions for mental illnesses are not strongly established. Gonçalves et al. (2012) argues that since 1990s, virtual reality technology has been successfully used in the treatment of post-traumatic stress disorder. However, anxiety and depression call for new programs which can address quite broad conditions. The library of Palo Alto includes content of how VR can be employed to treat claustrophobia, alcohol addiction and teenage depression. This makes a premise and genesis for considering VR as a potentially beneficial technology in dealing with mental health illnesses.

Carvalho et al. (2010) examines how virtual reality is employed as a mechanism for exposure therapy. The current VR content is primarily designed to support exposure therapy, a treatment for disorders of anxiety, where patients are exposed to stimuli that induces anxiety in a controlled and safe environment, which helps them to learn that the threats which they are worried about are actually not as dangerous as they think. For example, people who are scared of heights can actually be guided by therapist to visit taller buildings in VR context progressively and show an experience that helps them to understand that such buildings are not always dangerous. According to Gonçalves et al. (2012), conventional therapies allow exposure occurring in environments that are highly controlled. Nevertheless, VR can allow therapist to create such a safe and controlled environment within a headset. This is considered to be less expensive and much quicker. Additionally, the use of VR allows therapists to regulate the intensity of all the experiences of their patients, which might lead to better therapeutic outcomes. In another study Bouchard (2020), argues that VR allows patients to attempt things that they would not attempt in the real world such as jumping from the cliff. This can play a very important role in managing their fear and anxiety.

It is essential to note that the application of technology such as virtual realities, hitherto, does not present entirely unique interventions or therapeutic treatments. Instead, it enhances the efficacy of the already existing interventions. Carvallo et al. (2010) posits that in cognitive behavioral therapies, the use of interventions associated with exposure has already received validation, hence can only be extended to virtual reality contexts based on the specific needs of the patients. A number of studies such as Powers and Emmelkamp (2008); and Garcia et al. (2001) have shown that exposure within virtual contexts has proven to be effective in the management and treatment of several mental illnesses such as acrophobia and spider phobia respectively. Wald and Taylor (2003) evidenced the efficacy of exposure in virtual contexts in treatment of social phobia, while Klinger et al. (2005) found that the approach is effective in treating binge eating disorders. From a psychotherapeutic standpoint, Parsons and Rizzo (2008) argued that virtual exposure is comparatively effective in patients that are carefully selected and can reduce phobia symptoms as well as anxiety. All this evidence, however, points to how virtual realities are employed to enhance the outcomes of already existing interventions as well as expand the utilization of approaches and techniques which have already been applied. Consequently, it can be argued that the existing evidence does not support the VR as stand-alone therapeutic options for management of depression and anxiety, but points to the potential of this approaches when combined with traditional therapies. Through this, the VR technologies continue to uphold the fundamentals of psychotherapy such as the continued use of already tested interventions such as the CBT.

When incorporating virtual realities in the management of anxiety, some researchers such as Castelnuovo et al. (2003) argued that focus should not be placed on the technology being employed, but instead the psychotherapeutic intervention which is being improved by use of the specific technology. Based on this, it can be argued that VR and other strategies within this field should never be random, but instead be in strong conformity with the needs of the patients. This is especially important in an era where health organizations such as NHS and NICE continue to emphasize the importance and application of patient-centered approaches (Gruffydd-Jones & Loveridge 2011). Castelnuovo et al. (2003) argues that not all VR therapy content has been created effectively, hence the need for testing in relation with patient needs before application. Consequently, there is need for more studies in this field, particularly, to establish when VR technologies need to be employed in treatment of anxiety and depression. More specifically, there is need to focus on the analysis of who will actually respond positively to the VR experience. There have been some studies, for instance, indicating that PTSD patients that also suffer from depression are highly likely to respond positively to VR exposure as compared to other traditional treatment methods such as Quero et al. (2014). There needs to more of such studies on anxiety and depression.

5 Effectiveness of Virtual Reality Therapies over Traditional Therapies

Evidence-based practice requires that interventions are empirically tested and evidence analyzed before it is applied in practice. As such, despite the promise of virtual reality, evidence of the effectiveness of this measures is important to encourage application. Few studies that have been conducted on this topic have yielded varying results (Shah et al. 2015). Fodor et al. (2018) reviewed the existing body of evidence to establish the efficacy of VR therapeutic interventions in patients with mental illnesses. The findings showed that there were no significant differences between interventions based on VR and other forms of active therapies. Even though VR-based interventions outperformed other controlled therapies of depression and anxiety, there was no improvement in treatment drop-out. Potential publication biases, high levels of heterogeneity, a focus on waitlist controls and uncertain or high levels of risks of bias for most of the studies included in the review, however, questions the validity and reliability of the effects. On the other hand, Hedman et al. (2013) employed a randomized controlled analysis to examine the effectiveness of VR exposure therapy in the management of fears and social anxiety. The findings showed that compared to the controlled group, VR exposure therapy was considered to be more effective in the management of social fears and the improvement was maintained for one year. Nevertheless, the research employed a relatively smaller sample, which makes it challenging to generalize and apply them reliably in practice. Klinger et al. (2005) also compared the effectiveness of virtual realities therapies and cognitive behavior therapies in the management of social fears by use of a randomized controlled study. The findings indicated that the differences in terms of therapeutic outcomes among the two interventions were not significant. CBT had almost a similar outcome in the management social anxiety as compared to when virtual reality therapies were involved.

Another randomized controlled study by Mclay et al. (2017) compared the effectiveness of virtual reality exposure therapies and other control exposure therapies in patients with post-traumatic stress disorder. Service members who had been diagnosed with combat-related PSTD were selected randomly and placed to either VRET or CET for a period of nine weeks. A controlled cross-over component was also included in the study. The findings showed that the symptoms of PSTD did improve in all the treatments. However, there were no statistically significant differences in the outcomes of the two treatments. There was a 31% improvement on the CAPS for those who received the VRET treatment, compared to 37% for those in CET treatment. In fact, the outcomes were slightly better in CET as compared to VRET. However, the levels of dropout were high in VRET treatment as compared to CET. From this findings McClay et al. (2017) argued for the utility of exposure therapy in management of PSTD, but did show that the inclusion of VR therapies does not have any additional benefits as far as therapeutic outcomes are concerned. While the study adopted a rigorous methodology with randomized controlled data, it is notable that the sample size is also relatively limited, which may compromise the ability to generalize the data to wider settings. Among the most recent studies comparing the efficacy of VR based therapies to traditional therapies is Fodor et al. (2018). The randomized controlled study employs a gamified virtual reality-based exposure therapy that involves single sessions to assess the efficacy of VR therapy in treating spider phobia. The study is based on the assumption that conducting exposure therapy by use of commercially available, modern VR technology can have positive effects on the outcomes. The researchers also aimed to examine the cost-effectiveness of incorporation of VR technology in therapies. As the health budgets are continually strained, health institutions such as the NHS are advocating for less-costly but effective interventions, particularly in areas that pose significant health and budgetary burdens such as mental health (Gruffydd-Jones & Loveridge 2011). Consequently, even with the argued effectiveness of VR therapies it essential to launch inquiries into how the therapies balance between cost-effectiveness and benefits in terms of therapeutic outcomes. Nevertheless, the findings of the study have not been officially released, hence no conclusions can be drawn from the same. According to Page and Coxon (2016), however, VR technologies can help to enhance availability and accessibility of exposure therapy. Currently, VR technologies have become increasingly available and affordable, incorporation in mental health therapies can enhance acceptability, ease of access and effectiveness of treatment for anxiety. VR exposure therapies are simple to control and implement and given the entertainment aspect associated with the technologies, they are also more acceptable to patients in imaginal exposure or vivo (Wood et al. 2009)). VR also holds the potential for the evaluation and therapist standardization training. Presented as a scalable technology, VR is considered capable of providing augmented exposure to as well as enhance efficiency and effectiveness of exposure therapies (Boeldt & McMohan 2019). As such, the authors advocated for continued training and educational programs to enhance the application and use of VR therapies in anxiety and other mental health therapies. Based on this evidence, it is safe to argue that the evidence of the cost-effectiveness or rather benefits of VR over traditional interventions has not been strongly established in literature. It is also notable that they do not provide a new solution, but rather seek to enhance the efficacy of existing approaches such as exposure therapies and CBT models.

6 Conclusion

Virtual Reality technology has significantly grown since its conception in the 18th century through to the current modern world and it presently famed in the gaming and entertainment industry. With the fascination of the technology around the gaming industry, researchers have concept and inquired its potential in the medical industry, more specifically in treating mental illnesses such as depression and anxiety. This analysis reveals attempts by a number of studies to reveal the potential benefits of VR in treatment of anxiety and depression disorders. From the analysis, there is no strong evidence point to the benefits and effectiveness of VR incorporated technologies over traditional technology. In most cases hitherto, virtual realities technologies have been employed in attempt to enhance the efficacy of existing therapies such as CBT, IPT and exposure therapies employed in the treatment of anxiety and depression. While it is argued that commercial availability and growing affordability of VR technologies can enhance accessibility and acceptability of exposure therapies, there was limited empirical evidence supporting this view. Additionally, it is considered that VR can provide therapists with an opportunity to control the therapist based on the needs of the patients, hence improve accessibility and outcomes. However, the preliminary research conducted hitherto does not support this views. The review of recent literature on the issue showed varied outcomes. Randomized controlled studies analyzed in this report also show that there is no significant differences between VR incorporated therapies and conventional therapies. However, most studies focused on limited samples and the VR were not designed based on patient specific needs. There is need for more studies in this area to outline the benefits of using VR technology in treating anxiety and depression.

References

Baldwin, D.S., et al.: Evidence-based pharmacological treatment of anxiety disorders, post-traumatic stress disorder and obsessive-compulsive disorder: a revision of the 2005 guidelines from the British Association for Psychopharmacology. J. Psychopharmacol. **28**(5), 403–439 (2014)

Bandelow, B., Lichte, T., Rudolf, S., Wiltink, J., Beutel, E.M.: The diagnosis of and treatment recommendations for anxiety disorders. Dtsch. Arztebl. Int. **111**(27–28), 473 (2014)

Boeldt, D., McMohan, E.: Using virtual reality exposure therapy to enhance treatment of anxiety disorders: identifying areas of clinical adoption and potential obstacles (2019). https://www.ncbi.nlm.nih.gov/pmc/articles/PMC6823515/

Bouchard, S.: Could virtual reality be effective in treating children with phobias? (2020). https://www.researchgate.net/publication/49822052_Could_virtual_reality_be_effective_in_treating_children_with_phobias

Brown, H.K., Dennis, C.L.: Psychosocial, psychological, and pharmacological interventions for treating antenatal anxiety. Cochrane Database Syst. Rev. **2017**(11) (2017)

Bryman, A.: Social Research Methods. Oxford University Press, Oxford (2016)

Burdea, G.C., Coiffet, P.: Virtual Reality Technology. Wiley, Hoboken (2003)

Carvalho, M., Freire, R., Nardi, A.: Virtual reality as a mechanism for exposure therapy. World J. Biol. Psychiatry 11(2–2), 220–230 (2010)

Castelnuovo, G., Gaggioli, A., Mantovani, F., Riva, G.: From psychotherapy to e-therapy: the integration of traditional techniques and new communication tools in clinical settings. Cyberpsychol. Behav. 6(4), 375382 (2003)

Dixon, S.: A history of virtual reality in performance. Int. J. Perform. Arts Digit. Media 2(1) (2006)

Dollaghan, C.A.: The Handbook for Evidence-Based Practice in Communication Disorders. Paul H Brookes Publishing (2007)

Earnshaw, R.A. (ed.): Virtual Reality Systems. Academic Press (2014)

Eichenberg, C., Wolters, C.: Virtual realities in the treatment of mental disorders: a review of the current state of research. Virtual Real. Psychol. Med. Pedagog. Appl. 2, 35–64 (2012)

Fodor, L.A., Cotet, C.D., Cuijpers, P., Szamoskozi, S., David, D., Cristea, I.A.: The effectiveness of virtual reality based interventions for symptoms of anxiety and depression: a meta-analysis. Sci. Rep. 8(1), 1–13 (2018). https://www.nature.com/arti-cles/s41598-018-28113-6#article-info. Accessed 21 Nov 2019

Garcia-Palacios, A., Hoffman, H.G., See, S.K., Tsai, A., Botella, C.: Redefining therapeutic success with virtual reality exposure therapy. Cyberpsychol. Behav. 4, 341–348 (2001)

Gonçalves, R., Pedrozo, A.L., Coutinho, E.S.F., Figueira, I., Ventura, P.: Efficacy of virtual reality exposure therapy in the treatment of PTSD: a systematic review. PLoS ONE 7(12) (2012)

Gruffydd-Jones, K., Loveridge, C.: The 2010 NICE COPD guidelines: how do they compare with the GOLD guidelines? Prim. Care Respir. J. 20(2), 199–204 (2011)

Harris, S.R., Kemmerling, R.L., North, M.M.: Brief virtual reality therapy for public speaking anxiety. Cyber Psychol. Behav. 5(6), 543–550 (2002)

Hedman, E., et al.: Mediators in psychological treatment of social anxiety disorder: individual cognitive therapy compared to cognitive behavioral group therapy. Behav. Res. Ther. 51(10), 696–705 (2013)

Hollon, S.D., Beck, A.T.: Cognitive and cognitive-behavioral therapies. In: Bergin and Garfield's Handbook of Psychotherapy and Behavior Change, vol. 6, pp. 393–442 (2013)

Klinger, E., et al.: Virtual reality therapy versus cognitive behavior therapy for social phobia: a preliminary controlled study. Cyberpsychol. Behav. 8(1), 76–88 (2005)

Lipsitz, J.D., et al.: A randomized trial of interpersonal therapy versus supportive therapy for social anxiety disorder. Depress. Anxiety 25(6), 542–553 (2008)

Martin, S.: Virtual reality might be the next big thing for mental health (2019). https://blogs.scient ificamerican.com/observations/virtual-reality-might-be-the-nextbig-thing-for-mental-health/

Mazuryk, T., Gervautz, M.: Virtual reality-history, applications, technology and future (1996)

McDaniel, C., Gates, R.: Marketing Research. Singapore (2013)

McLay, R.N., et al.: A randomized, head-to-head study of virtual reality exposure therapy for posttraumatic stress disorder. Cyberpsychol. Behav. Soc. Netw. 20(4), 218–224 (2017)

Merrell, K.W.: Helping Students Overcome Depression and Anxiety: A Practical Guide, 2nd edn. Guilford Press, New York (2008)

Mynors-Wallis, L.: Problem Solving Treatment for Anxiety and Depression: A Practical Guide. Oxford University Press, Oxford (2005)

Page, S., Coxon, M.: Virtual reality exposure therapy for anxiety disorders: small samples and no controls? Front. Psychol. 7, 326 (2016)

Parsons, T.D., Rizzo, A.A.: Affective outcomes of virtual reality exposure therapy for anxiety and specific phobias: a meta-analysis. J. Behav. Ther. Exp. Psychiatry 39, 250–261 (2008)

Powers, M.B., Emmelkamp, P.M.: Virtual reality exposure therapy for anxiety disorders: a meta-analysis. J. Anxiety Disord. 22(3), 561–569 (2008)

Quero, S., Pérez-Ara, M.Á., Bretón-López, J., García-Palacios, A., Baños, R.M., Botella, C.: Acceptability of virtual reality interoceptive exposure for the treatment of panic disorder with agoraphobia. Br. J. Guid. Couns. **42**(2), 123–137 (2014)

Schroeder, R.: Defining virtual worlds and virtual environments. J. Virtual Worlds Res. **1**(1) (2008)

Shah, L.B.I., Torres, S., Kannusamy, P., Chng, C.M.L., He, H.G., Klainin-Yobas, P.: Efficacy of the virtual reality-based stress management program on stress- related variables in people with mood disorders: the feasibility study. Arch. Psychiatr. Nurs. **29**(1), 6–13 (2015)

Wald, J., Taylor, S.: Preliminary research on the efficacy of virtual reality exposure therapy to treat driving phobia. Cyberpsychol. Behav. **6**, 459–465 (2003)

Wood, D.P., et al.: Cost effectiveness of virtual reality graded exposure therapy with physiological monitoring for the treatment of combat related post traumatic stress disorder. Annu. Rev. Cyberther. Telemed. **7**, 223–229 (2009)

Zeng, N., Pope, Z., Lee, J.E., Gao, Z.: Virtual reality exercise for anxiety and depression: a preliminary review of current research in an emerging field. J. Clin. Med. **7**(3), 42 (2018)

Analysis of the Impact on Immersive Experience: Narrative Effects in First and Third Person Perspectives

Lin Liu[✉], Shizhu Lu, Yuqing Guo, Qiuyu Huang, Xiaolie Yi, and Jifa Zhang

Guangdong University of Technology, Guangzhou 510090, Guangdong, China
Nikki6060@hotmail.com

Abstract. This study conducted a comprehensive analysis using meta-analysis methods on data extracted from 9 papers (N = 6770), aiming to explore the differences in audience experience and influencing factors related to first-person and third-person narratives. Specifically, the research focused on the effects of first-person and third-person narrative styles on potential factors influencing immersion experience, including emotional engagement and behavioral intent. The results indicate that both first-person and third-person narratives did not significantly impact the audience's emotional engagement and behavioral intent. When combining emotional engagement and behavioral intent into a single outcome variable, there was no significant difference between the effects of first-person and third-person narratives. However, when considering emotional engagement and behavioral intent as separate outcome variables, the study found that first-person narratives were more effective in eliciting emotional engagement compared to third-person narratives, with no significant difference in behavioral intent. Additionally, the research highlights that individual cognitive difference among the audience may influence memory biases, thereby affecting immersion experience. In summary, this study provides a clearer perspective on the core issue of the impact of different narrative perspectives on immersion experience. It not only lays the foundation for further research on immersive experiences in cultural heritage sites but also offers practical solutions for cultural communication and identity.

Keywords: Narrative Perspective · Immersive Experience · Meta-Analysis

1 Introduction

In recent years, there has been a transformation in the socio-economic landscape from traditional economies to experience economies. Users no longer find satisfaction solely in the materialistic acquisition; instead, they place greater emphasis on the experiential usage of goods, proposing an economic behavior centered around "feeling" [1]. This concept has garnered widespread attention, particularly within the realm of tourism. Over the past few years, the tourism industry has undergone significant changes, shifting from merely providing products and services to actively cultivating a tourism experience. This transition includes the incorporation of immersive technologies such as virtual reality

© The Author(s), under exclusive license to Springer Nature Switzerland AG 2024
A. Marcus et al. (Eds.): HCII 2024, LNCS 14715, pp. 78–97, 2024.
https://doi.org/10.1007/978-3-031-61359-3_7

(VR) and augmented reality (AR), which have rapidly evolved due to their advantages in enhancing user tourism experiences [2]. Recent research has focused on the sensory experiences based on technological applications in the immersive experience of cultural heritage sites. This encompasses various domains, including virtual reality (VR), augmented reality (AR), and the integration of virtual and augmented reality [3, 4]. However, the actual technological developments have faced challenges in meeting audience expectations for fully immersive experiences, diverging from the goal of prioritizing authentic audience experiences. Consequently, in the realm of experiential emotional responses and behavioral stages, tangible indicators such as physical and sensory participation have become crucial [5]. These disparities present new challenges for the audience's emotional responses and behavioral intentions in the realm of digital immersive storytelling.

The quest for the optimal narrative mode to maximize immersive experiences has become a pivotal consideration for narrative constructors [6]. Within the immersive experience, the narrative perspective influences the audience's viewpoint, comprehension of the story, and engagement in behavior [7–9], necessitating the consideration of various choices in personal narrative perspectives. The selection of different personal narrative perspectives significantly impacts the audience's viewpoint alignment, engagement, as well as their immersive perceptions of cognitive abilities, value perceptions, and psychological states related to the story [2, 10]. Some studies suggest that the first-person perspective involves intentional possession of real or imagined phenomena and objects, connecting behavioral intent with our perceived reality [11]. The use of a first-person perspective allows for the contemplation of experiences, emotional dimensions, and the cultivation of introspective abilities [12]. Gregorians elucidated the relationship between core emotions and architectural experiences through a first-person perspective within the architectural environment, verifying the interconnections among three psychological dimensions of architectural experience: charm, coherence, and familiarity [13]. Conversely, other research indicates that a third-person perspective is associated with the perception of having a stronger cognitive ability than others, without an increase in negative emotional responses [14, 15], In terms of movement and spatial awareness, a third-person perspective can offer enhanced perception, simultaneously observing actions within the environment and influencing audience immersion [16, 17]. However, the impact factors of different personal narrative perspectives on the effectiveness of immersive experiences remain unclear, with discrepancies among research findings. It is imperative to integrate diverse dimensions and conduct comparative analyses of influencing factors.

In addition, the impact of other macro-level factors has not been considered, such as cognitive differences, types of tourism experiences, and pre-experience. As a result, several research questions have emerged, including whether the experiential effects vary based on different types of tourism experiences [18]? Are the effects of immersive experiences influenced by other participants [19]? Does prior experience of visiting the destination affect audience emotional responses and behavioral intentions [20],

Although these factors may influence the effectiveness of different personal narrative perspectives in immersive experiences, they have not been thoroughly investigated. We aim to address the following research questions:

- RQ1: To what extent do first-person and third-person narratives impact audience emotional responses and behavioral intentions?
- RQ2: Does narrative genre moderate the effects of first-person and third-person narrative on audience emotional responses and behavioral intentions?
- RQ3: How does narrative mode influence the effectiveness of first-person and third-person narrative effects on audience emotional responses and behavioral intentions?

To address these questions, a comprehensive research framework is required to systematically analyze antecedents, mediating factors, and outcomes of the first-person and third-person narrative effects in immersive experiences. The meta-analytic approach can more comprehensively elucidate the moderating factors of first-person and third-person narrative effects on the immersion experience. Construct a theoretical framework based on the relationships between antecedents, mediating factors, and outcomes, as well as variables. Validate the effectiveness of moderating factors on the impact of first-person and third-person narrative effects on audience emotional responses and behavioral intentions by encoding effect sizes of sample data from the literature.

2 Literature Review

2.1 Narrative Perspective

Since the development of narrative theory, the narrative perspective has become a crucial component in narrative construction. Narrative perspective refers to the physiological and psychological viewpoints presented in a story, guiding individuals in reading, interpreting, and understanding the inherent attributes of each narrative [21]. Narrative perspectives can be categorized into three types, as manifested in the narrative through the use of personal pronouns: first-person, second-person, and third-person. Among them, first-person and third-person narratives are the most prevalent narrative perspectives [22]. Research on different narrative viewpoints suggests that the nature of the relationship between the narrator and the story, as well as the narrator and the audience, is crucial for the immersive experience. This involves the distance between the audience and the story and the extent to which narrative constructors are willing to involve the audience in their interpretations [22, 23]. Different narrative perspectives convey information about the actions or event relationships between the narrator and the story [24]. In philosophy, diverse viewpoints reflect distinct cognitive patterns, where the first-person perspective is subjective and directed towards the cognitive subject's experience, while the third-person perspective is objective, providing a means to acquire objective knowledge [22]. Choifer has explicitly delineated cognitive differences between the first-person and third-person perspectives, defining the first-person perspective as a non-reflective experiential mode contrasting with the reflective nature of the third-person perspective. It is not merely a non-reflective, non-cognitive acquisition of consciousness experience, but rather, it pertains to "what it is like" [25]. The structural and typological aspects of the second-person narrative perspective align with the first-person perspective when the narrator is within the story and with the third-person perspective when the narrator is external to the story [20]. The second-person perspective is generally interpreted to have a generic meaning, particularly in descriptive language [26]. Consequently, the focal point of this study primarily revolves around the impact of first-person and third-person narrative effects.

As previously mentioned, narrative perspectives exhibit cognitive differences in subjectivity and objectivity, influencing the comprehension of narrative and informational texts differently. The impact of narrative dissemination on immersive effects is relative to the text mode, where audio and video image modes significantly enhance the salience of the narrator's characteristics. Narrative effects primarily facilitate audience immersion and improve the immersive experience through audience psychological responses [27].

2.2 Immersive Experience

The concept of the experience economy was first introduced in the Harvard Business Review, with particular emphasis on the transformative process from products to services and further to experiences, notably within the domain of the tourism industry. The necessity of "staged experiences" is underscored, highlighting the significance of immersion, absorption, and engagement in enhancing the tourism experience [3]. Experience is defined as an individually engaging event, and four types of customer experiences are discussed: aesthetic experience, entertainment experience, educational experience, and escapism experience, classified into two types: absorption and immersion [28]. Absorptive experiences occur when visitors indirectly acquire the influence of an experience [29], whereas immersive experiences occur when visitors actively participate in the experience [30]. Absorptive experiences captivate attention by introducing experiences to the human mind, while immersive experiences demand the audience to enter and become a physical part of the experience itself [28], Consequently, absorptive experiences typically precede immersive experiences, and individuals gain richer experiences when possessing more cognitive foundations or interests [30]. The concept of immersion is approached through two distinct dimensions: technology/system-centric immersion and audience-centric immersion. In the technological dimension, immersion is defined as the extent to which computer displays provide inclusiveness, surroundingness, vividness, and realism to human senses, considering immersion as an objective description enhancing the environment [31, 32]. On the psychological dimension, immersion is defined as the sensation of the self being surrounded by a continuous stimulus and an environment of experiential flow, interacting with it. In this context, immersion is considered a psychological response of individuals to the intermediary environment [32, 33]. Imagination and understanding are deemed necessary conditions for emotional contact with others, i.e., feeling what others feel. Greater ease in sensing the feelings of others occurs when there is a sufficient understanding and comprehension of their situations [34]. The transition of spectators to participants redirects their aesthetic appreciation towards value generation, stemming from the processes of immersive activities Given the emphasis of the experience economy on immersion, research on the concept of immersive experiences is particularly meaningful within various narrative perspectives [35].

Starr employs emotional perception, sensory input, and semantic data to delineate the psychological imagery during the immersion process, utilizing visualization techniques to assess a particular affective experience [36]. This description and apprehension of affect play a pivotal role in constructing meaningful and coherent psychological imagery, signifying the spontaneous and bottom-up process inherent in the formation of immersive experiences [37]. Therefore, this study adopts a viewer-centric approach, conceptualizing immersive experiences as a psychological state of immersion.

2.3 The Modulating Factors and Dependent Variables of Narrative Effects Application

Moderating Factors. In the genres of fictional and non-fictional narratives, narrative based on fictional content holds a greater potential for altering the real world to a higher degree, while narrative grounded in non-fictional content tends to exert a comparatively lower impact on the real world [38].

Beyond traditional textual narratives, with the widespread proliferation of digital media and the internet, diverse narrative modalities continue to emerge. Sound narration is produced, stored, and listened to through various means, thereby enabling individuals to more effectively engage with narrative content [39]; John Berger's visual theory, originating from the viewer's perspective, employs visual observation as a focal point for the analysis of images or visuals [40].

Dependent Variables. From the perspective of psychological responses, we can categorize the factors influencing psychological states during immersive experiences. These factors encompass flow, emotional engagement, satisfaction, and attitudes. Among these, emotional factors are regarded as intermediaries linking immersive experiences to audience psychological responses, achieving this by reducing psychological distance while concurrently enhancing engagement [41], Emotional engagement constitutes a composite concept encompassing emotions, affect, empathy, and similar elements [2]. Research suggests that Electrodermal Activity (EDA) can serve as a standard for measuring the degree of experiential intensity and can reflect emotional responses from data measured through various personal perspectives [42].

In the context of behavioral intent, it refers to the preparatory state towards a specific behavior, reflecting the audience's desire level for a particular action. Previous studies have employed three variables to delineate behavioral intent: attention, persuasiveness, and trust [43, 44], Casaló posits an association between behavioral intent and actual behavior [45], for instance, virtual reality technology can provide a try-before-buy experience, creating a destination image for potential audiences, stimulating positive behavioral intent, thereby resulting in actual behavior [46]. In this study, the primary focus is on the influencing factors of immersion effects, excluding the segment related to the implementation of audience behavior. Consequently, the sections addressing behavioral intent and the outcomes of behavior are consolidated into the concept of behavioral intent.

3   Method

3.1 Literature Retrieval and Screening

Building upon previous research, this study consolidates structures with similar meanings but different operationalizations into a single framework. The meta-analysis framework comprises two independent variables, two moderators and two dependent variables, aiming to investigate the effectiveness of narrative effects from different perspectives on the factors influencing immersive experiences.

Following Loureiro et al.'s text mining research [47], this study conducted literature retrieval on three major databases (Web of Science, Elsevier SDOL, Google Scholar). The selection of relevant studies was identified using the keyword "point of view" (POV)" narrative perspective" or "first person effect, third person effect (FPE, TPE)" and "immersive experience". To integrate unpublished research, ProQuest Dissertation & Theses platform was used to search for dissertations, aiming to minimize publication bias. In total, 952 papers were retrieved (see Fig. 1). The search method followed the steps commonly used in meta-analyses in the narrative field, covering both published and unpublished studies, forming a comprehensive literature list. However, this app-roach does not guarantee the inclusion of all available literature. Any missing literature should be due to random rather than systematic omissions and should not affect the research conclusions [48]. Additionally, we screened the references of included studies to identify relevant literature and excluded documents falling under the following cate-gories: interview and qualitative research literature, literature where metadata could not be obtained by contacting the author, literature not addressing the impact of narrative perspectives on audience emotional responses and behavior, and literature not related to immersive experiences. After excluding duplicate papers, we ultimately obtained 9 studies eligible for meta-analysis, encoding data from 41 studies involving 6,770 par-ticipants. Figure 1 illustrates the process of including or excluding research literature according to the PRISMA guidelines for meta-analysis.

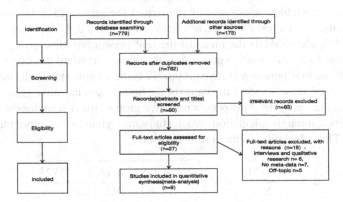

Fig. 1. Flow chart of the study selection process.

3.2 Literature Coding

Following the completion of literature search and screening, the coding process was con-ducted by two research assistants. Independently adhering to the specified coding criteria, each coder was responsible for coding the selected nine papers. The coded information encompassed details such as authorship, publication year, sample size, outcome vari-ables, effect sizes, emotional engagement, behavioral intention, narrative perspective, and narrative genre. Given that some papers included multiple outcome variables, each of them was treated as an independent analytical unit and distinguished by numerical labels (1), (2), (3), (4), etc.

3.3 Data Extracting and Effect Size Calculating

The analysis of selected papers revealed two scenarios in which the first-person and third-person narratives affect audience immersion experiences. One scenario result in an impact on either emotional involvement or behavioral intent, while the other scenario influences both emotional involvement and behavioral intent. In the meta-analysis, we coded and grouped conceptually similar variables into larger categories to analyze the relationships between more comprehensive variables [49]. Drawing on the ABC theory model from consumer behavior (which posits that attitudes comprise cognition, behavioral intent, and attitude), we conducted two separate analyses on the outcome variables: firstly, merging emotional involvement and behavioral intent into a single outcome variable; secondly, treating emotional involvement and behavioral intent as two separate outcome variables. This allowed us to examine the impact of different narrative perspectives on emotional involvement and behavioral intent during the immersive experience from two distinct perspectives.

Meta-analysis employs Cohen's d to represent the effects generated by first-person and third-person narratives in immersive experiences. It converts standard deviations, means, sample sizes, and F statistics from each study into indicators of research effects. Effect size is a measure of the strength of experimental effects or the strength of associations between variables, unaffected by the size of the sample [50]. In cases of large sample sizes, there is almost no difference between Cohen's d, Glass's, and Hedge's g effect sizes [51]. Here, M1 is the mean of the first-person narrative group, M2 is the mean of the third-person narrative group, S is the pooled standard deviation, N1 is the sample size of the first-person narrative group, N2 is the sample size of the third-person narrative group, S1 is the standard deviation of the first-person narrative group, and S2 is the standard deviation of the third-person narrative group. Effect sizes for each group of data are obtained through calculations (each study may yield one or more independent effect sizes). The calculation formula is as follows:

$$d = \frac{M1 - M2}{S} \qquad s = \sqrt{\frac{(N1 - 1)S1^2 + (N2 - 1)S2^2}{N1 + N2 - 2}}$$

If the study data reports sample size (N) and F-statistic, Cohen's d can be calculated based on the literature method, where F-statistic is converted to Cohen's d (with N1 representing the sample size of the first-person narrative group and N2 representing the sample size of the third-person narrative group). The calculation formula is as follows.

$$d = \sqrt{\frac{(N1 - 1)S1^2 + (N2 - 1)S2^2}{N1 + N2 - 2}}$$

The calculation of effect sizes in this study was conducted using the Review Manager 5.4 software. Therefore, in data coding, positive effect sizes indicate that in immersive experiences, the impact of third-person narratives on emotional engagement and behavioral intent is greater than that of first-person narratives. Conversely, negative effect sizes indicate that in immersive experiences, the impact of first-person narratives on emotional engagement and behavioral intent is greater than that of third-person narratives.

3.4 Publication Bias Assessment

Bias refers to systematic errors, specifically the deviation between research results or meta-analysis effect sizes and true values. It is one of the factors influencing the accuracy of meta-analysis. In the field of social sciences, literature bias is commonly present; hence, examining publication bias becomes crucial. This study employs a funnel plot to visually inspect potential bias in studies with smaller effect sizes. Furthermore, it utilizes both qualitative funnel plots and quantitative Begg's test to assess publication bias. Begg's rank correlation test is considered a statistical simulation of the funnel plot. If $Z > 1.96$ and $P < 0.05$, bias is present; if $Z < 1.96$ and $P > 0.05$, there is no evidence of bias. By adopting statistical measures, this study aims to evaluate the presence of bias in research results and reduce subjectivity in interpreting funnel plots [52].

3.5 Model Selection and Heterogeneity Test

The fixed-effects model and the random-effects model are two common models used in meta-analysis to assess the overall effect size of a sample [53]. When there are differences in study methods and objects among the included literature in a meta-analysis, the random-effects model is more suitable [54]. Given the diversity in research methods and subjects related to the impact of narrative perspective on audience emotional responses and behavioral intentions in this study, the random-effects model is employed. Additionally, to ensure accuracy, the results are compared with those obtained using the fixed-effects model. The heterogeneity test in the meta-analysis utilizes the statistics Q and I2 as indicators to measure the degree of heterogeneity [55].

4   Result

4.1 The Literature Coding Results

Based on the previous analysis, in the investigation, emotional engagement and behavioral intention were considered as dependent variables. The emotional engagement variable includes aspects such as empathy, emotion, and emotional response. On the other hand, the behavioral intention variable encompasses aspects like persuasiveness, attention, and trust. The encoding results are presented in Table 1.

4.2 Main Effect Test

When combining emotional involvement and behavioral intention into one outcome variable, the impact of first-person and third-person narratives on audience emotional involvement and behavioral intention is presented in Table 2. The meta-analysis included

Table 1. Original study coding results included in the meta-analysis.

Author (year)	Sample size	Outcome variable	Effect value	Narrative mode	Narrative genre
Zhang, Jin 2022 (1)	80	Emotional engagement (emotion)	0.52	Video, Image	Non-fiction
Zhang, Jin 2022 (2)	101	Behavioral intention (persuasion)	0.66	Video, Image	Fiction
Zhang, Jin 2022 (3)	101	Emotional engagement (emotion)	−0.4	Video, Image	Fiction
Zhang, Jin 2022 (4)	414	Behavioral intention (sense of trust)	0.28	Video, Image	Non-fiction
Zhang, Jin 2022 (5)	414	Emotional engagement (empathy)	−0.45	Video, Image	Non-fiction
Zhang, Jin 2022 (6)	890	Behavioral intention (sense of trust)	0.28	Text	Non-fiction
Zhang, Jin 2022 (7)	890	Emotional engagement (emotion)	−0.35	Text	Non-fiction
Kim, Nuri 2020 (1)	501	Behavioral intention (persuasion)	0.19	Text	Fiction
Kim, Nuri 2020 (2)	501	Behavioral intention (persuasion)	0.21	Text	Fiction
Kim, Nuri 2020 (3)	501	Behavioral intention (sense of trust)	0.08	Text	Fiction
Chang, Yaping 2019 (1)	76	Behavioral intention (attention)	1.05	Text	Non-fiction
Chang, Yaping 2019 (2)	76	Behavioral intention (persuasion)	−0.62	Text	Non-fiction

(continued)

Table 1. (*continued*)

Author (year)	Sample size	Outcome variable	Effect value	Narrative mode	Narrative genre
Chang, Yaping 2019 (3)	85	Behavioral intention (attention)	0.6	Text	Fiction
Chang, Yaping 2019 (4)	85	Emotional engagement (emotion)	−0.54	Text	Fiction
Chang, Yaping 2019 (5)	72	Emotional engagement (emotion)	1.46	Text	Non-fiction
Chang, Yaping 2019 (6)	72	Emotional engagement (emotion)	−3.33	Text	Non-fiction
Mulcahy, Melissa 2016 (1)	32	Behavioral intention (attention)	−0.06	Text	Fiction
Mulcahy, Melissa 2016 (2)	32	Emotional engagement (emotion)	−0.1	Text	Fiction
Mulcahy, Melissa 2016 (3)	32	Behavioral intention (sense of trust)	−0.24	Text	Fiction
Mulcahy, Melissa 2016 (4)	32	Emotional engagement (empathy)	0.19	Text	Fiction
Mulcahy, Melissa 2016 (5)	32	Behavioral intention (sense of trust)	−0.1	Text	Fiction
Mulcahy, Melissa 2016 (6)	32	Emotional engagement (emotion)	0.03	Text	Fiction
Mulcahy, Melissa 2016 (7)	32	Behavioral intention (sense of trust)	−0.14	Text	Fiction
Mulcahy, Melissa 2016 (8)	32	Emotional engagement (empathy)	0	Text	Fiction

(*continued*)

Table 1. (*continued*)

Author (year)	Sample size	Outcome variable	Effect value	Narrative mode	Narrative genre
Quintero 2021 (1)	159	Emotional engagement (emotion)	−0.81	Audio	Non-fiction
Quintero 2021 (2)	144	Emotional engagement (empathy)	−0.66	Audio	Non-fiction
Quintero 2021 (3)	159	Emotional engagement (emotion)	0.08	Audio	Non-fiction
Quintero 2021 (4)	144	Emotional engagement (empathy)	−0.21	Audio	Non-fiction
Hatton, Martin 2001 (1)	21	Emotional engagement (emotion)	−0.1	Video	Non-fiction
Hatton, Martin 2001 (2)	20	Emotional engagement (emotion)	−0.12	Video	Non-fiction
Hatton, Martin 2001 (3)	21	Behavioral intention (attention)	−0.4	Video	Non-fiction
Hatton, Martin 2001 (4)	20	Behavioral intention (sense of trust)	−0.56	Video	Non-fiction
Igartua, J. J. 2020	525	Emotional engagement (emotion)	0	Audio	Non-fiction
M. Shalom 2022 (1)	29	Emotional engagement (empathy)	−0.6	Video, Image	Non-fiction
M. Shalom 2022 (2)	26	Behavioral intention (persuasion)	−0.62	Video, Image	Non-fiction
M. Shalom 2022 (3)	29	Emotional engagement (empathy)	−0.57	Video, Image	Non-fiction

(*continued*)

Table 1. (*continued*)

Author (year)	Sample size	Outcome variable	Effect value	Narrative mode	Narrative genre
M. Shalom 2022 (4)	26	Behavioral intention (persuasion)	−0.56	Video, Image	Non-fiction
Wimmer, Lena 2021 (1)	72	Emotional engagement (emotion)	−0.05	Text	Fiction
Wimmer, Lena2021 (2)	87	Emotional engagement (empathy)	−0.81	Text	Fiction
Wimmer, Lena2021 (3)	84	Behavioral intention (attention)	−0.11	Text	Fiction
Wimmer, Lena2021 (4)	84	Behavioral intention (persuasion)	0.95	Text	Fiction

41 effect sizes (k = 41). Under the fixed-effect model, the effect size was d = −0.06, SD = 1.26, CI = −0.09-−0.03, with a two-tailed test result of Z = 4.06, p < 0.00001. Under the random-effect model, the effect size was d = −0.15, SD = 6.72, CI = −0.31–0.02, with a two-tailed test result of Z = 1.76, p = 0.08. The heterogeneity test showed Q = 923.62, I^2 = 96, indicating that 4% of the observed variation was due to sampling error. This situation is more suitable for analysis using the random-effects model. The results of the random-effects model analysis of the impact of first-person and third-person narratives on emotional involvement and behavioral intention in immersive experiences reveal that the narrative perspective does not significantly influence audience emotional involvement and behavioral intention. However, the first-person perspective is more effective than the third-person perspective in enhancing audience emotional involvement and triggering higher behavioral intention (k = 41, p > 0.05, d = −0.18).

Analyzing the result variables by dividing them into two components, audience emotional engagement and behavioral intent, it was found that the narrative perspective significantly influences audience emotional engagement with statistical significance (k = 23, p < 0.05, d = −0.26). However, the impact of narrative perspective on audience behavioral intent is not statistically significant. In comparison, third-person narrative seems to evoke higher behavioral intent in the audience than first-person narrative (k = 18, p > 0.05, d = 0.04), as shown in Table 3.

Moderation Effect Test. The heterogeneity test results for the impact of narrative perspective on emotional engagement and behavioral intent are significant (Q = 923.62, I2 = 96), indicating potential moderators between these two factors. In this study, narrative genre and narrative mode were selected as potential moderators. However, the results

Table 2. The meta-analysis results of narrative perspectives on audience impact (combined emotional engagement and behavioral intent).

Outcome variable	Model	k	Effect size	95% CI	Two-tailed test		Homogeneity			
					Z-value	P-value	Q-value	df	P-value	I^2
Emotional engagement	Fixed effects model	41	−0.06	[−0.09, −0.03]	4.06	0	923.62	40	0	96
Behavioral intent	Random effects model		−0.18	[−0.34, −0.02]	1.76	0.08				

Table 3. The separate meta-analysis results of narrative perspectives on audience emotional engagement and behavioral intent.

Outcome Variable	Model	k	Effect size	95% CI	Two-tailed test		Homogeneity			
					Z-value	P-value	Q-value	df	P-value	I^2
Emotional engagement	Fixed effects model	23	−0.24	[−0.28, −0.20]	12.13	0	564.67	23	0	96
	Random effects model	23	−0.26	[−0.50, −0.03]	2.2	0.03				
Behavioral intent	Fixed effects model	18	0.18	[0.14, 0.23]	7.89	0	166.92	18	0	89
	Random effects model	18	0.04	[−0.13, 0.21]	0.47	0.64				

indicate that neither narrative genre nor narrative mode played a moderating role, as shown in Table 4.

4.3 The Role of Narrative Genre

Narrative genres are classified into fiction and non-fiction based on whether the narrative content is factual. Fiction and non-fiction narratives have long been regarded as a categorization form distinguishing between fact and fiction [56]. When combining audience emotional engagement and behavioral intent into a single outcome variable, there is no significant difference in the effect size of narrative genre on the outcome variable from an inter-group perspective ($Q_{BETWEEN}$ = 0.010, p > 0.05). In the context of fictional narrative, first-person narration is more effective in eliciting audience emotional engagement and behavioral intent compared to third-person narration (d = −0.16, p < 0.05).

Table 4. The meta-analysis of moderator (narrative mode and narrative genre) on audience emotional engagement and behavioral intent.

Outcome variable	Moderator	Group	k	Effect size	95% CI	Two-tailed test			Homogeneity		
						Z-value	P-value	Q-value	df	P-value	I^2
Emotional engagement and Behavioral intent	Narrative genre	Fiction	19	−0.16	[−0.40, 0.08]	1.29	0.20	197.2	18	0.00	91
		Non-fiction	22	−0.17	[−0.42, 0.08]	1.11	0.18	672.62	21	0.00	97
		Total between						0.01	1	0.94	0
		Total within						870.56	40	0.00	95
Emotional engagement	Narrative genre	Fiction	8	−0.13	[−0.52, 0.25]	0.67	0.50	55.05	7	0.00	87
		Non-fiction	14	−0.38	[−0.71, −0.04]	2.22	0.03	449.37	13	0.00	97
		Total between						0.88	1	0.35	0
		Total within						512.83	21	0.00	96
Behavioral intent	Narrative genre	Fiction	11	−0.81	[−0.51, 0.15]	1.06	0.29	141.76	10	0.00	93
		Non-fiction	8	0.09	[−0.32, 0.18]	0.38	0.70	69.99	7	0.00	90
		Total between						0.88	1	0.35	0
		Total within						224.42	18	0.00	92
Emotional engagement and Behavioral intent	Narrative mode	Text	23	−0.11	[−0.37, 0.15]	0.84	0.40	716.71	22	0.00	97
		Video, Image	13	−0.29	[−0.56, −0.02]	2.11	0.03	96.57	12	0.00	88
		Audio	5	−0.1	[−0.46, 0.26]	0.55	0.58	51.28	4	0.00	92
		Total between						1.08	2	0.58	0
		Total within						870.56	40	0.00	95
Emotional engagement	Narrative mode	Text	10	−0.24	[−0.81, 0.34]	0.81	0.42	398.95	9	0.00	98
		Video, Image	7	0.45	[−0.69, −0.21]	3.66	0.00	19.93	6	0.00	70
		Audio	5	−0.1	[−0.46, 0.26]	0.55	0.58	51.28	4	0.00	92

(continued)

Table 4. (*continued*)

Outcome variable	Moderator	Group	k	Effect size	95% CI	Two-tailed test		Homogeneity			
						Z-value	P-value	Q-value	df	P-value	I²
		Total between						2.59	2	0.27	23
		Total within						512.83	21	0.00	96
Behavioral intent	Narrative mode	Text	13	0	[−0.26, 0.26]	0.02	0.98	198.81	12	0.00	94
		Video, Image	6	−0.05	[−0.47, 0.37]	0.23	0.82	26.29	5	0.00	81
		Audio	0	–	–	–	–	–	–	–	–
		Total between						0.04	1	0.84	0
		Total within						226.22	18	0.00	92

However, in the context of non-fictional narrative, there is no statistically significant difference between first-person and third-person narratives in eliciting audience emotional engagement and behavioral intent ($d = -0.17$, $p > 0.05$).

When dividing the outcome variable into emotional engagement and behavioral intent, there is no significant statistical difference in the moderating effect size of narrative genre on audience emotional engagement ($Q_{BETWEEN} = 0.880$, $p > 0.05$). In the context of non-fictional narrative, first-person narration is more effective than third-person narration in eliciting audience emotional engagement ($d = -0.38$, $p < 0.05$). Regarding audience behavioral intent, there is no significant difference in the effect size of narrative genre on the outcome variable ($Q_{BETWEEN} = 0.880$, $p > 0.05$). In the context of fictional narrative, first-person narration tends to be more effective than third-person narration in eliciting audience behavioral intent, although the result is not statistically significant ($d = -0.32$, $p > 0.05$). Conversely, in the context of non-fictional narrative, third-person narration tends to be more effective than first-person narration in eliciting audience behavioral intent, though again the result is not statistically significant ($d = 0.09$, $p > 0.05$).

4.4   The Role of Narrative Mode

When combining audience and behavioral intent into a single outcome variable, there is no significant difference in the effect size of narrative modes on the outcome variable ($Q_{BETWEEN} = 1.080$, $p > 0.05$). Under the conditions of video or image narrative modes, first-person narrative is more effective in eliciting emotional engagement and behavioral intent compared to third-person narrative ($d = -0.29$, $p < 0.05$). However, under the text narrative mode, there is no significant difference in emotional engagement and behavioral intent between first-person and third-person narratives ($d = -0.24$, $p > 0.05$). Similarly, under the audio narrative mode, there is no significant difference in emotional engagement and behavioral intent between first-person and third-person narratives (d = −0.10, p > 0.05).

When dividing the outcome variable into two variables, emotional engagement and behavioral intent, there is no statistically significant difference between first-person and third-person narratives in eliciting emotional engagement funnt ($Q_{BETWEEN}$ = 2.590, p > 0.05) and behavioral intent ($Q_{BETWEEN}$ = 0.040, p > 0.05). Regarding audience emotional engagement, under the narrative modes of video or image, first-person narratives are more effective in eliciting emotional engagement compared to third-person narratives (d = −0.45, p < 0.05).

4.5 Publication Bias Test

The funnel plot is characterized by its intuitiveness, allowing researchers to visually assess the presence of publication bias. The results displayed in the funnel plot, as illustrated in Fig. 2, indicate that the majority of study outcomes cluster in the upper-middle section of the funnel plot, closely centered around the combined effect size (d = −0.18). This initial observation suggests the absence of publication bias. The Begg's test result reveals Z = 1.76 < 1.96, p = 0.08 > 0.05, indicating a lack of publication bias in this study. Consequently, the combined effect size obtained in this research is considered relatively robust.

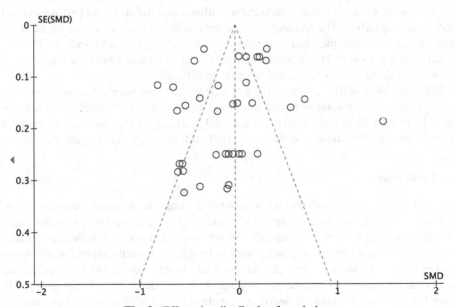

Fig. 2. Effect size distribution funnel plot.

5 Discussion and Conclusion

This study integrates findings from nine empirical articles on the effects of first-person and third-person narrative on immersive experiences. It conducts an analysis of outcome variables and moderating factors within the context of immersive experiences. With a particular focus on moderating factors—emotional engagement and behavioral intent, the results confirm (1) a higher capacity of first-person narrative, compared to third-person narrative, to evoke emotional engagement when the narrative genre involves non-fictional content, and (2) in visual narrative mode (utilizing images and videos), first-person narrative not only enhances emotional engagement but also triggers behavioral intent in the audience.

5.1 Significance

This study contributes to the theoretical advancement of immersive experiences in the tourism domain through a meta-analysis of narrative effects from various perspectives. The research synthesizes a substantial body of empirical literature, offering a referential research framework. Through 41 studies involving 6770 participants, it provides crucial research insights and directions for future in-depth investigations, supported by empirical evidence.

Upon investigating potential moderating factors, it was observed that narrative genre and narrative mode did not exert a moderating influence on the effects of first-person and third-person narratives. The relationship between emotional engagement and behavioral intent represents a complex research question. Meta-analysis results indicate that the impact of first-person and third-person narrative perspectives on emotional engagement and behavioral intent does not exhibit significant differences.

In future studies exploring the effects of immersive experiences, it is recommended to analyze emotional engagement and behavioral intent as distinct variables. Subsequent research efforts, both in theoretical constructs and practical applications, should consider a more refined and multidimensional analysis of audience experience measurements.

5.2 Limitation

Although utilizing meta-analysis for research offers numerous advantages, it is not without limitations. The literature incorporated in this study is restricted to results published in English-language journals, potentially introducing a language bias. Future research endeavors should encompass a broader array of languages, thereby expanding the scope of investigation in this field through additional empirical studies. The first-person and third-person perspectives are the primary focus of this study, both being commonly utilized in narrative contexts. However, the study does not address narratives from the second-person perspective. During the literature retrieval stage, no empirical studies were identified that simultaneously examined narratives from the first, second, and third person perspectives. There is only one study that investigated how the shift from the first or second person to the third person viewpoint affects the immersive experience of reading, proposing a system to address issues related to changing narrative perspectives.

However, this study does not explicitly differentiate between the effects of first-person and second-person narratives.

Acknowledgments. This study was funded by the National Social Science Foundation of China (19ZD27).

Disclosure of Interests. It is now necessary to declare any competing interests or to specifically state that the authors have no competing interests.

References

1. Wang, Z.: Innovative development of digital immersion cultural tourism in the perspective of experience economy. Jiangxi Soc. Sci. **42**(08), 190–197 (2022)
2. Fan, X., Jiang, X., Deng, N.: Immersive technology: a meta-analysis of augmented/virtual reality applications and their impact on tourism experience. Tour. Manag. **91**, 104534 (2022)
3. Lee, H., et al.: Experiencing immersive virtual reality in museums. Inf. Manag. **57**(5) (2020)
4. Jung, T., tom Dieck, M.C., Lee, H., Chung, N.: Effects of virtual reality and augmented reality on visitor experiences in museum. In: Inversini, A., Schegg, R. (eds.) Information and Communication Technologies in Tourism 2016, pp. 621–635. Springer, Cham (2016). https://doi.org/10.1007/978-3-319-28231-2_45
5. Mura, P., Tavakoli, R., Pahlevan Sharif, S.: 'Authentic but not too much': exploring perceptions of authenticity of virtual tourism. Inf. Technol. Tour. **17**(2), 159 (2017)
6. Chronis, A.: Tourists as story-builders: narrative construction at a heritage museum. J. Travel Tour. Mark. **29**(5), 444–459 (2012)
7. Yip, B.: The transformation of emotion: first and third person perspectives in developmental context. Australas. Philos. Rev. **5**(4), 395 (2021)
8. Chen, M., Bell, R.A.: A meta-analysis of the impact of point of view on narrative processing and persuasion in health messaging. Psychol. Health **37**(5), 545–562 (2022)
9. Allé, M.C., et al.: Differential influence of first- vs. third-person visual perspectives on segmentation and memory of complex dynamic events. Conscious. Cogn. **111**, 103508 (2023)
10. Sutin, A.R., Robins, R.W.: Correlates and phenomenology of first and third person memories. Memory **18**(6), 637 (2010)
11. Perregaard, B.: Experienced repetition. Integrational linguistics and the first-person perspective. Lang. Commun. **86**, 118 (2022)
12. Göken, J., Weger, U.: Advancing first-person access to experience through sense of certainty training. New Ideas Psychol. **72**, 101059 (2024)
13. Gregorians, L., et al.: Architectural experience: clarifying its central components and their relation to core affect with a set of first-person-view videos. J. Environ. Psychol. **82**, 101841 (2022)
14. Yang, J., Tian, Y.: Others are more vulnerable to fake news than I Am: third-person effect of COVID-19 fake news on social media users. Comput. Hum. Behav. **125**, 106950 (2021)
15. Chen, M., et al.: Character-defining elements comparison and heritage regeneration for the former command posts of the Jinan campaign-a case of Chinese rural revolutionary heritage. Buildings **13**(8) (2023)
16. Gorisse, G., et al.: First- and third-person perspectives in immersive virtual environments: presence and performance analysis of embodied users. Front. Robot. AI **4**, 33 (2017)

17. Hanashima, R., Ohyama, J.: How to elicit ownership and agency for an avatar presented in the third-person perspective: the effect of visuo-motor and tactile feedback. In: Yamamoto, S., Mori, H. (eds.) HCII 2022. LNCS, vol. 13306, pp. 111–130. Springer, Cham (2022). https://doi.org/10.1007/978-3-031-06509-5_9

18. Bogicevic, V., et al.: Virtual reality presence as a preamble of tourism experience: the role of mental imagery. Tour. Manag. **74**, 64 (2019)

19. Hudson, S., et al.: With or without you? Interaction and immersion in a virtual reality experience. J. Bus. Res. **100**, 468 (2019)

20. Kim, M.J., Hall, C.M.: A hedonic motivation model in virtual reality tourism: comparing visitors and non-visitors. Int. J. Inf. Manag. **46**, 249 (2019)

21. Fu, J., Yu, G.: First-person and third-person narrative effects in advertising: a study based on a meta-analytical paradigm. J. Southwest Minzu Univ. (Humanit. Soc. Sci. Ed.) **43**(07), 137–146 (2022)

22. Chen, M., Bunescu, R.: Changing the narrative perspective: from deictic to anaphoric point of view. Inf. Process. Manag. **58**(4) (2021)

23. Diasamidze, I.: Point of view in narrative discourse. In: 14th Language, Literature and Stylistics Symposium, Selcuk, Turkey (2014)

24. Bec, A., et al.: Management of immersive heritage tourism experiences: a conceptual model. Tour. Manag. **72**, 117–120 (2019)

25. Choifer, A.: A new understanding of the first-person and third-person perspectives. Philos. Pap. **47**(3), 371 (2018)

26. de Hoop, H., Tarenskeen, S.: It's all about you in Dutch. J. Pragmat. **88**, 175 (2015)

27. Jung, T., Chung, N., Leue, M.C.: The determinants of recommendations to use augmented reality technologies: the case of a Korean theme park. Tour. Manag. **49**, 86 (2015)

28. Pine, B.J., Gilmore, J.H.: The Experience Economy. Harvard Business Press (2011)

29. Hosany, S., Witham, M.: Dimensions of cruisers' experiences, satisfaction, and intention to recommend. J. Travel Res. **49**(3), 351–364 (2010)

30. Song, H.J., et al.: The influence of tourist experience on perceived value and satisfaction with temple stays: the experience economy theory. J. Travel Tour. Mark. **32**(4), 415 (2015)

31. Slater, M., Wilbur, S.: A framework for immersive virtual environments (FIVE): speculations on the role of presence in virtual environments. Presence Teleoper. Virtual Environ. **6**(6), 603–616 (1997)

32. Daassi, M., Debbabi, S.: Intention to reuse AR-based apps: the combined role of the sense of immersion, product presence and perceived realism. Inf. Manag. **58**(4), 103453 (2021)

33. Witmer, B.G., Singer, M.J.: Measuring presence in virtual environments: a presence questionnaire. Presence **7**(3), 240 (1998)

34. Meretoja, H.: Non-subsumptive memory and narrative empathy. Mem. Stud. **14**(1), 24–40 (2021)

35. Deighton, J., Grayson, K.: Marketing and seduction: building exchange relationships by managing social consensus. J. Consum. Res. **21**(4), 660–676 (1995)

36. Starr, G.G.: Feeling Beauty: The Neuroscience of Aesthetic Experience. MIT Press, Cambridge (2013)

37. He, Z., Wu, L., Li, X.: When art meets tech: the role of augmented reality in enhancing museum experiences and purchase intentions. Tour. Manag. **68**, 127–139 (2018)

38. Visch, V.T., Tan, E.S.: Categorizing moving objects into film genres: the effect of animacy attribution, emotional response, and the deviation from non-fiction. Cognition **110**(2), 265–272 (2009)

39. Catropa, A., Nesteriuk, S., Prado, G.: From Hörspiel to audio fiction: sound design perspectives for blind and visually impaired people. In: Duffy, V. (ed.) DHM 2018. LNCS, vol. 10917, pp. 268–279. Springer, Cham (2018). https://doi.org/10.1007/978-3-319-91397-1_23

40. Zhang, W.: "Another narrative": research on John Berg's visual narrative theory. Guangxi Normal University (2019)
41. Yung, R., Khoo-Lattimore, C.: New realities: a systematic literature review on virtual reality and augmented reality in tourism research. Curr. Issues Tour. **22**(17), 2081 (2019)
42. Hartung, F., et al.: Taking perspective: personal pronouns affect experiential aspects of literary reading. PLoS ONE **11**(5), e0154732 (2016)
43. Ladhari, R.: The movie experience: a revised approach to determinants of satisfaction. J. Bus. Res. **60**(5), 454–462 (2007)
44. Zeithaml, V.A., Berry, L.L., Parasuraman, A.: The behavioral consequences of service quality. J. Mark. **60**(2), 31–46 (1996)
45. Casaló, L.V., Flavián, C., Ibáñez-Sánchez, S.: Understanding consumer interaction on instagram: the role of satisfaction, hedonism, and content characteristics. Cyberpsychol. Behav. Soc. Netw. **20**(6), 369–375 (2017)
46. Marasco, A., et al.: Exploring the role of next-generation virtual technologies in destination marketing. J. Destin. Mark. Manag. **9**, 138–148 (2018)
47. Loureiro, S.M.C., Guerreiro, J., Ali, F.: 20 years of research on virtual reality and augmented reality in tourism context: a text-mining approach. Tour. Manag. **77**, 104028 (2020)
48. Eisend, M., et al.: A meta-analysis of the effects of disclosing sponsored content. J. Advert. **49**(3), 344–366 (2020)
49. Jiang, K., et al.: How does human resource management influence organizational outcomes? A meta-analytic investigation of mediating mechanisms. Acad. Manag. J. **55**(6), 1264–1294 (2012)
50. Zheng, H.-M., Wen, Z.-L., Wu, Y.: The appropriate effect sizes and their calculations in psychological research. Adv. Psychol. Sci. **19**(12), 1868–1878 (2011)
51. Hedges, L.V.: Distribution theory for Glass's estimator of effect size and related estimators. J. Educ. Stat. **6**(2), 128 (1981)
52. Leng, J.L.W.: Theory & practice of systematic review meta-analysis. Chin. J. Evid. Based Cardiovasc. Med. **5**(02), 115 (2013)
53. Hunter, J.E., Schmidt, F.L.: Fixed effects vs. random effects meta-analysis models: implications for cumulative research knowledge. Int. J. Sel. Assess. **8**(4), 292 (2000)
54. Koven, M.: Speaking French in Portugal: an analysis of contested models of emigrant personhood in narratives about return migration and language use. J. Sociolinguist. **17**(3), 354 (2013)
55. Higgins, J.P.T., Thompson, S.G.: Quantifying heterogeneity in a meta-analysis. Stat. Med. **21**(11), 1558 (2002)
56. Rothschild, J.M.Z.: Reading the difference between "fiction" and "nonfiction": the emergence of the narrator in English prose (Defoe, Derrida) (1987)

IMARISS: Story Creation Tools - Inspiration Mobile Augmented Reality Interactive Story System

Yaojiong Yu[(✉)] and Mike Phillips

School of Art, Design and Architecture, University of Plymouth, Plymouth, UK
{yaojiong.yu,m.phillips}@plymouth.ac.uk

Abstract. Traditional story creation tools currently lack effectiveness in fostering creative thought and expanding beyond-textual-narration, offering limited user experiences, functionality, interactivity, and system compatibility, thus failing to meet diverse needs in creative expression, education, and entertainment. IMARISS, presented by us, is an interdisciplinary approach combining technology, design, art, and user experience design, focusing on user interface, back-end logic, and data processing for enhanced user experience. This paper shows innovative narrative theories and creative writing applications in construction of stories, augmented reality's role in enhancing story element ideation, participatory design's significance, and the integration of gamified system design, while also discussing methodologies in creative writing, pedagogy, and user research for understanding and assessing user needs in story creation. A second experiment formally evaluated utilizing IMARISS against not utilizing it to measure system's support in areas such as immersion, creativity enhancement, and user satisfaction. The result shows its story creation benefits. This study discussed derive preliminary conclusions about the IMARISS's effectiveness and insights gained for future Narrative Interactive System Construction Model.

Keywords: User Center Design · Interactive Storytelling · Usability experiment

1 Introduction

1.1 Inspiration for the System Design

Storytelling is the oldest and most universal way, for humans to communicate knowledge, express emotions, and many purposes. With the growth of media and technology, it has not only told stories orally, but also used words as an important tool, then upgraded to movies, and now it is presented through interactive stories, which can describe stories in the interaction between players and scenes. As digital technology grows in popularity and inventiveness, storytelling (or called narration) face new opportunities and challenges. The current market of traditional storytelling tools reveals significant gaps in meeting the needs for guiding ideation and inspirating creative expansion during the story creative process. These tradition tools often fall short in offering a diversified and enriching user experience and exhibit limitations in functionality, interactive capabilities, and system compatibility [8, 10]. Such deficiencies hinder their effectiveness in satisfying the diverse needs of users across creative expression, educational application, and entertainment. Furthermore, with the introduction of digital technology, the expression of the story is richer, which brings users a good sense of immersion and makes people feel vivid, which was impossible to achieve before. This trend lays greater demands on how to structure a story, requiring new era story to be more adaptive, immersive, and entertaining. People are full of expectations for narrative logic and narrative structure. Multi-module Interaction is a novel approach to media engagement, which provides story with a more innovative narrative development direction. One interdisciplinary is called interactive storytelling (IS). IS allows the audience to affect the unfolding of the story by merging development technology and content [1–3]. In one branch of IS, the author will discover interactive narrative creation (INC), INC is obviously different from the way of presenting stories in the past, which guides people to participate actively through the branching of story plots, strong visual stimulation, and game-like content [6]. In this way, the story will be more touching, the characters in the story will be more diverse, and the narrative appeal will be enhanced [7]. The fundamental purpose is to create a creative environment that can inspire people to develop rich imagination, create boldly, establish critical thinking, and show their talents in narrative stories [8, 9]. With the inspiration of IS or INC, the authors consider whether is it possible to utilize card game cross story creation. A system design in human-computer interaction (HCI), The Inspiration Mobile Augmented Reality Interactive Story System (IMARISS) means a system integrating interactive storytelling creation and card game module through the lenses of augmented reality, artificial intelligence backstage, and streamlined user interfaces, and test how level this system can now reexamine narrative elements including story structure, visual discourse, character roles, and emotional stimulation.

1.2 Inspiration for the System Design

How to stimulate user's creation and the immersion of being invested in creating a story. This study embraces participatory design (PD) + customized design (CD) theories. The pursuit of good user experience is the foundation of PD, which is widely used in many fields, including software, medical, architecture and so on [12–14]. PD plays a guiding role in the development of this subject, which can bring about subversive changes. Users are not only simply observing, but also becoming the main body of design and creation. Under the support of PD, more diverse elements are supplied by participants, which trigger the system iteration. Not only PD, the research also further infuses the customizable design (CD) to amplify users' innovative and individualized characteristics. Customizable design (CD), a strategy empowering user to modify a product or service's attributes, functionalities, or aesthetics, is to align with their preferences [15]. Some scholars have found that CD can make users more satisfied, and they will not hesitate to make the same choice again when they need similar products in the future, and the products will create higher value in the market [15]. IMARISS opens up a new model, in which users can integrate a large number of personalized contents into the process of creating stories, and become the narrative subject, and even become the core force of the whole design activity. This study is innovative to embed feasible (PD, CD) theories into the core of the system design process. Users can weave stories according to their own imagination, become the main body in story creation, and promote the development of system towards diversification.

1.3 Character, Event, Prop, and Emotion in the Story

The IMARISS project takes design as an important content, At the core of this system design, it is a deep integration in the process of innovation, from events, emotions, characters, and other aspects of the design of user interface, each content is to allow users to immerse in the story scene, in order to create multiple stories for user diverse purpose. The reason why we should improve the narrative structure from these aspects is that each aspect can make the story more meaningful and achieve story innovation [16, 17]. In this way, the central character in the story is able to portray, all props can become metaphorical elements, events will develop step by step, which may lead to conflicts [18]. Conflicts may occur at any time in the development of the story, and it is uncertain at which time point there will be a turning point, thus forming a complete logical structure, forming a good narrative arc, and playing a guiding role in the birth and development of the story [18–22]. This is a structure that can achieve goals, enhance people's ability to meet challenges, and then develop reasonable solutions. As the other part, Emotions are more critical in the process of evaluation. In the process of creating stories, people can produce a variety of emotions, including joy, happiness and so on. In the face of loss, failure and achievement, people's reactions are obviously different. Dividing people's emotions into various types, the characters in the story are more likely to resonate with readers, the difficulty of emotional transmission is reduced, and cross-domain cognitive behavior will also occur [23–26]. Through in-depth analysis of creative writing and narrative theory, we can provide guidance for diversified creative methods and deeply feel the impact of characters, events, emotions, and props in the process of creating stories. This is a systematic research method, which plays a theoretical guiding role in the design of the user interface of the system, can enhance the applicability and universality, and will not limit the user's narrative experience.

2   Design of IMARISS

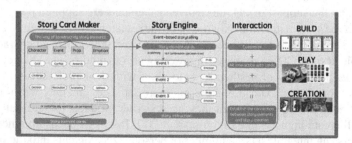

Fig. 1. Architecture of IMARISS

Yaojiong designed IMARISS as an end-to-end system. Consisting of three applications: the ability to customize the creation of story elements in an easy way, story plots, and experience story card play interaction and AR interactions during the creation process (See Fig. 1). The story card maker enabled users to input text into the corresponding category user interfaces, thereby generating desktop story cards containing specific categorized elements. After completed inputs in the four categories, IMARISS extensively organized story cards (inputted by the user) and generated them into a card game. Then, the story engine set the backend story element processing algorithm (Decision-Tree) integrates user input data into the story element database of the desktop application, allowing users to play with their created story cards for story creation under card game rules. When finished the card game, IMARISS generated a story instruction, allowing users to arrange and combine instructions based on elements that appear in the card game. In short, users can directly experience and adjust the stories they created through interaction with the desktop game cards. Additionally, IMARISS also generated story script templates, summarizing the storylines used for instructions after the user completed story instruction interactions, (or could be recognized after user playing role play card game) to assist users in decision-making during the story creation process. After completing this tabletop game-style instruction interaction, the system helped users summarize their storylines after the interactive instructions, which could be used as plot script cues for users in story creation, randomly and creatively providing directional thoughts and inspiration for further creation. More details will be elaborated in the later part of the text. Consequently, IMARISS provided users a diverse range of story instruction categories and content, enriching ways of story creation process. In detail, IMARISS consisted of four core functions to construct a seamless interactive story creation framework: 1). The user interface employed a story element card mode for information input; 2). The backend mechanism was responsible for organizing and processing these story elements; 3). Linear story element guide cards were used to direct story development; 4). The Augmented Reality (AR) module provided a visual representation of the story elements (Fig. 2). Augmented Reality (AR) technology, aimed at optimizing the overall experience of visualization story creation. Designed in this way, users' story creation phase would be more novel, immersive, and enjoyable. IMARISS could also reflect the development potential through the combination of multiple modals, such stories (narratives) were creative.

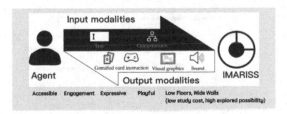

Fig. 2. Input/Output modalities diagram

The purpose of this study was to combine the characteristics of IMARISS platform to create an innovative story creation tool, which could effectively enhance the experience of all users in the process of creating stories (See Fig. 2). This creative method had a strong systematism, could introduce a large number of innovative elements into the story, could also promote the enrichment of the story database, could also play the advantages of augmented reality technology, could process story creation as playing card game. In fact, this way could make IMARISS satisfied by users, effectively interact the various variables in the creation of stories, and made people feel like designers of this system. This method could effectively reflect the advantages of IMARISS.

2.1 Evaluation Tools

This research project embarked on a thorough evaluation of the IMARISS through a comparative experimental approach. This experiment was designed to discern the relative strengths and weaknesses of utilizing the IMARISS in the process of story creation. This paper would predominantly focus on elucidating the methodologies employed for user usability testing. The objective is to gauge the efficacy of IMARISS in augmenting the story crafting process, informed by the outcomes of these assessments. Key performance indicators were identified to distinguish between scenarios whether IMARISS was used versus it was not, providing a clear measure of its impact on the user's experience in story creation, interaction, and satisfaction levels. To achieve this, the study adopted a mixed-methodology framework, intertwining qualitative and quantitative data. In the analysis of this paper, the product performance is evaluated from four aspects (See Fig. 3):

1) *Immersion Questionnaire (IQ)*: Quantified how immersive the user is during the interaction with the participants.
2) Emotional Feedback: To find out if the user has an emotional connection when interacting with the system.
3) User Engagement and Interaction Behavior Observation: Analyze whether user participation in authoring is differentiated using IMARISS or not.
4) Interactive Learning Cost: Evaluate the difficulty of creation story.

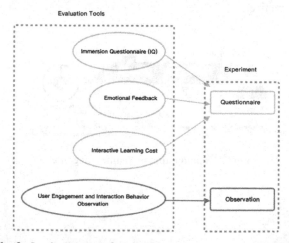

Fig. 3. Logic diagram of evaluation tools related to experiment.

These evaluation tools standards and processes were designed to make this study more in-depth, to grasp the effect of using IMARISS to create stories, and to deepen the understanding of user experience in the process of telling interactive stories.

3   Method

Volunteers would be randomly assigned to either an experimental group or a control group. The experimental group would use the IMARISS to create stories, while the control group would not use IMARISS to create stories. In experimental group. Each participant would have maximum 20 min to use IMARISS. Then he/she would have maximum 20 min to write a small story (700 words or less). Each participant would have to create a story based on a given narrative context (medieval fantasy theme) with at least three characters, three items, three events, and three emotions. In control group, participant would have maximum 20 min to preparation for story creation. Then he/she would have maximum 20 min to write a small story (700 words or less). Each volunteer would have to create a story based on a given narrative context (medieval fantasy theme) with at least three characters, three items, three events, and three emotions. (it is the same task as the experimented group). A group of participants would anonymously be compared with another group of participants. The comparison would use the same evaluation tools and data collection and analysis methods as the exercise and the evaluation. After completing a story creation exercise. The researcher would give each participant a handbook was written on corelated questions, (it will take user's 10 min to answer). The handbook was summarized as templates for the following three valuation tools. (1). Immersion Questionnaire (IQ), which assessed their level of immersion when using IMARISS or their own methods when they created story. (2). Creativity Support Index (CSI), which measured how well IMARISS, or their own methods supported your creativity. (3). User Experience Questionnaire (UEQ), which measured participants' satisfaction and task completion using statistics. They would have Q&A session after all experiment (10min or less). it usually would answer their questions or seek for the answer about several open-ended questions for discussion with the researcher. They would also be filmed by camera during the whole experiment. The researcher would anonymously record each participant's usability process during the test. The researcher would also collect their written stories and archive them for analysis. It was worth to notice the whole experiment (Using IMARISS [20min] + Creating Story [20min] + Questionnaires [10min] + Q&A [10min or not]) is approximately 1 h or less. Carry out the experiment as follows:

- Recruitment of participants: The number of volunteers should reach 10, at least 18 years old and no more than 35 years old. These volunteers had a strong interest in narrative creation. Ten volunteers were randomly divided into two groups: one was the experimental group, which used IMARISS in the creation, and the other was the control group, which only used the traditional method to create, with the same number (5) of people in both groups.
- Experiment Set-Up: A thorough introduction to the experiment's objectives and methodologies was provided to all participants. All volunteers were required to understand what procedures should be followed to manage data, and to understand the privacy protection policy to generate the necessary understanding.

- Introduction story writing tools: Participants of both teams developed the necessary understanding of the IMARISS and used story writing App – "Living writer" [30]. The control group, meanwhile, was not provided access to IMARISS but was given equal opportunity and time to craft stories using similar story writing App- "Living writer".
- Task: In the process of completing this task, all creators would weave their own understanding of the Middle Ages to develop their stories. Each story had a certain number of creative elements. At least three characters should be arranged. (there can be cunning thieves, creepy wizards, heroic and handsome knights, etc.). When designing props, we should pay attention to innovation and use at least three kinds. (For example, a magic book that everyone yearns for, a sword with infinite charm, and a map that can attract people's attention). There were at least three key events, (which may be a war between different countries, a betrayal of friendship, or a search for lost treasures). Showed diverse emotions through these elements, (such as fearlessness, loyalty and so on). The only difference between the two groups was the use or non-use of IMARISS, which required the participants of the two groups to conceive the story first, which lasted for 20 min.
- Analyze the data: After obtaining the data, we needed to make statistics and in-depth analysis to understand how the IMARISS could play a role in narrative and creation. In this link, we also focused on the user's style, creativity, content, interaction and so on.
- Write a report: Completed the research report, not only to introduce the experimental process and results, but also to notice their own experience, all participants would be an opportunity to learn about the outcomes of the research by contacting researchers through a variety of platforms to publish the report, such as social media, email, etc.

3.1 Usage of Questionnaire Described.

After using IMARISS, each of the 10 volunteers was given a manual with a questionnaire that took about 10 min to fill out. In this process, the options of each question in the questionnaire could be adjusted, and open-ended questions could be added to understand the real feelings of volunteers. In the questionnaire, we needed to understand the specific situation of volunteers in the creation, understand the specific situation of each link, and grasp their narrative process. This experiment formed a complete framework, the purpose was to understand the efficacy of IMARISS, but also to have a comprehensive understanding of its experience in the process of using the system (the full questionnaire is displayed in the appendix).

3.2 Crafting the Experimental Environment

To capture the essence of participants' interactions and emotional dynamics, a smart-phone stands, and a ring light were strategically placed before the session. Participants engaged using the IMARISS, conveniently pre-installed on their mobile devices. The experimental area was thoughtfully designed as a desktop testing zone, creating an optimal space for groups of 2–5 participants. This meticulously arranged setting ensures that all activities for each participant were uniformly conducted in this controlled environment.

3.3 Tools and Materials for the Experiment

In a meticulous comparative study on narrative creation with IMARISS, researchers employed an array of specialized tools and devices. We had thoughtfully prepared devices with "Living Writer" [30] installed for seamless testing. Positioned in front of the conference table was a Hisense large screen, complete with an HDMI interface, serving as an efficient medium for signal output. Behind this setup, researchers had installed a smartphone stand and ring light, not only for stability but also to activate a recording feature, meticulously capturing both video and audio for future analysis and media use. The technological ensemble extended to Apple Mac computers, iPad mini-6, and a variety of Apple or Android smartphones, each poised for recording with internet access and user store login capabilities. Complementing these were the smartphone stands and ring lights, alongside external recording devices (notably the Mac computer's recording feature). Furthermore, a card printer was readily available, tasked with bringing to life the creative story elements crafted by users.

Beyond the realm of recording and testing gear, after engaging with IMARISS, researchers distributed a carefully crafted handbook filled with pertinent questionnaires to participants. In the preparatory work, the more detailed and in-depth, the more effective the questionnaire handbook could be guaranteed, and the professional level of research could be improved. These handbooks were the experience accumulated in the long-term research, which could provide assistance for the effective development of user experience design. This user experience questionnaire template was ingeniously developed based on three foundational tools: (1) Immersion Questionnaire (IQ), (2) Creativity Support Index (CSI), (3) User Experience Questionnaire (UEQ) [27]. In the meticulous composition of this handbook, the author drew upon various experimental studies, forming a robust theoretical foundation for the questionnaire's design. Notably referenced are UEQ-S, UEQ, and diverse methodologies for analyzing user experience perspectives within the UEQ framework [28]. The UEQ-S focused on two specific scales: "Usability Quality" and "Hedonic Quality," while the broader UEQ spanned six scales for a more nuanced assessment. Additionally, researchers incorporated 20 user dimensions and corresponding explanations from UEQ-b for in-depth, face-to-face interviews and user experience tests (as detailed in Appendix). These interviews, structured as a continuous 10-min dialogue with participants, invited them to express their subjective experiences, thereby providing a holistic framework for product user experience analysis. For an intimate understanding of the primary user group, we also implemented the "Engaging User Persona" experiential method as a guiding framework [29]. By embracing these diverse evaluations, we were equipped to delve deeper into customers' perceptions and needs, fostering innovation and optimization. The purpose of these experiment tools was to analyze how IMARISS attracts users, try to be objective and reasonable, grasp the specific characteristics of user models, and analyze the differences of user behavior. Through these tools and materials, the common characteristics of all users could be gathered together, which could help to extract information (Referencing see Appendix for comprehensive details).

3.4 Documentation, and Archival Techniques

At the end of the filling out questionnaire, we would send a notice to the participants to let them know that all the tasks they have undertaken in this activity have been completed. We would collect written data extensively and store them in electronic files, each of which had a unique identifier and a brief introduction, including date, number, completion level and so on. If one participant initially agreed to be filmed and later decided to remain anonymous, he/she film would need to be edited to maintain its anonymity. This might include blurring your face, changing his/her voice, or even deleting his/her footage altogether if anonymity could not be guaranteed. Typically, filming would only capture the page of the device, and his/her hand movements, with a textual record of the question this participant were asking (named as PARTICIPANT + NUMBER).

3.5 Statistical Analysis

Utilizing qualitative and quantitative lens, this study meticulously examined and interpreted observational and questionnaire data to unearth recurring themes, discernible patterns, and pivotal insights. The research team embarked on an exhaustive data review journey, extracting pivotal information pertinent to user engagement, preferences, and usability hurdles. The observed behavior was analyzed, and when classifying the data, the statistical analysis method was adopted, the interactivity was emphasized, and the development trend was predicted. A deep dive into questionnaire data through thematic analysis would be conducted, where we would pore over transcripts, categorizing key segments to uncover recurring themes, participant viewpoints, and actionable suggestions. Following this, a holistic review of the coded observational and questionnaire data would be undertaken to identify overarching themes, strengths, weaknesses, and potential areas for enhancement. Putting all the findings together could guide the iteration the system design and could also provide a large amount of information for the effective enrich the database of the IMARISS. In this link, it was necessary to enhance the reliability of research data, to make reasonable explanations for specific problems, and to obtain more reasonable improvement in the process of system iteration.

3.6 Iterative Comparative Trend Charting

After the statistical analysis, all kinds of data collected should be stored and kept comprehensively, so as to prepare for the more intuitive presentation of IMARISS in the subsequent operation. During this period, we would draw a comparison chart to describe the changes of user experience in different diagrams in an intuitive way. With the help of specific data, according to the trend chart, we would predict to getting the following gains: 1. We could find out what advantages IMARISS has compared with the traditional creative tools, such as the ability to suitable integrate card game elements, optimize the user interface layout, and enhance the design interaction, so as to provide support for users to make higher satisfaction evaluation. 2. We could analyze the shortcomings of the system, point out the existing bottlenecks, so that the user experience can be improved. 3. Be able to grasp which functions would directly affect the user experience, make reasonable design decisions, and focus on this in the next iteration. 4. Took that test result as a reference, gave correct instructions for the design and development system, and carried out sequencing. Generally speaking, making iterative comparative trend charting in this way could lay a foundation for the feasible and reasonable suggestions for its optimization, prepare for its continuous iteration, and provide better services for the core user groups.

4 Result

In this study, the core data set was relatively comprehensive, which was a summary of the opinions of 10 volunteers. The conclusions drawn here were rooted in the rich data these ten individuals provided. Among the pivotal findings: Comparative assessments of story creation, both with and without the IMARISS (system), alongside controlled variable experiments, underscore that the IMARISS (system) had garnered an impressive 95% satisfaction rate among participants. This satisfaction spanned personalization, user contentment, and the enriching experience of immersive interactive story crafting and gaming. This highlighted a marked advancement in the realm of human-computer interaction and overall user experience. The system's prowess in weaving comprehensive story frameworks was evident from our data. Behavioral observations revealed that a striking 70% of participants were able to autonomously create story element cards, with the remaining 30% achieving this with minimal guidance, showcasing the system's adeptness in story element generation. During the narrative construction phase, all users (100%) successfully engaged with story scripts, finding the card game element refreshingly novel, which underscored the IMARISS system's exceptional capability in offering captivating story creation guidance. Moreover, an overwhelming 95% of users expressed their satisfaction with the system's personalized, gratifying, and enthralling interactive narrative and gaming experience. For statistical validation, paired sample t-tests were employed, a method ideal for comparing the performance or measurements of the same participants under varied conditions, assessing the significance of these conditions on the outcomes.

4.1 Detailed in Results.

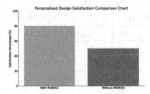

Fig. 4. Personalized Design satisfaction

1) Enhanced satisfaction with personalized design (participatory design satisfaction) recorded a notable rise: 80% compared to 50% (p-value at a significant level of 0.05). This was ascertained through a paired sample t-test, yielding a t-value of 4.32 and a

p-value < 0.05, clearly indicating heightened satisfaction with personalized design (Refer to Fig. 1: [Personalized Design Satisfaction Comparison Chart]). This chart visually contrasted user satisfaction levels, with the orange bar indicating the use of the IMARISS system and the gray bar depicting scenarios without its use (Fig. 4).

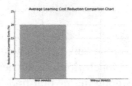

Fig. 5. Average Learning Cost Reduction Comparison Chart

2) A significant decrease in average learning cost: 20% versus 0% (p-value at 0.01 significance level) (The decline in average learning cost determined by $Z = -3.76$, significance level p-value <0.01, using the Wilcoxon signed-rank test). This graph illustrated the magnitude of learning cost reduction and its statistical significance, with the orange bar signifying the learning costs associated with the IMARISS system, contrasted against the gray bar for the non-IMARISS scenario (Fig. 5).

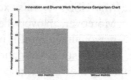

Fig. 6. Innovation and Diverse Work Performance

3) A surge in innovation and diversity in work performance: 70% over 50% (p-value at 0.05 significance level), as determined by a z-test ($z = 2.01$, significance level p-value <0.05). This chart offered a comparative view of the proportions of innovative and diverse works produced, with the orange bar representing narratives crafted using the IMARISS system, while the gray bar showed those created without it (Fig. 6).

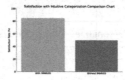

Fig. 7. Satisfaction with Intuitive Categorization

4) Elevated Satisfaction with Intuitive Categorization: Achieving a notable 85% satisfaction rate over 50% (p-value at a significant level of 0.05). This marked increase in satisfaction with intuitive categorization (Paired sample t-test, t = 3.21, p-value < 0.05) further underscored that the IMARISS system's innovative narrative theory and intuitive approach to creative writing categorization were instrumental in reducing the learning curve for users (Fig. 7).

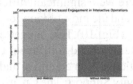

Fig. 8. Increased Engagement in Interactive Operations

5) Amplified Engagement in Interactive Operations: A substantial raised to 90% from 50% in user engagement (p-value 0.01 significance level), as evidenced by a one-tailed t-test (t = 6.52, p-value < 0.01). This chart vividly showcased the heightened level of engagement experienced during interactive processes, with the orange bars depicting participants who utilized the IMARISS system, in contrast to the gray bars representing non-users (Fig. 8).

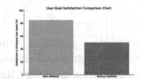

Fig. 9. User Goal Satisfaction

6) User Goal Achievement: A significant increase to 85% satisfaction in achieving user goals from 50% (p-value 0.05 significance level), validated by a one-tailed t-test (t = 3.75, p-value < 0.05). This chart offered a comparative view of user satisfaction across different categorization methodologies, with orange bars indicating participants using the IMARISS system, contrasted against the gray bars for non-users (Fig. 9).

7) User Immersion Level: The IQ questionnaire could be used to understand what kind of immersion the user had in the process of using the system. The average IQ scores of the experimental group and the control group were 4.12 and 3.12, respectively. According to the T test, the difference between the two groups in this respect was significant (t (28) = 4.86, p < 0.001), which was enough to prove that the five volunteers in the experimental group had a higher degree of immersion. According

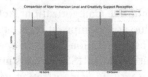

Fig. 10. User Immersion Level & Creativity Support Perception

to the analysis of variance, there were significant differences in the three dimensions ($F (2,56) = 15.24$, $p < 0.001$), and the most obvious one was the emotional dimension ($F (1,28) = 26.78$, $p < 0.001$) (Fig. 10).This suggested that the experimental group experienced greater joy, excitement, and fulfillment using the system, significantly boosting user immersion, particularly in cognitive and emotional aspects.

8) Perception of System's Creativity Support: The Creativity Support Index (CSI) evaluated the system's effectiveness in nurturing user creativity. The experimental group's average CSI score stood at 4.23 (standard deviation 0.54), markedly outperforming the control group's average of 3.17 (standard deviation 0.63). A t-test revealed a substantial difference in total CSI scores ($t (28) = 5.34$, $p < 0.001$), indicating that the experimental group perceived a higher level of creative support from the system. Through ANOVA analysis, we found that each CSI item was different ($F (3,84) = 16.87$, $p < 0.001$), and the most obvious difference was the challenge dimension, from which we could see that all participants of the experimental group unanimously found that this was a challenging and innovative system, and they were supported in the process of creating stories (Fig. 14).

5   Discussion

The writing of this paper could bring enlightenment to more story creators and narrative designers, provide a breakthrough story creation tool, play the role of story element cards, and highlight the value of augmented reality technology. Research in an interdisciplinary way could integrate psychological, artistic, and other professional knowledge, enhance human-computer-interaction, reflect personality, enhance user's interest in participation, provide favorable conditions for the development and design of similar system design, made user's experience more diversity, and feel the importance of interactive narrative. Although The development of this study had a unique insight into product development, there were also shortcomings, and breakthroughs should be made in the next step of development and design.

5.1   Reflection on Study Limitations

Although our pursuit of comprehensive in the research process, but inevitably there were deficiencies. In the initial research, the scope was not wide enough, but limited to certain situations or users, which required careful investigation to get more convincing and applicable results. Although qualitative analysis was insufficient and quantitative methods were used to make up for it, from the perspective of creativity evaluation, this study was disturbed by subjective factors in judgment. In the next phase of the survey, more indicators that could describe creativity should be aggregated. Although this study could make users feel the superiority of the new system, it had not been fully promoted because of the constraints of many factors in the process of system design. In the next stage of research, we need to get rid of the shackles, deal with more challenges, and improve the system in the next stage.

5.2 Prospective Discussions on Future Developments

With the development of this study, we had a deep understanding of interactive narrative and the use of augmented reality technology in games and look forward to the future development combined with the actual situation. The development of this study predicted what kind of effect technological innovation could achieve, which was conducive to enhancing narrative expansibility and preparing for the development of personalized story creation. With the support of artificial intelligence, the user experience would be gradually enhanced, especially to make good use of a series of advanced technologies, including augmented reality, language models, Generative Adversarial Networks and so on.

Looked forward to the next stage of development, focusing on the following points: 1. Inclusion and diversity: The in-depth research should focus on the inclusion strategy, so that the needs of users with different cultural backgrounds can be met.2. Long-term participation: played the role of the system in mobilizing users' enthusiasm for participation, enhance users' creativity, increase emotional investment and get good returns.3. Technology exploration: It was necessary to innovate the technology and follow the changes of users' needs. With the passage of time, users would put forward diversified needs and have new expectations for the system, which required technology upgrading to make users' experience stronger.4. User feedback: Mobility was the basic feature of user feedback. We should be aware that user needs would never remain unchanged for a long time. In the process of advancing this study, interactive narrative could gradually achieve development, research will be more in-depth, and innovation would be achieved in this process. Human-computer interaction would have a more prominent performance, and development could be achieved through innovation. When designing games, we should make appropriate adjustments so that user satisfaction can be greatly improved.

5.3 Enhanced Conclusion

To analyze the essence of this study, user data-driven was an effective method in the process of constructing narrative interaction system, and IMARISS model analyzed and clarified the specific situation in all aspects, which was ready for the promotion and development of this innovative model. System design should focus on user experience. By analyzing the content generated by users, we could fully see the degree of personalization and creativity and could use as for next focus point on system development. In the future, we would explore more insights from interactive system, help users achieve personal goals, has more excellent performance in story content arrangement, deep excavation of the story, and promote the expansion of module about narrative contents. Through the organization of experiments, combined with the situation found in the analysis of data, in-depth analysis would be carried out in the next stage of the survey to meet the interests and needs of more users and develop a more advanced IMARISS (system).

Acknowledgments. I would like to acknowledge the support of CSC scholarship and the assistance of i-DAT team at University of Plymouth during this study.

A APPENDICES

A.1   AI Application/Algorithm

IMARISS was used to process user input in creative storytelling, including categorizing various elements such as characters, events, props, and emotions, and then generating story instructions for role-playing games. AI application / algorithm - Decision tree algorithms would be suitable for this application. First, it could manage both categorical and numerical data (story elements) and provide a clear logic (labeled) for decision-making, which aligned well with the system's need to process diverse story elements and user inputs. Decision trees could offer intuitive explanations for why certain story elements were grouped or sequenced in a particular way, which could be beneficial for both developers and users when understanding the story structure. (e.g. one story how to combine with character, events, props, and emotions). And it is very intuition for applied storyline combination of story elements). For the IMARISS, which involved categorizing and processing creative story elements, the Decision Tree algorithm seemed most appropriate. It efficiently handled varied data types and could intuitively map the decision-making process behind story development. This algorithm's ability to deal with non-linear relationships and its suitability for feature selection made it ideal for the complex task of organizing and suggesting narrative elements in the story creation process. It was good for systems requiring a clear logic flow, like IMARISS, which needed to make logical connections between different story components. In the phase of story element combination and organization, IMARISS offered a gamified.

A.2 Experiment

A.2.1 Immersion Questionnaire (IQ)

Immersion Question, which is an evaluation tool for measuring the subjective experience of being immersed while playing a video game, which you can found by Jennett et al. [2]. The IQ or IEQ (Immersive Experience Questionnaire) consists of 31 items that assess six dimensions of immersion: cognitive involvement, real world dissociation, emotional involvement, challenge, control, and empathy. Each item is rated on a 5-point scale, from 1 (strongly disagree) to 5 (strongly agree). The total score ranges from 31 to 155, with higher scores indicating higher levels of immersion (Table 1).

A.2.2 User Experience Questionnaire (UEQ)

Give examples. Make a document for the UEQ. This user experience questionnaire template was developed from the UEQ user questionnaire template [6] (Table 2).

Table 1. An example of a video game that was rated using the IEQ can be found in the article by Iacovides et al. (2015) [3].

Item	Rating
Cognitive involvement	X
Real world dissociation	X
Emotional involvement	X
challenge	X
control	X
empathy	X

Table 2. Figure 4: A sample of scale efficiency.

To achieve my goals, I consider the product as							
Slow	o	o	o	O	o	o	o	Fast
Inefficient	o	o	o	O	o	o	o	Efficient
Impractical	o	o	o	O	o	o	o	Practical
Cluttered	o	o	o	O	o	o	o	Organized
I consider the product property described by these terms as							
Completely irrelevant	o	o	o	O	o	o	O	Very important

The chart covers a variety of topics, such as product speed, efficacy, practicality, and general organization. Each component is rated on dimensions such as "slow" to "fast," "ineffective" to "effective," "impractical" to "practical," and "disorganized" to "organized," allowing researchers to gain a full understanding of the product's user perceives in various aspects.Several measures were performed to adapt and validate the UEQ questionnaire: Part 1: Initially, the questionnaire used for interviews was assessed by user experience professionals or academics. Experts in user experience were also involved in the pre-assessment of the outcomes. This guaranteed that the UEQ questionnaire maintained a high level of professionalism and effectively gathered relevant user experience information. These validation data and insights would help researchers improve and optimize the user experience design more systematically. UEQ-S, UEQ, and UEQ use distinct assessment methodologies to analyze user experience ideas across the UEQ questionnaire [7]. Researchers also employed UEQ-b's 20 user dimensions and related explanations for questionnaire and user experience testing (see Fig. 6). This interview consisted of continuous 10-min conversations with participants who were asked to circle their subjective feelings. These characteristics give a thorough framework for analyzing the product's user experience. By taking all these factors into account, researchers can gain a greater understanding of customer perceptions and demands for the product, allowing for innovation and optimization.

A.2.3 Questionnaire Sheet

Attractiveness:
1. This product makes me feel delighted. [ ] 1 [ ] 2 [ ] 3 [ ] 4 [ ] 5 [ ] 6 [ ] 7
2. I find this product visually appealing. [ ] 1 [ ] 2 [ ] 3 [ ] 4 [ ] 5 [ ] 6 [ ] 7
3. I have a positive overall impression of this product. [ ] 1 [ ] 2 [ ] 3 [ ] 4 [ ] 5 [ ] 6 [ ] 7
4. I would recommend this product to others. [ ] 1 [ ] 2 [ ] 3 [ ] 4 [ ] 5 [ ] 6 [ ] 7

Perspicuity:
5. I quickly became familiar with how to use this product. [ ] 1 [ ] 2 [ ] 3 [ ] 4 [ ] 5 [ ] 6 [ ] 7
6. I find the operation of this product easy to understand. [ ] 1 [ ] 2 [ ] 3 [ ] 4 [ ] 5 [ ] 6 [ ] 7
7. I find the interface of this product clear. [ ] 1 [ ] 2 [ ] 3 [ ] 4 [ ] 5 [ ] 6 [ ] 7
8. I find the functions of this product well-defined. [ ] 1 [ ] 2 [ ] 3 [ ] 4 [ ] 5 [ ] 6 [ ] 7

Efficiency:
9. I can complete tasks in this product quickly. [ ] 1 [ ] 2 [ ] 3 [ ] 4 [ ] 5 [ ] 6 [ ] 7
10. I find the response time of this product to be fast. [ ] 1 [ ] 2 [ ] 3 [ ] 4 [ ] 5 [ ] 6 [ ] 7
11. I find the performance of this product to be good. [ ] 1 [ ] 2 [ ] 3 [ ] 4 [ ] 5 [ ] 6 [ ] 7
12. I feel that using this product doesn't waste my time. [ ] 1 [ ] 2 [ ] 3 [ ] 4 [ ] 5 [ ] 6 [ ] 7

Dependability:
13. I have confidence in the results produced by this product. [ ] 1 [ ] 2 [ ] 3 [ ] 4 [ ] 5 [ ] 6 [ ] 7
14. I find the functions of this product to be dependable. [ ] 1 [ ] 2 [ ] 3 [ ] 4 [ ] 5 [ ] 6 [ ] 7
15. I feel that this product won't encounter errors or malfunctions. [ ] 1 [ ] 2 [ ] 3 [ ] 4 [ ] 5 [ ] 6 [ ]
7
16. I believe this product can handle various situations. [ ] 1 [ ] 2 [ ] 3 [ ] 4 [ ] 5 [ ] 6 [ ] 7

Stimulation:
17. Using this product makes me feel excited. [ ] 1 [ ] 2 [ ] 3 [ ] 4 [ ] 5 [ ] 6 [ ] 7
18. Using this product makes me feel refreshed. [ ] 1 [ ] 2 [ ] 3 [ ] 4 [ ] 5 [ ] 6 [ ] 7
19. Using this product makes me feel entertained. [ ] 1 [ ] 2 [ ] 3 [ ] 4 [ ] 5 [ ] 6 [ ] 7
20. Using this product makes me feel delighted. [ ] 1 [ ] 2 [ ] 3 [ ] 4 [ ] 5 [ ] 6 [ ] 7

Novelty:
21. I perceive innovative features in this product. [ ] 1 [ ] 2 [ ] 3 [ ] 4 [ ] 5 [ ] 6 [ ] 7
22. I believe this product stands out from others. [ ] 1 [ ] 2 [ ] 3 [ ] 4 [ ] 5 [ ] 6 [ ] 7
23. I consider this product to have a unique style. [ ] 1 [ ] 2 [ ] 3 [ ] 4 [ ] 5 [ ] 6 [ ] 7
24. I perceive this product to incorporate cutting-edge technology. [ ] 1 [ ] 2 [ ] 3 [ ] 4 [ ] 5 [ ] 6 [ ]
7

Please fill out this questionnaire to provide feedback on your experience with the product.

A. 3 Result Analysis

A dataset was analysis by researcher. Based on the outcomes of 10 participants. Here are six percentages of data for 1). Personalized design satisfaction, 2). Learning cost reduction, 3). Innovation and diversity performance, 4). Intuitive categorization satisfaction, 5). User goal satisfaction, 6). Interaction engagement and user goal satisfaction. Each percentage was derived from a specific section of the questionnaire. Here are examples of Participant 1 (Figs. 11 and 12):

$$\text{Total Attractiveness Score} = \frac{\sum_{i=1}^{4}\text{Participant}_i\text{'s Attractiveness Scores}}{4}$$

$$\text{Total Perspicuity Score} = \frac{\sum_{i=5}^{8}\text{Participant}_i\text{'s Perspicuity Scores}}{4}$$

$$\text{Total Efficiency Score} = \frac{\sum_{i=9}^{12}\text{Participant}_i\text{'s Efficiency Scores}}{4}$$

$$\text{Total Dependability Score} = \frac{\sum_{i=13}^{16}\text{Participant}_i\text{'s Dependability Scores}}{4}$$

$$\text{Total Stimulation Score} = \frac{\sum_{i=17}^{20}\text{Participant}_i\text{'s Stimulation Scores}}{4}$$

$$\text{Total Novelty Score} = \frac{\sum_{i=21}^{24}\text{Participant}_i\text{'s Novelty Scores}}{4}$$

Fig. 11. Calculation of total percentage

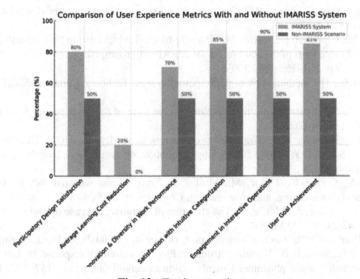

Fig. 12. Total comparison

References

1. Cavazza, M., Young, R.M.: Introduction to interactive storytelling. Handbook of digital games and entertainment technologies, pp. 377–392 (2017)
2. Xiong, J., Hsiang, E.L., He, Z., Zhan, T., Wu, S.T.: Augmented reality and virtual reality displays: emerging technologies and future perspectives. Light: Sci. Appli. **10**(1), 216 (2021)
3. Eiranen, R., Hatavara, M., Kivimäki, V., Mäkelä, M., Toivo, R.M.: Narrative and experience: interdisciplinary methodologies between history and narratology. Scand. J. Hist. **47**(1), 1–15 (2022)
4. Boris, V.: What makes storytelling so effective for learning. Harvard Business Learning (2017)
5. Peterson, L.: The science behind the art of storytelling. Harvard Business Publishing (2017). (Retrieved 21 May 2019)

6. Green, M.C., Jenkins, K.M.: Interactive narratives: processes and outcomes in user-directed stories. J. Commun. **64**(3), 479–500 (2014). https://doi.org/10.1111/jcom.12093
7. Oestreich, K.F.: Immersion vs. Engaged Interactivity in The Autobiography of Jane Eyre's Storyworld; Or What We Can Learn from Paratextual Traces, Adaptation, vol. 16(2), Pp. 166–184 (August 2023). https://doi.org/10.1093/adaptation/apad016
8. Skains, R.L.: Teaching digital fiction: integrating experimental writing and current technologies. Palgrave Commun **5**, 13 (2019). https://doi.org/10.1057/s41599-019-0223-z
9. Xu, E., Wang, W., Wang, Q.: The effectiveness of collaborative problem solving in promoting students' critical thinking: A meta-analysis based on empirical literature. Humanit. Soc. Sci. Commun. **10**, 16 (2023). https://doi.org/10.1057/s41599-023-01508-1
10. Rahiem, M.D.H.: Storytelling in early childhood education: time to go digital. ICEP **15**, 4 (2021). https://doi.org/10.1186/s40723-021-00081-x
11. Dünser, A., Hornecker, E.: An observational study of children interacting with an augmented story book. In: Technologies for E-Learning and Digital Entertainment: Second International Conference, Edutainment 2007, pp. 305–315. Springer, Berlin (2007). https://doi.org/10.1007/978-3-540-73011-8_31
12. Sanders, E.B.N., Stappers, P.J.: Co-creation and the new landscapes of design. Co-design **4**(1), 5–18 (2008)
13. Müller, M., Charypar, D., Gross, M.: Particle-based fluid simulation for interactive applications. In: Proceedings of the 2003 ACM SIGGRAPH/Eurographics Symposium on Computer Animation, pp. 154–159 (July 2003)
14. Spinuzzi, C.: The methodology of participatory design. Technical Commun. **52**(2), 163–174 (2005)
15. Piller, F.T.: Mass customization: reflections on the state of the concept. Int. J. Flex. Manuf. Syst. **16**, 313–334 (2004)
16. Hühn, P., Sommer, R.: . The role of characters in stories. In: Hühn, P., Meister, J.C., Pier, J., Schmid, W. (eds.) The living handbook of narratology. Hamburg University Press, Hamburg (2012)
17. Mar, R.A., Oatley, K., Djikic, M., Mullin, J.: Emotion and narrative fiction: Interactive influences before, during, and after reading. Cogn. Emot. **25**(5), 818–833 (2011).
18. Murtagh, F., Ganz, A., McKie, S.: The structure of narrative: the case of film scripts. Pattern Recogn. **42**(2), 302–312 (2009)
19. Foster-Harris, W.: The basic patterns of plot. University of Oklahoma Press, Norman (1959)
20. Escalas, J.E., Stern, B.B.: Narrative structure: Plot and emotional response. In: Lowrey, T.M. (ed.) Psycholinguistic phenomena in marketing communications, pp. 157–175. Lawrence Erlbaum Associates Publishers, Mahwah, NJ (2007)
21. Psychology Today. Conflict, the ultimate character development workout, February 15 (2016)
22. Carroll, N.: Narrative closure. Philos. Stud. **135**(1), 1–15 (2007)
23. Ekman, P.: Basic emotions. In: Dalgleish, T., Power, M. (eds.) Handbook of Cognition and Emotion, pp. 45–60. John Wiley & Sons Ltd., Chichester, UK (1992)
24. Fox, A.S., Lapate, R.C., Shackman, A.J., Davidson, R.J. (eds.) The nature of emotion: Fundamental questions, 2nd ed. Oxford University Press, New York (2018)
25. Keltner, D., Kring, A.M.: Emotion, social function, and psychopathology. Rev. Gen. Psychol. **2**(3), 320–342 (1998).
26. Wargo, E.: Understanding the interactions between emotion and cognition. Observer **23**(7), 10–13 (2010)
27. Hinderks, A., Schrepp, M., Mayo, F.J.D., Escalona, M.J., Thomaschewski, J.: Developing a UX KPI based on the user experience questionnaire. Comput. Stand. Interf. **65**, 38–44 (2019)
28. Santoso, H.B., Schrepp, M., Hasani, L.M., Fitriansyah, R., Setyanto, A.: The use of User Experience Questionnaire Plus (UEQ+) for cross-cultural UX research: evaluating Zoom and Learn Quran Tajwid as online learning tools. Heliyon **8**(11) (2022)

29. de Villiers, R.: Design Thinking as a Problem-Solving Tool. In: The Handbook of Creativity & Innovation in Business: A Comprehensive Toolkit of Theory and Practice for Developing Creative Thinking Skills, pp. 223–242. Springer Nature Singapore, Singapore (2022)

30. Livingwriter (2024). https://livingwriter.com/?gad_source=1&gclid=EAIaIQobChMI55a zmYrIgwMVOItLBR1FOApAEAAYASAAEgIoLfD_BwE

31. Abras, C., Maloney-Krichmar, D., Preece, J.: User-centered design. In: Bainbridge, W. (ed.) Encyclopedia of Human-Computer Interaction, vol. 37(4), pp. 445–456. Sage Publications, Thousand Oaks (2004)

32. Birchfield, D., et al.: Embodiment, multimodality, and composition: convergent themes across HCI and education for mixed-reality learning environments. In: Advances in Human-Computer Interaction (2008)

33. De Villiers, R.: Design Thinking as a Problem-Solving Tool. In: The Handbook of Creativity & Innovation in Business: A Comprehensive Toolkit of Theory and Practice for Developing Creative Thinking Skills, pp. 223–242. Springer Nature Singapore, Singapore (2022). https:// doi.org/10.1007/978-981-19-2180-3_11

34. Heard, D.: Statistical inference utilizing agent-based models (Doctoral dissertation, Duke University) (2014)

35. Price, S., Rogers, Y.: Let's get physical: The learning benefits of interacting in digitally augmented physical spaces. Comput. Educ. 43(1–2), 137–151 (2004)

36. Schuler, D., Namioka, A. (eds.) Participatory design: Principles and practices. CRC Press (1993)

37. Serafini, F.: Reading multimodal texts in the 21st century. Res. Sch. 19(1), 26–32 (2015)

38. Smith, J.: Designing multi-channel user interfaces: challenges and opportunities. In: Proceedings of the ACM Conference on Human Factors in Computing Systems, pp. 123–132. ACM (2019). https://doi.org/10.1145/1234567.1234567

39. Sweller, J.: Cognitive load theory. In: Psychology of Learning and Motivation, vol. 55, pp. 37–76. Academic Press (2011)

40. Thorne, B., Young, R.M.: Generating stories that include failed actions by modeling false character beliefs. In: Proceedings of the AAAI Conference on Artificial Intelligence and Interactive Digital Entertainment, vol. 13(2), 244–251) (2017)

Virtual Reality Image Creation in the Era of Artificial Intelligence

Antong Zhang[1,2(✉)]

[1] School of Arts and Communication, Beijing Normal University, Beijing 100875, China
202221110050@mail.bnu.edu.cn
[2] Faculty of IT and Design, The Hague University of Applied Sciences, The Hague 2521EN, Netherlands

Abstract. In recent years, with the epoch-making development of artificial intelligence (AI) technology, new media visual arts have been profoundly influenced in terms of creative ideas, production processes, and the final presentation of works. The question of whether AI can replace creators in image design has become a hot topic of discussion. Concurrently, as a significant form of new media visual arts, virtual reality (VR) imagery has undergone iterative development in production standards and product applications. In many VR image works and applications, we can observe the impact and changes brought about by the development of AI technology. This paper starts from the development and application of AI and VR imaging technology, analyze the integration of these two technologies, and present its own perspective on the creation of VR imagery in the era of AI.

Keywords: Virtual Reality · Artificial Intelligence · Image Creation · Visual Arts

1 Introduction

The development of AI has undergone multiple evolutionary stages, with each period's technological advancements and expanded application areas collectively illustrating the rich landscape of AI [1–3]. In its early stages, AI was shaped as a rule-based thinking, emphasizing the simulation of human intelligence through symbolic logic [4, 5]. However, over time, the development of AI transitioned into the connectionist era, introducing neural networks and machine learning, injecting more learning capabilities into AI. In the knowledge-based era, researchers focused on knowledge representation and reasoning, attempting to extract and apply knowledge from data, propelling AI towards more complex cognitive levels. Entering the 21st century, with the rise of big data, the statistical learning era opened a new chapter [6, 7]. Methods such as support vector machines, decision trees, and random forests became mainstream, emphasizing learning models from data. The wave of deep learning emerged as a new engine for AI, with architectures like convolutional neural networks and recurrent neural networks making significant progress in areas such as image recognition and natural language processing, laying the foundation for achieving higher levels of intelligence [8, 9]. Currently, the field of AI is in an era of deep reinforcement learning and self-learning, emphasizing training intelligent systems through trial and error and rewards, enabling them to possess autonomous learning and adaptive capabilities. Representative technologies during this period include reinforcement learning and meta-learning, marking the beginning of a new stage in the continuous evolution of AI capabilities. On the application front, AI demonstrates immense potential across various domains [10]. Natural language processing supports intelligent assistants, speech recognition, and machine translation. Computer vision enhances the accuracy of image recognition, object detection, and facial recognition. Autonomous driving technology introduces new possibilities for intelligent traffic systems and self-driving vehicles. In the healthcare sector, AI is applied to disease diagnosis, drug discovery, and personalized treatment. The influence of AI extends to profound transformations in finance, manufacturing, education, social media, and other fields.

The rapid development of VR technology in recent years has sparked a digital revolution, ushering people into a new era of immersive experiences. The evolution of this technology spans multiple domains, including hardware, software, and content creation, driving innovation and application in the virtual world. First and foremost, advancements in hardware technology have been a key driver in the rapid development of VR technology. Continuous upgrades to head-mounted displays enable users to access more lightweight and comfortable devices, while improvements in resolution and field of view enhance the realism of virtual environments. Advanced sensor technologies such as gyroscopes, accelerometers, and laser tracking make users' movements in virtual environments more accurate, further enhancing immersion. Progress in real-time rendering and graphics technology injects new vitality into VR. Engines and tools like Unity and Unreal Engine provide powerful real-time rendering capabilities, allowing developers to easily create high-quality virtual scenes [11]. The development of ray tracing technology enhances the realism of lighting and shadows in virtual environments, giving VR scenes a more intricate and captivating appearance. In terms of content creation and experience, VR technology offers creators entirely new possibilities. 360-degree videos and panoramic images allow users to freely navigate a virtual environment in 360 degrees, providing a lifelike experience. VR games have become leaders in VR technology, offering users immersive and highly interactive gaming experiences. In the field of education, virtual laboratories provide students with opportunities to conduct practical scientific experiments without the need for physical laboratory equipment. Enterprises are also actively adopting VR technology for employee training, enhancing training effectiveness through simulated real-world scenarios. The medical field is another notable area of application for VR technology. Doctors can use VR for surgical simulation and training, improving surgical skills and reducing patient risks. Additionally, VR is widely applied in pain management and psychotherapy, providing patients with an immersive and attention-diverting means to alleviate suffering. Social VR has garnered significant attention in recent years. Virtual social platforms enable users to interact with others in virtual environments, engaging in various activities and communication. Virtual meetings provide remote teams with a more realistic collaborative experience, overcoming communication barriers imposed by geographical distances.

2 Integration of AI Technology and VR Imaging

The fusion of AI technology with VR imaging is leading a revolution in digital experiences, making virtual environments more realistic and interactive. Simultaneously, it brings profound transformations to various fields. From AI-generated virtual content to emotion recognition and interactive experiences, applications in areas such as healthcare, education, and creative endeavors, the intersection of AI and VR becomes a crucial domain for technological innovation and societal progress. The rapid development of AI technology empowers computers with creativity. Through technologies like Generative Adversarial Networks, AI can create realistic virtual landscapes, architectures, and characters. This provides diverse and vibrant materials for the creation of virtual environments, enabling creators to build imaginative and expressive virtual scenes more easily. From envisioning future cities to fantastical virtual worlds, AI's creative power is pushing the boundaries of the VR experience [12]. Emotion recognition and interactive experiences are breaking the boundaries between digital and reality. AI's emotion recognition technology enables virtual environments to intelligently perceive users' emotional states. Through the analysis of facial expressions, speech, and movements, the elements of the virtual environment can be adjusted to provide a more personalized and interactive experience. Users can feel a more realistic and lifelike interaction in virtual space, where virtual characters respond intelligently to changes in the user's emotions. Real-time rendering plays a crucial role in VR technology, and AI's intervention makes real-time rendering more intelligent. By dynamically adjusting the details of the virtual scene based on the user's gaze and movements, AI provides a smoother and more realistic experience. Additionally, AI can be used for image enhancement and noise reduction, improving the visual effects of the virtual environment and reducing visual fatigue during prolonged use [13]. AI is emerging prominently in the creation of virtual scripts. Through natural language generation technology, AI can collaborate with creators to generate scripts and storylines for virtual environments. This collaboration not only enhances efficiency in storytelling but also injects more creative and emotional elements into the virtual world, providing users with a more captivating story experience in virtual environments.

VR imaging technology has evolved beyond conceptual design, now optimizing and enriching user experiences through the application of hardware products, with AI playing a pivotal role in this transformative process [14]. In 2023, both Apple and Meta introduced influential products, Vision Pro and Quest 3, showcasing the integration of AI with applications in these devices. In Vision Pro, AI features include digital avatars, emotion detection, smart input, and motion recognition. Digital avatars involve capturing user characteristics and projecting a virtual representation in the virtual space, providing a more immersive experience. Vision Pro utilizes front-facing cameras to scan facial information, employing machine learning techniques and advanced neural network encoding to generate a "digital avatar" for users. During FaceTime calls, the digital avatar dynamically mimics the user's facial and hand movements, retaining a sense of volume and depth. AI development, particularly in spatial audio computation, eye movement tracking, and hand behavior capture, contributes to Vision Pro's innovation. Apple, supported by M2 and R1 chips, successfully achieves the localized deployment of AI. Similarly positioned as Mixed Reality devices, Quest 3 allows users to switch between AR and VR functionalities. As a benchmark product, Quest 3 boasts powerful AI capabilities. Meta, following the release of the Llama 2 open-source language model, introduces its Meta AI, joining the AI chatbot arena. Meta AI seamlessly integrates with applications such as WhatsApp, Instagram, and Messenger. Based on the Llama 2 language model, Meta AI serves as a versatile AI assistant, handling diverse applications, from summarizing group chat messages to answering user queries. Meta also collaborates with Microsoft Bing, providing real-time web search results during conversations, distinguishing Meta AI from other AI tools lacking up-to-date information. In addition to Meta AI, Meta introduces 28 AI-generated virtual characters in its messaging app, representing well-known personalities or movie characters. Users can engage in conversations with these characters, all generated by Meta's AI. Beyond Meta's developments, numerous third-party software applications with AI capabilities exist across various VR headsets. AI technology is shaping diverse ways for people to engage with the digital world, and the convergence of these two technologies is evolving to deeper levels.

3   Impact of AI on VR Image Creation

During the filming stage of a movie, AI can automatically recognize key objects, scenes, and actions through image recognition and processing technologies. This enhances the efficiency of filming and reduces the workload for filmmakers. This technology can assist in organizing and backing up imported image materials during the material importing phase, ensuring data integrity and security. In the post-production phase, AI technology optimizes traditional post-production processes through intelligent enhancements such as image stitching, color correction and adjustment, and special effects addition [15, 16]. For example, deep learning algorithms can be used in color correction tools to automatically identify color deviations in images and make real-time adjustments, improving the accuracy and speed of post-processing. Additionally, technologies like generative adversarial networks are widely employed for creating vivid and captivating elements in virtual environments, adding more lively aspects to VR films. In the exporting and publishing phase, AI technology helps export the completed VR images in formats that comply with VR device standards. It can also intelligently select suitable platforms for uploading and sharing. This streamlines the entire production process, enhancing the dissemination and viewing effects of VR images. Furthermore, AI technology plays a crucial role in optimizing the VR experience. Through user interaction design and performance optimization, it ensures that users can smoothly and comfortably explore panoramic scenes in the virtual environment. This includes performance optimization tailored for different VR devices to ensure a consistent high-quality experience across various devices, avoiding stuttering or delays. This intelligent optimization maintains a consistent high-quality experience for VR images on different devices [17]. In summary, AI technology, by optimizing the production process and various stages of VR image creation, improves efficiency, accuracy, and creativity. This intelligent impact not only streamlines the production process but also provides creators with more possibilities for innovation and expression, driving progress and development in VR image creation.

AI technology has played a pivotal role in the acquisition and creation of digital resources, providing creators with richer and more diverse materials and sources of creativity in the process of VR image creation. Firstly, through image recognition and analysis technology, AI can automatically label and categorize many images, providing creators with more convenient digital material search and management tools. This enables creators to quickly access materials that meet their needs, whether for constructing scenes in virtual environments or adding creative elements. Secondly, by training neural networks, AI can generate high-quality virtual images, including landscapes, characters, objects, etc., offering a more extensive range of digital resources for VR image creation [18]. In the audio domain, speech synthesis and sound generation technologies allow creators to flexibly craft sound elements in VR. Whether it's the voice guidance of a virtual guide or the environmental sound effects in a virtual scene, AI technology provides more diverse and innovative possibilities for audio creation. Additionally, AI technology can analyze user preferences and behavior to generate personalized digital resources. By understanding users' interests and preferences, the system can automatically adjust elements in virtual scenes to better align with users' tastes, providing a more personalized VR experience.

The major impact of AI technology on VR image creation involves the optimization of interactive experiences between users and image content in virtual environments. On one hand, it includes the interaction experience between users and image content in virtual environments, and on the other hand, it involves the intelligent analysis of user behavior and feedback to achieve a more intelligent and personalized interactive experience [19]. Through AI technology, VR creators can achieve adaptive interactive scene design. The system can monitor user behavior, gaze points, gestures, and other data in real-time, intelligently adjusting elements in the virtual environment based on user feedback. This includes adjusting the position of objects, changing the atmosphere of the scene, providing personalized virtual guides, and more, enriching the user experience and aligning it with individual preferences. AI's speech recognition and natural language processing technologies provide a higher level of intelligence for dialogues with virtual characters. Through deep learning algorithms, virtual characters can respond more naturally to user voice commands, provide information, and even engage in emotional communication. This intelligent dialogue and interactive experience enhance the immersion of virtual images, making users feel more integrated into the virtual environment. Utilizing deep learning and computer vision technologies enables intelligent capturing of user gestures and movements. This means that user gestures and movements in the virtual environment can be more accurately recognized and understood, achieving a more natural and precise interaction. For example, users can interact and select virtual objects through gestures or perform other actions related to interaction in the virtual environment. Using machine learning algorithms, user behavior can be predicted. By analyzing users' historical behavior data, the system can predict users' possible next actions or choices, enabling corresponding adjustments to the virtual environment in advance. This intelligent behavior prediction makes interactions smoother and more natural, enhancing the overall user experience. In summary, the optimization of interaction and feedback mechanisms through AI technology in VR image creation not only improves the interactive experience between users and virtual environments but also allows creators to intelligently understand and meet users' needs. This intelligent interactive experience propels VR images towards a more personalized and deeply immersive direction, opening broader possibilities for the application of VR technology.

4 Possibilities of VR Image Creation in the Era of AI

By analyzing the integration of AI with VR images and its impact on creation, we can see that AI has expanded and extended the development of image experiences in various dimensions [20, 21]. Considering the influence of AI technology, how can VR images better integrate the characteristics of these two technologies and adhere to certain creative principles in the future? Firstly, VR images can leverage emotional computing brought by AI to better meet users' emotional needs. A significant characteristic of VR images is the reshaping of time and space. Users immerse themselves in a virtual environment with a 360-degree field of view using VR headsets, and behind the high-degree freedom of movement lies a form of emotional expression. Although many current features and works involve emotional expression, they often serve more as emotional conduits, and their interactivity may not fully meet users' emotional needs. Due to the current limitations of AI technology in handling complex emotions, achieving emotionally driven designs to satisfy user needs is challenging. However, from a creator's perspective, providing more interactive mechanisms for emotions is crucial. In the digital age, there exists an intangible "social distance" between individuals, and even a state of absence. AI can precisely fill the role of an emotional confidant. VR serves as an excellent space for psychological healing, not only because of the reshaped virtual environment but also because users' senses can escape the influence of physical reality in such a virtual space, providing a sense of envelopment [22]. Many current VR headset products have their own intelligent assistants, and I believe that AI, as a form of social robot, can be more deeply utilized in VR images. Beyond the functionalities of the system itself, more intelligent emotional design can be incorporated into interactions. Gestures, eye movements, actions, and emotion capture can all be further optimized with the development of AI technology.

In addition, AI can play a significant role in the creation of VR image works. Taking VR movies as an example, many current works adopt a multi-linear narrative strategy, which is a prominent feature of VR itself. Undoubtedly, in the high-degree freedom of virtual space, user participation can influence the development of the plot. If AI's intelligent analysis is integrated in the future to make immediate adjustments based on user participation, it should bring about a better sense of experience [23]. The future development direction should include increasing user involvement in the creation of virtual environments. Through intelligent creative tools and interactive design, users may be able to participate in the creation of virtual scenes more directly, thereby increasing their engagement with the VR experience. This aligns with the fundamental attribute of VR interactivity, where users find themselves in a highly open virtual world—being both an experiencer and a creator [24]. Undoubtedly, this can bring more enjoyment to the VR image experience.

5 Conclusions

To dive deeper into the implications of AI in the VR image creation, the multifaceted advancements have ushered in an era where creativity converges seamlessly with technological innovation. The transformative influence is discernible across the entire spectrum of tools, where AI injects a level of intelligence that streamlines the creative process for artists and designers. This not only expedites the realization of imaginative concepts but also enables creators to push the boundaries of what is achievable in the VR landscape.

Content generation, a pivotal aspect of VR image creation, undergoes a paradigm shift as AI introduces unprecedented levels of personalization. The ability of AI algorithms to comprehend user preferences, behaviors, and engagement patterns empowers content generators to tailor experiences that resonate more intimately with individual users. This heightened level of personalization fosters a sense of connection and engagement that was previously elusive in traditional VR content.

Interactive experiences within virtual environments receive a significant boost through adaptive scene design, a hallmark of AI integration. The dynamic monitoring of user behaviors, gaze points, and gestures allows the virtual environment to evolve in real-time, responding intelligently to user inputs. This not only enhances the immersive quality of VR experiences but also ensures that users are active participants in shaping the narrative, fostering a more engaging and participatory form of storytelling.

The amalgamation of speech recognition and natural language processing technologies in virtual dialogue and interactions marks a notable stride toward more authentic and meaningful user engagement. Virtual characters responding organically to voice commands adds a layer of realism and emotional depth to the interactive experiences, creating a more compelling and authentic connection between users and the virtual world.

In the world of gesture and motion capture, the application of deep learning and computer vision technologies propels the accuracy and naturalness of user interactions to unprecedented levels. This ensures that users can engage with the virtual environment in an intuitive and instinctive manner, eliminating barriers between the digital and physical worlds.

The intelligence-driven analysis of user behavior and feedback represents a pinnacle in personalized interaction. AI technologies, encompassing personalized content recommendations, emotion recognition, behavior prediction, and optimization, elevate the interactive experience to new heights. Users find themselves immersed in an environment that not only caters to their preferences but also anticipates and adapts to their evolving needs, creating a dynamic and ever-evolving virtual landscape.

Looking forward, the continued evolution of AI promises to deepen and enrich VR image creation. As AI algorithms become more sophisticated and attuned to user intricacies, the potential for creating highly personalized, emotionally resonant, and intellectually stimulating virtual experiences becomes limitless. The synergy between human creativity and artificial intelligence in the VR space holds the promise of redefining the boundaries of imagination and storytelling in ways that were once only dreamed of.

References

1. Moor, M., et al.: Foundation models for generalist medical artificial intelligence. Nature **616**(7956), 259–265 (2023)
2. Krenn, M., et al.: On scientific understanding with artificial intelligence. Nat. Rev. Phys. **4**(12), 761–769 (2022)
3. Huynh-The, T., Pham, Q.V., Pham, X.Q., Nguyen, T.T., Han, Z., Kim, D.S.: Artificial intelligence for the metaverse: a survey. Eng. Appl. Artif. Intell. **117**, 105581 (2023)
4. Skilton, M., Hovsepian, F.: The 4th industrial revolution. Springer Nature (2018)
5. Miller, C.H.: Digital Storytelling 4e: A creator's guide to interactive entertainment. CRC Press (2019)
6. Gong, Y.: Application of virtual reality teaching method and artificial intelligence technology in digital media art creation. Eco. Inform. **63**, 101304 (2021)
7. Cavazza, M., et al.: Intelligent virtual environments for virtual reality art. Comput. Graph. **29**(6), 852–861 (2005)
8. Luck, M., Aylett, R.: Applying artificial intelligence to virtual reality: intelligent virtual environments. Appl. Artif. Intell. **14**(1), 3–32 (2000)
9. González-Zamar, M.D., Abad-Segura, E.: Implications of virtual reality in arts education: research analysis in the context of higher education. Educ. Sci. **10**(9), 225 (2020)
10. Baduge, S.K.: Artificial intelligence and smart vision for building and construction 4.0: Machine and deep learning methods and applications. Autom. Construct. **141**, 104440 (2022)
11. Cavedoni, S., Chirico, A., Pedroli, E., Cipresso, P., Riva, G.: Digital biomarkers for the early detection of mild cognitive impairment: artificial intelligence meets virtual reality. Front. Hum. Neurosci. **14**, 245 (2020)
12. Kim, K., Lee, M.: Flocking in interpretation with visual art design principles. Wireless Pers. Commun. **93**, 211–222 (2017)
13. Winkler-Schwartz, A., et al.: Artificial intelligence in medical education: Best practices using machine learning to assess surgical expertise in virtual reality simulation. J. Surg. Educ. **76**(6), 1681–1690 (2019)
14. van der Maden, W., Lomas, D., Hekkert, P.: A framework for designing AI systems that support community wellbeing. Front. Psychol. **13**, 1011883 (2023)
15. Visser, F.S., Stappers, P.J., Van der Lugt, R., Sanders, E.B.: Contextmapping: experiences from practice. CoDesign **1**(2), 119–149 (2005)
16. Norman, D.A.: Design for a better world: Meaningful, sustainable, humanity centered. MIT Press (2023)
17. Liu, W., Lee, K.P., Gray, C.M., Toombs, A.L., Chen, K.H., Leifer, L.: Transdisciplinary teaching and learning in UX design: a program review and AR case studies. Appl. Sci. **11**(22), 10648 (2021)
18. Desmet, P.M., Xue, H., Xin, X., Liu, W.: Demystifying emotion for designers: a five-day course based on seven fundamental principles. Adv. Design Res. **1**(1), 50–62 (2023)
19. Wu, X., Liu, W., Jia, J., Zhang, X., Leifer, L., Hu, S.: Prototyping an online virtual simulation course platform for college students to learn creative thinking. Systems **11**(2), 89 (2023)
20. Bullock, B., Learmonth, C., Davis, H., Al Mahmud, A.: Mobile phone sleep self-management applications for early start shift workers: a scoping review of the literature. Front. Public Health **10**, 936736 (2022)
21. Desmet, P., Hekkert, P.: Framework of product experience. Int. J. Des. **1**(1), 57–66 (2007)
22. Liu, W., et al.: Designing interactive glazing through an engineering psychology approach: Six augmented reality scenarios that envision future car human-machine interface. Virt. Reality Intell. Hardware **5**(2), 157–170 (2023)

23. Schrepp, M., Hinderks, A., Thomaschewski, J.: Design and evaluation of a short version of the user experience questionnaire (UEQ-S). Inter. J. Interactive Multimedia Artifi. Intell. **4**(6), 103–108 (2017)
24. Zhu, Y., Tang, G., Liu, W., Qi, R.: How post 90's gesture interact with automobile skylight. Inter. J. Hum.-Comput. Interact. **38**(5), 395–405 (2022)

Technology, Design, and Learner Engagement

Research on Strategies of Virtual Reality Technology to Promote Astronomy Science Popularization Education in Primary Schools

ZiYi Chen[1], WenXi Wang[1], ZiYang Li[1(✉)], JinYi Zhao[2], and ZiYue Chen[3]

[1] Art and Design Academy, Beijing City University, Beijing, China
li.ziyang@qq.com
[2] RDFZ Shi Jing Shan School, Xiu Fu Street, Beijing, Shi Jing Shan District, China
[3] Zhong Guan Cun Third Primary School, No. 23 Wan Liu Zhong Street, Beijing, Hai Dian District, China

Abstract. Teaching popular science in primary school science courses has gained significant attention due to the national strategy for promoting science and education. 12.5% of the sixth-grade science curriculum is focused on astronomical content, but the scope and format of astronomical popular science in primary school curricula are relatively limited. After conducting an investigation, it has been found that there are few existing extracurricular astronomical popular science teaching methods. The issues with existing methods include low alignment with textbook content, lack of systematic teaching, limited interactivity, and difficulties in stimulating students' initiative. Fun-based teaching using virtual reality technology is an emerging teaching method with unique interactivity and experience. It allows students to immerse themselves in interactive environments and have a rich learning experience. This study aims to offer students practical hands-on opportunities by designing challenging tasks and activities. This approach deepens students' understanding and application of knowledge. Virtual reality technology based on game-based learning enables students to apply scientific knowledge in simulated scenarios, fostering problem-solving skills and innovative thinking. This method enhances students' depth of understanding and promotes their practical skills, sparking a strong interest in astronomical popular science among primary school students.

Keywords: Primary school science education · Fun-based teaching · Virtual Reality · Astronomy popular science

1 The Current Status and Issues of Popular Science Platforms in Informal Learning

Popular science platforms play a crucial role in disseminating scientific knowledge, advocating scientific methods, spreading scientific ideas, and promoting the spirit of science through the organization of informal educational activities. Relevant government departments have recognized the importance of popular science platforms and have

A. Marcus et al. (Eds.): HCII 2024, LNCS 14715, pp. 129–141, 2024.
https://doi.org/10.1007/978-3-031-61359-3_10

issued related documents to guide and regulate them. For example, both the "Opinions on Further Strengthening the Popularization of Science and Technology in the New Era" in 2022 and the "Outline of the Action Plan for Improving Scientific Literacy Nationwide (2021–2035)" in 2021 emphasize the importance of utilizing technology education platforms and other extracurricular teaching resources to enhance the cultivation of scientific literacy in youth.

In order to respond to the spirit of these documents, we should make full use of the valuable resource of popular science platforms and strive to build an integrated science education system both inside and outside primary and secondary schools. This will provide students with a broader space for scientific exploration and more diversified learning opportunities.

1.1 Definition of the Concept

The Concept of Non-formal Education. Education that occurs outside of the campus is collectively referred to as informal education, as defined by Gerber et al. Informal education is elaborated into two parts, the first part is in the form of an organized classroom, but different from a formal classroom. For example, independent study and completion of a list of tasks in an informal learning place. The second part is the use of informal learning methods to gain knowledge and experience, such as in the form of visiting museums, watching documentaries, and so on [1]. The knowledge acquired through this type of learning reaches more than 75% of the individual's total knowledge [2].

The Concept of Interesting Teaching and Learning. The idea of teaching with fun was first put forward by Liang Qichao, who wrote articles such as "Education with Fun". The concept of "fun" in teaching is found in his teaching activities. He believed that "fun" is the driving force and source of life, and that life will lose its color if it is devoid of fun. Education should focus on cultivating students' interest in learning and making learning interesting and meaningful. In the process of teaching, we should not only focus on the transfer of knowledge, but also pay attention to the learning experience of students, through the design of interesting teaching games and activities, to stimulate students' interest and enthusiasm in learning, so that they can acquire knowledge and skills in a happy way.

The Concept of Virtual Reality. The main advantage of virtual reality technology lies in the ability to simulate the real world does not exist or the naked eye is difficult to see the scene, so that the experience of the person immersed in the scene, to obtain a more intuitive feeling. Virtual environment allows users to enter the three-dimensional world from the two-dimensional plane to experience and subjective operation in the virtual environment, personal experience and interaction breaks the previous teaching methods and concepts, which helps to make up for the defects in the traditional two-dimensional teaching environment, presenting a more three-dimensional, interesting three-dimensional teaching environment [3].

Concept of Astronomical Science Popularization. Astronomy popularization is the scientific popularization of astronomical knowledge. Astronomy is the science of celestial bodies (objects outside the atmosphere) and the universe [4]. The scope of astronomical knowledge referred to in this paper is the content covered in Unit 3, Universe, in the second book of the sixth grade of the elementary school science textbook, such as the "solar system", "moon phases" and other astronomical knowledge and concepts. Popularization of science is the process of disseminating scientific knowledge, scientific methods, and the scientific ideas and the spirit of science integrated in them, which have been researched and developed by human beings, to the society through various methods and channels, so that they can be understood by the public [5]. Popularization of astronomy helps people to further understand the universe, to recognize the significance of astronomical research, and to feel the romance of the universe and the infinite charm of astronomy.

1.2 Status of the Platform for the Popularization of Astronomical Sciences in Informal Education

At present, astronomy science popularization platforms in informal education at home and abroad are mainly conducted through planetariums, museums, libraries and other venues. The general forms include paper-based media dissemination such as popular science books, journals and books, multimedia publicity such as television, radio and programs, online and offline lectures for the community, astronomical observations, museum-themed summer camps and so on.

With the development of digital means and the change of people's way of acquiring information, the demand for flexible learning increases, and science popularization activities relying on online platforms have more research prospects and application value. Current astronomical science popularization platforms take online dissemination as the main way to attract the interest of the public through games, co-branding and live broadcasting. (see Fig. 1).

Author	Ways to popularize science	Concrete content	Platforms to popularize science	Existence of continuity with the school curriculum
Zan Zhang	Astronomical Observation Activities; Science and Innovation Tournament	Basic astronomy knowledge	Offline	No
QiuSha Shen	live broadcast; Game; Jointly; Digital collections	Cloud planetarium	Online	No
Xi Guan	Models and inductive interactive devices	Astronomical knowledge	Offline	No
JiaWen Yao	Telescope popular science observation	Sun related science popularization	Online&Offline	No
Lei Zhang	Network media; Mini knowledge seminar	Meteorite science popularization	Online	No
HaiMing Tang	Webcast	Astronomy popularization	Online	No
Bo Zhang	Virtual reality	Astronomy popularization	Online	No
ZhangFeng Pi	Virtual reality	Astronomy popularization	Online	Yes

Fig. 1. Basic information on current astronomical science popularization

The popularity of smartphones and tablets has become a major tool for informal learning. Learners can learn anytime and anywhere in their daily lives without being restricted by time, space and other conditions, showing a high degree of flexibility. In mobile devices, the proportion of learning using educational games is much higher than that of reading e-books, watching live broadcasts or documentaries. Fundamentally, educational games are more interactive and can constantly guide students to find problems, ask questions and solve problems.

1.3 Problems with the Popularization of Digital Astronomy in Informal Education

Digital astronomy science activities can break through the limitations of time and space and provide a more convenient way of learning, but there are also some problems. Common ways to popularize digital astronomy science include online courses, astronomy software, cell phone applications and so on.

Online courses on astronomical science and technology are characterized by diversity and interactivity. These courses utilize the convenience of the Internet to provide flexible learning methods and rich learning resources. There are certain disadvantages of online classes, as the number of people online in the classroom is large, it is impossible to get timely feedback and guidance from the teacher, which weakens its interactive characteristics. Over time, students will reduce communication with others and participate in activities less frequently, leading to a decline in attention teaching results are not satisfactory.

The operation process of some astronomical software is complicated, and primary school students need to spend a longer time to familiarize themselves with the functions and operation of the software when using it, which increases the learning cost. Elementary school students usually have a weak understanding of complex interfaces and operational processes. Too many interfaces and complicated operations may cause them to get lost in the software and reduce their interest in the application. Meanwhile, the lack of effective connection between the content in the software and the school curriculum leads to the inconsistency between the popularization activities and the students' focus, weakening the role of popular science education.

The use of augmented reality is predominantly used in cell phone applications to combine the virtual world with the real world to create an immersive user experience. By superimposing digital information onto the real scene, users can obtain richer and more realistic visual effects, which enhances user perception and interaction.

VR games are more advantageous while meeting the characteristics of mainstream applications, and through head-mounted devices, they can provide users with a fully immersive environment that makes them feel as if they are in the universe. The influence of external factors can be blocked to achieve a better sense of immersion and experience. Users can experience astronomical phenomena more deeply and enhance their knowledge and interest in the universe. From the point of view of knowledge acquisition and deep learning, learners have a deeper impression of the knowledge and skills acquired through personal experience, observation and exploration.

2 Integration of Virtual Reality Technology and Astronomy Popularization

The application of digital means in popularizing elementary school astronomy knowledge has transformed the traditional one-way teaching format. The widespread use of electronic devices such as computers, smartphones, VR glasses, etc., in popular science education has made digital media an indispensable auxiliary tool in teaching. However, existing applications lack immersion, and students are greatly influenced by their surrounding environment, making it difficult for them to maintain focus for an extended period, thereby diminishing the effectiveness of teaching. This paper primarily explores the positive impact of virtual reality technology on informal learning environments for elementary school astronomy popularization.

The use of virtual reality technology is one effective approach to cultivate students, providing them with a better learning experience and igniting their interest in learning. Virtual reality technology meets the diversification of learning resources, featuring simplicity in operation, and is conducive to inquiry-based learning. Currently, virtual reality technology is primarily applied in the entertainment sector, but as the technology matures, its application in education has gradually gained attention, contributing to the rise of research on gamified teaching. Despite its relatively late start, scholars increasingly recognize and focus on its value and significance as it rapidly develops. In recent years, the number of studies on this topic has continued to grow. With the advent of the artificial intelligence era, its impact on education is becoming increasingly significant. The integration of VR technology has transformed the forms and methods of education.

Building upon the Learning Retention Pyramid, the effective utilization of VR technology enables active learning. Through hands-on practices and immediate application scenarios, it achieves the effects equivalent to the sixth level of the pyramid, resulting in an average retention rate of 75% for the learning content. VR technology provides learners with a more immersive, vivid, and engaging learning experience, fostering their acquisition and mastery of knowledge (See Fig. 2).

2.1 The Advantages of Virtual Reality Technology

By simulating a three-dimensional environment, virtual reality technology provides users with both first-person and third-person perspectives. The first-person perspective allows users to feel as if they are physically present, while the third-person perspective enables users to observe the surrounding environment from a god-like viewpoint, offering a highly immersive experience. This immersion allows users to gain a deeper understanding and experience of the simulated environment or situation.

Virtual reality technology allows users to interact naturally with the virtual environment, such as through gesture recognition. This interactivity enables users to explore and manipulate the virtual world more freely, enhancing their engagement and overall experience. VR can simulate five scenarios, including situations that no longer exist, scenarios that are difficult to access, structures that are challenging to dissect, situations that are hard to observe, and scenarios that are difficult to simulate. This creative capability provides users with a space to unleash their imagination, fostering innovative thinking and broadening perspectives.

THE
LEARNING PYRAMID

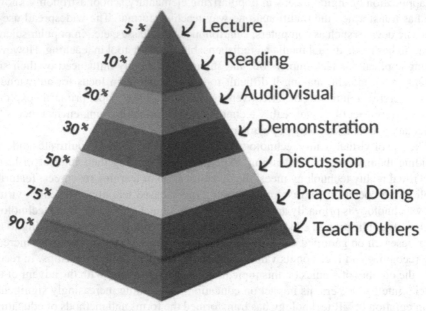

5 %   ↙ Lecture

10%   ↙ Reading

20%   ↙ Audiovisual

30%   ↙ Demonstration

50%   ↙ Discussion

75%   ↙ Practice Doing

90%   ↙ Teach Others

Fig. 2. Learning Retention Pyramid (Image from Baidu)

Users can simulate various high-risk or hazardous operations, such as flight simulations or circuit simulations, without concerns about real-world safety issues. This safety aspect positions virtual reality technology with extensive applications in fields such as training and education.

2.2 The Advantages of Virtual Reality Technology in Astronomy Popularization

The constructivist theory fully embodies the idea that knowledge is constructed through the interaction between individuals and their environment. The authentic environment allows people to construct and understand knowledge through hands-on experiences, leading to a deeper understanding of the world. VR educational games can provide students with an immersive virtual environment, making them feel as if they are in the universe. This experiential immersion enhances students' perception and cognition, improving learning outcomes. The interactivity and exploratory nature can stimulate students' proactive learning spirit. By completing tasks, solving problems, and engaging in other activities, students actively participate in the learning process, fostering independent learning and problem-solving abilities.

This immersive experience significantly increases learners' engagement and hands-on skills, thereby deepening their understanding and memory of the learning content.

Diverse learning modes can meet the needs of different students, incorporating various sensory experiences such as visual, auditory, and tactile, enhancing the interest and effectiveness of learning. In a virtual environment, factors can be precisely controlled and adjusted according to students' learning progress and ability levels, allowing for difficulty customization. This controllability enables students to better manage the learning process, improving learning outcomes. Conducting astronomy popularization education through VR educational games avoids issues related to weather, safety, and other objective conditions that may limit observations.

3 The Strategies for Utilizing VR in Informal Learning Settings for Astronomy Popularization Education

Utilizing the immersive and interactive features of virtual reality technology, combined with specific classroom teaching content, to stimulate student interest and enhance learning effectiveness. Specific strategies include, but are not limited to: creating immersive learning experiences; providing personalized learning paths to meet the diverse needs of students; encouraging innovation and exploratory spirit, and more. These strategies, implemented through the assistance of VR technology in informal learning settings, enable students to better understand and master astronomical knowledge, enhancing their scientific literacy and practical skills.

3.1 Environmental Virtualization

The Situated Cognition Theory posits that knowledge is constructed through the interaction between individuals and their environment, and it is acquired through interactive processes. The knowledge acquired in a real learning environment is active knowledge that can be applied in practical situations [6] Immersion Theory is also relevant in this context, suggesting that individuals immersed in an activity tend to unconsciously disregard irrelevant perceptions. VR can render highly realistic teaching environments, assisting learners in immersive experiences and sparking their interest in learning. In scenarios like a space environment, VR can simulate and concretize abstract concepts, creating diverse and otherwise inaccessible scenes to help students practically acquire knowledge.

The interactivity provided by VR technology allows students to actively manipulate elements within the virtual environment during exploration, deepening their understanding of abstract concepts. This interactive engagement significantly enhances students' interest and motivation, encouraging them to actively participate in the learning process.

3.2 Activity Fun

The Emotion Theory emphasizes the significant role of emotions in learning. By incorporating interesting game plots and challenges within educational games, positive emotions can be elicited in students, thereby enhancing the learning experience. The game is divided into three levels of difficulty—easy, medium, and hard—allowing students to choose learning content based on their individual learning progress and abilities. This approach ensures that students can appropriately elevate and challenge themselves at a level they find acceptable.

This approach to popular science can accommodate students with different learning styles; some are visual learners who can utilize VR's visual effects for learning, while others prefer hands-on practices and can engage in simulated experiments. This accommodates diverse learning needs, ultimately boosting students' motivation to learn.

3.3 Interaction Simplicity

User Experience (UX) Theory suggests that overly complex interaction designs for child users may lead to confusion or helplessness, thereby reducing their willingness to use. For mobile applications targeting children, a simple and intuitive interaction design should be adopted, allowing child users to easily understand and use the application. This helps improve the acceptance and satisfaction of children users, ultimately increasing the frequency and duration of their app usage. User Experience Theory also emphasizes the importance of addressing children's aesthetic and psychological needs in design, aiming to provide interesting content as much as possible to stimulate children's interest and curiosity.

3.4 Knowledge Systematization

Bruner believes that any knowledge in the cognitive process must be constructed into a network of basic theories interconnected with each other. This is beneficial for students to memorize and apply knowledge. With the use of VR technology, students can construct a virtual knowledge map, linking the knowledge they have learned. This allows them to visually see the relationships between each knowledge point, facilitating a better understanding and memory of the knowledge.

4 Interesting Science Popularization in Virtual Reality

The use of digital games in education and teaching has received more and more attention and importance, and many researchers and educators have made positive contributions to it. Through the use of digital means to assist the interesting teaching, not only can make the learning process more vivid and interesting, stimulate students' enthusiasm for knowledge learning, enhance their sense of independent learning and comprehensive literacy; it can also cultivate students' innovative thinking and ability to adapt to the digital era, laying a solid foundation for their future learning and development. The interesting popularization of astronomical knowledge in virtual reality presents astronomical phenomena and principles in a vivid and interesting way by integrating astronomical knowledge into virtual reality scenes. The immersive, interactive, exploratory, and interdisciplinary integration features of this approach attract students to participate and enhance their understanding and memory of astronomical knowledge. Developing a universe exploration game based on virtual reality technology allows users to explore the universe, planets, stars, and other celestial bodies in the game. Through the tasks and challenges in the game, users can learn about astronomy while enjoying the game. This gamification can increase students' learning autonomy and their interest in astronomy. (See Fig. 3).

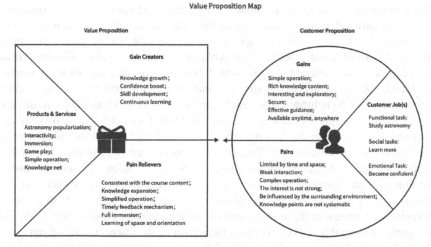

Fig. 3. Value Proposition Map

4.1 Game Scene Design

Theme Scene. In the scene design of the VR astronomy knowledge science game, we mainly use the real space as the background to increase the realism of the game. In order to ensure that students have a better experience in the game, we have added an Observation Deck Mode to choose from. This mode allows the player to choose an observation deck in space and stand in a bright and safe environment to observe the starry sky, avoiding the insecurity that may come from standing directly in the vastness of the universe. In addition, the game provides a number of interactive safety barriers that allow the player to maintain a certain sense of security while exploring space. In terms of visual design, we also paid special attention to creating a comfortable and friendly environment to reduce students' sense of tension. (See Fig. 4).

Fig. 4. Starry sky interface created in the VR scene

Teaching Scenario. Provide astronomical knowledge and content that is compatible with local educational content according to the cultural and educational needs of the target market in order to increase the appeal and applicability of the game. Accurately calculate the orbits of celestial bodies such as planets, moons, asteroids and comets using Kepler's laws or other relevant astrophysical formulas. Consider factors such as mass, velocity, and distance of celestial bodies to simulate realistic gravitational interactions and orbital changes. Synchronize the simulation of celestial motions based on the real-world rate of time passing. For example, it takes one year for the Earth to revolve around the Sun and one month for the Moon to revolve around the Earth. Provide options for time acceleration or deceleration so that users can observe changes in celestial motions over long time scales. Simulate astronomical events such as solar and lunar eclipses to ensure that the time, location, and visibility of their occurrences correspond to reality. Maintain accuracy of relative sizes and distances between celestial objects so that users can perceive the vastness of the universe and the great variety of celestial objects. Provide zoom functions to enable users to explore the universe on different scales from macro to micro. (See Fig. 5).

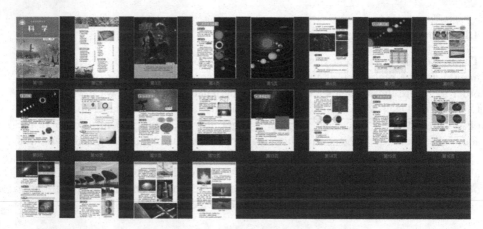

Fig. 5. Primary 6 Science Textbook, Unit 3

4.2 Interactive Design

VR-assisted astronomy popularization interaction design enables users to explore the mysteries of the universe in an immersive way by creating an immersive virtual astronomy experience. This design focuses on interactivity and user participation, enabling users to interact with the virtual environment, gain in-depth knowledge of astronomy through interactive manipulation, and increase their interest in and understanding of astronomical phenomena. Through VR technology, Interaction design for astronomical science aims to provide a novel and interesting way of learning, so that users can harvest knowledge and have fun in the process of exploring the universe (See Fig. 6).

The Interface Can Reach Up to Three Levels. Through the research and analysis, it is found that the interface of the application for elementary school students does not exceed

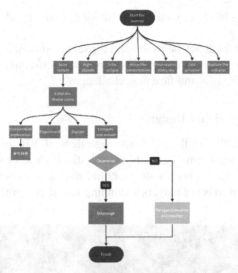

Fig. 6. Conceptual design drawing

four levels at most, and three levels account for the most. Elementary school students usually have a weak understanding of complex interfaces and operation processes. By limiting the interface to fewer levels, the learning cost can be reduced and the application can be simpler and easier to use. Intuitive and clear design helps children to quickly get started and enjoy the application.

Elementary school children are easily distracted, and too many interface layers may cause them to get lost in the interface, reducing their interest in the application. Simplifying the interface structure helps keep kids focused and makes it easier for them to find the target content.

Too many layers can lead to elementary students getting lost in the app and not knowing how to return or find what they need. By limiting the number of layers, the potential for confusion and disorientation can be reduced and the user experience improved.

Easy Operation. Elementary school students have a relatively low cognitive level and limited understanding of complex operations and abstract interactions. Simple interactions are easier for them to understand and remember, and complex interactions may make them lose interest.

Elementary school students' motor coordination is still developing, and complex operations may challenge their motor control. Simple interactions can reduce the difficulty of manipulation and make it easier for students to participate and enjoy.

Timely Feedback Mechanisms. Elementary school children have a relatively short attention span and they are more likely to lose interest in a short period of time. By providing timely feedback, interesting information can be provided to keep their attention on the game before their interest fades.

Elementary school students are more likely to reinforce learning through timely positive feedback. When they receive an immediate reward or recognition for their behavior, they are more likely to view that behavior as correct and worthy of repetition, thus deepening learning.

Immediate positive feedback helps to build the self-confidence of elementary school students. Successful experiences can quickly boost their self-confidence and make them more willing to try new tasks and face new challenges.

4.3 Full Sensory Experience Design

Visual Experience. Utilizing the 3D rendering effect of VR technology, it presents players with realistic cosmic environments and celestial bodies. From nebulae, galaxies, stars to planets, each celestial body's shape, color, size, and movement trajectory have been carefully designed to bring players a stunning visual enjoyment. (See Fig. 7).

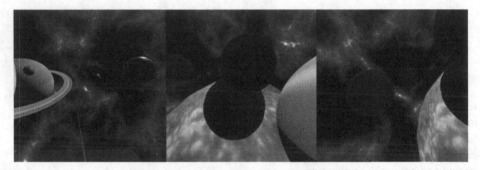

Fig. 7. Modeling the scene of the visual effect

Auditory Experience. The immersive sound design includes the quiet background sound of the cosmic space, sound effects generated by celestial movements, and soundtracks related to the game's plot. These sound elements enhance the realism of the game and channel the emotional resonance of the player.

Tactile Experience. Although the player can't really touch the virtual universe environment, but through the vibration feedback or tactile feedback technology of the VR handle, the player can feel the interaction with the virtual object during the game, such as the vibration sense of touching the surface of the planet, the feedback of operating the device, and so on.

5 Conclusion

With the rapid development of science and technology, digital means have gradually become an important auxiliary tool for teaching and learning, especially in the field of astronomical science popularization. This study emphasizes the unique advantages of VR technology in astronomy science education through in-depth analysis of the current situation of learning styles and equipment used in informal learning places. VR technology not only provides an immersive learning experience to enhance students' interest and efficiency, but also promotes students' learning and mastery of knowledge through perfect real-life exercises and immediate application scenarios. In future productions I will include a virtual lecture space. Students can be immersed into a virtual lecture hall or conference room and feel the atmosphere and effect similar to the real scene. This application of simulated speech space can help speakers to simulate and rehearse their speeches and improve their speaking skills and self-confidence. It enables them to reach the seventh level of the absorption rate pyramid to pass on to others and increase the average knowledge retention rate to 90%. VR technology has significant advantages and potentials in astronomy science teaching, and has become an important way of astronomy science teaching with its features of immersion, interactivity and spatial sense. By reasonably utilizing VR technology, it can enhance the learning experience, help students better master science knowledge, and cultivate their scientific literacy and innovative spirit.

References

1. Sefton-Green J. Literature review in informal learning with technology outside school [EB/OL]. (2004–01–01) [2019–06–04]. https://www.nfer.ac.uk/publications/FUTL06/FUTL06.pdf
2. Yu, S., Mao, F.: Informal learning-a new field of e-Learning research and practice. E-education Res. **10**, 19–24 (2005)
3. Hua, Z., Ouyang, Q., Zheng, K., Cai, J.: Yu, S., Mao, F.: Construction and validation of virtual reality teaching utility model. Mod. dis. educ. res. **33**(02), 43–52 (2021)
4. Su, Y.: A new survey of astronomy, 4th edn. Science Press, Beijing (2009)
5. Lv, Y., et al.: Construction of a distinctive experimental teaching demonstration center. Laboratory Res. Explorat. **28**(08), 101–103 (2009)
6. Wang, X.: A study on the design and development of English mobile learning resources in primary schools based on the theory of situational cognition. Hebei Normal University (2014)

Analysis of Gamification Strategies for Children's Safety Popularization Education Based on AR Technology

Yan Hao[1], WenXi Wang[1], ZiYang Li[1(✉)], and Meng Wang[2]

[1] Art and Design Academy, Beijing City University, Beijing, China
li.ziyang@qq.com
[2] Beijing Chen Jing Lun High School Jia Ming Branch, No. 86 Bei Yuan Road,
Chao Yang District, Beijing, China

Abstract. The progress of China's science and technology sector has drawn attention to the need to science popularization education, especially for children. Educating primary school students about safety popularization education is essential, as they are curious about the world but often need more safety awareness. Safety popularization education is urgently needed to address the need for more safety awareness. Children should be taught to understand safety hazards and dangerous factors in their daily lives, which can improve their safety awareness and self-protection ability. Gamified design is effective in science popularization education as it engages children to enhance their understanding of science knowledge and could play the same role in home safety popularization education. Research methods like surveys and interviews can explore how Augmented Reality (AR) technology can improve Safety popularization education. Based on the theory of immersive experience, this study analyzes the design of home Safety education games for children, investigating methods for immersive safety popularization education. By analyzing the cognitive development level of children and the elements of user experience, Safety education games can be designed to meet the needs and characteristics of children. This study helps explore how AR technology can enhance safety education, offering innovative strategies for children's future safety popularization education development.

Keywords: Children's Interactive Experience · Safety Popularization Education Gamification · AR Technology

1 The Current Status and Issues of Children's Science Popularization Games

1.1 Development Status

The primary school stage is an important phase for children to form their knowledge systems, values, and ways of thinking. Science education guides children to explore scientific questions, cultivating their innovative thinking and imagination, and enhancing their scientific literacy. The emergence of science games as a combination of educational and entertaining experiences is an important way to improve the effectiveness of science popularization. Disseminate scientific knowledge and promote learning through interactive and fun gaming experiences. Liao Hong, Vice Minister of Popular Science Department of the China Association for Science and Technology, pointed out that playing games is human nature, and stimulating people's curiosity in exploring the mysteries of science with the help of the charm of games is an initiative in the development of popular science work. With the in-depth study of game theory and the continuous development of digital technology, popularizing scientific knowledge through gamified methods can make the learning process more interesting and interactive. "Gamification" refers to the use of game design elements and game thinking in non-gaming scenarios to motivate user behavior and satisfy human psychological motivations and needs [1]. Gamified science popularization is an innovative educational approach. It draws on the design principles of games, integrating scientific knowledge into various aspects of the game. This allows children to learn science popularization knowledge while playing, effectively enhancing the learner's enthusiasm.

1.2 Problem

- Imbalance Between Education and Entertainment

    Overemphasizing educational content can make a game lose its fun, while excessively pursuing entertainment can diminish its educational value. Some games lack innovation, leading to a monotonous and repetitive experience for players.
- Insufficient Evaluation and Feedback Mechanisms

    Science popularization games often lack effective assessment tools to track and measure learning outcomes, making it difficult to determine whether players truly understand and absorb the scientific knowledge.
- Lack of Interactivity

    Knowledge is often presented directly in the form of pop-up boxes, not departing from the passive education model. The games do not offer an in-depth interactive experience, such as slow response time, child-unfriendly interfaces, poor visual effects, etc., affecting the player's engagement and immersion.

2 The Current Status and Issues of Children's Science Popularization Games

2.1 Advantage of AR Technology

AR technology overlays virtual information onto the real environment, allowing users to interact with virtual elements on interactive devices, thereby enhancing their perception of the real world.

1. AR technology presents abstract scientific knowledge in an intuitive and dynamic manner. For instance, students can use AR technology to view dynamic models of the Earth, understanding concepts like the Earth's rotation and revolution. This type of visualized teaching aids children in better understanding complex concepts and processes.

2. Compared to traditional learning methods, AR technology offers a more vivid and interesting learning experience. Through interaction with virtual objects, children can learn while playing, thereby stimulating their interest and curiosity in science popularization knowledge.
3. In science popularization education involving experiments or dangerous scenarios, Augmented Reality technology can provide a safe, risk-free learning environment. Children can perform practical operations in a virtual setting, thereby reducing the risks associated with real-life operations.

2.2 Filed Research

To gain a deeper understanding of the development and practice of science popularization education, field research was conducted at the China Science and Technology Museum and the Tianjin National Marine Museum. The research focused on three aspects: the content displayed, the methods of interaction, and the interactive experience and level of engagement. The purpose of this research is to explore interactive methods in safety education, the effectiveness of AR technology in exhibitions, and to observe children's interactive experiences within the museums.

Display Content. At the China Science and Technology Museum, the display content of safety knowledge was researched. The content covered practical safety skills such as earthquake resistance, emergency calls, escape methods, and fire extinguishing techniques. This content transforms safety knowledge into an easily understandable form and encourages learning through hands-on operations, effectively increasing children's interest in learning about safety. However, there are certain issues: the depth of safety education is not sufficient to meet the needs of visitors seeking in-depth learning, lacking comprehensiveness and systematization; safety knowledge is presented independently, not forming a coherent knowledge system.

Interaction Methods. The China Science and Technology Museum employs a variety of display methods, such as model displays, multimedia explanations, operational devices, and touch screens. These methods transform abstract knowledge concepts into multi-sensory learning experiences, which helps to enhance understanding and memory retention of the information. The National Maritime Museum of China boasts a rich collection of marine biological specimens and provides an immersive interactive experience using digital technology, comprehensively displaying the nature, history, and civilization of the ocean. When lifting the AR guide camera in the hall for identification, the screen fills with many lifelike marine elements, allowing for photo-taking and check-in records. When pointed at specimens, it provides explanations. However, there are some limitations: the device's response time is slow, and the screen cannot zoom in or out; after the AR guide camera scans the exhibits, the displayed image is static, lacking sufficient immersion; and the relatively dim environment inside the museum can also affect the device's rapid recognition capabilities. The learnability, stability, and fluidity of interactive devices can impact the visitor experience. Malfunctions or sluggishness in the devices might lead to a loss of interest among visitors. For instance, in the rocket launch control experience, parents may feel confused about which button to press. Additionally, some control panels have joysticks that are not sensitive enough, diminishing the children's interest in the exhibit.

Interactive Experience and Engagement. With the advancement of technology and the growing demand for enriched experiences, museums are continuously exploring ways to enhance visitors' interactive experiences and engagement, thereby increasing the appeal and educational effectiveness of science popularization. Interactive experiences often combine visual, auditory, tactile, and other sensory elements, providing visitors with an immersive experience. The information obtained through interaction is easier to understand and remember, and can stimulate the interest and emotions of the audience, making the experience more multidimensional and profound. Jean Piaget emphasized that children construct knowledge through actively exploring their environment. The interactive exhibits provided by the China Science and Technology Museum allow children to personally experience and explore through touching, operating, experimenting, etc. This process of active participation enables them to effectively understand the knowledge. However, the large number of visitors and the long waiting time for each exhibit, coupled with weak audio from the displays and interference from ambient noise, made it difficult for visitors to receive information clearly. These factors led to a decline in children's interest in the experience.

Based on the above analysis, the experience process of children is depicted in a user journey map, divided into four stages: initial contact, participation in interaction, immersive experience, and sharing (see Fig. 1). This is of significant value for formulating game strategies and enhancing the immersive experience. Safety education content should not only include basic safety knowledge but also delve into practical application aspects. According to the research results, employing AR technology to create an immersive interactive experience can enhance children's interest and participation in safety education. In game design, consider the cognitive level and interests of the users, providing suitable content and difficulty, and creating entertaining, highly interactive game elements. Additionally, to ensure a smooth user experience, optimize the performance of AR devices to enhance response speed and recognition capabilities, ensuring a stable and fluid operational experience.

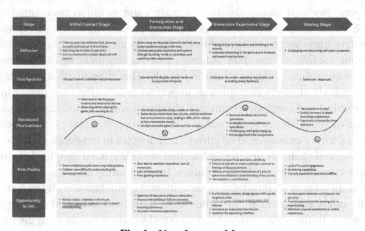

Fig. 1. User Journey Map

3 User Analysis and Theoretical Foundation Analysis

3.1 User Research

Parents have a deep understanding of their children's daily life and learning, allowing them to intuitively grasp their children's needs and behaviors. Through survey questionnaires, gaining insights into parents' perspectives on safety education, its content and objectives, as well as the channels for acquiring safety knowledge, can help in determining the specific content of safety education games.

According to the survey data (see Fig. 1), it is evident that most parents wish for their children to start learning about safety knowledge in the preschool stage, highlighting the importance of early cultivation of safety awareness. Among the various aspects of children's safety education, traffic safety and home safety are seen as the primary areas of concern. The safety knowledge that children need to strengthen includes traffic safety, internet safety, and home safety. This reflects parents' comprehensive thinking and profound understanding regarding safety education knowledge (Fig. 2).

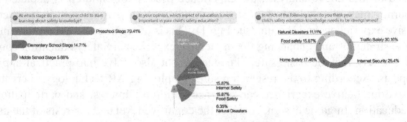

Fig. 2. Research Data Visualization

From the data (see Fig. 3), it is observed that parents expect their children to master basic self-protection skills, the ability to recognize various potential dangers and learn how to respond, as well as the ability to remain calm in emergency situations. This shows the high level of concern and expectation parents have for safety education. Although safety knowledge is acquired through media campaigns, classroom teaching, and community activities, the data indicates that parents believe these channels are insufficient to meet their children's learning needs. This suggests that parents perceive the current methods of safety education as imperfect or less effective, indicating a need for more resources and methods to enhance children's safety awareness and skills.

Synthesizing the results of the survey, it is clear that parents place high importance on their children's safety education. The current deficiencies in the depth of content, methods of learning, and channels of safety education provide crucial insights for strengthening and improving children's safety education. Internet safety education emphasizes the cultivation of awareness of information security and compliance with laws and regulations. Traffic safety education, on the other hand, focuses on practical operational skills and adherence to traffic safety rules. Science popularization games struggle to simulate real-life situations, which can impact the effectiveness of education.

Teachers, as direct participants in the educational process, have observations and insights that are critical to the design strategy of AR safety education games. Through

Fig. 3. Research Data Visualization

interviews with teachers, a comprehensive understanding can be gained about the learning situation of safety knowledge, classroom performance, and challenges in teaching practice.

1. Students possess some knowledge of traffic safety, electrical safety, and drowning prevention, and are also aware of natural disasters like earthquakes and fires. Teachers observe that students have a superficial understanding of internet safety, attributing this to the inherent complexity of internet safety, which makes it challenging for students to comprehend. Additionally, considering the strong curiosity of primary school students, overemphasis on these topics may paradoxically encourage them to explore these unknown areas.

2. In teaching, teachers use various methods such as classroom lectures, discussions, and games to teach safety knowledge. Classroom observations reveal that students' understanding of safety education knowledge needs enhancement, but they demonstrate high enthusiasm. Schools are working on integrating disciplines, incorporating moral education into various subjects to strengthen students' understanding of safety knowledge.

3. Schools have thematic class meetings and drills, where students know how to respond during exercises, but their reactions in actual dangerous situations are uncertain. Due to limitations in campus and classroom conditions, some risky situations cannot be simulated, which sometimes leads to students not taking them seriously. Therefore, it is recommended to further develop and integrate based on existing educational resources, while also encouraging students to step out of the classroom or introducing new course resources.

The current educational content in schools is biased towards general knowledge, whereas real-life issues tend to be more varied and richer in detail. Based on questionnaires and interviews, family safety knowledge is integrated into game design. Dr. Martin, the founder of the Global Children's Safety Organization, believes: "There are no accidental accidents, only preventable injuries." The home is a crucial setting in children's daily lives, where the "Compulsory Education Labor Curriculum Standards (2022 Edition)" set labor goals for students at different educational stages. Since children's cognitive and physical coordination abilities are not yet mature, their judgment is insufficient, and they are lively and active, home safety occupies a relatively high proportion in children's safety issues. Through the popularization of safety knowledge, it helps them to recognize and understand the difference between safety and danger, and to establish a sense of safety.

3.2   User Analysis

The United Nations Convention on the Rights of the Child defines a child as any person under the age of 18. The "2020 China Child Population Status: Facts and Data" classifies the developmental stages of children by age. This research focuses on children in the primary school stage, specifically targeting 8–11-year-old students in higher grades. At this age, according to Jean Piaget's theory of cognitive development, children are in the concrete operational stage. They have developed certain reading abilities and basic logical thinking skills, beginning to understand the mechanisms of the world and capable of reverse thinking. Furthermore, according to Jerome Seymour Bruner, an American psychologist who built upon cognitive development theory and his understanding of children's ways of representing the world, children at this stage are in the iconic representation stage of intellectual development.

Conduct an in-depth analysis of children's characteristics from four aspects: physiological, psychological, cognitive, and behavioral (see Fig. 4). At the physiological level, the text in games should use a larger and clearer font to ensure that children can read easily. At the same time, presenting information through a combination of pictures and text makes the content more intuitive and easier to understand. Moreover, bright and harmonious color design creates a visually friendly and pleasant environment. This not only helps to protect children's eyesight but also enhances the attractiveness of the game. At the psychological level, game design should provide children with a sense of achievement, display progress bars for tasks, and enhance children's self-confidence. By offering appropriate challenges and timely support to accommodate children's emotional fluctuations, children can feel pleasure during the gaming process. At the cognitive level, the difficulty of the game should gradually increase according to the child's age and cognitive level, making the gaming process more challenging and interesting. Use visual elements to attract children's attention and interest, while presenting complex concepts in an easy-to-understand manner, to help them learn about safety knowledge, thereby effectively learning and memorizing. At the behavioral level, the theory of reinforcement of learning motivation provides important guiding principles. Positive reinforcement plays a key role in game design. Designing a reward system in the game, such as points, badges, or achievements, motivates children to complete game tasks. Design challenging tasks and problems to encourage children to solve problems through practice and exploration, enhancing their sense of self-efficacy. The game design should include a sharing feature, allowing children to showcase their achievements to peers or parents, satisfying their need for recognition and social interaction.

Through the above analysis, a deeper understanding of children's characteristics and needs in various aspects helps in designing science popularization content and game elements that better meet user needs, ensuring children's continued participation and deeper exploration of safety knowledge. Designing more challenging and exploratory tasks stimulates children's curiosity and desire for knowledge, thereby promoting the enhancement of their scientific literacy.

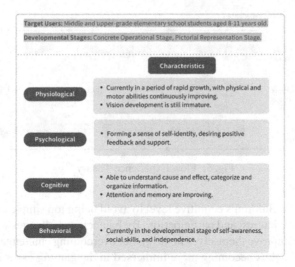

Fig. 4. User Analysis

3.3 Flow Experience Theory

The concept of "immersion" was first proposed from a psychological perspective by psychologist Mihaly Csikszentmihalyi in 1975. William Lidwell, in "Universal Principles of Design," interprets immersion in the context of Flow Theory. Mihaly Csikszentmihalyi conceptualizes the flow experience as a strong interest in an activity or object that induces an individual to fully engage in it. It's a comprehensive emotional state, encompassing elements like pleasure and interest. This experience is driven by the activity itself, rather than any external objective. Csikszentmihalyi also identified nine characteristics of the immersive experience. Hoffman and Novak, based on the flow experience process, proposed three categories of factors that lead to the emergence of flow: Factors of Condition, Factors of Experience, and Factors of Outcome [2]. Chen and others further classified these into three stages of flow: the pre-experience stage, the experience stage, and the effect stage [3]. In flow theory, challenge and skill are identified as two critical factors. They need to achieve a certain level and maintain a balance to create an immersive state. (see Fig. 5).

3.4 Combining AR Children's Safety Education Games with Flow Experience

- The Preconditions of Immersive Experience

  Safety knowledge should be aligned with children's age, comprehension abilities, and learning stages, transforming complex safety concepts into simple, easy-to-understand points for children to grasp and understand. In the game, there are clear learning objectives and directions. Children can explore hidden safety hazards in a home setting using AR technology, completing game tasks. When children complete tasks or fail them, providing immediate visual and auditory feedback can help them understand the importance of safe behavior and learn from mistakes, enhancing their learning experience. The game's level of difficulty and the complexity of operations

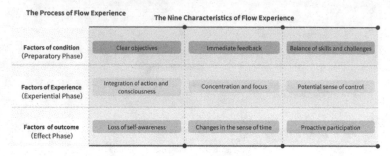

Fig. 5. Flow Experience Theory

should match the children's cognitive level to avoid being too simple or too complex, maintaining their interest and participation. By balancing challenges with skills, children gradually improve themselves in the game, overcoming challenges and boosting their confidence, thus becoming more immersed in the gaming experience.

- The Process of Immersive Experience

  AR technology allows virtual elements to interact with the real world, such as through touching, moving, and manipulating, closely integrating perception and cognitive processes, thus engaging children in the game. AR technology transforms complex or abstract knowledge into intuitive, concrete information, incorporating various forms such as virtual images and videos, enriching the sensory experiences of children. To maintain children's focus, the game interface should be designed to be simple, and tasks should be progressed in stages, minimizing distracting elements to ensure children can concentrate. By allowing children to autonomously choose their exploration paths and methods of problem-solving, their sense of control over the game process is enhanced. This approach encourages their decision-making abilities and creative thinking, making them feel that their choices have an impact on the game's outcome.

- The Effects of Immersive Experience

  The interactivity and immersion of AR games fully engage children in learning and exploration. To achieve this goal, the game's storyline, characters, and scene designs should closely align with children's interests to maintain their sustained involvement in the game. When children are fully immersed in an AR game, they often lose track of time, which is a hallmark of the flow experience. The game continuously captivates their participation and interest to the extent that they are unaware of the length of time they have been playing. By designing a variety of interactive elements, the science popularization content becomes more appealing, encouraging children to actively explore and learn, rather than passively receive information.

4 Design Strategy for Augmented Reality-Based Children's Safety Popularization Education Games

Based on user experience elements and immersion experience theory, combined with user analysis and research, design safety popularization education games that meet the needs and characteristics of children (see Fig. 6).

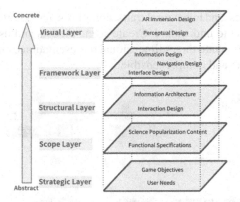

Fig. 6. Design Strategy Framework

4.1 Strategic Layer

User Needs. Based on preliminary user analysis, children enjoy learning new knowledge through games and interactive activities and show a strong interest in animations, storylines, and role-playing. The content of the game should be easy to understand, aligned with children's cognitive levels, and effectively convey knowledge related to home safety. Children's attention is easily influenced by external factors, so maintaining their focus through the creation of virtual characters, storylines, and dynamic visual effects is crucial. As children in this age group begin to develop independent thinking abilities, increasing the challenge and interactivity of the game through interactive elements can fulfill their need for interactive experiences.

Game Objectives. By incorporating safety knowledge into game design, children are encouraged to independently explore home safety knowledge based on game tasks, helping to build their awareness of safety. Utilizing augmented reality technology to simulate real-life scenarios allows children to enhance their interest and engagement in learning through interactive experiences, thus motivating them to gain a deeper understanding of home safety-related knowledge.

4.2 Scope Layer

Functional Specifications. Design game levels related to home safety, allowing children to learn about home safety knowledge through practical operations within the game. When players successfully identify safety hazards, they earn points or unlock new areas of the home, increasing the game's enjoyment and appeal. In the game, every choice is provided with immediate feedback, showing the safe or dangerous consequences of the children's decisions. This enhances their understanding of decision-making and helps them comprehend the importance of safe behavior.

Science Popularization Content. Ensure the accuracy of safety knowledge to provide correct guidance for children. The game primarily focuses on electrical safety, fire safety, and general safety knowledge (see Fig. 7). Based on children's learning levels, cognitive characteristics, and behavioral traits, complex safety knowledge is transformed into forms that are easy to understand. Create scene models and use AR technology to transform flat information into three-dimensional representations, making abstract safety concepts more concrete and comprehensible.

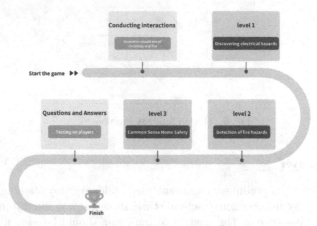

Fig. 7. Game Architecture

4.3 Structural Layer

Interaction Design. The game controls should be intuitive and easy to understand, such as simple swiping and tapping actions, suitable for children's hand gestures. Using a mobile device to scan a flat image and then presenting a three-dimensional model, children can rotate and zoom in for viewing. These models have dynamic effects. Players are required to place cards in corresponding areas. If placed correctly, a safety mascot will provide science popularization information; if incorrect, a prompt appears for repositioning (see Fig. 8). In the game, operations provide timely and accurate feedback through animations, sound effects, and text prompts, helping children understand the consequences of their actions. Focus on user experience to ensure a smooth gameplay process. Considering the unpredictability of user behavior, implement fault-tolerant design, providing effective error prompts and solutions, guiding users to complete the gaming experience.

Information Architecture. In the AR safety education game for children, the guided interactive segments require children to identify unsafe behaviors related to electricity and fire use, such as using old electrical wires, overloading power strips with too many appliances, touching switches and sockets with wet hands, and not closing natural gas valves. In the level-clearing segment of the game, it is divided into "discover electrical hazards," "detection fire hazards," "common sense home safety," with video explanations on safety knowledge. The game features multiple home scenarios, including bedrooms, living rooms, kitchens, bathrooms, and balconies, each hiding different safety hazards.

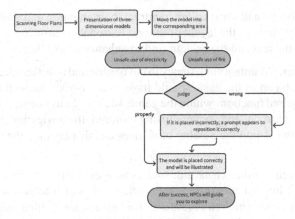

Fig. 8. Interaction Process

The child's task is to find all the hazards in the scene to unlock that room. Unlocking all the rooms reveals the entire home scenario (see Fig. 9). For each safety hazard identified, children can choose to learn related information from the NPC. The knowledge quiz section, through challenges and problem-solving, cultivates children's ability to analyze issues and find solutions.

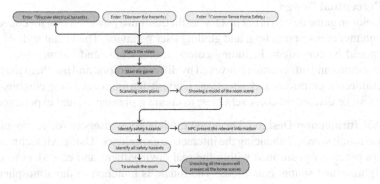

Fig. 9. Game Level-Clearing Process

4.4 Framework Layer

Interface Design. The number of layers in the interactive interface should be simplified as much as possible, controlled within 3–4 levels. Excessive layers of interaction can affect the fluidity of children's operations and judgment, hindering their ability to achieve an immersive interactive experience. The interface layout should be intuitive and easy to understand, avoiding excessive complexity or crowding, enabling children to easily find the functions they need. Design characters and graphics that align with children's aesthetics, using bright and vivid colors to attract their attention and make the interface more user-friendly. Arrange the layout of the text reasonably, ensuring there is sufficient contrast between the text and the background to enhance readability.

Navigation Design. Maintain consistency in navigation and interface elements throughout the game. Each part of the game should have clear instructions so that children can easily find the required functions within the game, such as "Start Game," "Next," "Return to Main Menu," and so on. To avoid confusing children, the navigation menu should be as simple as possible. Limit the number of choices and display only the most important functional options.

Information Design. Utilize visual aids such as images or icons to replace textual information, aiding children in better understanding the game's instructions and information. Before starting the game, children should watch a video to learn about safety knowledge, preparing them for the challenges within the game. Utilizing augmented reality technology, information is dynamically presented, enhancing interactivity and enjoyment. Establish a clear hierarchy of information to ensure orderliness and comprehensibility. Employ appropriate contrast and color to highlight key information, drawing the user's attention.

4.5 Visual Layer

Perceptual Design
Color in game design is not just for aesthetics, but a powerful tool for conveying emotions, enhancing understanding, and guiding user behavior. The visual style of the entire game should be consistent, including colors, fonts, icons, and layout styles. Understand the emotions and information conveyed by different colors, and use them judiciously to guide children's emotions and attention. Choose harmonious color combinations, avoiding harsh or discordant color schemes, to create a pleasant visual experience.

AR Immersion Design. The scene models allow users to rotate, zoom, or move them via touch screen, enhancing the interactive experience. Using AR technology, the models are precisely positioned within the real environment and can adapt to the surrounding lighting and spatial conditions. The music is matched to the atmosphere of the scene, such as using relaxing music to create a calming environment, thereby enhancing the sense of immersion. The game provides clear usage instructions to help users understand how to interact with the AR experience.

5 Conclusion

This research, through initial investigations, has found that augmented reality technology stimulates children's interest and participation in safety education. Compared to traditional safety education methods, the application of AR technology avoids physical harm to children. By simulating real-life scenarios to explore safety knowledge in areas like electricity and fire use, the interactive experience becomes more engaging. In the game, children can learn about home safety while also enjoying the gameplay. This study comprehensively recognizes the potential and value of AR technology in children's safety education. In future designs, there will be a continued focus on optimizing game segments and user experience, enriching the content of science popularization, and enhancing the game's enjoyment and interactivity to promote the development of children's safety popularization education.

References

1. McGonigal, J.: Reality Is Broken. M. Zhejiang People's Publishing House. Hangzhou (2012). Lu, J, translate
2. Novak, T.P., Hoffman, D.L., Yung, Y.F.: Measuring the customer experience in online environments: a structural modeling approach. J. Mark. Sci. **19**(1), 22–42 (2000)
3. Chen, H., Wigand, R.T., Nilan, M.S.: Optimal experience of web activities. J. Comput. Hum. Behav. **15**(5), 585–608 (1999)
4. Xu, X.Y., Li, F.Y., Yang, P.: Research review of product interaction design based on flow theory. Package. Eng. (2020)
5. Wang, S.: Design and implementation of children's popular science educational game in interactive context. Beijing University of Technology (2020)
6. Li, T.N., Wang. J.: Research on Gamification Design of Museum Online Science Popularization Services Based on Flow Experience. Grand View (2021)
7. Werbach, K., Hunter, D.: Gamification Thinking. M. Zhejiang People's Publishing House. Hangzhou (2017). Zhou, K., Wang. X.D. translate
8. Deng, Y.X.: The research on the experience design of children's immersive learning in smart museum. Jiangnan University (2021)
9. Song, X.N.: Research on AR interactive science popularization products based on children's cognition——Taking marine life science popularization as an example. China Academy of Art (2022)
10. Xu, L., Liu, C.N.: Research on Science Popularization Service Design from the Perspective of Game Elements. Chemical fiber and textile technology (2022)
11. Wang, Y.S.: Gamification design of a carbon neutral science app for children based on the octagon behavior analysis model (2023). https://doi.org/10.1007/978-3-031-48060-7_24

The Impact of Innovative Education Driven by Design Thinking and Training Model of Innovative Talents on Student Engagement: The Moderating Role of Background of Blockchain Technology

Rong Li[1] , Shunyuan Zhang[1]([⊠]) , Leong Mow Gooi[2] , and Yan Wang[3]

[1] Xiangtan Institute of Technology, Xiangtan 411100, China
3569716715@qq.com
[2] SEGi University Kota Damansara, Jaya, Malaysia
[3] Xiangtan Institute of Technology, Xiangtan 411100, China

Abstract. This study aims to examine the influence between innovative education driven by design thinking and student engagement, emphasizing the crucial role of training model of innovative talents and the impact of the background of blockchain technology. Data were collected through a questionnaire survey of 325 students from higher education institutions in Hunan, China. Insights were obtained through structural equation modelling analysis. The research results indicate that innovative education driven by design thinking positively influences the development of creative skills and student engagement. In this process, the mediating role of the training model of innovative talents did not receive empirical support. However, there was empirical support for the negative moderating effect of the background of blockchain technology in this context, filling a gap in the current research. These findings underscore the value of incorporating design thinking into educational programs aimed at promoting innovation to enhance student engagement. The study includes limitations and provides recommendations for future research.

Keyword: Innovation Education · Design Thinking · Blockchain Technology · Student Engagement

1 Introduction

In today's dynamic and ever-evolving marketplace, innovation is increasingly becoming essential for organizations to maintain a competitive edge (Vrontis, El Chaarani, El Abiad, El Nemar, & Yassine Haddad, 2022). As a response, the role of innovation education in cultivating creative talents across diverse sectors such as business, engineering, and design is being recognized more than ever. This recognition is particularly evident in the realm of higher education, where there is a growing focus on nurturing innovative minds (Nguyen, Mai, & Anh Do, 2020; van den Beemt et al., 2023). The effectiveness of these educational programs, however, largely depends on the teaching methodologies applied. A notable method is the integration of design thinking in innovation education (Lynch, Kamovich, Longva, & Steinert, 2021), which prioritizes the development of both creative and analytical abilities. This method is geared towards understanding and addressing problems through a user-centric approach, as noted by Sarooghi, Sunny, Hornsby, & Fernhaber (2019).

Additionally, the burgeoning field of blockchain technology necessitates its integration across various sectors, including the realm of education (Kuleto et al., 2022). Known for its secure, transparent, and decentralized methods of data storage and sharing (Zutshi, Grilo, & Nodehi, 2021), blockchain technology holds significant potential in higher education. It can be utilized for validating academic qualifications, managing student databases, and ensuring secure financial transactions. Despite its growing relevance, the literature shows a gap in the thorough exploration of how blockchain technology can be effectively blended with innovation education that is grounded in design thinking principles (Mourtzis, Angelopoulos, & Panopoulos, 2022).

The current academic discourse extensively covers both innovation education influenced by design thinking principles and the application of blockchain technology in higher education settings. However, studies examining the intersection of these two domains remain sparse (Bucea-Manea-Ţoniş et al., 2021; Zhang et al., 2022). Specifically, there is a noticeable absence in scholarly work addressing how design thinking-led innovation education, in the context of blockchain technology, impacts the development of creative talent (Seidel, Marion, & Fixson, 2020). While existing research has separately delved into either the impact of design thinking on innovation education or the role of blockchain technology in academic environments, a comprehensive examination that unifies these two elements to assess their collective effect on fostering innovative capabilities is yet to be extensively explored (Bucea-Manea-Ţoniş et al., 2021; Seidel et al., 2020).

This research is designed to address a notable gap in existing studies. The primary focus is on innovation education steered by design thinking as the independent variable. This aspect of the study investigates a training approach that integrates both creative and analytical skills for problem-solving, centering on user needs (R. Li, Qian, Chen, & Zhang, 2019). Additionally, the study incorporates the context of blockchain technology as a critical moderating variable. This is further broken down into three distinct sub-variables: the student's comprehension of blockchain technology, their confidence in its applications, and their overall familiarity with its concepts (Sundarakani, Rajamani, & Madmoune, 2023). These sub-variables aim to gauge how students' understanding and confidence in blockchain technology might influence their level of engagement and ultimately, the effectiveness of the innovation education model.

To encapsulate, this study is poised to explore the interplay between innovation education, propelled by design thinking, and the implementation of blockchain technology within higher education settings, particularly in cultivating innovative capabilities. Central to this research is the examination the influence of blockchain technology's context as a moderating factor in the relationship between training model of innovative talents and student engagement. The identified research gap underscores the necessity for further inquiry into the synergistic impact of these two concepts in nurturing creative talents. The outcomes of this study are anticipated to provide significant insights for devising effective educational strategies for the development of innovative talents in higher academic institutions.

The focus of this research is to address the current gap in knowledge. It explores the impact of design thinking-driven innovation education as the primary independent variable. This aspect of the study concentrates on a training methodology for nurturing innovative capabilities, highlighting the integration of creative and analytical abilities for problem-solving through a user-centric lens (R. Li, Qian, Chen, & Zhang, 2019). Additionally, the study examines the role of blockchain technology background as a moderating variable, encompassing three distinct facets: understanding of blockchain technology, confidence in its application, and familiarity with its concepts (Sundarakani, Rajamani, & Madmoune, 2023). These facets gauge the level of students' knowledge and confidence in blockchain technology, influencing their participation and the efficacy of the educational model.

2 Literature Review

2.1 Theory and Conceptual

The objective of this literature review is to elucidate the various elements utilized in the study titled "Exploring the Development of Innovative Talent Training Strategies in Education: The Role of Design Thinking in the Era of Blockchain Technology". This research is focused on analyzing the framework for developing innovative talent through innovation education that is guided by design thinking principles, and it also assesses the influence of blockchain technology as a potential moderating factor. Key components of this research include the role of design thinking in driving innovation education (serving as the independent variable), the level of student participation (acting as a mediating factor), and the influence of blockchain technology (considered as a moderating variable, subdivided into three aspects: comprehension of blockchain technology, confidence in blockchain technology, and the degree of familiarity with blockchain technology).

Student Engagement. "Rahimi and Zhang (2022) define student participation as the level of commitment and enthusiasm that students display in their learning journey. This factor is crucial for student achievement and success. Engaged students typically exhibit behaviors such as regular class attendance, active participation in discussions, timely completion of assignments, and a positive approach to learning, as observed by Bailey, Almusharraf, and Hatcher (2021). In contrast, disengaged students tend to miss classes, fail in assignment submission, and exhibit a negative attitude towards their learning process, a pattern noted by Haoting Li (2022).

2.2 Hypotheses Development

Education in innovation, shaped by principles of design thinking, represents a progressive pedagogical method for imparting innovative skills, particularly within tertiary education settings, as underscored by Androutsos and Brinia (2019) and Sándorová, Repáňová, Palenčíková, and Beták (2020). This approach has seen a growing implementation in various educational contexts, with notable adoption in China, as to and Liu (2021) point out. The primary objective of this education method is to cultivate the necessary knowledge and skills for solving complex problems and driving innovation. In a broader context, blockchain technology is recognized as a transformative force capable of revolutionizing multiple sectors, a perspective shared by da Rosa Righi, Alberti, and Singh (2020). Although still in its early phases of incorporation into educational frameworks, there is a growing fascination with investigating its potential to enrich creative education, as suggested by Bhaskar, Tiwari, and Joshi (2021), along with Mackey, Bekki, Matsuzaki, and Mizushima (2020). This investigation seeks to evaluate the effectiveness of the training model for cultivating innovative talents within the realm of education in innovation, influenced by design thinking, and contextualized by the backdrop of blockchain technology. In this study, we put forward the following hypotheses:

Auernhammer and Roth (2021), along with Wolcott, McLaughlin, Hubbard, Rider, and Umstead (2021), have identified that innovation education, underpinned by design thinking, focuses on nurturing students' problem-solving and creative skills through a user-centric methodology. According to Guaman-Quintanilla, Everaert, Chiluiza, and Valcke (2022), it is anticipated that students engaging in such design thinking-driven innovation education will cultivate innovative talents, thereby significantly enhancing their capabilities to tackle complex problems.

Lynch et al. (2021) and Pande & Bharathi (2020) have established in their research that innovation education and design thinking are highly effective in fostering innovative capabilities. Design thinking, as explained by Auernhammer & Roth (2021) and Foster (2021), is a problem-solving approach that places a strong emphasis on human-centered innovation. Foster (2021) also highlights its focus on understanding the needs and desires of end-users to develop appropriate solutions. In comparison, innovation education, as Eisenbart et al. (2022) point out, prepares students with the necessary knowledge, skills, and attitudes for innovation and creating novel solutions. Lin, Wu, Hsu, and Williams (2021) predict that integrating design thinking into innovation education will likely enhance the development of innovative skills in students. What distinguishes this study is its exploration of the synergy between design thinking-driven innovation education and the training model for innovative talent.

H1: Innovation education driven by design thinking has a positive effect on the training model of innovative talents.

Design thinking principles in education enhance student engagement, as evidenced by academic research. Lor (2017) notes that design thinking fosters creativity, collaboration, and problem-solving, aligning well with learning goals like critical thinking and adaptability. Goldman (2016) highlights its emphasis on empathy and user-centered problem solving, making learning more relevant and engaging. Razzouk and Shute (2012) support this, pointing out that the iterative process of design thinking, involving ideation, prototyping, and testing, promotes continuous learning and active student involvement. Carroll, Cameron, and Rosson (2014) emphasize design thinking's role in fostering collaborative learning environments, enhancing engagement through teamwork. Noweski (2012) found that design thinking in higher education increases student motivation and interest, leading to more meaningful learning experiences. Overall, innovation education driven by design thinking positively impacts student engagement by emphasizing creativity, collaboration, real-world problem solving, and iterative learning (Henriksen et al., 2017; Razzouk & Shute, 2012; Carroll et al., 2014; Noweski et al., 2012).

Hence, the study proposed the hypothesis:

H2: Innovation education driven by design thinking has a positive effect on the Student Engagement.

Innovative talent training models significantly enhance student engagement, supported by various academic studies. Malik (2018) emphasizes the importance of developing innovative talents in students for the challenges of the new era, with Wagner (2010) advocating for education systems to foster critical thinking, collaboration, and adaptability. Such training models, prioritizing these skills, lead to greater student engagement due to their relevance to real-world scenarios. Bozic (2013) and Zhao (2012) also highlight the benefits of innovative talent training models in increasing student engagement, particularly through personalized education that caters to individual needs and interests. This approach motivates students by allowing them to explore their passions and strengths.

Additionally, Hoidn and Kärkkäinen (2014) examined the global impact of innovative talent training on student engagement. Their study indicates that educational approaches emphasizing innovation and creativity effectively engage students from diverse backgrounds, preparing them for success in a rapidly changing global economy. Innovative talent training models positively affect student engagement by developing critical 21st-century skills such as creativity, critical thinking, and problem-solving. Studies demonstrate that learning environments prioritizing innovation and personalization result in higher student motivation and involvement (Wagner, 2010; Zhao, 2012; Scott et al., 2004; Hoidn & Kärkkäinen, 2014).

H3: Training model of innovative talents has a positive effect on the Student Engagement.

The training model of innovative talents serves as a mediator between design thinking-driven innovation education and student engagement, as indicated by various academic studies. Wagner (2010) and Zhao (2012) stress the importance of nurturing innovative talents in students, advocating for education systems to prioritize skills like creativity, critical thinking, and adaptability. Wagner (2010) notes that training models emphasizing these skills result in greater student engagement, while Zhao points out that personalizing education to individual needs and interests enhances motivation and engagement.

Scott, Leritz, and Mumford (2004) found that higher education programs focusing on creativity and innovation significantly improve student engagement and performance, with students more actively involved when encouraged to think creatively and solve problems innovatively. Hoidn and Kärkkäinen (2014) examined the global impact of innovative talent training on student engagement, concluding that educational approaches emphasizing innovation and creativity effectively engage diverse student populations, preparing them for a rapidly changing global economy.

The innovative talent training model acts as a mediator in the relationship between design thinking-based innovation education and student engagement. This mediation, supported by Wagner (2010), Zhao (2012), Henriksen et al. (2017), Scott et al. (2004), and Hoidn & Kärkkäinen (2014), suggests that the effectiveness of design thinking in engaging students is enhanced when paired with a training model focused on developing innovative talents, creating a more dynamic and effective learning environment.

H4: Training model of innovative talents mediation the relationship between Innovation education driven by design thinking and student engagement.

The background of blockchain technology moderates the relationship between the training model of innovative talents and student engagement, as evidenced by research in educational technology and innovation. This moderation implies that students' familiarity or expertise in blockchain technology can influence the impact of a training model focused on developing innovative talents on their learning engagement. Tapscott and Tapscott (2016) discuss blockchain technology's transformative potential in various sectors, including education. They propose that blockchain's principles of decentralization, transparency, and security can significantly alter educational content delivery and reception, making learning more engaging and relevant for students with a blockchain background, especially in technology, finance, or digital innovation courses.

Iansiti and Lakhani (2017) explore blockchain's influence on business and organizational processes, noting that understanding blockchain enhances students' engagement in discussions on digital transformation and innovation. This background knowledge fosters more active participation in courses incorporating blockchain concepts. Zhao (2012) emphasizes the importance of aligning educational models with students' interests and backgrounds, suggesting that a training model accounting for students' pre-existing knowledge in areas like blockchain leads to more personalized and engaging learning experiences. Additionally, Swan (2015) highlights blockchain's potential to revolutionize various societal aspects, including education. She argues that familiarity with blockchain technology empowers students to engage more deeply with digital innovation and emerging technologies content.

Blockchain technology's context acts as a moderating factor in the relationship between innovative talent training frameworks and student engagement. Research by Tapscott and Tapscott (2016), Iansiti and Lakhani (2017), Zhao (2012), and Swan (2015) indicates that students' acquaintance with blockchain technology can enhance their involvement in educational settings focused on fostering innovative capabilities. This moderation effect is particularly relevant in educational contexts where blockchain technology is integrated into the curriculum or discussed in digital innovation and transformation.

H5: Background of blockchain technology moderates the relationship between the training model of innovative talents and student engagement (Fig. 1).

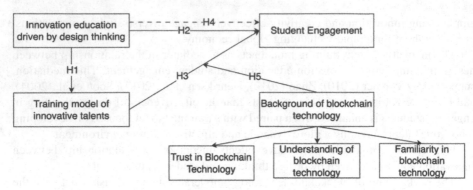

Fig. 1. Research model

3 Methodology

3.1 Population and Sampling

The objective of this research is to explore the interconnectedness between education in innovation influenced by design thinking, student involvement, and the historical development of blockchain technology. As well as their collective impact on the model for cultivating innovative talents among students in higher education institutions in Hunan Province, China conducted a study in using a quantitative research design. The sample consisted of 325 students from different Hunan Province higher education institutions. Convenience sampling was used to choose the participants, and students who satisfied the inclusion requirements and were willing to participate were requested to complete an online survey. Being enrolled in a Hunan higher education program, having a rudimentary understanding of blockchain technology, and agreeing to participate in the study were the requirements for inclusion.

3.2 Data Collection Research Instruments

In this research, data collection was conducted using various sections of an electronic survey. The initial section gathered demographic data, covering aspects such as age, gender, academic discipline, and academic year. The primary independent variable, education in innovation shaped by design thinking, was assessed with a seventeen-item scale developed by Huaizhong Li and Chang (2017), using a 5-point Likert scale. Additionally, the mediator variable, student engagement, was measured by an eight-item scale, adapted and revised from Bertolani, Mortari, and Carey (2014), also on a 5-point Likert scale. The study then examined the moderating variable, the historical aspect of blockchain technology, using a ten-item scale by Kim and Lee (2022) to evaluate understanding, confidence, and acquaintance with blockchain technology. In the final part of the survey, the dependent variable, the training framework for developing innovative talent, was evaluated. This evaluation employed fifteen questions designed to assess students' perceptions of the effectiveness of their innovation education in enhancing innovative skills, based on models by Yang (2020) and refined by Fang, Chen, Zhang, Dai, and Tsai (2020).

3.3 Data Analysis

In this study, data analysis was performed using the Partial Least Squares Structural Equation Modeling (PLS-SEM) method. This statistical approach is particularly effective for studies with smaller sample sizes, enabling simultaneous evaluation of both measurement and structural models. The analysis commenced with a confirmatory factor analysis (CFA) to verify the validity and reliability of the elements within the evaluation framework. Following this, the structural model was applied to investigate the proposed relationships among variables such as education in innovation driven by design thinking, student participation, comprehension of blockchain technology, and the framework for developing innovative talents. Additionally, the research explored the potential moderating effect of blockchain technology background on the relationship between innovation education guided by design thinking and the training model for innovative talent. Ethical standards for research involving human participants were rigorously adhered to throughout the investigation. Participants were informed about the objectives and methods of the study and gave their informed consent before participating. The privacy and anonymity of the participants were scrupulously preserved. All collected data were treated as confidential and used exclusively for this research.

4 Results

4.1 Descriptive Analysis

The analysis of latent variables, as depicted in Table 1, reveals that the average scores for variables such as design thinking-led innovation education, the model for developing innovative talents, student engagement, trust in blockchain technology, comprehension of blockchain technology, and acquaintance with blockchain technology were 3.973, 4.237, 4.467, 3.923, 4.232, and 4.412, respectively. In line with Kline's (2011) prior studies, both skewness and kurtosis values were observed to be below the established thresholds of +3 and +10, respectively, as shown in Table 1. This absence of multicollinearity suggests that the model is well-suited for subsequent statistical evaluations.

4.2 Measurement Model

The data in this study were quantitatively analyzed using the Partial Least Squares (PLS) method within Structural Equation Modeling (SEM). This approach was selected for its ability to bypass the need for traditional assumption testing, a feature emphasized by Hair et al. (2017). The latent nature of the variables required the application of PLS-SEM, as direct quantification was impractical, a point highlighted by Ramayah et al. (2018). As a result, the assessment of the variables was based on well-established theoretical models. This evaluation incorporated various measures, such as factor loadings, Cronbach's alpha, Composite Reliability (CR), and Average Variance Extracted (AVE), as outlined by Shrestha (2021). Convergent validity, the degree to which an item correlates with others within the same construct, was evaluated using factor loadings, CR, and AVE. For significance, factor loadings should exceed 0.70. Items with factor loadings in the range of 0.40 to 0.70 were considered for exclusion only if it improved the CR or AVE

Table 1. Descriptive statistics and correlation analysis

	Mean	SD	Skewness	Kurtosis
1. Innovation education driven by design thinking	3.973	0.873	0.839	−0.268
2. Training model of innovative talents	4.237	0.694	0.618	−0.593
3. Student engagement	4.467	0.852	0.412	−0.821
4. Trust in Blockchain Technology	3.923	0.912	0.303	−1.129
5. Understanding of Blockchain Technology	4.232	0.876	0.143	−1.435
6. Familiarity of Blockchain Technology	4.412	0.895	−0.102	−1.941

Source: Authors' calculation

values, following the guidance of Hair, Howard, & Nitzl (2020). Given that all factor loading, CR, and AVE estimates exceeded their respective thresholds, the measurement model was confirmed to exhibit convergent validity, as shown in Table 2.

All collected data were treated as confidential and used exclusively for this research. Discriminant validity (DV) is defined as a scenario in which it is established that two indicators are statistically distinct, a concept elaborated by Islam et al. (2019). Fornell and Larcker (1981) proposed a conventional method for assessing DV, which encompasses two distinct procedures. The initial method involves a comparison between the square root of the Average Variance Extracted (AVE) and the correlation coefficients; essentially, the AVE's square root should be contrasted with the squared correlation values. In recent developments, scholars have innovated in the calculation of DV, critiquing the traditional metric as inadequate. Henseler, Ringle, and Sarstedt (2016) introduced an alternative approach, the heterotrait-monotrait ratio (HTMT) of correlations, for evaluating DV. In this study, both the traditional Fornell-Larcker criterion and the HTMT method were applied. According to the conventional Fornell-Larcker approach, the square root of the AVE for each construct exceeds its corresponding correlation coefficients in each row, as shown in Table 3, thereby affirming the DV of the constructs. Following the guidelines of Henseler et al. (2016), the HTMT threshold is set at 0.90 for theoretically similar constructs and 0.85 for conceptually different variables. As depicted in Table 4, the HTMT ratios for all constructs are below 0.85. Additionally, Hair et al. (2016) noted that the variance inflation factor (VIF) is instrumental in assessing multicollinearity, with a recommended threshold below 5. The analysis indicated that the VIF values are under 5, thereby meeting the DV criteria, as evidenced in Table 4.

Table 2. Construct validity and reliability

Constructs	Items	Factor Loadings	Alpha	CR	AVE
Innovation Education driven by Design Thinking	IEDT1	0.890	0.975	0.975	0.716
	IEDT2	0.902			
	IEDT3	0.889			
	IEDT4	0.851			
	IEDT5	0.885			
	IEDT6	0.842			
	IEDT7	0.847			
	IEDT8	0.855			
	IEDT9	0.775			
	IEDT10	0.846			
	IEDT11	0.858			
	IEDT12	0.844			
	IEDT13	0.807			
	IEDT14	0.803			
	IEDT15	0.843			
	IEDT16	0.816			
	IEDT17	0.821			
Training Model of Innovative Talents	TMIT1	0.831	0.970	0.970	0.702
	TMIT2	0.783			
	TMIT3	0.784			
	TMIT4	0.788			
	TMIT5	0.850			
	TMIT6	0.858			
	TMIT7	0.852			
	TMIT8	0.847			
	TMIT9	0.883			
	TMIT10	0.857			
	TMIT11	0.856			
	TMIT12	0.776			
	TMIT13	0.869			
	TMIT14	0.861			

(continued)

Table 2. (*continued*)

Constructs		Items	Factor Loadings	Alpha	CR	AVE
		TMIT15	0.867			
Student Engagement		SE1	0.838	0.942	0.942	0.711
		SE2	0.830			
		SE3	0.835			
		SE4	0.853			
		SE5	0.863			
		SE6	0.839			
		SE7	0.848			
		SE8	0.838			
Background of Blockchain Technology	Trust in Blockchain Technology	TBT1	0.848	0.909	0.909	0.786
		TBT2	0.912			
		TBT3	0.868			
		TBT4	0.916			
	Understanding of Blockchain Technology	UBT1	0.884	0.871	0.872	0.795
		UBT2	0.912			
		UBT3	0.878			
	Familiarity of Blockchain Technology	FBT1	0.899	0.883	0.884	0.810
		FBT2	0.910			
		FBT3	0.891			

Note (s): Alpha = Cronbach's Alpha, CR = Composite reliability, AVE = Average variance extracted
Source: Authors' calculation

4.3 Structural Model

After completing the measurement model, the structural equation model was computed. Our analysis, following the approach of Ramayah et al. (2018), focused on investigating the mediating role of the innovative talent training model and the moderating influence of blockchain technology background. To evaluate the direct and indirect impacts within the structural models, four key criteria were utilized: First, the variance distribution across all constructs was determined by calculating the R^2 values for the endogenous latent variables, in line with Hair et al. (2017). Although acceptable R^2 values vary depending on the study's context, as Cohen (1988) notes, typically, values of 0.26, 0.13, and 0.09 are considered high, moderate, and low, respectively. In this research, the R^2 values, as depicted in Table 5, were above 0.9, demonstrating the model's strong predictive capability. Second, the model's predictive relevance (Q^2) was examined using a cross-validation redundancy approach, which assesses the model's significance, following the guidelines of Hair et al. (2017). The results, shown in Table 5, validate the direct effect model's significance, as indicated by Q^2 values greater than zero.

Table 3. Fornell – Larcker criterion

	BBT	FBT	IEDT	SE	TBT	TMIT	UBT
BBT	0.963						
FBT	0.876	0.923					
IEDT	0.879	0.888	0.964				
SE	0.913	0.841	0.938	0.943			
TBT	0.867	0.903	0.954	0.908	0.938		
TMIT	0.907	0.904	0.878	0.837	0.916	0.987	
UBT	0.895	0.905	0.875	0.823	0.904	0.938	0.891

Note: In the correlation matrix, the bold figures along the diagonal represent the square roots of the Average Variance Extracted (AVE). The elements situated beneath the diagonal, off-diagonal, denote the correlations existing between the constructs
Source: Authors' calculation

Table 4. HTMT criterion.

	BBT	FBT	IEDT	SE	TBT	TMIT	UBT	BBT*TIMIT	VIF
BBT	0.832								4.232
FBT	0.789	0.834							3.456
IEDT	0.812	0.843	0.821						4.178
SE	0.798	0.849	0.849	0.823					3.132
TBT	0.846	0.811	0.832	0.833	0.842				4.675
TMIT	0.849	0.821	0.841	0.847	0.812	0.846			3.257
UBT	0.821	0.834	0.849	0.834	0.849	0.838	0.823		3.989
BBT*TIMIT	0.815	0.832	0.843	0.848	0.832	0.803	0.814	0.833	

Source: Authors' calculation

Table 5. Predictive relevance of the model.

	R2	Q2
Training Model of Innovative Talents	0.912	0.915
Student Engagement	0.903	0.881
Trust in Blockchain Technology	0.959	0.960
Understanding of Blockchain Technology	0.949	0.950
Familiarity of Blockchain Technology	0.922	0.924

Source: Authors' calculation

The results show that H1, the direct impact of IEDT on TMIT, is positive and significant (b = 0.955, t = 94.797, p < 0.000). Furthermore, H2, the direct impact of IEDT on SE (b = 0.382, t = 3.901, p < 0.000) is also positive and significant. But H3, the direct impact of the influence of TMIT on SE, indicated by a beta value of 0.096 and a t-value of 0.951 (p = 0.342), was found to be statistically insignificant. Consequently, while the first two direct hypotheses, H1 and H2, were supported, H3 did not receive empirical validation. In the subsequent analysis, the indirect mediating role of TMIT in the IEDT-SE relationship was also not statistically significant, as evidenced by a beta value of 0.066 and a t-value of 0.952 (p = 0.342). Additionally, the moderating influence of BBT on the TMIT-SE relationship was observed to be negative yet significant (b = −0.181, p < 0.000). This suggests that while the indirect mediating hypothesis H4 was not substantiated, the moderating hypothesis H5 received empirical support (Fig. 2 and Table 6).

Table 6. Direct and indirect effects hypotheses test results.

Hypotheses	Structural Path	Coefficient	t-statistics	P Values	Remarks
	Direct effect				
H1	IEDT-> TMIT	0.955	94.797	0.000	Supported
H2	IEDT-> SE	0.382	3.901	0.000	Supported
H3	TMIT-> SE	0.096	0.951	0.342	Not supported
Indirect effect					
H4	IEDT-> TMIT-> SE	0.066	0.952	0.171	Not supported
H5	BBT*TMIT-> SE	−0.181	6.661	0.000	Supported

Notes: one-tailed test. Source: Authors' calculation

5 Discussion and Conclusion

5.1 Discussion

This research endeavors to examine the nexus between education in innovation propelled by design thinking and student participation, alongside the intermediary function of models for developing innovative talents and the conditional influence of blockchain technology background. Analyzing survey responses from 325 university students in Hunan province led to the formulation of five hypotheses. The findings of the study reveal that three of these hypotheses received empirical support, whereas two were not substantiated.

The research substantiates the initial two hypotheses concerning direct correlations, specifically that education in innovation, steered by design thinking, exerts a favorable influence on the cultivation of innovative talents and markedly boosts student engagement. The data reveal a notably positive correlation between innovation education fueled by design thinking and the model for nurturing innovative talents. This suggests that universities can adeptly employ design thinking as a pivotal method in innovation education to foster innovative capabilities. Concurrently, a significant positive link is observed

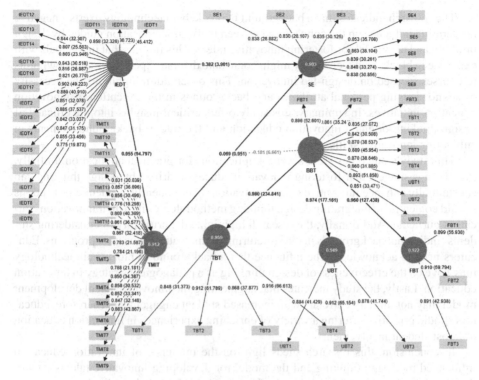

Fig. 2. Structural model (R2, Factor Loadings, t-values and p-values)

between design thinking-oriented innovation education and student engagement, indicating that universities can leverage design thinking as a key strategy to augment students' active involvement in academic pursuits. The outcomes of this study highlight the beneficial impacts of design thinking-led innovation education on both the development of innovative talents and student engagement, offering valuable insights for academic institutions aiming to effectively promote innovation and student participation.

The data affirmed the fifth hypothesis, which suggests that the background in blockchain technology acts as a moderating factor in the link between the model for cultivating innovative talents and student engagement. The outcomes demonstrate that knowledge and proficiency in blockchain technology have a negative moderating effect on this relationship. This implies that an increased level of understanding and familiarity with blockchain technology tends to be linked with a decrease in student engagement.

This study's results reveal a significant positive correlation between innovation education influenced by design thinking and the model for nurturing innovative talents. This is consistent with theories of innovation, which argue that education in innovation bolsters individual creative thinking and inventiveness. The ethos of design thinking further underscores the importance of embracing user-centric problem-solving methods and generating novel solutions. Consequently, the favorable influence of design thinking-led innovation education on the innovative talent development model aligns with expectations.

The research indicates that a background in blockchain technology exerts a negative moderating influence on the connection between innovation education guided by design thinking and the model for fostering innovative talent. This implies that individuals with expertise in blockchain technology might contribute diverse experiences and viewpoints to courses focused on design-led innovation. This observation highlights the necessity of acknowledging personal attributes and backgrounds in the execution of innovation education initiatives. In summary, this study offers critical insights into the efficacy of design thinking-oriented innovation education and the role of background elements in cultivating innovative skills.

This study's outcomes yield several implications for practical application. Initially, the findings suggest that fostering innovation education driven by design thinking can substantially enhance innovative talent cultivation. Consequently, academic institutions should contemplate integrating design thinking methodologies into their innovation education curricula. Additionally, the research highlights the criticality of considering students' individual backgrounds in the structuring of innovation education programs. Educators need to acknowledge the influence that a background in blockchain technology may have on the effectiveness of design thinking as a pedagogical strategy in innovation education. Lastly, the study indicates that augmenting the innovative talent development model may not directly correlate with increased student engagement. Therefore, educators should prioritize offering a variety of enriching experiences in innovation education to boost student involvement.

In conclusion, this research sheds light on the influence of innovation education influenced by design thinking and the model for developing innovative talents on student participation, especially within the framework of blockchain technology expertise. The findings from this study can guide universities in devising successful approaches to nurture innovative capabilities, enhance innovation education initiatives, and foster increased student engagement in educational activities.

5.2 Conclusion

To summarize, the objective of this research was to investigate the effects of innovation education propelled by design thinking on student engagement, considering models for cultivating innovative talents as a mediating factor and the background in blockchain technology as a moderating element. The findings reveal a notably positive influence of design thinking-oriented innovation education on models for developing innovative talents, thereby validating Hypothesis 1. Additionally, a substantial positive correlation was observed between innovation education guided by design thinking and student engagement, affirming Hypothesis 2.

Moreover, the outcomes of the study reveal that the model for developing innovative talents does not positively influence student engagement, leading to the rejection of Hypothesis 3. Furthermore, this model does not act as a conduit linking innovation education influenced by design thinking with student engagement, resulting in the dismissal of Hypothesis 4. Nonetheless, the findings indicate that innovation education, driven by design thinking, exerts a positive effect on student engagement, underscoring the significance of this educational method in enhancing student involvement and motivation.

Furthermore, the study found that the blockchain technology background moderates the relationship between innovative talent development models and student engagement, supporting Hypothesis 5. The research results indicate that students' understanding, trust, and familiarity with blockchain technology can decrease student engagement in the innovative talent development model. Importantly, there is no significant relationship between the innovative talent development model and student engagement, but the blockchain technology background negatively moderates the relationship between the two.

In summary, this research underscores the importance of innovation education influenced by design thinking in boosting student engagement and the contribution of blockchain technology within this educational framework. These insights carry practical relevance for educational entities and policymakers, stressing the necessity to amalgamate innovative educational strategies and contemporary technologies to equip students for the challenges and prospects in the 21st century.

5.3 Implications and Limitation

This study's results bear considerable consequences for the application and investigation of innovation education, design thinking, and blockchain technology. Primarily, they emphasize the critical role of innovation education, steered by design thinking, in augmenting student engagement. Secondly, the study elucidates the function of innovation education and models for developing innovative talents in fostering student engagement. Although the hypothesis regarding mediation was not supported, the observed positive effect of innovation education on student engagement implies that institutions of higher learning should cultivate a learning atmosphere that encourages active involvement, teamwork, and critical analysis. Thirdly, this research pinpoints the moderating influence of blockchain technology expertise in the dynamic between models for cultivating innovative talents and student engagement. This discovery implies that integrating blockchain technology into educational frameworks could have diverse impacts on student engagement in innovative talent development, contingent upon students' comprehension, confidence, and acquaintance with the technology. Consequently, institutions of higher education should take into account the blockchain technology background of students when crafting innovative education initiatives that include blockchain applications.

This research offers insightful results, yet it's crucial to recognize its limitations. Initially, the survey's exclusive focus on students from Hunan province restricts the applicability of its findings to broader contexts. Conducting analogous studies in varied geographical locations or nations to examine how cultural, societal, and economic variances might impact the relationships identified in this research would be beneficial. Secondly, the reliance on student self-reports introduces possible biases and tendencies towards socially desirable responses. Subsequent studies might utilize alternative approaches like observational techniques or interviews to gather more impartial data. Thirdly, the research concentrated solely on the model for developing innovative talents, omitting other potential influencers of innovation such as leadership abilities, resources, and organizational culture. Future investigations could delve into these elements and their interplay with the innovative talent development model, offering a more holistic view of innovation education.

Considering the limitations identified, various avenues for future research can be suggested. Firstly, it would be valuable to explore the connection between innovation education driven by design thinking and additional outcomes like creativity, problem-solving abilities, and entrepreneurial aspirations. Such research could enrich our comprehension of design thinking's value and efficacy in innovation education. Secondly, future studies might investigate the effects of diverse instructional techniques and strategies on student engagement and the model for developing innovative talents. For example, comparative analyses of the effectiveness of online versus traditional classroom learning, or the impact of gamification and simulation in innovation education, could be insightful. Thirdly, there is scope for further exploration into the applications of blockchain technology in innovation education, beyond its moderating role. Future studies could, for instance, delve into blockchain-based peer assessment, digital certification, and collaborative projects within the context of innovation education.

In summary, this research offers significant insights into the dynamics between innovation education influenced by design thinking, models for developing innovative talents, and student engagement, along with the moderating influence of blockchain technology expertise. Nonetheless, this study is not without its limitations. Future research endeavors can aim to overcome these constraints and venture into new areas to deepen our comprehension of innovation education.

References

Alam, A.: Platform utilising blockchain technology for eLearning and online education for open sharing of academic proficiency and progress records. In: Smart Data Intelligence: Proceedings of ICSMDI 2022, pp. 307–320. Springer, Boston (2022). https://doi.org/10.1007/978-981-19-3311-0_26

Albayati, H., Kim, S.K., Rho, J.J.: Accepting financial transactions using blockchain technology and cryptocurrency: a customer perspective approach. Technol. Soc. **62**, 101320 (2020)

Anderson, N.: Design thinking: employing an effective multidisciplinary pedagogical framework to foster creativity and innovation in rural and remote education. Aust. Int. J. Rural Educ. **22**, 43–52 (2012)

Androutsos, A., Brinia, V.: Developing and piloting a pedagogy for teaching innovation, collaboration, and co-creation in secondary education based on design thinking, digital transformation, and entrepreneurship. Educ. Sci. **92**, 113 (2019)

Appl. Math. Stat. **9**(1), 4–11

Auernhammer, J., Roth, B.: The origin and evolution of stanford university's design thinking: from product design to design thinking in innovation management. J. Prod. Innov. Manag. **38**(6), 623–644 (2021)

Bailey, D., Almusharraf, N., Hatcher, R.: Finding satisfaction: Intrinsic motivation for synchronous and asynchronous communication in the online language learning context. Educ. Inf. Technol. **26**, 2563–2583 (2021)

Bertolani, J., Mortari, L., Carey, J.: Formative evaluation of eccomi pronto ['Here I Am Ready']: a school Counselor-Led, research-based, preventative curriculum for Italian primary schools. Int. J. Adv. Couns. **36**, 317–331 (2014)

Bhaskar, P., Tiwari, C.K., Joshi, A.: Blockchain in education management: Present and future applications. Interact. Technol. Smart Educ. **18**, 1–17 (2021)

Bozic, C., Dunlap, D.: The role of innovation education in student learning, economic development, and university engagement. J. Technol. Stud. **39**(2), 102–111 (2013)

Bucea-Manea-Țoniș, R., et al.: Blockchain technology enhances sustainable higher education. Sustainability **13**, 12347 (2021)

Cohen, J.: Statistical Power Analysis for the Behavioral Sciences, pp. 19–74. Routledge Academic, New York (1988)

Daradkeh, M.: The Nexus between business analytics capabilities and knowledge orientation in driving business model innovation: the moderating role of industry type. In: Informatics, vol. 10, pp. 19 (2023)

Eisenbart, B., Bouwman, S., Voorendt, J., McKillagan, S., Kuys, B., Ranscombe, C.: Implementing design thinking to drive innovation in technical design. Int. J. Des. Creativity Innovation **10**, 141–160 (2022)

Fang, Y.C., Chen, J.Y., Zhang, X.D., Dai, X.X., Tsai, F.S.: The impact of inclusive talent development model on turnover intention of new generation employees: the mediation of work passion. Int. J. Environ. Res. Public Health **17**, 6054 (2020)

Fornell, C., Larcker, D.F.: Evaluating structural equation models with unobservable variables and measurement error (1981)

Foster, M.K.: Design thinking: a creative approach to problem solving. Manag. Teach. Rev. **6**, 123–140 (2021)

Galikyan, I., Admiraal, W.: Students' engagement in asynchronous online discussion: the relationship between cognitive presence, learner prominence, and academic performance. Internet High. Educ. **43**, 100692 (2019)

Gleason, B., Jaramillo Cherrez, N.: Design thinking approach to global collaboration and empowered learning: virtual exchange as innovation in a teacher education course. TechTrends **65**, 348–358 (2021)

Goldman, S., Kabayadondo, Z.: Taking design thinking to school: How the technology of design can transform teachers, learners, and classrooms. In: Taking Design Thinking to School, pp. 21–37. Routledge (2016)

Hair, J.F., Jr., Howard, M.C., Nitzl, C.: Assessing measurement model quality in PLS-SEM using confirmatory composite analysis. J. Bus. Res. **109**, 101–110 (2020)

Henriksen, D., Richardson, C., Mehta, R.: Design thinking: a creative approach to educational problems of practice. Think. Skills Creativity **26**, 140–153 (2017)

Hofmann, F., Wurster, S., Ron, E., Böhmecke-Schwafert, M.: The Immutability Concept of Blockchains and Benefits of Early Standardization, pp. 1–8. IEEE, Piscataway, United States (2017)

Hoidn, S., Kärkkäinen, K.: Promoting skills for innovation in higher education: A literature review on the effectiveness of problem-based learning and of teaching behaviours (2014)

Inder, S.: Factors influencing student engagement for online courses: a confirmatory factor analysis. Contemp. Educ. Technol. **14**, ep336 (2021)

Jaag, C., Bach, C.: Blockchain Technology and Cryptocurrencies: Opportunities for Postal Financial Services, pp. 205–221. Springer, Boston, United States (2017). https://doi.org/10.1007/978-3-319-46046-8_13

Jiang, C., Pang, Y.: Enhancing design thinking in engineering students with project-based learning. Comput. Appl. Eng. Educ. **31**, 814–830 (2023)

Kim, K.-J., Lee, M.-S.: Blockchain technology and the creation of trust: focusing on transparency, immutability and availability. J. Korea Soc. Comput. Inf. **27**, 79–90 (2022)

Kucukaltan, B., Kamasak, R., Yalcinkaya, B., Irani, Z.: Investigating the themes in supply chain finance: the emergence of blockchain as a disruptive technology. Int. J. Prod. Res. 1–20 (2022)

Kuleto, V., et al.: The potential of blockchain technology in higher education as perceived by students in Serbia, Romania, and Portugal. Sustainability **14**, 749 (2022)

Li, H.: Classroom enjoyment: relations with EFL students' disengagement and burnout. Front. Psychol. **12**, 6602 (2022)

Li, H., Chang, S.J.: Does 'Just in Time' Design Thinking Enhance Student Interest and Appreciation of Customer Needs in the Design of Machine Elements? In: Annual Conference of the Australasian Association for Engineering Education, pp. 606–612. Australasian Association for Engineering Education, Sydney, Australia (2017)

Li, R., Qian, Z.C., Chen, Y.V., Zhang, L.: Design thinking driven interdisciplinary entrepreneurship. A case study of college student's business plan competition. Des. J. **22**, 99–110 (2019)

Malik, R.S.: Educational challenges in 21st century and sustainable development. J. Sustain. Dev. Educ. Res. **2**(1), 9–20 (2018)

Nguyen, H.D., Mai, L.T., Anh Do, D.: Innovations in creative education for tertiary sector in Australia: present and future challenges. Educ. Philos. Theory **52**, 1149–1161 (2020)

Nusantoro, H., Sunarya, P.A., Santoso, N.P.L., Maulana, S.: Generation smart education learning process of blockchain-based in universities. Blockchain Front. Technol. **1**, 21–34 (2021)

Olivier, E., Archambault, I., De Clercq, M., Galand, B.: Student self-efficacy, classroom engagement, and academic achievement: comparing three theoretical frameworks. J. Youth Adolesc. **48**, 326–340 (2019)

Ramayah, T.J.F.H., Cheah, J., Chuah, F., Ting, H., Memon, M.A.: Partial least squares structural equation modeling (PLS-SEM) using smartPLS 3.0. An updated guide and practical guide to statistical analysis, 2nd edn. Pearson, Kuala Lumpur, Malaysia (2018)

Shrestha, N.: Factor analysis as a tool for survey analysis. Am. J. Appl. Math. Stat. **9**(1), 4–11 (2021)

Singh Sandhawalia, B., Dalcher, D.: Developing knowledge management capabilities: a structured approach. J. Knowl. Manag. **15**, 313–328 (2011)

Strebinger, A., Treiblmaier, H.: Profiling early adopters of blockchain-based hotel booking applications: demographic, psychographic, and service-related factors. Inf. Technol. Tourism **24**, 1–30 (2022)

Sundarakani, B., Rajamani, H.-S., Madmoune, A.: Sustainability study of electric vehicles performance in the UAE: moderated by blockchain. Benchmarking: Int. J. **31**(1), 199–219 (2023).https://doi.org/10.1108/BIJ-10-2021-0624

Swan, M.: Blockchain thinking: the brain as a decentralized autonomous corporation [commentary]. IEEE Technol. Soc. Mag. **34**(4), 41–52 (2015)

Tapscott, D., Tapscott, A.: Blockchain Revolution: How the Technology behind Bitcoin is Changing Money, Business, and the World. Penguin (2016)

Thi-Huyen, N., Xuan-Lam, P., Thanh Tu, N.T.: The impact of design thinking on problem solving and teamwork mindset in a flipped classroom. Eurasian J. Educ. Res. **96**, 30–50 (2021)

To, S.-M., Liu, X.: Outcomes of community-based youth empowerment programs adopting design thinking: a quasi-experimental study. Res. Soc. Work. Pract. **31**, 728–741 (2021)

Wolcott, M.D., McLaughlin, J.E., Hubbard, D.K., Rider, T.R., Umstead, K.: Twelve tips to stimulate creative problem-solving with design thinking. Med. Teach. **43**, 501–508 (2021)

Wrigley, C., Straker, K.: Design thinking pedagogy: the educational design ladder. Innov. Educ. Teach. Int. **54**, 374–385 (2017)

Yang, B.: Training model of innovative talents in physical education major. Int. J. Emerg. Technol. Learn. (iJET) **15**, 176–190 (2020)

Zhang, L., Carter, R.A., Jr., Qian, X., Yang, S., Rujimora, J., Wen, S.: Academia's responses to crisis: a bibliometric analysis of literature on online learning in higher education during COVID-19. Br. J. Edu. Technol. **53**, 620–646 (2022)

A Study on the Application of Digital Products Designed to Improve Primary School Students' Literacy Skills

Hong Liu[✉], Shan Shan Lu, and Meng Wei Zhang

Beijing City University, No. 269 Bei Si Huan Zhong Lu, Hai Dian District, Beijing, China
1h1h312@126.com

Abstract. Literacy skills underpin reading comprehension and writing ability and serve as an important way for primary school students to grasp the theme of articles and expand their horizons. Therefore, exploring the application of digital products designed to improve primary school students' literacy skills can help improve learning efficiency and promote their language development. In this study, on-site observation, questionnaire surveys, and in-depth interviews are adopted to analyze and study students' experiences in Chinese classes and their satisfaction with literacy teaching by Chinese language teachers. Additionally, the gaps in improving primary school students' literacy skills are investigated, and the characteristics of cognitive development are identified. In-depth research has been conducted on user needs using empathy maps from service design methods. Based on the observation and analysis of the Chinese character culture in classical poetry suitable for primary school students, a digital platform for literacy skills centered on classical poetry is proposed. This platform aims to organically integrate characters, words, sentences, and contexts, effectively addressing the problems of weak literacy skills and limited understanding of Chinese characters among primary school students. Furthermore, an extension is made based on Chinese characters. The semantic diversity of Chinese characters in the context of ancient poetry can be expanded; more methods can be offered to students to learn characters; their understanding of Chinese characters can be strengthened. As a result, their vocabulary can be significantly improved, their literacy skills are greatly promoted, and their learning efficiency is enhanced. At the same time, this study also aims to promote the preservation of ancient Chinese poetry culture and explore new approaches for the application of digital products designed to improve literacy skills in primary schools.

Keywords: Digitization · Literacy Skills

A. Marcus et al. (Eds.): HCII 2024, LNCS 14715, pp. 175–184, 2024.
https://doi.org/10.1007/978-3-031-61359-3_13

1 The Necessity of Improving Primary School Students' Literacy Skills for their Learning and Development

1.1 Improving Learning Efficiency

Literacy is the foundation for reading and writing. A large vocabulary and fast character recognition promote reading speed and comprehension. It greatly enhances the ability to understand the meanings of Chinese characters and thereby the ability to comprehend questions and learning efficiency.

1.2 Facilitating Language Development

The primary school stage is crucial for language development, and literacy skills are vital for this development. Literacy instruction helps primary school students transition from oral language to written language, enabling them to better understand and use Chinese characters, improve their writing and reading abilities, and have a better grasp of language usage.

1.3 Promoting Cognitive Competence

Students in lower grades with weak literacy skills and insufficient perceptual abilities may have an incomplete understanding of Chinese character culture and primarily rely on unconscious and mechanical memorization. Reading, writing, and listening stimulate the perceptual systems of primary school students, enabling them to acquire a broader and richer range of information stimuli and continuously improve their literacy skills. At the same time, students' cognitive competence witnesses constant development.

2 Research and Analysis of Primary School Students' Literacy Skills

2.1 Analysis of Primary School Students' Poor Literacy Skills

Research has found that literacy instruction mainly involves two groups of people: students and teachers. Intensive research was conducted on these two groups to better understand user needs. Five pain points were identified (Fig. 1) after the research on primary school students in Miyun District, Beijing. Firstly, most teachers use simple teaching methods for literacy such as reading, writing, memorizing, and reciting. The teaching lacks stories, and the content is boring. Students can only rely on mechanical memorization and study Chinese characters through reading, writing, and recognition. Secondly, when students encounter new characters or words, they tend to ask their teachers for help or consult dictionaries, leading to a lack of solid mastery. Thirdly, students tend to get confused between visually similar characters and characters with similar sounds. Fourthly, students have a narrow understanding of the meanings of Chinese characters. They are unable to apply their knowledge of word combinations and sentence construction effectively due to their failure to thoroughly understand the origins, meanings, as well as the history and culture of Chinese characters. Fifthly, rote learning is a common problem, and students focus only on surface meanings when learning ancient Chinese poetry. The deeper meanings and emotions contained in the characters, words, and lines of the poems are neglected.

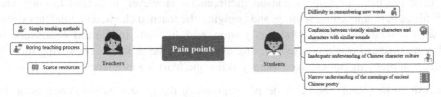

Fig. 1. Pain point analysis

2.2 User Research and Analysis

2.2.1 Analysis of User Needs

The target users were sufficiently studied in the earlier stages, and a user journey map was created. The map shows the needs and pain points of users, allowing us to identify areas for improvement and opportunities. The following is an analysis of the real needs of users (Fig. 2).

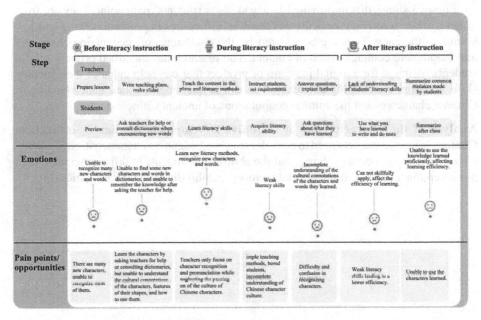

Fig. 2. User journey map

Figure 2 suggests that students' weak literacy skills affect their problem-solving abilities and learning efficiency and lead to an incomplete understanding of Chinese character culture. Additionally, rote learning results in confusion and difficulty in remembering information in some students.

The research has found that when students see new characters or words, they either ask their teachers for help or consult dictionaries. However, they tend to encounter difficulties in memorizing, writing, and applying the learned characters. Students struggle with limited vocabulary, slow recognition, and difficulty in learning characters. In addition, a lack of thinking after learning exacerbates the problem. Improving literacy instruction methods can enhance literacy skills and learning efficiency.

Analysis of the Real Needs. A deeper analysis of the most pressing concerns of the users was conducted using a user empathy map to find better solutions. To address the improvement of literacy skills, the following seven questions were asked to analyze and study the real needs of the users.

- Who found the problem?
- What did the user hear?
- What did the user see?
- What were the user's real thoughts and feelings?
- What did the user say and do?
- What was the user's pain point?
- What did the user want to achieve?

Figure 3 shows that improving literacy skills is students' pain point. They are frustrated by their weak literacy skills that result in difficulties in problem-solving and low learning efficiency. They are bewildered by the challenges of recognizing characters and incomplete comprehension of content. The research has identified primary school students' demand for a digital platform or product that can help enhance their literacy skills and improve learning efficiency. The aim is to strengthen their understanding of Chinese characters and the cultural connotations of ancient Chinese poetry.

Analysis of the Characteristics of Cognitive Development. In literacy instruction, Chinese language teachers need to consider students' cognitive characteristics. Students' cognitive competence is evolving, and the abilities of students in different grades, such as perception, attention, thinking, and memory, exhibit different characteristics (Fig. 4).

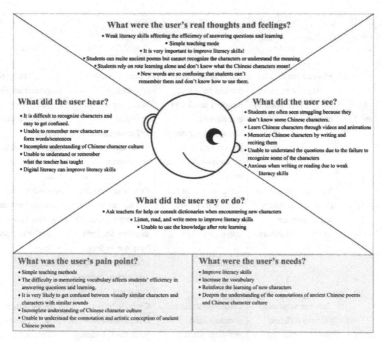

Fig. 3. User empathy map

Analysis of Competitors in Digital Literacy Instruction. In the field of education applications for children, gamified design is becoming more popular. There are now many applications designed to help children learn Chinese characters and ancient poetry, such as Dr. Panda (熊博士识字), Maitianshizi (麦田识字), iHuman Chinese (洪恩识字), Maodouaigushi (毛豆爱古诗), and Beibeigushi (贝贝古诗). They provide various learning modes to meet the needs of users at different levels. However, there are also some shortcomings. For example, the gamified approaches used to help students learn Chinese characters or understand the cultural connotations of characters often lead to sensory memory, causing difficulties in remembering and confusion. Currently, applications designed to help children learn Chinese characters and help them learn ancient poetry exist independently, indicating that there is room for developing applications integrating the two aspects.

Characteristics of cognitive development				
Grade/Cognitive characteristics	Perception	Attention	Memory	Thinking
Grades 1 and 2	Students can feel the outline of a character but lack perception of details.	They can only stay focused for a short time in a small area and are easily distracted by external objects, unable to concentrate for a long time.	Conscious memory is gradually increasing, but the ability of self-organization is weak, and memory only remains direct.	They can make simple judgments and reason based on some concepts. Abstract thinking has improved, but the level of thinking is not high.
Grades 3 and 4	They can observe the shape of a character and analyze the structure and features of it.	Attention is unstable, not sustained, and closely related to interest.	Conscious memory and unconscious memory continue to improve. Students have deeper levels of memory through associations between characters.	Abstract thinking is the main form, and the level of thinking gradually increases.
Grades 5 and 6	They can accurately perceive different parts of a character and detect the main features of it.	Conscious attention dominates and self-control and observation skills gradually increase.	Concrete image recognition and mechanical memory play a big part, and memory gradually improves.	Creative imagination gradually develops with some logical thinking.

Fig. 4. Characteristics of cognitive development

3 Innovative Strategies for Designing Digital Products to Improve Literacy Skills

This project is based on the current status of literacy instruction in primary schools in China. The guideline is the 2022 New Curriculum Standards for Chinese Language Teaching for primary schools, which stipulates the required number of Chinese characters for students in each grade. Based on factors such as students' interest in literacy, their motivation, learning habits, and their mastery of Chinese characters, a comprehensive understanding of the current status of literacy among primary school students was obtained, and the problems underlying the current situation were analyzed. In addition, the strengths and weaknesses of traditional literacy instruction in China were summarized. Based on this, we aim to explore new approaches to enhance the literacy skills of primary school students by incorporating digital media technology in literacy instruction and developing a digital teaching system to improve primary students' literacy skills (hereinafter referred to as the System).

Ancient poetry, one of the diverse art forms in traditional Chinese culture, plays a crucial role in Chinese language teaching at the primary school level. Traditional literacy instruction often focuses on the form and meaning of characters, neglecting the practice of pronunciation. As a result, students cannot experience the rhythmic beauty of the Chinese language during the process of learning characters. The combination of recitation and character recognition can help students better understand the meaning expressed by Chinese characters and appreciate the meanings and characteristics of words and sentences. The artistic conception and context can also strengthen the understanding of new characters and enhance the memorization of new words. As a result, students can understand both pronunciation and meaning. Additionally, teaching methods should be tailored to the cognitive and psychological characteristics of primary school students in different grades.

The design ideas for the System (Fig. 5) are centered around ancient Chinese poetry. Its creativity lies in the approach of teaching Chinese character culture using ancient poetry. Based on preliminary research and analysis, the design ideas were proposed through four modules: function introduction, target users, technical implementation, and operational strategies.

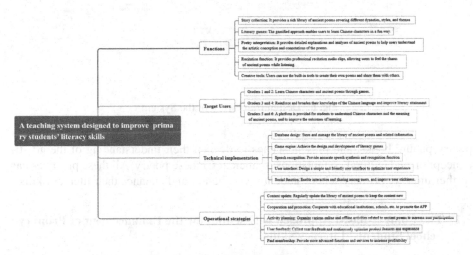

Fig. 5. Design ideas for the System

The functional framework (Fig. 6) focuses on primary school students in different grades, and the design of functional attributes has several parts, Recommendation, Ancient Poetry Picture Books, Word Reinforcement, Task List, and Character Library Selection.

The concept diagram of the System (Fig. 7) presents the entire process of character learning. Students can choose ancient poems suitable for their age and narrate the stories of the poems based on animations of the plots, which helps cultivate divergent thinking. The coloring game requires students to color the fonts or scenes of digital illustrations, making the learning process more interesting. The main focus is on reinforcing the learning of new words, which is achieved by deepening the understanding of the cultural connotations of Chinese characters through the implied meanings and scenes in ancient poetry. Task List provides personalized recommendations and schedules for students in different grades. It also enables students to create their own font library, generate ancient

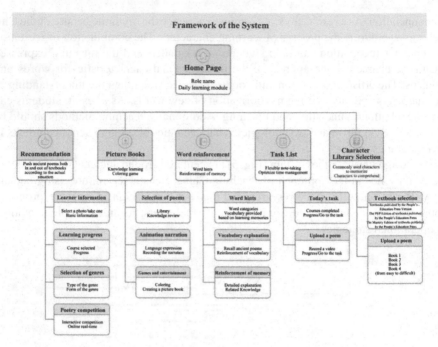

Fig. 6. Design framework of the System

poetry picture books, and present scenes to deepen their understanding of the artistic conception and cultural connotations of ancient Chinese poetry. All these practices can further improve primary school students' vocabulary and enhance their literacy skills.

3.1 The Context-Based Approach is Essential for the Enhancement of Primary School Students' Literacy Skills

Context-based and digital literacy teaching resources can help students strengthen their memory and optimize teaching methods. Ancient Chinese poetry, as a pivotal part of the Chinese language curriculum, lacks substantial teaching. Some schools focus only on recitation and memorization while neglecting the meaning and cultural value of ancient poetry as a kind of heritage. Based on the example of the poem Xiaochi (小池), a study was conducted through the design of the System. 池 (pond) in the title is a new character. First, the thinking on Chinese characters can be broadened to associate, supplement, and create based on the left-right structure of the character, in order to visualize the imagery of the poem. The teaching of character recognition is carried out using new characters in the lines of ancient poetry, guiding students to connect the context and situation with the roles and meanings of characters in the poem, and helping them quickly learn characters such as 泉 (spring), 惜 (treasure), and 露 (dew) and reinforce the learning. With the help of the System, students can deepen their understanding from characters to words. For example, the character 蜻, when used together with other characters in ancient poetry, forms the word 蜻蜓 (dragonfly), reminding people of the line 早有蜻蜓立上头

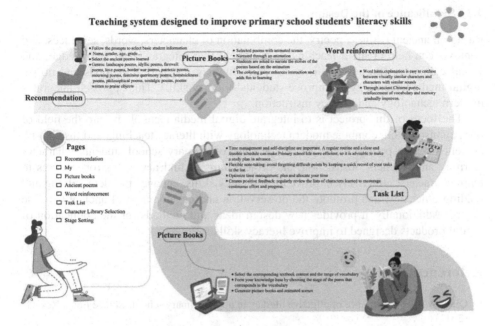

Fig. 7. Concept diagram of the System

(Long ago, dragonflies already perched above). This allows students to appreciate the connotations of characters in words and sentences. The contexts in ancient poems create a learning environment for students to understand characters, and digital illustrations help students gain a deeper understanding of the form, structure, and pronunciation of Chinese characters. This strengthens their perception of Chinese character culture and the artistic conception in ancient poetry. Consequently, primary school students can learn and master Chinese characters more firmly, and the effects of learning and their literacy skills can be ensured.

4 The Value of the Application of Digital Products Designed to Improve Primary School Students' Literacy Skills and Its Significance

4.1 The Value of the Application

In the context of information-based teaching, the application of digital media technology in literacy instruction in primary schools has gradually gained attention. The System improves students' understanding of Chinese characters through the interpretation of cultural connotations in ancient Chinese poetry. It also promotes their comprehension and memory of Chinese characters, accelerates the speed of character recognition, and enhances efficiency in literacy skills. This approach can effectively motivate students, broaden their cultural horizons, and enhance their cultural literacy.

4.2 Significance of the Design

Based on ancient Chinese poetry, the combination of characters, words, sentences, and contexts can help create a teaching environment that integrates fun, knowledge, and visual elements. The purpose is to diversify literacy instruction methods and utilize digital media technology to improve students' literacy skills. This approach integrates modern technology and literacy instruction.

The focus of this project is to integrate digital media technology into the field of literacy instruction, combine modern technology with literacy teaching, and fuse it with ancient Chinese poetry. From the perspectives of primary school students' character learning and teachers' instruction, the project aims to find new ways for students to learn characters, effectively improve their literacy skills, enhance problem-solving and reading efficiency, and promote the preservation and development of ancient Chinese poetry. Additionally, it provides new design ideas and methods for the application of digital products designed to improve literacy skills.

References

1. Qian, W.: The importance of effective literacy in upper primary school. Course Educ. Res. (1) (2017)
2. Tingting, K.: Research on diversified teaching methods for primary school students' literacy improvement. Ability Wisdom (16) (2018)
3. Die, M., Chenrui, Z.: Research on the problems of literacy teaching in primary school language and the solutions. W. China Qual. Educ. 4(13), 216–217 (2018)
4. Wei, L.: Research on the Problems of Language Literacy Teaching for Primary School Students and the Solutions. Harbin Normal University (2019)
5. Yun, D.: Research on the Strategy of Integrating Chinese Character Culture in Literacy Teaching in Lower Grades of Primary Schools. Shanghai Normal University (2019)
6. Zhuo, Y.: Exploration and Practice of Literacy Teaching in Lower Grades of Primary Schools based on Excellent Traditional Cultural Inheritance. Liaoning Normal University (2020)
7. Hong, Z.: Research on the strategy of integrating the cultural connotation of Chinese characters into literacy teaching in primary schools. Primary Sch. Times (07) (2020)
8. Yongjun, C.: Exploration of literacy teaching strategies in context-based classrooms. Way Success 642(14), 101–102 (2020)

Bridging Cello Learning with Technological Innovations: An Exploration of Interaction Design Opportunities

Kexin Sha, Yeon-Ji Yun, and Cheryl Zhenyu Qian(✉)

Purdue University, West Lafayette, IN 47907, USA
qianz@purdue.edu

Abstract. Incorporating emotional design, user-centered design, music education insights, and cognitive load management, this study investigates the integration of AI into cello learning. Through competitive analysis and qualitative user research, including detailed observations and interviews, we introduce interaction design solutions of "Goal-Oriented Three Practice Modes", "Interactive Learning", and "Personalized Practice Plans". This research aims to make classical music education more efficient, accessible and personalized, addressing economic and geographical limitations. By integrating technological innovations, we seek to enrich the classical music tradition, enhance the cello learning experience, and expand the community for cello learners and enthusiasts.

Keywords: User Experience · Qualitative User Research · Artificial Intelligence · Cello · Music Education · Interaction Design Solutions

1 Introduction

The cello, a cornerstone of classical music with centuries of history, commands a unique and revered place in the orchestral and solo performance realms. Renowned for its deep, resonant tones that closely mimic the range and timbre of the human voice, the cello offers a profound emotional depth and versatility unmatched by other string instruments. Its rich, sonorous sound, capable of conveying a wide spectrum of emotions, from melancholic whispers to exuberant jubilations, has cemented its role as a pivotal element of symphonic compositions and solo repertoire alike. This instrument's breadth in lower sound ranges allows it to serve as the backbone of the string section in orchestras, providing a critical counterpoint to the brighter violins and violas, and harmonizing with the double basses to create a full, cohesive sound.

However, cultivating cellists presents significant challenges due to high entry barriers. Firstly, mastering the cello demands precise technique and posture, challenging for beginners and potentially risky for professionals due to the long practice sessions required [1]. Secondly, a career in cello performance necessitates lifelong practice to learn new pieces and maintain skills, which are crucial for performances [2]. Moreover, the cello's size contributes to higher learning costs and transportation difficulties, compounding the challenge of finding and affording quality instruction, especially in less developed regions [3]. These barriers restrict access for those with limited resources, narrowing learning and career opportunities. Consequently, this impedes the popularization of the cello, reducing the number of learners and professionals, and potentially affecting the spread and development of classical music in the digital age.

The advent of Artificial Intelligence (AI) has ushered in a new era of interdisciplinary integration, challenging and expanding the boundaries of traditional domains, including the arts. Innovations such as MidJourney [4] and DALL-E 3 [5] have not only demonstrated AI's capability to collaborate within creative fields but have also ignited a conversation about the role of AI in understanding, creating, and even critiquing art. This dialogue encompasses AI's potential to grasp the nuances of artistic expression, make aesthetic judgments, and perhaps most provocatively, the extent to which it could complement or even substitute human artists. The rapid evolution of AI technologies hints at an expansive future for their application in the arts, promising unprecedented tools for creative expression and interpretation.

In light of these advancements, our exploration delves into how AI technology can be specifically leveraged to revolutionize cello education and daily training. By identifying and harnessing opportunities in interaction design, we propose the development of a user-centered, technologically advanced cello practice platform. This initiative is grounded in the application of music education principles and cognitive load theories, supplemented by an analysis of existing market solutions and insights from qualitative user research. Our aim is to dismantle economic and geographical barriers that hinder access to cello learning, thereby enhancing the learning experience for cellists.

2   Literature Review

This research delves into the learning motivation, practice processes, and experiences of cello players to uncover opportunities for applying AI technology in enhancing cello practice. To attain a comprehensive understanding of the experiences and needs of our target users, the theoretical framework of this study synthesizes insights from several interconnected domains. Specifically, we review literature on emotional design, music education, and working memory from cognitive studies. This multidisciplinary approach enables us to explore how emotional engagement influences learning, the pedagogical strategies that most effectively support music education, and the role of working memory in mastering complex skills.

Firstly, Donald Norman's theory of emotional design [6] underscores the importance of addressing users' emotional needs to enhance the appeal and usability of products. In the context of designing an application to boost learning motivation and practice efficiency for cello players, Norman's insights are invaluable. Our approach integrates user-centered design principles [7], which place the needs, preferences, and behaviors of users at the core of the development process.

In the realm of music education, the Dalcroze Eurhythmics method emerges as a pivotal approach, underscoring the essence of sensing, feeling, and listening as fundamental attributes of a musician [8]. This perspective is further enriched by Rosalind Ridout [9], a renowned flute performer, who articulates the multifaceted challenge of mastering a classical music piece. According to Ridout, achieving excellence in performance demands not only advanced instrumental technical skills and flexibility but also cognitive prowess for interpreting notation and rhythm. Furthermore, it requires a creative interpretation of techniques and musical colors, alongside a profound musical understanding to captivate and engage audiences. Adding to this discourse, Schiavio et al. [10] spotlight the ensemble as a crucial learning environment that fosters the ability to listen and respond to others, emphasizing the significance of time management, self-comparison within a group context, and the cultivation of responsible learning methodologies. Collectively, these perspectives illuminate the critical role of sensory engagement and listening in the process of music education. They delineate the array of skills and competencies essential for delivering a compelling performance, laying a solid theoretical foundation for the design and functional emphases of our music learning application.

Our design approach is deeply influenced by the working memory model proposed by Baddeley and Hitch [11], which serves as a pivotal framework for managing cognitive load in the development of applications for instrument learning. This model underscores the importance of preventing information overload to avoid overwhelming users. Further expanding on this foundation, the enhancements brought forth by Cowan's Embedded Process model [12] highlight the dynamic nature of working memory and its capacity limits, offering nuanced insights into how information is temporarily stored and manipulated. Additionally, the concept of cognitive load theory by Sweller [13] provides essential guidelines for instructional design, emphasizing the need to minimize extraneous load while optimizing intrinsic and germane loads for better learning outcomes.

The synthesis of literature not only presents the critical roles of emotional connection, pedagogical efficacy, and cognitive capacity in music education but also sets a theoretical backdrop for integrating AI in cello practice. As we pivot from theoretical insights to practical applications, we next explore existing projects in AI-assisted music education.

3 Related Work

3.1 Advancements in AI for Music Performance and Analysis

The intersection of artificial intelligence with music performance and analysis has seen remarkable advancements. Weinberg et al. [14] have harnessed computer vision to dissect drummers' movements, providing insights into the nuanced interplay between human performers and their instruments. In a comprehensive exploration, Miranda's book [15] compiles studies on various dimensions of AI in music, including the intricate dynamics of human-machine interactions. Similarly, Duke et al. [16] leverage computer vision technology to translate visual cues into musical notes, opening new avenues for interpreting performances. Blanco et al. [17] delve into analyzing the movements and sound quality of violinists, employing AI to discern the sound characteristics of a violin, categorizing them into descriptors such as "Gentle," "Excited," "Warm," and "Tight" [18].

Furthermore, Dalmazzo and Ramirez [19] have developed a model capable of classifying the bowing techniques of violinists, showcasing the potential of AI to understand and replicate complex musical gestures.

Recent developments in AI have ventured beyond analysis to the replication of human vocal nuances, creating content that increasingly blurs the boundaries between authentic and synthetic sounds. YouTube's introduction of the AI-powered Dream Track [20] enables users to emulate the voices of renowned singers, allowing the creation of short musical pieces tailored with specific lyrics and emotional tones. Additionally, the proliferation of AI voice cloning tools [21] empowers users to produce songs and speeches in any language, utilizing samples of existing voices. These technological leaps forward herald a future where AI could not only analyze and recognize individual performance styles for personalized enhancement but also generate new performances that faithfully mirror a particular artist's unique style.

3.2 Existing Music Learning Products Review

The market is currently filled with a variety of products designed for music learning, available on platforms including smartphones, tablets, and VR headsets. In pursuit of an innovative design, we have carefully selected and analyzed five applications focused on musical instrument practice (see Table 1). Our selection criteria were based on product popularity, integration of AI technology, and the specific relevance to cello instruction. The evaluation of the advantages and disadvantages of each application was informed by real user reviews gathered from the applications' official websites, as well as feedback from the App Store, Google Play Store, and Meta Quest App Store [22–26].

Beyond the applications listed in the table, we observed that tools specifically designed for cello learners are scarce and often limited in functionality. This gap presents a significant opportunity for leveraging AI technology in cello education, aiming to provide advanced cello players with a more efficient, comprehensive, and intelligent learning experience. Moreover, despite numerous demonstrations of technology's benefits, many musicians remain wary of incorporating such tools into their practice. Our preliminary survey revealed that only one out of 57 musicians regularly uses AI in their work, specifically the MyPianist app. This reluctance may be attributed to the deep-rooted traditions in music or apprehensions about AI, including fears of job displacement. However, an overwhelming 91% of respondents indicated a willingness to explore the potential of technology. Through this review, our goal is to develop digital solutions tailored to the unique challenges faced by cello players, with a focus on user-friendly interfaces that facilitate meaningful and transformative practice experiences.

Table 1. Existing music learning products review

Product Name	MyPianist	PianoVision	Yousician
Type	Mobile app	MR glasses app	Mobile app
Target Music Instrument	Any instrument	Piano	Guitar, Singing and Bass
Main User	All skill levels instrumentalists	All skill levels Piano player	Beginners and intermediate learners
Main Feature	Provides adaptive piano accompaniment based on live classical music playing	Turns surfaces into virtual keyboards with Meta Quest for 3D music interaction	· Instant performance feedback · Structured learning paths · Gamified learning experience
Technology	· AI · Real-time Audio Signal Processing	· Mixed Reality · Computer Vision	Real-time Audio Signal Processing
Pros	· Responsive accompaniment improves playing · Automatic tempo adjustment simplifies practice · Simulated ensemble enriches string practice	· Enhances practice immersion and enjoyment · Increases accessibility for beginners and amateurs with intuitive design	· Professional structured learning · Engaging interaction to keep learners motivated
Cons	Recognition accuracy is unstable when instrument sound blending it with piano accompaniment	· Prevent practicing sight-reading · Functions more as a musical game than a learning tool	· Unable to assess beginners' formation of correct playing habits · Lacks advanced content for experienced players

Product Name	Violy		Cello Coach
Type	Mobile app		Mobile app
Target Music Instrument	Mainly Violin and Piano		Cello
Main User	Music educators and learners		Intermediate or above cellists with a grasp of basic techniques
Main Feature	· Score-synced demonstration videos · Adjustable practice accompaniment. · Intonation and rhythm correction		· Real-time feedback on intonation and scale practice · Adjustable tuning · Progress tracking
Technology	· AI scoring · Real-time Audio Signal Processing		· Audio Signal Processing · Tailored Feedback Algorithms
Pros	· Comprehensive functions		· Professional content Targets cello

(continued)

Table 1. (*continued*)

	· Hands-free music initiation through unique interaction · Instructional videos for effective learning · Detailed practice reports aid in error correction	practice · Effective for tuning and refining intonation and note accuracy
Cons	· Low scores discourage young learners · Correction and repetitive practice is not motivating · No customization when version is different between app and textbook	· Limited basic functions · Insufficient guidance for beginners · Practice is repetitive and lack motivation

4 Methodology of the User Research

4.1 Design of the Research

This article adopts qualitative research methodologies to conduct user experience studies, focusing on observations of one-on-one cello lessons and interviews with cello players. By observing and engaging with users about their motivations for learning the cello, along with their experiences and emotions during the learning and practice processes, this study aims to uncover both the technical and emotional needs of cello practitioners. Additionally, by analyzing firsthand learning and practice experiences, we explore opportunities for translating these insights into interaction design and for the potential integration of AI technology to support cello practice. The research is guided by the following questions:

1. When do musicians typically encounter challenges during practice?
2. What type of guidance do they seek to enhance their performance skills?
3. How do musicians perceive the role of AI assistance within the context of music practice?

4.2 Recruitment of Participants

This research received approval from the Institutional Review Board (IRB) at Purdue University with approval study number IRB-2023-551. Participants were recruited through a variety of channels, including postings on social media platforms and through personal networks, to ensure a diverse and representative group of participants.

To maintain the validity of the research, all participants underwent a review process before inclusion in the study. Each participant was required to have at least one year of experience learning the cello and to have been regularly practicing the cello in the past year. This criterion was set to ensure that participants could provide insightful feedback on the learning process. Prior to participation, all participants were informed about the study purpose, which is to design digital assistance for enhancing the cello learning and practice experience and efficiency. Interviews were recorded with the consent of the interviewees, and participants were assured that these recordings would be used exclusively for research documentation and not for any other purposes. Furthermore, participants were informed that they might be invited to partake in usability testing and evaluation of the designed digital assistance in the future, with their consent obtained at each stage to ensure their comfort and agreement.

The study involved a total of 7 participants, comprising 5 females. Their experiences with the cello varied and included: one cello musician and university professor, one master's student specializing in cello, two undergraduate students specializing in cello, one cello enthusiast also specializing in piano, one amateur cello player who participates in orchestra performances, and one beginner cello player (see Table 2).

Table 2. Data of participants

No	Gender	Occupation	Cello Experience Level
1	Female	Cello musician/ Educator	Professional
2	Male	Cello major graduate student	Professional
3	Female	Cello major undergraduate student	Advanced
4	Male	Cello major undergraduate student	Advanced
5	Female	Piano major undergraduate student	Intermediate
6	Female	Software engineer	Intermediate
7	Female	Data Analyst	Beginner

4.3 Method of Observation

We conducted observations of one-on-one, in-person cello studio classes, each lasting 30 min, completing two sessions in total. The participants in these sessions were numbered 4 and 5, respectively. Our observations focused on various aspects of cello practice, including the procedural steps under the guidance of a professional teacher, methods employed in learning new pieces, challenges encountered by the learners, and the instructional support provided by the teacher. Throughout these observations, researchers meticulously documented the interactions between the participants and the teacher, as well as between the participants and both the cello and their surrounding environment, using detailed field notes.

4.4 Format of the Interview

This study utilized semi-structured interviews, conducting six one-on-one sessions with participants numbered 1, 2, 3, 5, 6, and 7. Each session varied in length from 30 min to an hour. The interviews were conducted using video conferencing software (e.g., Zoom) and were audio-recorded with the participants' prior consent. Researchers captured data through notes taken during the interviews in addition to the audio recordings. The primary aim of the interviews was to gather participants' feedback on their learning experiences, instructional preferences, and views on traditional versus modern learning methods, with a particular focus on digital support. With the consent of the participants, the sessions were audio-recorded to enhance the thoroughness of data collection and analysis.

4.5 Grounded Theory in Data Analysis

Drawing on Khan's insights into qualitative research [27], our study adopts a grounded theory approach for the analysis of data garnered from interviews and observations. This method, characterized by its bottom-up analytical strategy, embraces the inherently unstructured nature of the collected data to unearth patterns and themes organically. By eschewing biases inherent in the functionalities of existing applications, this approach ensures that our analysis remains unencumbered by preconceived notions about the challenges and types of assistance required during cello practice. This not only guarantees that our findings are rooted in fresh insights gleaned from the collected data but also facilitates a thorough examination of the nuanced interactive experiences of cello practice. Consequently, this method paves the way for the formulation of a user experience model that unveils innovative design opportunities, firmly anchored in empirical evidence.

5 Data Analysis

5.1 Data Preparation

Data from the two observations were meticulously recorded in detailed field notes, which included mappings of the scene, observations of participant behavior, language used, interactions observed, and comments from the observer. Additionally, six semi-structured interviews were audio-recorded and subsequently transcribed to facilitate analysis.

For data processing and analysis, thematic analysis [28] was employed. The process began with the identification of noteworthy and relevant quotes from the field notes and interview transcripts. Following this, coding was conducted manually using these quotes to create an affinity diagram, which helped in identifying emerging themes. This led to the construction of a network of interconnected themes. The analysis ultimately highlighted several dominant themes, each substantiated by direct quotes from the participants.

5.2 Thematic Analysis of the Challenges in Cello Practice

Observation. During our in-person observations of one-on-one cello classes, we concentrated on the interactions between learners and teachers, as well as the interactions between learners, their instruments, and the surrounding environment. The objective was to grasp the learning and practice processes of the cello, identify the challenges faced by participants, and understand the support and guidance provided by teachers. These observations helped us pinpoint design opportunities for transferring offline cello learning experiences into an online setting.

Throughout the observation of cello classes, significant quotes were noted on sticky notes from the field notes (see Fig. 1), and an affinity diagram was employed to code and categorize similar quotes pertaining to various aspects of cello practice (see Fig. 2). This approach resulted in the identification of five key themes:

1. Posture Challenges: The importance of correct posture in cello learning was evident, with teachers frequently making real-time corrections.
2. Practice Process: Classes typically begin with the basics, such as playing scales and confirming intonation by singing, progressing to reading scores and playing sections together before moving on to solo practice. This sequence reflects the comprehensive steps and methods involved in learning new pieces.
3. Timely Feedback: Teachers provide crucial, timely feedback during practice, offering both encouragement and constructive critique.
4. Guidance from the Teacher: One-on-one instruction facilitates invaluable guidance, blending professional expertise with personalized analysis for a thorough evaluation and strategic planning.
5. Physical and Cognitive Load: Participants encounter both physical and cognitive challenges, including maintaining posture, managing muscle soreness, juggling score pages and notes while holding the bow, and concentrating on multiple elements simultaneously, such as score reading, sound quality, posture, finger and bow positions, and dynamics. For instance, a participant was observed repeating a section inadvertently due to attention overload.

Our analysis of these themes revealed several insights into the nuanced challenges of cello practice, highlighting areas for potential intervention and support through digital solutions.

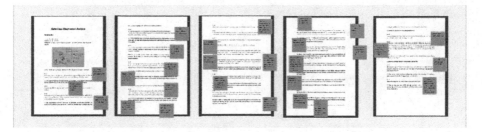

Fig. 1. The process of quoting from observation field notes.

Interview. During the semi-structured interviews, we focused on the participants' cello learning experience and motivation, challenges they face, the guidance they seek, and their opinions on AI technologies.

After the interviews, quotes were noted on sticky notes from the transcripts (see Fig. 3).

The analysis process employed a two-stage thematic analysis. Initially, the quotes were coded to identify primary themes. Subsequently, a more granular coding was conducted within these broad themes to define secondary themes, allowing for a nuanced

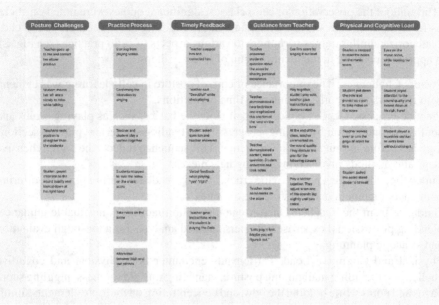

Fig. 2. Affinity diagram of cello practice themes from observational quotes.

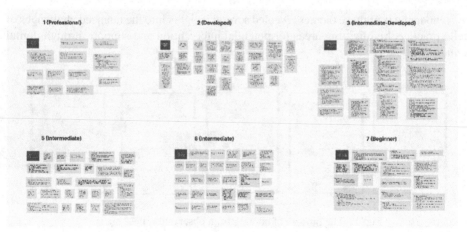

Fig. 3. Quotes from the six interview transcripts.

understanding of the interview data. The results of the two-level themes are presented in the affinity diagram (see Fig. 4). This approach resulted in the identification of seven primary themes and the secondary themes of each primary theme:

1. Motivation: Participants are driven to practice the cello due to their "love for music", desire for "interaction with people" through ensembles, and aims for "academic and career development". Many have dedicated significant time and effort towards specific

objectives like auditions, exams, competitions, and performances, either solo or with an orchestra.

2. Challenges: Common obstacles include the mental and physical exhaustion from "long and repetitive practice sessions", the struggle with "limited attention and self-awareness" in solitary practice without a teacher, and difficulties in mastering cello techniques such as "maintaining proper posture, fingering, and bowing", achieving "correct intonation", and realizing the desired "music interpretation".

3. Guidance/Method: To overcome these challenges, participants adopt strategies like creating a "practice plan" and focusing on individual techniques. They value expert advice, seeking "personal tips shared by professionals" and emulating performances from master videos. Tools like tuners and metronomes are utilized, alongside finding "accompaniment practice with timely feedback" crucial.

4. Practice Process: Practices commence with a review of "basic skills" across all skill levels, progressing methodically when "learning a new piece" until mastery is achieved.

5. Emotional Needs: The importance of "encouragement and support from friends and teachers" is emphasized for a more enjoyable practice experience, with one participant noting a profound "connection with the cello".

6. Criteria for Solo and Orchestra: While personal interpretation is acknowledged, there is consensus on evaluating orchestras based on technique and interpretation uniformity, and solos primarily on musicality.

7. Thoughts on AI: There is optimism that AI can offer "humanized interaction" and "personalized plans" through machine learning. "Timely and responsive feedback" from AI is seen as beneficial for efficiency, with its "accuracy and rigor" being particularly useful for orchestral practice. Concerns are raised about AI's capability in "music interpretation" for solo performances, given its subjective nature.

Following the identification of primary and secondary themes, we arranged these themes into a thematic network (see Fig. 5), focusing on their logical connections and relevance. This organization led to the following key observations:

1. Participants' motivation for practicing the cello is pivotal in setting their goals and refining their approach to practice, necessitating targeted methods for diverse evaluation criteria in auditions and competitions.

2. Our analysis of practice challenges, alongside participants' emotional needs and AI capabilities, has informed the conceptualization of our application's guidance features.

3. The perception of AI's credibility across musical aspects has been instrumental in tailoring our application's functions to meet user expectations.

4. AI's unique features address varied needs, with "personalized plans" enhancing practice sessions and "accuracy and rigor" in evaluations aiding in meeting orchestra performance criteria.

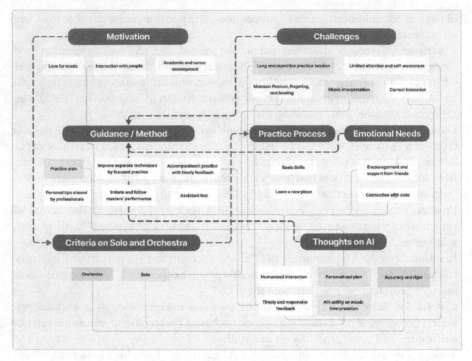

Fig. 4. The network of themes.

6 Design Directions

6.1 Synthesis of Design Principles

Our design direction is underpinned by a theoretical framework that integrates emotional design, user-centered design, the principles of sensing and listening from music education, and cognitive load management. These guiding theories emphasize the creation of interfaces that resonate emotionally, enhance usability, foster musical skill development through sensory engagement, and ensure cognitive loads are manageable. Our objective is to refine the learning experience, making practice more efficient and enjoyable for cello players.

A critical analysis of existing music education applications highlighted the necessity to amalgamate the best features while eliminating the least effective ones. Initially, identifying the target user group and categorizing users based on their objectives is crucial. This allows for the design of varied modes that cater to the specific needs of different user groups, striking a balance between professionalism and entertainment. Furthermore, our design seeks to integrate multiple functionalities to obviate the need for multiple devices during practice, thereby addressing the gap in comprehensive cello education software. Lastly, it is essential to explore new interaction modes that are conducive to cello practice scenarios.

6.2 Design Solutions

To address the identified needs and enhance the learning experience for cello players, we propose three major design solutions: Goal-Oriented Three Practice Modes, Interactive Learning, and Personalized Practice Plan.

Goal-Oriented Three Practice Modes. Insights from user interviews revealed the importance of aligning practice modes with user goals. Consequently, we introduced three distinct practice modes: Piece Learning, Orchestra Prep, and Soloist. The Piece Learning mode concentrates on score analysis, familiarizing users with musical scores, and understanding musical emotions. Orchestra Prep mode is designed for rigorous pitch and rhythm training, including accompaniment practices to refine performance precision. The Soloist mode offers flexibility, allowing users to explore pitch and rhythm, and analyze styles of cello masters for personalized musical interpretation.

Interactive Learning. This feature is refined to offer real-time, AI-driven feedback on posture through computer vision and intonation accuracy via sound recognition. Instructions and encouragement tailored to real-time progress during practice sessions will keep high engagement. During practice, the music score will automatically scroll to align with the progress, and highlight the section being played, minimizing the need to manually turn pages, which ensures a smoother practice session and aids in maintaining concentration. Voice and instrumental interaction for annotating scores directly and AI-driven highlights for areas needing improvement streamline the learning process by allowing continuous play without the interruption of traditional note-taking methods.

Personalized Practice Plan. The system crafts a personalized practice plan aligned with the user's long-term goals, breaking them down into daily, detailed schedules tailored to the user's skill level and specific objectives. Leveraging AI technology, the plan adjusts dynamically based on practice evaluations and interruptions, supporting continuous progress. AI also customizes practice duration based on the learner's physical and mental state, suggesting rest periods to prevent fatigue. Post-session, an analytical review identifies errors, summarizes challenges, and offers targeted recommendations, thus fostering sustained motivation and improving practice efficiency.

7 Credibility and Dependability

This study's participants spanned from beginners to professionals, ensuring a broad perspective on cello learning and practice experiences. Interviews delved into relevant topics like practice challenges and learning experiences, while observations highlighted effective learning strategies and interactions. These insights directly address the research goals, confirming the study's validity. The credibility of our findings is further supported by contributions from university professors specialized in cello performance among the research team and participants. Their expertise, combined with the consistency of themes across diverse interviews, such as practice routines and performance standards, enhances the study's reliability.

8 Future Plan and Limitations

The rapid advancements in AI within music education present a duality of excitement and concern among cellists. Enthusiasm exists for AI's potential to improve practice efficiency and concentration; however, doubts persist regarding its capacity to assess human musicality and the fear of it supplanting certain teaching roles. This ambivalence mirrors historical reactions to the industrial era's shift towards mechanization, which made goods more accessible and lessened wealth disparities but at the expense of the hand-made items' distinctiveness. In a similar vein, AI's evolution in music education could democratize access to classical instrument learning, like the cello, by boosting practice efficiency and tailoring the educational experience. AI aims to augment rather than replace human musicians or educators, thereby freeing up more time for creative expression. Additionally, generative AI applications could offer a deeper emotional connection to music than traditional educational software has achieved.

This study recognizes the challenge for interaction designers without a cello background in creating a comprehensive cello learning tool. Nevertheless, through empathetic user engagement and a robust understanding of user needs derived from observations and interviews, we have identified significant opportunities for innovative interaction designs. Future research will explore these avenues further, with plans for collaboration with professional musicians and comprehensive usability testing to refine and validate our design solutions.

9 Conclusion

This research aimed to uncover interaction design opportunities by applying AI technology to the specific challenges of cello learning. We developed solutions like Goal-Oriented Three Practice Modes, Interactive Learning, and Personalized Practice Plans, grounded in user-centered design, music education insights, cognitive load management, competitive analysis, and qualitative user research.

Our integration of AI into cello practice seeks to make classical music education more accessible, engaging, and personalized, addressing economic and geographical limitations. This initiative strives to improve the cello learning experience, widen access to classical music education, and democratize the learning process. By leveraging AI innovations, we aim to enhance the classical music tradition with new learning opportunities and creative possibilities, making cello practice more appealing and fostering a broader community of learners and enthusiasts.

Acknowledgement. The authors gratefully acknowledge the financial support provided by the National Science Foundation (NSF) under Grant No. 23–543 "Collaborative Research: FW-HTF-RM: Using Artificial Intelligence to Transform Music Performer' Skills and Productivity".

References

1. Rietveld, A.B.M.: Dancers' and musicians' injuries. Clin. Rheumatol. **32**, 425–434 (2013)

2. National Endowment for the Arts.: Artists and other cultural workers: A statistical portrait. NEA, Washington, District of Columbia (2019)
3. Beveridge, T.: Does music education have a poverty problem? Update: Appl. Res. Music Educ. **40**(2), 10–18 (2022)
4. MidJourney Homepage. https://www.midjourney.com/home. Accessed 14 Feb 2024
5. DALL·E 3 Homepage. https://openai.com/dall-e-3. Accessed 14 Feb 2024
6. Norman, D.A.: The Design of Everyday Things: Revised and Expanded Edition. Basic Books (2013)
7. Garrett, J.J.: The Elements of User Experience: User-Centered Design for the Web and Beyond (2nd Edition). New Riders (2011)
8. Jaques-Dalcroze, E.: Rhythm, Music and Education, Trans. H. F. Rubenstein. The Dalcroze Society, London (1967)
9. Ridout, R., Habron, J.: Three flute players' lived experiences of Dalcroze eurhythmics in preparing contemporary music for performance. Front. Educ. **5**, 18 (2020)
10. Schiavio, A., Küssner, M.B., Williamon, A.: Music teachers' perspectives and experiences of ensemble and learning skills. Front. Psychol. **11**, 291 (2020)
11. Baddeley, A., Hitch, G.: Working Memory. Psychol. Learn. Motiv. Adv. Res. Theor. **8**, 47–89 (1974)
12. Cowan, N.: An embedded-processes model of working memory. Models Working Mem. Mech. Act. Maintenance Executive Control **20**(506), 1013–1019 (1999)
13. Sweller, J.: Visualization and instructional design. In: Proceedings of the International Workshop on Dynamic Visualizations and Learning, vol. 18, pp. 1501–1510 (2002)
14. Weinberg, G., et al.: "Watch and Lear"—Computer Vision for Musical Gesture Analysis. In: Robotic Musicianship: Embodied Artificial Creativity and Mechatronic Musical Expression, pp. 189–212 (2020)
15. Miranda, E.R.: Handbook of Artificial Intelligence for Music: Foundations, Advanced Approaches, and Developments for Creativity. 2nd edn. Springer International Publishing AG (2021)
16. Duke, B., Salgian, A.: Guitar Tablature Generation Using Computer Vision. In: Bebis, G., et al. (eds.) ISVC 2019. LNCS, vol. 11845, pp. 247–257. Springer, Cham (2019). https://doi.org/10.1007/978-3-030-33723-0_20
17. Blanco, A.D., Tassani, S., Ramirez, R.: Real-time sound and motion feedback for violin bow technique learning: a controlled. Randomized Trial. Front. Psychol. **12**, 648479 (2021)
18. Musical performance & education with AI. https://www.artificia.pro/musical-performance-education-with-ai/. Accessed 15 Feb 2024
19. Dalmazzo, D., Ramírez, R.: Bowing gestures classification in violin performance: a machine learning approach. Front. Psychol. **10**, 344 (2019)
20. An early look at the possibilities as we experiment with AI and Music, https://blog.youtube/inside-youtube/ai-and-music-experiment/. Accessed 14 Feb 2024
21. Retrieval-Based-Voice-Conversion-WebUI. https://github.com/RVC-Project/Retrieval-based-Voice-Conversion-WebUI. Accessed 14 Feb 2024
22. MyPianist: A.I. accompanist. https://apps.apple.com/us/app/mypianist-a-i-accompanist/id1460393665. Accessed 14 Feb 2024
23. PianoVision. https://www.meta.com/experiences/5271074762922599/. Accessed 14 Feb 2024
24. Violy SyncedDemo & MusicSheet. https://apps.apple.com/us/app/violy-synceddemo-musicsheet/id1357516375. Accessed 14 Feb 2024
25. Yousician: Learn & Play Music. https://apps.apple.com/us/app/yousician-learn-play-music/id959883039. Accessed 14 Feb 2024
26. Cello Coach. https://play.google.com/store/apps/details?id=net.precise_team.cellocoach&hl=en_US&gl=US. Accessed 14 Feb 2024

27. Khan, S.N.: Qualitative Research Method: Grounded Theory. (n.d.). International Journal of Business and Management (2014)
28. Braun, V., Clarke, V.: Thematic analysis. In: Cooper, H., Camic, P. M., Long, D.L., Panter, A.T., Rindskopf, D., Sher, K. J. (eds.) APA Handbook of Research Methods in Psychology, Vol. 2, pp. 57–71. American Psychological Association (2012)

Unlocking Interactive Learning: Applying Bioecological Theory to Parent-Child Interaction in Educational Product Design

Chuxia Shen and Fan Yang[✉]

Guangzhou Academy of Fine Arts, No. 257, Changgang East Road, Haizhu District, Guangzhou, China
antony4d@hotmail.com

Abstract. The existing educational products of parent-child interaction have lost the two-way reciprocal nature of parenting education. The Bioecological Theory concept of interaction between multi-layer systems is consistent with the theory of Product Design Theory. In view of this, the purpose of this study is to explore the potential links between these two areas and to explore whether Bioecological Theory can help improve product innovation for children and parents. We conducted a case study with an industry-leading provider in Shenzhen. In the first stage, we distributed questionnaires to 99 parents of K6-K9 children to understand their views, daily interactions with children, communication styles, and preferences for learning devices. In the second stage, 12 children and their parents were selected from people in the first stage of the study for Non-participatory observation. From the data obtained, we established a framework to describe the interaction model based on the concept of interaction between multi-layer systems of Bioecological Theory, and sorted out an improvement strategy 'Dynamic Interaction, Two-way Reciprocity, Long-term Participation, Adaptability'. These outputs were subsequently evaluated with company experts and received positive feedback. This study affirms the two-way reciprocal and dynamic development of parent-child interaction. The Bioecological Theory reveals that the complex interaction between different systems needs to be considered in the design of parent-child interactive education products. At the same time, it also provides a reference for how to correctly apply Bioecological Theory in the study of parent-child relationship.

Keywords: Product Design · Bioecological Theory · Parent-child Interaction · Educational Science Popularization Products

1 Research Background

Educational Science Popularization at home play a vital role in the current children's education. By extending the learning environment outside the classroom, it provides children with educational resources and activities to explore at home, encourages parents and children to learn together, and uses the power of parent-child interaction to enrich the educational experience. Professor Zhou Yuru points out that the theme of parent-child interaction in education is everyone in the parent-child relationship, emphasizing the importance of 'together' [1]. How to achieve meaningful parent-child interaction has always been a dynamic and evolving challenge. The digital divide of parent-child interaction and the emergence of multi-form smart devices have led to an imbalance in the interaction mode of parents, children and products in the educational products interaction process [2]. In the process of using educational products, children place their emotions on the products, and the emotional collision between parents and children and the human-computer interaction are less, becoming a role that can be replaced by others at any time [3]. Xiao Cuihong pointed out that the monotony, inequality, content limitations in parent-child interaction education will have a negative impact on children's development, and the way of parent-child interaction in family education and parents' own factors will have a certain impact on children's development [4].

In the initial research, we revealed some problems exposed by parent-child interactive Educational Science Popularization products on the market. The following three points are listed here: 1) The boundary between play and teaching is not clear; 2) The sense of parent-child is weak, which does not reflect the particularity of parent-child role; 3) Lack of long-term interest in a positive learning environment. The second point is particularly important, forming a common problem in the industry's products. The specific performance is that the existing parent-child interaction products are more confined to the one-way level of children's cognitive and emotional needs, ignoring the role positioning and needs of parents, so that the Educational Science Popularization products lose the two-way reciprocal nature of parent-child interaction.

The factors that influence the imbalance of parent-child interaction in Educational Science Popularization products come from many aspects. In addition to the characteristics of children's own development, they also include factors to parents. The field of psychology is one of the main research fields of parent-child interaction. The earliest American psychologist D. Baumrind in 1971, through the study of family environment and parents' behavior, explored parent-child interaction in parenting style and child development characteristics, and emphasized the one-way behavior of parents in parent-child interaction [5]. In the study of parent-child interaction, we found that parents' behavior and participation attitude Attitude have a two-way effect on children. Close parent-child relationship and effective parent-child interaction can stimulate children's curiosity and exploration. In the face of children's curiosity about why, parents who are impatient and do not understand parent-child interaction will inhibit the multiple possibilities of children's development, and choosing not to answer will reduce children's interest in exploration; choosing perfunctory answers or wrong answers is more likely to cause the consequences of wrong education for growing children [6]. Carson J L et al. (1996) examined the relationship between preschool children's peer interaction ability and their negative emotional performance in games with their parents. If parents respond negatively to a child's negative emotional performance, the child's sharing behavior is less, aggressive behavior is more, and avoidance behavior is more [7]. Nowadays, the more mature development in this field is the Bioecological Theory proposed by psychologist Urie Bronfenbrenner in 1979. The theory is rooted in the two-way nature of the influence between parents and children, which emphasizes the importance of considering the complex interactions between multi-layer systems when exploring human development. These systems extend from inside to outside in turn are: the Micro system refers to the direct environment of individual activities, the Mesosystem refers to associated with multiple micro systems, the Exosystem refers to the indirect generation of Microsystems, the Macro system refers to the cultural and social environment that exists in the above three systems, and the Chronosystem that reveals the environmental system and its mechanism of action varies from time to time [8].

This theory was supported by Sameroff et al. (2003), who proposed a transactional models of development, which indicates that development is complex, interrelated and interactive [9]. The work of both scholars emphasizes the dynamics and reciprocity of parent-child interaction. On the basis of Sameroff's transactional models of development, Zhang Xiao, Chen Huichang et al. (2008) in the Department of Psychology of the University of Hong Kong proved that there is a two-way interaction between parent-child relationship and children's problem behavior in the early parent-child interaction of children's growth, and improved the interaction model of early parent-child relationship and children's problem behavior [10].

We sort out the viewpoints in the existing literature, as shown in Table 1, and find that many studies have similarities, indicating that parent-child interaction is a complex system intertwined with multiple influencing factors, and different factors are interrelated and bidirectional.

However, we note that the current research on parent-child interaction is often limited to the field of Psychological Education and Preschool Education, and the research conclusions are too single. For the complex system of Product Design Theory, the research reference provided is often not comprehensive enough. The concept of Bioecological Theory considering the interaction between multi-layer systems is consistent with Product Design Theory. In view of this, the purpose of this study is to explore the potential links between these two areas and to explore whether Bioecological Theory can help improve product innovation for children and parents.

2 Methods

In order to study the applicability of Bioecological Theory in Educational Science Popularization products design, we conducted a case study with an industry-leading provider in Shenzhen. The selected target population is K6-K9 children (grades 1–4 of Chinese primary schools). The research method is divided into two parts. The first part distributed online questionnaires to the parents of the target children to collect learning needs in different family backgrounds, the frequency of daily parent-child interaction, and the main types of educational products used. In the second part, considering the principle of convenient sampling, we selected 12 children and their parents from those who participated in the first stage to use the Educational Science Popularization products, and adopted non-participatory observation, that is, the observer does not directly intervene in the middle of the observation object, but after recording the video, observe the process of parent-child game, and only collect the interactive video to objectively record and analyze the process of interaction. At the end of the study, we evaluated these outputs with company experts and conducted follow-up visits to families involved in the study.

Table 1. Research on the influencing factors of parent-child interaction

Influencing factor	Scholar	Main viewpoints
Parents' attitudes and behaviors	Symonds Carson J L, Parke R D Napier C Kildare C A, Middlemiss W	In the face of children's questions, parents' inappropriate answers may inhibit children's development [5] Parents' negative emotional expression in the game has an impact on children's peer interaction ability [6] Parents who turn on the TV during the interaction are less sensitive to their children, and the noise of the TV can hinder parent-child communication [11] Parents who use mobile phones in parent-child interaction are not sensitive to their children's verbal or nonverbal reactions, which reduces the quality of parent-child interaction [12]
Characteristics of a mother	Cox A D, Puckering C, Pound A et al McMahon C A, Meins E Cao Ruixin, Xia Meiping, Chen Huichang et al Lu Shan, Si Chen, Wang Zhengyan et al	The quality of interaction between depressed mothers and their children is poor [8] Mothers with higher sensitivity use a more positive state when playing with their children [13] Mother's speech can predict the non-compliance behavior of toddlers [14]
		The speech style of Chinese mothers has its own characteristics. There are differences in the speech style of mothers from different income families in parent-child interaction [15]

(*continued*)

Table 1. (*continued*)

Influencing factor	Scholar	Main viewpoints
Characteristics of the father	Cabrera N J, Shannon J D, Tamis-LeMonda C Schwartz J I	Low-educated fathers often find it more difficult to develop positive and sensitive relationships with their children [16] Compared to mothers, fathers are more likely to use more direct and closed questions, which may hinder interaction with their children [17]
Characteristics of children	Katainen S, Raïkkönen K, Keltikangas-Järvinen L Yu Shoujuan	There is a low to moderate stability between children's temperament dimension and mother's parenting attitude [18] The difference in the age of the child will affect the way the mother guides her reading [19]
Family economic level	Wu Yan, Lin Tong, Li Wen et al Tao Cuiping Mccormick, C.E. & Mason, J.M Yu Shoujuan	Families with higher annual income are more likely to have a higher level of parent-child interaction [20] Highly educated and high-income families will pay more attention to the development of parent-child reading activities [21] The economic level of the family has a certain influence on the development of children's early reading ability. Families with high economic level pay more attention to the development of children's reading ability [10] Mothers with higher education have a more comprehensive understanding of parent-child reading, and pay more attention to guiding children to participate in reading and express their own ideas [19]

2.1 Date Collection

In the first stage of the study, we designed a questionnaire survey for quantitative research. The main content was to investigate the frequency of parent-child interaction and the Educational Science Popularization products used in different family backgrounds. In order to make the credibility of the research information and the reference value of the research results to the follow-up practice, the sample selection of this questionnaire is positioned as the parents of K6-K9 children. The questionnaire is edited and accurately delivered to the WeChat group of primary school parents through the Questionnaire Star. The problem setting is divided into the following four aspects: 1) Basic information of the target user's parents, to understand the situation of their family children and the brief family economic and cultural background; 2) Daily interaction mode, to understand the types of activities and interaction methods of daily parent-child interaction. For example, RQ1: 'What are the types of activities that interact with children on a daily basis?' and RQ2: 'usually enhance communication?' 3) Home Education Popular Science products, to understand the use of such products and the use of feelings, such as RQ3: 'What are the factors that affect your experience of parent-child interaction in Education Popular Science products?' 4) The proportion and optimal expectation of parental involvement in household education science popularization products and parent-child interaction. And at the end, we set up open questions to encourage them to leave contact information for subsequent research. For example, 'is it convenient to leave your contact information as a follow-up interview. The whole process is confidential only for research'.

In the second stage of the study, we used a purposive sampling method to select 12 children and their parents from the participants in the first stage of Guangdong Province for non-participatory observation. In order to facilitate the experimental comparison and reference, all the subjects recruited were from different family backgrounds. There were 8 pairs of parents who had been exposed to family parent-child education products, of which 5 pairs were still insisting on using such products to improve family parent-child education, and the other 3 pairs were no longer using such products. There are also 4 pairs of parents who have heard of but have not used such products. We explained the purpose of the study to parents and children and obtained written consent. The twelve families were designated as F1-F12, and the process of each use of home-based parent-child interactive education products with children was recorded by the observer using a two-camera camera tool at home. The experiment was divided into four groups, each group was controlled at about 30–45 min. We sorted out the basic information table of the research object, as shown in Table 2.

Four groups of experiments included four types of products, and these participants were asked to use them separately during the observation period. These four products are selected by the cooperative enterprises from the four aspects of educational value, interest, re-play, and applicable parent-child education for K6-K9 children in the market, aiming to cultivate children's attention, emotional management and rule awareness. Includes AR globes made by partner vendors, online learning software called 'Epic Audio Book', Blue Orange's board game 'My Planet' and DK's paper book 'Fun stereo encyclopedia Space'. The basic information of the four experimental materials is shown in Table 3 below.

Table 2. User basic information table

Numbering	User	Occupation	Children information	Basic information of users and families
F1	Ms. Shao	Mentor	10-year-old son	As a geography teacher, he often guides questions with children and purchases after-school education products to assist
F2	Ms. Xing	Civil servant	9-year-old daughter	Attaches great importance to children's communication, after work will be free together parent-child activities
F3	Ms.Cheng	State-owned enterprise staff	9-year-old son	Busy work, occasionally use holidays to play with
F4	Mr. Huang	Designer	10-year-old daughter	Working time flexibility, use of this type of product, but allow more willing to apply for research classes
F5	Ms. Guo	Doctor	10-year-old daughter	Purchased parent-child education products, but because of work, most of them are used alone by their children
F6	Mr. Zhou	Businessman	14 years old daughter 9 years old son	Most of the time you need to travel, pay attention to communication with children, but do not know how to communicate
F7	Danny	Lawyer	9-year-old son	Purchased this type of product, the child likes, sometimes the parent-child sometimes the child completed independently

(*continued*)

Table 2. (*continued*)

Numbering	User	Occupation	Children information	Basic information of users and families
F8	Ms. Chen	Housewife	10-year-old son	Time is abundant, and there is a fixed time to interact with it after school every day
F9	Ms. Lee	Company employees	7-year-old daughter	No such products are purchased, but in the expected preparation
F10	Ms. Wu	Liberal profession	year-old 8-year-old son	Most of the time need to take care of the little daughter, son weekend interested in counseling, did not buy this kind of product
F11	Ms. Gong	Teacher	8-year-old son	I've bought a lot of this type of product, but kids are interested in it for a while
F12	Mr. Xu	Fitness coach	8-year-old daughter 12-year-old son	Communicate with children more in daily life, subject class rarely involves active discussion

2.2 Date Analysis

Based on the audio data obtained from the experiment, we compare and analyze the materials from two aspects according to the influence concept of different systems of Bioecological Theory, that is, different experimental materials are based on the same experimental family group, and the summary of the influencing factors of the materials on children; the same experimental material is located in different experimental family groups, and the differences in the interaction between different systems and individuals are compared. It includes the Microsystem directly related to children, the Mesosystem associated with each micro-system, and the Exosystem that children do not directly participate in but have an impact. Since the source of the experiment is the interaction between parents and children at a single stage, which is a short-term experimental result, the Macro system and the Chronosystem here are not considered. We classify the influencing factors of the disorder by universality and difference, link the interaction between multi-layer systems, establish a framework to describe the interaction mode, and determine the key influencing factors. Subsequently, these outputs were assessed with the company's experts, and follow-up visits were conducted to the families involved in the study.

Table 3. Basic information of experimental materials

Product	'Epic Audio Book ' Online learning software	AR globe	Board game 'My Planet'	Paper album ' Fun Stereo Encyclopedia Space'
Target population	Children aged 7-9 years	Children aged 6-10 years	Children aged 6+	Children aged 9-10 years
Product positioning	The bilingual education software that focuses on children 's audio picture books and reading combines education and entertainment content in depth.	A hardware product that uses AR intelligence to make geography knowledge 3D emerge.	Geographical theme scene desktop game suitable for multi-person reasoning mechanism.	A 3D stereoscopic book about children 's interesting space knowledge popularization.
Functional design	1) Contents related to disciplines, children 's science, DIY, educational Lego, bilingual interaction, etc. 2) Presentation methods include dynamic audio books and experimental mini-tests. 3) Promoting the experience of question and answer sessions. 4) Reward mechanisms such as medals and coins.	1) Basic knowledge of children 's geography, including astronomy, culture, domestic and foreign geography. 2) Using AR stereo suspension and point reading pen. 3) AI voice question answering assistant. 4) Knowledge game experience.	1) Spatial planning of hexahedron planet. 2) Abundant game accessories, easy to operate. 3) Understanding of subject knowledge in the game. 4) Multi-person joint interaction to enhance the sense of experience.	1) Pulling three-dimensional design, breaking the rigid traditional paper atlas. 2) Funny small questions and answers to improve reading interaction. 3) Scan code video real-time viewing.

3 Result

3.1 Questionnaire Survey Analysis

A total of 99 online questionnaires and 20 offline questionnaires were received in this survey. A total of 119 questionnaires were screened out of 12 invalid questionnaires, and 107 valid questionnaires were finally obtained. Among the parents surveyed, 89.9% were from Guangdong Province, with different family backgrounds and educational backgrounds. Through investigation, we found that the proportion of multi-child second-child families in this area was 56.57%. Except for working days, 37.37% were arranged interest counseling courses on weekends. Most parents (86.86%) have a high degree of participation in their children's after-school counseling.87.88% of parents have purchased household popular science products, but only 50% of them have actually used such products for parent-child interaction. The reason is that 79.31% of parents do not understand geographical knowledge, and 41.38% of parents are in a passive state of answering questions, which makes more than half of parents (50%) feel mediocre or bad about the experience of existing parent-child interaction products. At the same time, due to factors such as time, energy, communication, content, and children themselves, 63.64% of parents want to intervene in the use of educational products by their children. The proportion is 15–35%.

We analyzed and summarized the questionnaire survey data, as shown in Table 4, and found that the new user information is consistent with the parent-child interaction problems shown in previous studies. The questionnaire shows that most parents (85.32%) attach importance to the interaction with their children, but many factors lead to the difficulty of forming a real two-way interaction between parents and children, and the imbalance of participation experience between parents and children. These multifaceted effects include parents' lack of active awareness of parent-child interaction, failure to play a good way of guiding, and different angles of thinking between parents and children will produce certain communication barriers, which will accelerate the consumption of energy and patience in the process of parent-child interaction. In the use of educational science products, parents' cognitive status of this type of product is in two states: Knowing and using it and Knowing but not using it. The understanding and use of parents in the two-way interaction to pursue a deeper level of demand, specifically reflected in the reasonable proportion between parent-child intervention and children's independence, as well as the quality control screening of such products in content communication and interactive experience. The research results also show that the influencing factors of parent-child interaction experience come from energy, time, communication, product elements and so on. For the existing family Education Popular Science products on the market, from the perspective of purchase rate, parent-child interaction frequency, and children's interest, the selection of paper-based atlas products is the highest, followed by online software learning platforms, intelligent hardware products, and multi-person interactive board games. For those parents who know but have not used it, they also give their reasons. Most parents (79.31%) are familiar with the following stages of geography science knowledge, so they are more willing to spend money on professional after-school counseling for their children. At the same time, they put forward some doubts on the choice of educational popular science products on the market. Due to children's learning content is rich and broad, while the replacement iteration of paper-based map products is high. Online software learning platforms need to borrow smart devices such as mobile phones or ipads. If they do not strictly control the duration of use, they are worried that children will become overly addicted.

Table 4. Research summary table

	Parent-child interaction mode	Educational science products	
Background	Most parents attach importance to the interaction between children	Know and use	Understood but not used
Questions	It is difficult to form a real two-way interaction between parents and children, and there is an imbalance Parents lack the awareness of parent-child interaction and do not know how to interact Parents and children lack patience in interaction Different angles of thinking lead to certain communication barriers	Parents prefer to bring two-way satisfaction and happiness in the interaction The proportion between parent-child intervention and children's independence and autonomy can have a reasonable effective value Most parents prioritize content communication and interactive experience when choosing this type of product The factors that affect the interactive experience are limited energy, lack of time, communication difficulties, content one-way From the purchase rate, parent-child interaction frequency, children's interest in the use of factors such as View album > Software > Hardware > Desktop games	Most parents are familiar with the following stages of geography science knowledge There are additional after-school tutoring for children, and there is too little free time Paper version brochure products have high replacement iterations, and software products have limited usage time, worrying about excessive addiction Hope that interactive products are creative

3.2 Analysis of Non-participatory Results

According to the observation and analysis of the parent-child interaction of 12 groups of families in the game process, we classify the current situation and behavior categories of parent-child interaction, as shown in Table 5. Sort out common practices when children interact with their parents and their behaviors when children encounter difficulties in games, and substitute them into the family numbers of the experimental group. We found that the typical parent-child interaction model can be roughly divided into three categories: 1) Guiding type, in the interaction process does not give an answer, focusing on throwing questions to guide children to think independently; 2) Explanation type, along with the interaction from the beginning to the end of the role of teachers to play the role of children to explain the game; 3) Instructional type, the way of parent-child interaction is mostly followed by instructions. For the guided experimental group, the overall quality of parent-child experience is high, and the proportion of parent-child intervention is balanced with the proportion of children's independent thinking. By observing the video and audio, we found that the parent-child interaction audio is intermittent when the parents are in a spectator state, which reduces the child's concentration. Compared with mothers, fathers' interaction tends to be more directive or directly giving answers, lacking children's sense of experience, and it is easy to develop a dependence on directly asking questions without understanding the questions to get answers. From the side, it also proves that the father of the previous study may interact with the child in a more direct and closed way. For products with unclear parent-child division of labor, experimental groups that have not been exposed to this type of product are prone to be transformed into parent-led, thus lacking experience.

According to the influence concept of different systems of Bioecological Theory, we compared the differences in the interaction between different systems and individuals in the same experimental material located in different experimental family groups. By sorting out the universality and difference of the messy influencing factors and linking the interaction between multi-layer systems, a framework describing the interaction mode is established, and the key influencing factors are determined. As shown in Fig. 1, which contains:

Microsystem. Direct contact with children. Although the twelve groups of subjects are located in K6-K9, the children's own cognitive characteristics are controlled in a large range. However, there are still differences. For children who have been exposed to such products, they are more active in the process of interaction and more adaptable to the products. Children with different personality traits perform differently in the interaction process of the same experimental material. Boys are more active and less patient than girls.

Mesosysystem. The interrelated system between each Microsystem, which is embodied in the characteristics of parents, parents' educational ideas, brothers and sisters of multi-child families in different experimental groups. These factors will produce differences in parents' attitudes and behaviors, which will lead to differences in the impact of parent-child interaction. Individual families in the experimental group have added diversity of medium-system influencing factors to children's interest counseling.

Table 5. Experimental group observation summary table

Interactive status	Type of behaviour	Typical user number
Common practices when interacting with children	Watch the children play on the sidelines and give help if necessary	F3, F5, F10
	Cooperate with the child after being invited by the child	F2, F7, F12
	Actively invite children and negotiate to play together	F1, F4, F8, F11
	Let the children follow their parents' ideas	F6, F9
Parents' practice when children encounter difficulties in the game	Let the child think of his own way, depending on the situation	F8, F10, F12
	After the child 's' help', tell the solution	F3, F4, F5, F11
	After noticing, immediately give hand-in-hand help	F2, F6, F9
	Guiding throw prompts for children to solve	F1, F7

Exosystem. Children are not directly involved but have an impact, including differences in the nature and income level of parents' work, family background and living environment. It shows that parents' work has different class backgrounds and income levels, and the emphasis on children's parent-child interaction will be different. The higher the family's economic level, the more comprehensive the understanding of children's parent-child interaction.

Macrosystem. The experimental groups are all from China, so the social and cultural background here, the core education system did not see significant differences.

For different experimental materials based on the same experimental family group, the summary of the material's influence factors on children, we selected 20 influencing factors from the latitude of product content and experience mode to designate a Likert scale, 1 is the lowest impact, 5 is the highest impact. And the adults of these 12 groups of families were scored on the Educational Science Popularization products elements that affect parent-child interaction, so as to screen out the positive influencing factors of 50% of the participants as the higher factors affecting the parent-child experience obtained from our experimental results. As shown in Table 6, We found that the changing needs and interests of parents and children require products to have adaptive and personalized functions. In addition, factors such as interactive tests, collaborative activities and appropriate discussion tips in Educational Science Popularization products will affect the two-way interaction between parents and children. Good forms of interaction can generate meaningful communication and dialogue in the process of interaction. For example, user-friendly interface, different views, language and cultural elements of

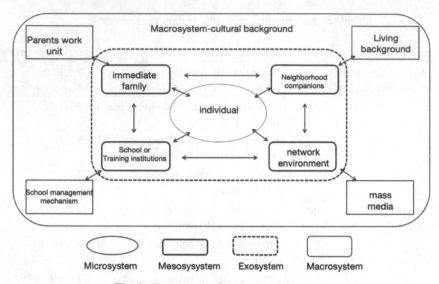

Fig. 1. Framework of the interaction pattern

Table 6. Factors affecting parent-child experience in experimental materials

	Product elements	Embodiment
Dynamic interaction	Dynamic changes in demand	Customizable content, progress tracking and personalized learning paths in our products ensure that the educational experience is tailored to the unique dynamics of each parent-child relationship and to the changing needs and interests of parents and children
Two-way reciprocity	Two-way interactive function	Interactive tests, collaborative activities or shared exploration models in Educational Science Popularization products can integrate the functions of encouraging two-way interaction between parents and children
	Communication Enhancement Tools	Discussion tips or collaborative projects can encourage parents and children to have meaningful conversations while exploring geographical concepts

(*continued*)

Table 6. (*continued*)

	Product elements	Embodiment
Adaptability	Cultural sensitivity and inclusiveness	Integrating different perspectives, language and cultural elements into Educational Science Popularization products can resonate between parents and children with different experience backgrounds
	User-friendly interface for all ages	Ensure that the product is friendly to parents and children of different ages. The interface should be intuitive to meet the diverse needs of users in parent-child relationship
Long-term participation	feedback mechanism	In-product progress reports, achievement badges, or parent-child feedback loops create a continuous and positive learning environment
	Characteristics of long-term participation	Gamification methods, progressive courses, or reward systems that encourage long-term continuous participation and learning can develop elements that promote continuous interest and participation
	Family-centered activities	Family-centered challenges, collaborative projects, or multi-person models can enhance shared learning experiences and strengthen parent-child relationships

all ages resonate with different backgrounds of parent-child pairing; the gamification method, progressive curriculum and learning reward system can create a continuous and positive learning environment for long-term participation.

By combining the characteristics described by multiple product elements, we have sorted out an improvement strategy. For example, expressing educational experience requires 'dynamic interaction' that is suitable for the dynamic needs of parents and children; stimulate parent-child two-way interaction in the product, enhance the communication between the two sides of the 'two-way reciprocity'; integrate into different experience backgrounds to meet the 'adaptability' of friendly content of all ages; the multi-person model with feedback mechanism, progressive curriculum and family-centered development can promote the 'long-term participation' of parent-child sustainable development.

4 Discussion and Conclusion

The purpose of this study was to explore the potential link between Bioecological Theory and product research and design through non-participatory observations of purposeful sampling experimental groups to see whether Bioecological Theory can help improve product innovation for children and parents. In the initial research, we revealed the nature of the loss of two-way reciprocity between parents and children exposed by the existing parent-child interaction products through the investigation of Educational Science Popularization products on the market. It affirms the problems of monotony, inequality and content limitation in parent-child education pointed out by (Xiao Cuihong et al., 2007) [4]. Through the questionnaire survey of a large number of experimental samples, we found that most parents attach importance to the interaction with their children and are in the process of understanding or purchasing family Educational Science Popularization products. However, the results are derived from China's first-tier developing cities and do not have the universality of the results in other regions. From the side, it also puts forward whether urban culture and economic level have a certain impact on parent-child interaction education? Most parents choose to send children to interest counseling classes because of their lack of good guidance awareness of parent-child interaction and lack of understanding of geography popular science knowledge, which occupies the rest time that children should have, and also accelerates the reduction of parent-child communication quality. As the scholar Zhou Yuru mentioned, the theme of parent-child interaction in education is everyone in the parent-child relationship, emphasizing the importance of 'together' [1]. In the study of parent-child interactive education products, if the key nature of two-way reciprocity is ignored, it will still be criticized by the industry today.

Through the observation and analysis of 12 groups of experimental subjects, we found that the influencing factors of these problems come from many aspects. In addition to the characteristics of children themselves, they also include the attitudes and behaviors of parents in the process of interaction, and these factors are influenced by the characteristics of father or mother, family economic level and so on. In other words, parent-child interaction is a complex system intertwined with multiple influencing factors, and different factors are interrelated and bidirectional. This further confirms the potential link between Bioecological Theory and Product Design Theory, both of which consider the importance of complex interactions between multi-layer systems. Through the typical behavior classification of the two interaction states of parents' common practices when interacting with children and parents' coping performance when children encounter difficulties in the game, we find that the performance of parents in the whole process of parent-child interaction has a certain impact on stimulating children's curiosity and exploration desire. The best parent-child interaction is the two-way cooperation between parents and children, focusing on the guiding consciousness of solving problems. Parents who lack the awareness of correct parent-child interaction will inhibit the multiple possibilities of children's development. And the characteristics of differences between parents are not the same as the sensitivity of children's emotional state.

In the study, based on the Macro, Meso and Micro perspectives of Bioecological Theory, we link the interaction between multi-layer systems from the perspective of the relationship between Multiple systems and Microsystems of parent-child interaction and the direct environmental level of individual activities, establish a framework to describe the interaction mode, and determine the key influencing factors. The theory is not limited to the current sample data. For parent-child interaction in different countries, substituting its cultural background and sample data of each system can also provide us with a clear link between multi-layer systems of parent-child interaction. At the end of the experiment, we screened out the factors that affect the parent-child experience in the parent-child interaction education products by scoring the influencing factors in the experimental materials by the parents of the experimental group, and proposed an improvement strategy 'Dynamic Interaction, Two-way Reciprocity, Long-term Participation, Adaptability'. That is, when designing parent-child interaction for educational products, we need to think about how the product affects children and parents, and how their interaction evolves over time; consider how both sides shape each other's behavioral experience in the learning process; how to promote the continuous interest in geography and develop a positive and collaborative learning environment over time; how to allow flexibility and adapt to the changing needs and interests of both sides. We use this improvement strategy for partner experts and relevant participating users to evaluate. Almost all participants in the strategy improvement satisfaction survey pointed out that these influencing factors are effective in solving the criticism of parent-child interaction education products on the market today, and said that the design practice guided by the strategy may help parents improve their true understanding of parent-child interaction when using such products.

Acknowledgments. This study was supported by Guangdong Planning Office of Philosophy and Social Science (Grant No. GD24CYS41); and the Department of Education of Guangdong Province (Grant No. 2023WTSCX052, and Grant No. 2023GXJK347).

References

1. Yuru, Z., Niyu, H.: Review of the relationship between parent-child reading emotional speech and children's emotional understanding ability. J. Educ. Sci. Res. **55**(3) (2010)
2. Yazhi, Z.: Research on Emotional Design of Parent-Child Interaction Products. Southeast (2022).https://doi.org/10.27014/d.cnki.gdnau.2020.002786
3. Chiasson, S., Gutwin, C.: Design princles for children's technoligy. Interfaces **7** (2005)
4. Cuihong, X.: Parent-child interaction and children's socialization. Educ. Pract. Res. (Primary School Edition) **09**, 4–6 (2007)
5. Baumrin, D.: Current patterns of parental authority. Developmental Psychology Monographs 4 (1971)
6. Symonds. Origins of personality. Dailer W R. Readings in psychology of human growth an development New York. Holt, Rinehart & Winston Inc. (1962)
7. Carson, J.L., Parke, R.D.: Reciprocal negative affect in parent-child interactions and children's peer competency. Child Dev.ild Dev. **67**(5), 2217–2226 (1996)
8. Bronfenbrenner, U., Ceci, S.J.: Nature-nuture reconceptualized in developmental perspective: a bioecological model. Psychol. Rev. **101**(4), 568 (1994)

9. Sameroff, A.J., Machenzie, M.J.: Research strategies for capturing transactional models of development: the limits of the possible. Dev. Psychopathol. **15**, 613–640 (2003)

10. Zhang, X., Chen, H., Zhang, G., et al.: A Dynamic Interaction Model of Parent-Child Relationship and Problem Behavior: A Longitudinal Study of Early Childhood. University of Hong Kong (2008)

11. Napier, C.: How use of screen media affects the emotional development of infants. Primary Health Care **24**(2), 18–25 (2014)

12. Kildare, C.A., Middlemiss, W.: Impact of parent's mobile device use on parent-child interaction: a literature review. Comput. Hum. Behav. **75**, 579–593 (2017)

13. McMahon, C.A., Meins, E.: Mind-mindedness, parenting stress, and emotional availability in mothers of preschoolers. Early Child Res. Q. **27**(2), 245–252 (2012)

14. Ruixin, C., Meiping, X., Huichang, C., et al.: Children's noncompliance at 2 years of age predicts social adjustment between 4 and 11 years of age. Chin. J. Psychol. **42**(5), 581–586 (2010)

15. Shan, L., Chen, S., Zhengyan, W., et al.: A preliminary study on mother 's speech input style in early parent-child interaction. Chin. J. Child Health **22**(3), 258–260 (2014)

16. Cabrera, N.J., Shannon, J.D., Tamis-LeMonda, C.: Fathers' influence on their children's cognitive and emotional development: from toddlers to pre-K. Appl. Dev. Sci. **11**(4), 208–213 (2007)

17. Schwartz, J.I.: An observational study of mother/child and father/child interactions in story reading. J. Res. Child. Educ. **19**(2), 105–114 (2004)

18. Katainen, S., Raïkkönen, K., Keltikangas-Järvinen, L.: Childhood temperament and mother's child-rearing attitudes: stability and interaction in a three-year follow-up study. Eur. J. Pers. **11**(4), 249–265 1997

19. Yu, S.: Research on Parent-Child Co-Reading Mode of Different Types of Picture Books for Children Aged 4–6. Shanghai Normal University (2018)

20. Yan, W., Tong, L., Wen, L., et al.: A cross-sectional survey of parent-child interaction and early childhood development in new kindergarten children in Shanghai. Chin. J. Evid.-Based Pediatr. **15**(6), 406 (2020)

21. Cuiping, T.: Investigation on the Current Situation and Influencing Factors of Parent-Child Reading in Urban Children's Families. Shenyang Normal University, Shenyang (2013)

Research on an Educational Toy for Preschool Children's Oral Care Based on Persuasive Design

Xiaoying Tang⬤, Silu Zheng⬤, Yibing Chen(✉)⬤, and Zitao Liu⬤

Guangdong University of Technology, No. 729 Dongfeng Road, Yuexiu District, Guangzhou, Guangdong, China

cyb1224@126.com

Abstract. In China's rapid urbanization, the dietary structure of preschool children tends to be high in sugar, fat, and salt. Due to increased economic and employment pressures, some Chinese families have adopted intergenerational education where children are cared for by their grandparents, who are usually not educated in modern oral health care knowledge, which leads to a lack of proper understanding of children's oral care and makes it difficult for them to effectively guide their children in proper oral care behaviors. The prevalence of early childhood caries in younger children is alarming. The main objective of this study was to develop a science-based toy product on oral care knowledge aimed at encouraging preschoolers to perform proper oral care and prevent dental caries. This study is guided by the FBM model and refers to Professor Fogg's persuasion technique, which was developed in five stages: identifying persuasive behaviors -identifying target users -analyzing the elements of user behavioral persuasion --Selecting appropriate persuasion strategies -Designing practices. By designing the children's game-based brushing method, we guide children to complete the oral care process in a fun way while fighting with monsters, correcting incorrect brushing postures in time, and ensuring the duration of children's brushing, to realize the correct process of brushing teeth on their own. We hope that this product can guide children to change bad oral care methods, establish healthy oral care habits, realize the stimulation of children's internal drive to care for their teeth and prevent children's dental caries.

Keywords: Persuasion design · oral care · preschoolers · science toy design · principal component analysis

1 Introduction

Oral problems are an important part of ensuring the overall health and quality of life of children [1–5]. Early childhood caries (ECC) is defined as a preschooler with one or more decayed teeth that have been lost or filled due to dental caries. The prevalence of ECC has become a global public health problem, especially due to its high prevalence which has triggered widespread concern [6–9].

© The Author(s), under exclusive license to Springer Nature Switzerland AG 2024
A. Marcus et al. (Eds.): HCII 2024, LNCS 14715, pp. 219–237, 2024.
https://doi.org/10.1007/978-3-031-61359-3_16

During China's rapid urbanization and modernization, the dietary structure of preschool children has changed from coarse grains and vegetables to one dominated by refined grains, meat, and a large amount of highly processed foods and beverages [10], which is an important reason for the dramatic increase in the rate of dental caries. Along with the increase in economic and employment pressures, some Chinese families have adopted intergenerational education, where children are cared for by their grandparents, who are mostly uneducated in modern oral health care knowledge and lack a correct understanding of children's oral care, making it difficult to effectively guide children to form good oral care habits [11–14]. Therefore, it is of vital significance to use special means to guide children to perform oral care correctly and develop good oral care habits. In this paper, we will combine the theory of persuasive design to explore the design opportunities in the process of children's oral care, to guide preschool children's dental care behaviors with gamified brushing, to help them develop good oral care habits, and to ultimately improve children's oral health.

2 Related Work

2.1 Current Status of Research on Children's Oral Care

According to the Fourth National Oral Health Epidemiologic Survey of the National Health Commission of China, the prevalence of tooth decay among 5-year-old children in China has increased by 5.8% from 66.1% to 70.9% over the past decade [15]. Children's reluctance to brush their teeth, incorrect brushing methods, and insufficient brushing time all increase the risk of dental caries. Therefore, guiding children to establish proper oral care habits during the preschool years is the key to improving children's oral health.

In the fields of dentistry, child health, and public health, scholars have generally paid attention to the importance of oral care education for children and have explored different educational methods and technological approaches in the prevention and treatment of ECC [16–19], including studies on the prevalence of dental caries in preschool children and the influencing factors leading to the occurrence of dental caries [11, 20, 21], different oral care methods and techniques in the prevention and treatment of dental caries in children [22–24], oral health education programs for preschool children and parents [25], and studies on the effectiveness and delivery of oral health education [26, 27]. These studies have provided valuable theoretical support and practical references for protecting preschoolers from dental caries, but scholars have not yet fully utilized science toys as an intervention tool to guide preschoolers through oral care.

2.2 Main Oral Health Education Methods and Features

Developing good oral care habits and self-drive through correct brushing methods, reasonable dietary habits, and regular oral checkups is an important way to maintain preventive ECC and oral health [28–30], and oral health education for preschoolers is crucial for lifelong oral education. The current oral health education methods for preschoolers mainly include: first, story picture books similar to "What's New on Tooth Street" convey correct oral health care information through interesting characters and plots, but the perspectives are mostly difficult to transform into the children's first perspective to be applied in self-oral care scenarios; second, the use of visual display carriers, such as pictures and videos, increases the degree of participation and helps the children to understand the correct oral hygiene methods intuitively. Oral hygiene methods, but may lack in-depth learning [23]; third, educators conduct imitative demonstrations in the classroom or at home through imitative learning theory to enable children to observe correct brushing postures and methods in depth, but may ignore children's differences and ability to learn on their own [24]. The current main oral health education methods and characteristics can be seen in Table 1.

Table 1. Oral Health Education Methods and Features

Method	Medium	Children's Abilities	Advantages	Disadvantages
The educator explains and demonstrates, that children imitate	Picture books, storybooks	Understand story plots and information	Enhances educational effectiveness, guides interest	May overlook other influencing factors, oversimplify content, insufficient for covering complex issues
Display educational materials, guide children to observe and imitate	Visual presentation forms such as pictures, videos	Visual and auditory perception	Intuitively demonstrates correct methods, improves learning effectiveness	This may lead to superficial understanding, lack of in-depth comprehension
The educator demonstrates children imitate	Teaching demonstrations, imitative tasks	Observation and imitation of others' behavior	Facilitates learning of correct postures and methods	May neglect individual differences and independent learning ability

It is important to guide user behavior and build an internal drive for children's dental care through children's oral care science and toy service systems. Oral care products are those products that clean human teeth or oral mucosa, reduce bad odors, maintain the oral cavity, and keep it in good condition by washing, scraping, rubbing, and gargling [31]. Toys are model objects used for children's entertainment, and are a bridge between young children and the real material world [32]; science toys are model objects used for teaching and entertainment. In China, the market for children's oral care products has great potential. Compared with developed countries such as Europe and the United States, the Chinese science toy market has serious homogenization problems, and the differentiation and professionalism of brands and products need to be improved.

2.3 Persuasive Design Theory

Persuasive Design or Persuasion Design, as a specific practice of persuasion theory, analyzes the content of users' behaviors with the help of psychological theories and methods and guides them in an appropriate way to change their attitudes or behaviors [33]. As Xin Xiangyang scholars proposed in 2020 "lifestyle is the context of design" [34], we can guide the occurrence of behavior by designing lifestyle. Persuasive design theory seeks to understand and explain how people change their self-behavior to achieve specific goals and is an important way to promote positive behavior change.

Professor BJ Fogg, a Stanford psychologist, proposed the Fogg Behavior Model (FBM) in 2009, which argues that behavior occurs when the three conditions of sufficient motivation, sufficient ability, and effective triggers are simultaneously met [35, 36]. Motivation is the source of behavior generation and represents the intrinsic or extrinsic drivers of user behavior [37]. Capability includes the ability of the target user and the ability to achieve the use behavior, which can be enhanced by improving the usability and ease of use of the product and reducing the difficulty of use to improve the capability factor. Behavioral triggers include Spark, Facilitator, and Signal. Depending on the scenario and the user's motivation and ability, appropriate triggers can be selected. In this study, we will take the FBM model as a guide, refer to Professor Fogg's persuasive technology to guide the design and practice of the relevant steps [38] and follow the idea of "determining persuasive behaviors - identifying the target users - analyzing the elements of user behavioral persuasion - selecting appropriate persuasive strategies - designing and practicing" to carry out the persuasive design of the children's oral care science and technology toys.

3 Defining Child Oral Care Persuasive Behaviors

Before executing the persuasive behaviors, we used a top-down goal decomposition technique to identify the child's oral care behaviors to be achieved by the persuasion in a goal-oriented manner, to quantify the tasks, and to plan the behavioral measures. The core process included:

Clarifying Goals. We clarify the goal of persuasion as assisting children to understand the importance of oral health and to develop good brushing habits, to improve children's oral health, and to prevent and reduce the occurrence of oral diseases such as low-grade caries.

Formation of Indicators. Combining the elements of persuasion design, we break down the objectives into persuasive indicators, including motivation indicators, i.e., actively brushing their teeth every morning and evening, and brushing for two minutes; and ability indicators, i.e., adopting correct brushing postures and methods.

Formulation Steps. We then developed the steps needed to reach the indicator. The team followed and recorded the dental cleaning process of the interviewees throughout the process and analyzed the children's main behaviors before, during, and after brushing, as shown in Fig. 1, capturing the children's emotional experiences within the steps of getting up, getting the toothbrush, squeezing the toothpaste, putting it in the mouth, brushing in the same position, asking for attention to be praised, brushing style, rinsing to finish, and encouraging style. We found that brushing style and encouragement were the sessions where children's emotions rose and fell, and were the core and foundational steps of oral care [30]. To achieve the motivation and competence indicators, we developed a series of steps including: purchasing appropriate oral care products and placing them in a place where children could easily focus on them as a reminder to brush their teeth; choosing appropriate ways to help children to perform oral care correctly; developing a plan to ensure the length of children's dental care; and praising or rewarding children after completing daily oral care tasks to increase their motivation.

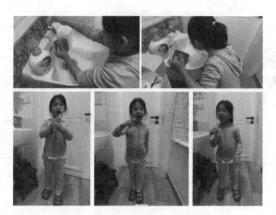

Fig. 1. User Behavior Observation Chart

Assessing Behaviors. Finally, we assess the appropriate persuasive behaviors to ensure that the child can achieve a sense of satisfaction, enjoyment, confidence, accomplishment, and contentment throughout the oral care process. This includes the following three main areas:

Motivational factors - Enhance internal and external drivers by designing fun oral care processes, setting rewards and praise, etc. to enhance the fun of the oral care process, thus satisfying children's psychological need to have fun.

Competence factor - Improve the ease of use, fault tolerance, and feasibility of the process of oral care products, which greatly reduces the difficulty for children to perform oral care correctly.

Trigger Factor - Help children develop proper dental care behaviors by encouraging them, providing teaching assistance, and giving positive feedback.

4   Identify Target Users

4.1   Analyzing the Target Population

Preschool children are the main users of oral care science toys. In this study, we interviewed and observed 4-year-old children and mapped the story world (see Fig. 2). During the interview, we recorded several salient events, and summarized and recorded the perceptions and expectations of the interviewee. As preschool-aged children, their main places of activity were home and kindergarten. In terms of oral hygiene, their behavior is mainly influenced by parents, kindergarten teachers, and pediatric dentists [39]. Parents supervise and assist their children in oral cleaning and check their oral health care daily; kindergarten teachers use a variety of methods to educate their children about the need to maintain a good habit of brushing their teeth daily; and children visit dentists and general practitioners regularly for dental and general health checkups. The motivation for oral care behaviors of the respondents came mainly from the extrinsic drivers of parents, teachers, and dentists, while the children's intrinsic drivers were relatively weak.

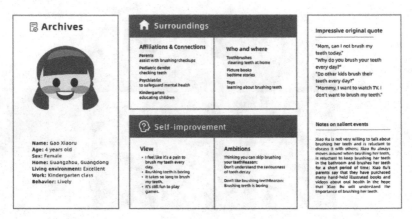

Fig. 2. StoryWorld

4.2 Needs and Expectations of the Target Population

Through our interviews, we gained insight into the fact that preschoolers' oral care behaviors are influenced by a variety of external influences, their interests, and their receptivity. When developing an oral care persuasion strategy, we felt it was important to consider these factors and design a strategy that was both fun and educational.

We were particularly concerned that children prefer simple, clear instructions during brushing, and that complex brushing procedures may be confusing. Therefore, we emphasized the importance of providing simple, easy-to-understand brushing instructions to ensure that oral care persuasion is more relevant to the needs and expectations of the target population.

4.3 Assessing User Abilities

At the beginning of the project, we conducted an in-depth ability assessment of the target users, preschoolers, involving physical, psychological, and cognitive characteristics and learning abilities, including strength characteristics, coordination, emotion, personality, exploration ability, autonomy, initiative, language comprehension, concentration, perception, life skills, and learning styles, etc. We collected data from various authoritative sources and used the three-level coding method of qualitative research to organize, deeply analyze, and compare the relationship between the categories to obtain the four themes of preschool children's behavioral abilities. The results of the coding of preschool children's abilities are shown in Table 2.

Table 2. Coding Results of pre-school children's abilities

Selective Encoding (Core Category)	Central Axis Encoding (Main Category)	Open Encoding (Initial Category)
Physiological Features	Tooth Development	Children's deciduous teeth development is completed, and cavities are common, requiring daily dental care
	Strength Characteristics	Small muscle development in 3–6-year-olds is incomplete, making it difficult to regulate muscles well and prone to fatigue
	Coordination Ability	Preschool children can imitate, independently perform simple movements, and engage in basic games
Psychological Features	Emotions	Children aged 3–6 exhibit strong emotions, often leading to greater behavioral instability
	Personality	Children are naturally playful and lively during this period, showing a strong preference for games
	Exploratory Ability	Preschoolers have a strong curiosity, begin to explore their surroundings, and gradually develop more concrete thinking
	Behavioral Aspects	Children possess some autonomy and initiative, and psychological characteristics gradually stabilize
Cognitive Features	Language	3–6-year-olds can understand conversations and provide simple responses based on the situation

(*continued*)

Table 2. (*continued*)

Selective Encoding (Core Category)	Central Axis Encoding (Main Category)	Open Encoding (Initial Category)
	Attention Span	Preschoolers predominantly exhibit unintentional attention, gradually forming intentional attention, focusing more on things of interest
	Sensory Perception	Concrete, prominent, and vivid objects can stimulate children's perception, prompting observation and usage
Learning Features	Life Skills	Children gradually learn activities like brushing their teeth, changing clothes, and putting on shoes during this stage
	Learning Methods	Children primarily engage in learning through imitation, requiring proper guidance
	Enthusiasm	Continuous and detailed rewards can enhance children's interest in learning. Considering children's learning characteristics, using educational toys as a medium can cultivate good oral hygiene habits and stimulate children's interest in learning

5   Analyzing Elements of Behavioral Persuasion

5.1   Data Collection

In the persuasion of children's oral care behaviors, we summarized eight elements that may influence children's acceptance and adherence to oral care behaviors in terms of motivation, competence, and triggers: fun, rewards, feasibility of the process, ease of use of the product, tolerance, encouragement, teaching, and supervision (see Table 3). A scale survey was conducted to evaluate the eight observed variables on a five-point scale from "disagree" (1 point) to "strongly agree" (5 points). The scale questionnaire was distributed to a sample of 115 families with children aged 3–6 years in urban China, and 115 questionnaires were returned, of which 110 were valid and 5 were invalid because they did not pass the lie detector test.

Table 3. Translates to "Design table of latent variables and observed variables

motivation	Fun X1, Reward X2
Ability	Process feasibility X3, Product ease of use X4, Fault tolerance X5,
Trigger	Encouragement X6, Teaching X7, Supervision X8

5.2 Principal Component Analysis

To better understand and quantify the main factors influencing children's oral care behaviors, we used Principal Component Analysis PCA, a statistical downscaling method.

KMO Values and Bartlett's Test. Before performing the Principal Component Analysis, we performed the KMO value and Bartlett sphericity test on the data. The results show that the KMO value is greater than 0.6 and the p-value is less than 0.05, indicating that these data are suitable for principal component analysis.

Extraction of Principal Components. We used SPSS26.0 software to analyze and find out the main components through the table of variance explained. The eigenvalues of the first two principal components are greater than 1 and the contribution rate reaches 68.632%, so two principal components are extracted to replace the original eight influence indicators.

Analysis of Factors Influencing Children's Oral Care. This study used principal component analysis to gain a deeper understanding of the factors influencing children's oral care behaviors and resulted in two main components. As shown in Table 4, the matrix of component score coefficients shows that the first principal component is mainly influenced by the factors of teaching, process feasibility, fault tolerance, and product ease of use, while the second principal component is mainly influenced by rewarding, supervising, encouraging notification, and fun. Therefore, we named the first principal component "behavioral guidance" and the second principal component "behavioral interaction" as the main influences on children's oral care behaviors (see Table 5 for specific meanings).

Due to their young age, variable personality, and incomplete development, children are unable to perform oral care tasks independently. The "Behavioral Guidance" component emphasizes lowering the competency requirements for proper oral care behaviors by teaching and using easy-to-understand care processes and easy-to-use products that can help children perform oral care tasks more easily." The "Behavioral Interaction" component emphasizes increasing children's interest and motivation in oral care by providing incentives, supervision, and introducing fun to motivate children and help them develop good oral care habits.

Table 4. Matrix of ingredient score coefficients

	Ingredient	
	1	2
Fun X1	0.307	−0.042
Reward X2	0.338	−0.097
Process feasibility X3	−0.019	0.299
Product Ease of Use X4	−0.074	0.329
Fault Tolerance X5	−0.043	0.3
Teaching X6	−0.124	0.358
Encouragement Notification X7	0.332	−0.08
Supervision X8	0.292	−0.034

Table 5. The main influencing factors of children's oral care

Principal Components	Implications
Behavioral guidance	Reducing the competencies required for proper oral care behaviors
Behavioral Interaction	Increase internal motivation for interest in oral care behaviors

6 Persuasive Design Strategies for Children's Oral Care Science Toys

Based on children's oral care behaviors and their influencing factors, and guided by the theory of persuasive technology, we propose a persuasive design strategy for oral care educational toys for children.

6.1 Behavioral Guidance Strategy

To guide children to develop good oral hygiene habits by reducing the cognitive and operational difficulties of correct oral care behaviors.

Simplified Teaching. Use audio-visual language and product semantics to convey oral hygiene knowledge in the form of interesting animation [40, 41].

Simple Process. Emphasize the simple and intuitive product process to ensure that children are easy to understand and implement.

Timely Correction. For possible problems in the process of dental care, timely reminders and corrections are provided in a variety of ways to gradually guide children to the correct way and time of brushing.

User-friendly. Combine the concepts of human factors engineering and structural design to design oral care toys that are suitable for children's physiological development and operating habits.

6.2 Behavioral Interaction Strategies

Increase children's intrinsic interest in oral care behaviors and encourage them to participate more actively in oral care activities.

Game-Based Design. The oral care process is skillfully integrated into the game to stimulate children's interest through interesting plots and challenging tasks [42].

Reward Mechanism. Use of medals, sound effects, and other forms of positive feedback to strengthen the formation of correct oral care behavior.

Technology Integration. Real-time data transmission is realized through the introduction of several technologies to improve the realism and interactivity of the game.

Prompted Feedback. Introduce a variety of prompted feedback to make the oral care process more interesting and popularization of science, and cultivate children's willingness to participate spontaneously.

7 Design Practice and Validation

7.1 Workflows that Characterize Persuasion

We apply behavioral guidance and behavioral interaction design strategies to the design of children's oral care toys. "Teeth is a smart oral care toy for preschoolers aged 3–6 years old. In the face of the target user's resistance to dental care, boredom with the oral cleaning process, and high caries rate, we designed a children's game-based brushing method (designing a lifestyle), so that the user can complete the oral care process during the game (guiding the behavioral content), correct the incorrect brushing posture promptly and ensure that brushing time (changing the lifestyle), and help them to develop a healthy oral care habit (establishing a healthy life value), and ultimately realize the independent oral care system. Healthy life values), and ultimately realize the correct process of brushing teeth on their own (generating internal motivation to construct lifestyles).

7.2 Children's Oral Care Popularization Toy Design Practice

This product puts forward the concept of playful brushing, allowing children to complete the process of dental care in a fun way while fighting monsters, and persuading them to develop good oral care habits. Visualize the steps of brushing, use the visual language and product semantics that children love to correct incorrect brushing posture, ensure the length of children's brushing, create a comfortable oral care environment and atmosphere, and help children develop healthy oral care habits.

Modeling Design. In the modeling and color-matching design of children's oral care science toys, we fully consider the psychological and behavioral characteristics of preschool children. Animal anthropomorphic character images were introduced into the design practice as the visual and semantic elements of the product to enhance affinity and an oral care set including a children's intelligent toothbrush and oral care science toys were designed to assist children in brushing their teeth on their own (shown in Fig. 3, and the details are shown in Fig. 4). The toothbrush is specially designed with a small center and two large ends, and is equipped with a silicone non-slip handle to provide good anti-slip effect.

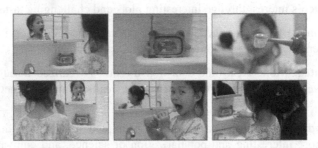

Fig. 3. Product image

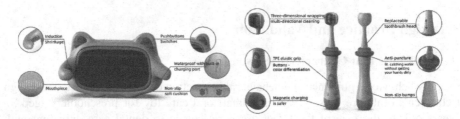

Fig. 4. Product detail diagram

Interactive Interface Design. The design of the interactive interface in the "Tooth and Tooth" smart screen echoes Professor BJ Fogg's persuasive technique, follows Nielsen's usability principles, and takes into account the three major elements of efficiency, effectiveness, and satisfaction, and designs a simple and intuitive game interface that is easy for children to understand and operate, and provides timely feedback, to guide children to carry out oral care process.

At the motivation (M) level, we took advantage of children's natural interest in games to make the brushing process more interesting and appealing through interactive games with interesting interfaces (see Fig. 5); and stimulated children's active brushing motivation through rewards (see Fig. 6).

In terms of ability (A), the interface is presented through the oral angle interface so that children can visualize the correctness of the brushing action (see Fig. 7). Meanwhile, the in-game voice assistant provided real-time brushing instructions to ensure that children cleaned each tooth correctly, thus improving their brushing ability.

Fig. 5. Interactive game interface

Fig. 6. Reward interface

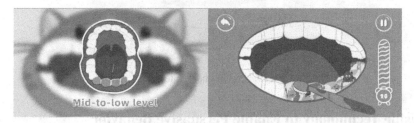

Fig. 7. Oral Angle interface

In the prompt (P) section, the interaction interface is designed with multiple forms of prompts, such as visual prompts, voice prompts, and vibration feedback, to remind children to perform oral care, such as when the toothbrush leaves the mouth and the brushing time is insufficient, the system will give corresponding reminders (see Fig. 8), which further encourages children to persist in completing the brushing task.

We make full use of the advantages of multimodal interaction, visually designing a game screen that attracts children's attention, and audibly through music and sound effects, as well as tactilely through the vibration feedback of the toothbrush, to attract children's participation in an all-round way, so that the process of brushing teeth is no longer a single tedious task, but an interesting and interactive experience. In addition, parents can keep abreast of their children's oral cleaning habits through the toy interface, to provide appropriate guidance and encouragement (see Fig. 9).

Fig. 8. Reminder interface

Fig. 9. Parent check interface

8   Using Technology to Enable Persuasive Behavior

To optimize children's brushing experience and oral care process, the Toothbrush Kit utilizes the latest infrared sensing and 5.3 Bluetooth technology. The smart toothbrush has built-in infrared sensors to accurately capture children's brushing movements. Information on the toothbrush's collision with the teeth, the angle of use, and the duration of use are transmitted to the play toy in real time via 5.3 Bluetooth technology (see Fig. 10).

The smart interactive screen displays the "Kitten Brushing Adventure" game, which translates the brushing behavior into character actions within the game. The voice assistant in the "Tooth and Tooth Kit" provides real-time brushing instructions to ensure that the child cleans each tooth correctly. The voice assistant can also act as a character in the game, making the brushing process and the gameplay more fun and relevant. The app on the child's parent's phone collects and analyzes the child's brushing data synchronously, providing parents with timely feedback on their child's oral cleaning habits. At the same time, the difficulty of the games on the smart interactive screen will increase as the child's brushing habits improve, thus maintaining the child's interest and motivation in brushing.

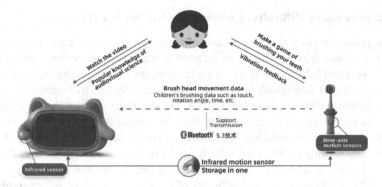

Fig. 10. Product technical drawing

8.1 Precise Positioning

A triaxial magnetometer is a sensor that can measure the strength of the magnetic field in three spatial directions, and it plays a key role in the design of our smart toothbrush. With the triaxial magnetometer, the product can accurately sense and record changes in the direction and angle of the toothbrush during brushing. The working principle of the 3-axis magnetometer is based on the earth's magnetic field. As the smart toothbrush rotates in space, the Triaxial Magnetometer detects changes in the Earth's magnetic field on the toothbrush's three axes. By parsing this data the direction of the toothbrush can be determined, thus realizing the precise positioning of the toothbrush. A smart toothbrush with precise positioning will help children better understand and master brushing techniques. When they do not cover all surfaces of the teeth while brushing or brush at an incorrect angle, the Smart Toothbrush will send tips and instructions to the product display through the app to help users correct their brushing skills and ensure a fully clean mouth.

8.2 Toothbrushing Behavior Monitoring

A nine-axis inertial sensor is a combination of a three-axis gyroscope, a three-axis accelerometer, and a three-axis magnetometer. In our smart toothbrush design, the nine-axis inertial sensor is used to track and record the movement and speed during brushing, which can monitor the dynamic information of children's hands and toothbrushes during brushing in real-time, including direction, angle, speed, and acceleration. Through the real-time analysis of these data, the mobile application can accurately track and record the brushing movements, thus realizing the monitoring of tooth brushing behavior.

The tooth brushing behavior monitoring function will help children identify and correct problems in their brushing techniques promptly. For example, when they brush their teeth for too short a period, with too much force, or with incomplete coverage, the mobile application will send reminders and provide correct brushing instructions to help them develop good brushing habits.

8.3   Adaptive Game Difficulty: Customized Oral Science Games

Adaptive game difficulty is a key feature in the design of science toys. The goal of the product is to allow the game difficulty to be automatically adjusted according to children's brushing skills and habits, thus providing a challenging but not frustrating playing environment. The Smart Toothbrush has a built-in embedded system that includes a nine-axis inertial sensor and a three-axis magnetometer. These sensors monitor children's brushing movements and toothbrush orientation in real-time, generating a large amount of data. By analyzing this data in real-time, the system can accurately assess children's brushing skills and habits, being used to adjust the difficulty of the oral science game in the mobile app. And then using advanced graphic processing techniques, the data analysis results are mapped to the movements and difficulty of the game characters. For example, if the system detects an improvement in children's brushing skills, the game difficulty will be increased accordingly to keep it challenging and engaging.

8.4   Daily Reminders: Towards the Development of Tooth Brushing Habits

Children need to develop good brushing habits. For this reason, we have included a smart reminder system in our science toys to help children brush their teeth regularly in their daily lives. Our smart toothbrush can record children's brushing time and frequency. When the set brushing time is reached, or when children do not brush their teeth during the day, the smart toothbrush will send a reminder via the mobile app to remind children to brush their teeth. Our reminder system can not only set up regular reminders but also personalize the reminder according to the child's brushing habits. For example, if the system detects that children often forget to brush their teeth at night, it will send reminders at night. In this way, our science toy can help children develop good brushing habits, thus protecting their oral health.

9   Conclusion

We have proposed and implemented a novel gamified persuasion solution to the oral care challenges faced by preschoolers. By gamifying the daily oral care tasks, the "Tooth and Tooth" kit not only changed children's oral care behaviors but also successfully motivated children to brush their teeth and successfully guided them to form good oral care habits. The design concepts from this study can inspire other product designs that focus on children as a primary target group, especially those that wish to promote behavioral change in children through interaction and gamification. We plan to further develop this product to optimize the design and personalize the settings to meet the needs of more children through user testing and data collection. In addition, we will also validate the effectiveness of the "Teething Fun" kit in real-life environments to further ensure its feasibility and validity in real-life situations.

Through the integration of design thinking, behavioral psychology principles, advanced technology, and data analysis, this study has innovatively designed a product that can effectively guide and motivate children to change their behavior. This result has important practical value for current children's oral care and provides new insights and directions for our future research.

Acknowledgments. This study was funded by the 2023 General Program of the National Social Science Foundation of China in Art (23BC048); Ministry of Education Industry-University Cooperation Collaborative Breeding Program (220900316224726); Ministry of Education Industry-University Cooperation Collaborative Education Program (202102199034); Guangdong Philosophy and Social Science Planning 2022 Regular Program (GD22CYS01).

Disclosure of Interests. The authors have no competing interests to declare that are relevant to the content of this article.

References

1. Bhatia, S.K., et al.: Characteristics of child dental neglect: a systematic review. J. Dent. **42**, 229–239 (2014). https://doi.org/10.1016/j.jdent.2013.10.010
2. Guarnizo-Herreño, C.C., Wehby, G.L.: Children's dental health, school performance, and psychosocial well-being. J. Pediatr. **161**, 1153–1159.e2 (2012). https://doi.org/10.1016/j.jpeds.2012.05.025
3. McGrath, C., Broder, H., Wilson-Genderson, M.: Assessing the impact of oral health on the life quality of children: implications for research and practice. Commun. Dent. Oral Epidemiol. **32**, 81–85 (2004). https://doi.org/10.1111/j.1600-0528.2004.00149.x
4. Sheiham, A.: Dental caries affects body weight, growth and quality of life in pre-school children. Br. Dent. J. **201**, 625–626 (2006). https://doi.org/10.1038/sj.bdj.4814259
5. Low, W., Tan, S., Schwartz, S.: The effect of severe caries on the quality of life in young children. Pediatr. Dent. **21**, 325–326 (1999)
6. Kawashita, Y., Kitamura, M., Saito, T.: Early childhood caries. Int. J. Dent. **2011**, e725320 (2011). https://doi.org/10.1155/2011/725320
7. Anil, S., Anand, P.S.: Early childhood caries: prevalence, risk factors, and prevention. Front. Pediatr. **5**, 157 (2017). https://doi.org/10.3389/fped.2017.00157
8. Davies, G.N.: Early childhood caries-a synopsis. Commun. Dent. Oral Epidemiol. **26**, 106–116 (1998)
9. Seow, W.K.: Early childhood caries. Pediatr. Clin. **65**, 941–954 (2018)
10. Drivers of children's dietary change: the current state of the market for highly processed foods and beverages (summary) | United Nations Children's Fund. https://www.unicef.cn/reports/market-highly-processed-food-and-drink-driving-childrens-diets-briefing. Accessed 24 Nov 2023
11. Zhang, Y., Zhang, X., Jiang, X., Wang, X., Chen, C.: Effects of grandparent-related factors on children's oral health under intergenerational parenting. China School Health **43**, 952–955+960 (2022). https://doi.org/10.16835/j.cnki.1000-9817.2022.06.036
12. Guo, G., Wu, H.: Current situation and problem analysis of the research on grandparent participation in parenting in China. J. Huzhou Normal College **45**(47–54), 13 (2023)
13. Duan, F., Li, J.: An overview of the research on intergenerational parenting in the past ten years. Shanghai Educ. Res. Center, 13–16 (2012). https://doi.org/10.16194/j.cnki.31-1059/g4.2012.04.034
14. Yu, X., Shangguan, Y., Liu, H.: New rural insurance, intergenerational care and children's health. China Rural Econ., 125–144 (2019)
15. 4th National Oral Health Epidemiology Survey Results Released_Scrolling News_Chinese Government Website. https://www.gov.cn/xinwen/2017-09/20/content_5226224.htm. Accessed 12 Feb 2023

16. Brignardello-Petersen, R.: Prevention strategies at school may be effective in reducing the incidence of early childhood caries. J. Am. Dent. Assoc. **151**, E49–E49 (2020). https://doi.org/10.1016/j.adaj.2020.01.009

17. Faghihian, R., Faghihian, E., Kazemi, A., Tarrahi, M.J., Zakizade, M.: Impact of motivational interviewing on early childhood caries: a systematic review and meta-analysis. J. Am. Dent. Assoc. **151**, 650–659 (2020). https://doi.org/10.1016/j.adaj.2020.06.003

18. Ramos-Gomez, F., Kinsler, J., Askaryar, H.: Understanding oral health disparities in children as a global public health issue: how dental health professionals can make a difference. J. Public Health Policy. **41**, 114–124 (2020). https://doi.org/10.1057/s41271-020-00222-5

19. Wazurkar, S., Madhu, P.P., Chhabra, K.G., Reche, A., Tidke, S., Fulzele, P.: Motivational interviewing for prevention of early childhood caries. J. Pharm. Res. Int. **33**, 501 (2010). https://doi.org/10.9734/JPRI/2021/v33i45B32824

20. Qingping, Y., et al.: Oral health risk behavior aggregation and influencing factors among 12-year-old children in Beijing. China Public Health **38**(11–14), 21 (2022)

21. Liu, L., Li, L.: Progress in the study of factors influencing children's oral health based on Anderson's model. China School Health. **42**, 476–480 (2020). https://doi.org/10.16835/j.cnki.1000-9817.2021.03.036

22. Chen, Y., Guo, P., Wang, X., Shi, X.: Evaluation of the effectiveness of an Internet+ integrated management platform to guide parents in promoting children's oral health. China Health Educ. **36**, 656–659 (2020). https://doi.org/10.16168/j.cnki.issn.1002-9982.2020.07.016

23. Xu, X., Liu, Y., Li, W., Wang, L., Yu, X., Tian, Y.: Evaluation of the effect of children's oral drama health education on the knowledge, belief and behavior of oral health care among 10-year-old children. Shanghai Stomatol. **29**, 304–307 (2020). https://doi.org/10.19439/j.sjos.2020.03.014

24. Zhang, L., Cheng, D.: Application of role-playing method in children's oral health education. J. China Med. Univ. **45**, 378–379 (2016)

25. Li, J., Shi, M., Yang, Y., Wang, L., Zhang, Z.: Impact of oral health interventions on oral health of kindergarten children and parents' perception of oral hygiene. Modern Preventive Medicine. Mod. Prev. Med. **48**, 1592–1594+1613 (2021)

26. Zeng, X., et al: A survey on the knowledge, beliefs, and behaviors of oral health among children with disabilities and their parents in Shanghai. Shanghai Stomatol. **30**, 379–383 (2021). https://doi.org/10.19439/j.sjos.2021.04.008

27. Niu, J., Dong, N., Wang, X., Zuo, L.L.: Effects of kindergarten continuous oral health education on preschool children's oral health care behavioral compliance. Nurs. Res. **32**, 1132–1134 (2018)

28. Laranjo, E., Baptista, S., Norton, A.A., Macedo, A.P., de Andrade, C., Areias, C.: Early childhood caries: an update. Revista Portuguesa de Medicina Geral e Familiar **33**, 426–429 (2017)

29. Pitts, N., Zero, D.: White paper on dental caries prevention and management. FDI World Dental Fed., 3–9 (2016)

30. Raison, M.H., Corcoran, R., Burnside, G., Harris, R.: Oral hygiene behaviour automaticity: are toothbrushing and interdental cleaning habitual behaviours? J. Dent. **102**, 103470 (2020). https://doi.org/10.1016/j.jdent.2020.103470

31. Classification and Terminology of Oral Hygiene Care Products:GB/T 35919-2018 (2018)

32. Li, X.: Playing with toys: play attributes and selection strategies of toys. People's Educ., 36–39 (2022)

33. Fogg, B.J.: Persuasive technology: using computers to change what we think and do. Ubiquity **2002**, 2 (2002). https://doi.org/10.1145/764008.763957

34. Xin, X.Y.: The butterfly effect of design: when lifestyle becomes the object of design. Packag. Eng. **41**, 57–66 (2020). https://doi.org/10.19554/j.cnki.1001-3563.2020.06.009

35. Fogg, B.: A behavior model for persuasive design. In: Proceedings of the 4th International Conference on Persuasive Technology, pp. 1–7. Association for Computing Machinery, New York, NY, USA (2009). https://doi.org/10.1145/1541948.1541999

36. Cao, E., Lou, S., Deng, R.: Persuasive design in sports and health apps. Packag. Eng. **38**, 232–235 (2017). https://doi.org/10.19554/j.cnki.1001-3563.2017.16.051

37. Wang, S.: A review of persuasive design research. Packag. Eng. **43**, 32–46 (2022). https://doi.org/10.19554/j.cnki.1001-3563.2022.22.004

38. Fogg, B.: Creating persuasive technologies: an eight-step design process. In: Proceedings of the 4th International Conference on Persuasive Technology, pp. 1–6. ACM, Claremont California USA (2009). https://doi.org/10.1145/1541948.1542005

39. Duijster, D., de Jong-Lenters, M., Verrips, E., van Loveren, C.: Establishing oral health promoting behaviours in children – parents' views on barriers, facilitators ' views on barriers, facilitators and professional support: a qualitative study. BMC Oral Health **15**, 157 (2015). https://doi.org/10.1186/s12903-015-0145-0

40. Graetz, C.: Toothbrushing education via a smart software visualization system. J. Periodontol. **84**, 186–195 (2013)

41. Zhang, L.: Exploring the animation design of user interface in digital media art. Art & Design (Theory). **2**, 84–86 (2021). https://doi.org/10.16824/j.cnki.issn10082832.2021.08.021

42. Groos, K.: The play of man. Nature. **65**, 78–78 (1901). https://doi.org/10.1038/065078e0

Optimizing the Student Evaluation System in Higher Education: A Comprehensive Approach from the Perspective of Student Experience

Qiong Yang[✉]

Academic Affairs Office, South China University of Technology, Guangzhou 510006, China
jwqyang@scut.edu.cn

Abstract. As an important component of the teaching quality assurance system at universities, students' evaluation of teaching plays a pivotal role in implementing teaching quality monitoring. This paper first investigates the status quo of students' evaluation of teaching at universities from the perspective of student experience; then critically points out issues such as the lack of student centrality, formalism in evaluation activities, uniformity in evaluation indicators, and the inadequacy of feedback mechanisms; finally, with a focus on student learning outcomes, it provides corresponding solutions following the approach of the PDCA cycle ("Plan", "Do", "Check" and "Action"), in order to build a student-based evaluation system of teaching performance. This paper is expected to bring into full play students' evaluation in ensuring teaching quality, encourage teachers to improve teaching quality, and enhance the quality of undergraduate talent cultivation comprehensively.

Keywords: Student Experience · Student Evaluation system · Talent Cultivation

1 Introduction

The student evaluation system is not only a crucial component of the higher education quality assurance system but also a key element in implementing teaching quality monitoring. Student evaluation allows students to assess whether the teacher's instructional activities meet their needs and provides teachers with a significant avenue for self-assessment regarding the effectiveness of their teaching objectives.

Currently, there is extensive research in academia on the construction of student evaluation systems. Analyzing the significant position of student evaluation in higher education activities, researchers such as Dunrong Bie have identified issues such as the lack of student empowerment, a focus on the form rather than the substance of student evaluation, misuse of student evaluation for teacher management, and systemic design flaws. Correcting these issues is vital to establish a proper understanding of student evaluation, construct a scientific student evaluation system, and harness the core role of student evaluation in ensuring the quality of higher education [1]. Jianzhong Wang and others have studied cases and tools for student evaluation in four universities in the United States, Europe, and Australia. They propose that the value orientation of student evaluation should be centered around students, aligning with contemporary demands in the higher education market and the human-centric characteristics of the era. Considering the timely and comprehensive aspects in the implementation of student evaluation is essential [2]. Tingting Zhou analyzed the student evaluation indicator systems in some universities, conducting theoretical analysis from five perspectives: curriculum design, teaching, exercises and assessment, student feedback, and experimental operations. Effective student evaluation indicator systems should be student-centered, reflect the fundamental principles of higher education, value the personalized teaching performance of teachers, and address issues related to course quality and teaching materials that closely correlate with teaching quality and effectiveness [3]. Yudong Sheng studied the American experience in evaluating undergraduate education's path and values, proposing a shift from traditional dominance based on resources and reputation (such as university rankings) to student-centered educational practices (students' learning behaviors and campus experiences). Establishing correct views on quality and assessment is fundamental to improving undergraduate education quality [4].

This paper aims to build upon previous research by focusing on the perspective of student experience. It examines the current state of student evaluation in higher education, optimizing and constructing a "comprehensive, all-encompassing, closed-loop, continuous improvement" student evaluation indicator system based on the student experience perspective.

2   Key Issues in the Current Student Evaluation Indicator System

2.1   Lack of Student Centrality

In recent years, there has been a paradigm shift in higher education from "teacher-centered teaching" to "student-centered learning." The concept of "student-centered education" encompasses three aspects: centering on student development, learning, and learning outcomes [5]. However, the current design of student evaluation indicator systems in higher education focuses excessively on teacher instruction. These indicators involve aspects such as the teacher's teaching attitude, content, methods and skills, and teaching effectiveness. This approach places more emphasis on the teacher's performance in teaching activities, using teaching terminology in questions that exceed students' professional and judgment capabilities. Furthermore, when designing and formulating student evaluation indicator systems, universities are predominantly led by teaching management departments, rarely involving students or seeking their opinions. Consequently, the designed student evaluation indicators often reflect the goals and needs of school teaching management without adequately considering the student's central role in evaluation.

2.2   Formalism and Student Evaluation Fatigue

Currently, due to the lack of student empowerment in evaluation, student evaluation tends to be perfunctory. Students do not receive effective feedback after participating in evaluations, resulting in many students not fully recognizing the importance of student evaluation and struggling to muster enthusiasm for it. Some schools bundle student evaluation with processes such as course selection and grade inquiries, obliging students to conduct evaluations. Some students believe that student evaluation is not closely related to their academic development. Consequently, some students approach student evaluation with a negative attitude, considering it a mere formality. Student fatigue towards evaluation significantly impacts the reliability and validity of student evaluation data. Teachers find it challenging to derive meaningful feedback from student evaluation data, making it difficult to utilize the data to improve teaching in subsequent sessions.

2.3 Uniformity in Indicators

Currently, student evaluation indicators in universities are highly similar, mainly focusing on dimensions such as teaching attitude, content, methods and skills, and teaching effectiveness [6]. Most university student evaluation systems emphasize common teaching characteristics, rarely considering the characteristics of disciplines, majors, courses, class nature, and student diversity. Some universities categorize student evaluation into theoretical courses, laboratory courses, and physical education/art skills courses, but the evaluation indicators remain standard and do not reflect the unique features that courses should possess. This uniformity leads to low student approval of evaluations, and some students exhibit a dismissive attitude or even a negative stance towards the process.

2.4 Lack of Effective Closure and Feedback

Issues raised by students in evaluations often lack timely and effective feedback. Some universities schedule student evaluations after the course concludes, making students realize that evaluation results no longer have relevance to their course learning. This significantly reduces students' motivation to participate actively in evaluations. In some cases, student evaluation results are only used as a means for teaching management, faculty title evaluation, and teaching assessment. The collected student evaluation information is rarely processed, updated, or maintained effectively. There is a lack of meaningful utilization and analysis of student evaluation data, and teachers seldom reflect on and improve teaching based on student evaluation data. The importance of student evaluation in improving student learning outcomes and promoting teachers' teaching proficiency is overlooked. Some teachers even believe that students, as learners, lack the knowledge and competence to assess the teaching proficiency of teachers.

3 Application of PDCA Cycle in Student Evaluation Indicator Systems

The PDCA (Plan-Do-Check-Act) cycle, also known as the Deming Cycle, is a management philosophy that achieves continuous improvement through iterative stages. Applying the PDCA cycle to student evaluation constructs a student evaluation indicator system with continuous improvement capabilities, reinforcing effective connections and closed-loop processes in various stages of student evaluation.

In the construction of the student evaluation indicator system from the perspective of student experience, the four stages of the PDCA cycle (Plan, Do, Check, and Act) are explored in terms of indicator design, evaluation implementation, data collection, and feedback and improvement. This exploration aims to build a student evaluation indicator system that is "comprehensive, all-encompassing, closed-loop, and continuously improving" (as shown in Fig. 1). This recursive approach dynamically manages the quality of classroom teaching, promoting continuous improvement in teaching quality and ensuring a spiral rise in classroom teaching quality.

Indicator Design

Departing from traditional paradigms, design evaluation indicators from a student experience perspective. Construct a student-centered system, incorporating both qualitative and quantitative elements and a mix of standard and distinctive indicators.

Data Collection

Implement evaluations using a combination of process-oriented and results-oriented assessments. Ensure that the evaluation process covers the entire spectrum of student learning experiences. Leverage various methods, including surveys, student discussions, and online and offline channels.

Feedback and Improvement

Analyze process-oriented and results-oriented evaluations to extract information for improving teaching quality. Provide timely and efficient feedback to departments and teachers. Establish a responsive mechanism for rectification and continuous improvement.

Evaluation Implementation

Establish a mechanism for collecting and processing student evaluation data. Develop a data management system to analyze and evaluate feedback comprehensively. Implement quality control and tracking based on student evaluation data, ensuring effective closed-loop management.

A closed-loop and continuous improvement model that covers four fundamental stages: indicator design, evaluation implementation , data collection, and feedback and improvement.

Fig. 1. Undergraduate Classroom Teaching Quality Assurance System Based on Student Experience.

4 Optimization of Undergraduate Classroom Teaching Quality Assurance System Based on Student Experience

4.1 Indicator Design (Plan)

The paradigm shifts from teacher-centric to student-centered education requires educational evaluations to listen to students' voices, focusing on students' learning experiences and feelings. The shift toward student-centered assessment aligns with the new perspective on international higher education quality assessment, emphasizing value-added evaluations based on students [7]. Scholars like E. Kuh and Y.S. Lincoln propose that evaluation should be an interactive process where all involved, especially evaluators and their subjects, interact to construct a unified viewpoint. When designing student evaluation indicator systems, students as evaluators and teachers as subjects should actively participate [8]. This paper constructs a student-centered evaluation index system from the following four aspects (as shown in Fig. 2).

Firstly, design the student evaluation indicator system from the perspective of student experience, constructing a student-centered system that revolves around questions related to student learning and development. It should be able to effectively guide teaching activities based on students' cognitive levels and psychological activities, arrange teaching content reasonably to meet students' learning needs, and enhance student learning outcomes. Scientifically formulated evaluation indicators can genuinely reflect students' requirements for good teaching [9].

Secondly, student evaluation indicators should emphasize the combination of quantitative and qualitative evaluations. On the basis of selective questions, additional open-ended questions should be added to allow students a more comprehensive and free space to express their opinions on teaching. Students can provide specific descriptions of their learning experiences and needs, offering teachers concrete suggestions, making evaluation data more adaptable and targeted, thus improving the validity of student evaluation results.

Thirdly, student evaluation indicator systems should incorporate both standard and distinctive indicators. Standard indicators primarily reflect common issues in teacher instruction, while distinctive indicators reflect the characteristics and teaching effectiveness of different majors and courses. Scientifically establishing evaluation indicators that combine standard and distinctive elements, based on the perspective of student experience, can fully motivate students to actively participate in evaluations and enhance the involvement of students in the evaluation process. Additionally, it provides teachers with a diversified space and multiple perspectives to grasp students' learning outcomes.

Lastly, when educational authorities formulate student evaluation indicators, they should invite experts in education, school teachers, and students to participate collaboratively. Seeking opinions from a broad range of faculty and students ensures that the established evaluation criteria are more scientific, applicable, and continually updated and improved in the subsequent processes of educational management.

4.2   Evaluation Implementation (Do)

After determining the evaluation indicators, it is essential to conduct student evaluation activities through a reasonable process.

Firstly, it is crucial to continuously optimize the evaluation methods, adhering to a combination of process-oriented and results-oriented evaluation methods. Ensure that student evaluations cover the entire process of student course learning. During the teaching process, students conduct process-oriented evaluations based on learning experiences and learning outcomes at different stages, providing timely feedback to teachers regarding issues in their teaching. Through process-oriented evaluations, teachers can understand students' learning methods, resources, and difficulties during the teaching process, addressing students' learning needs and continuously improving in subsequent teaching. After the course concludes, students conduct results-oriented evaluations from the overall perspective of course learning, comprehensively perceiving the experience and gains from course learning. Through results-oriented evaluations, teachers further understand students' learning needs, enhancing and improving teaching in future sessions.

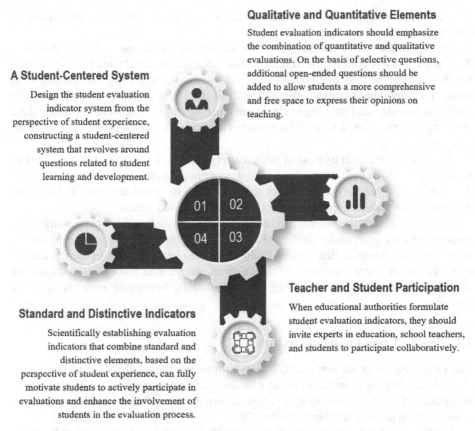

A Student-Centered System

Design the student evaluation indicator system from the perspective of student experience, constructing a student-centered system that revolves around questions related to student learning and development.

Qualitative and Quantitative Elements

Student evaluation indicators should emphasize the combination of quantitative and qualitative evaluations. On the basis of selective questions, additional open-ended questions should be added to allow students a more comprehensive and free space to express their opinions on teaching.

Standard and Distinctive Indicators

Scientifically establishing evaluation indicators that combine standard and distinctive elements, based on the perspective of student experience, can fully motivate students to actively participate in evaluations and enhance the involvement of students in the evaluation process.

Teacher and Student Participation

When educational authorities formulate student evaluation indicators, they should invite experts in education, school teachers, and students to participate collaboratively.

Fig. 2. A Student-Centered Evaluation Index System.

Secondly, it is essential to leverage information technology to conduct student evaluations through various channels. Methods such as surveys, student discussions, and learning achievement sharing events can be employed online and offline to obtain students' feelings and opinions about teachers' course instruction.

Lastly, it is crucial to strengthen the publicity and educational efforts about student evaluations. Ensure that students have a correct understanding of the role and significance of student evaluations. Help students recognize that student evaluations are closely related to their academic development and learning interests. Make them realize that student evaluations can change teachers' classroom teaching methods, thereby improving students' learning outcomes. Encourage students to provide authentic and objective student evaluations.

4.3 Data Collection (Check)

Higher education institutions should establish mechanisms for collecting and processing student evaluation data, creating a student evaluation information management data system, and conducting effective data processing to ensure the reliability and validity of student evaluation data.

Firstly, create individual data files for each teacher based on student evaluations. Record the process-oriented and results-oriented evaluations conducted by students during the teaching process comprehensively and truthfully. Utilize big data mining techniques for comprehensive evaluation and analysis of student evaluation data. Implement quality monitoring and tracking of classroom teaching based on student evaluation data, ensuring effective closed-loop and continuous improvement in the quality of classroom teaching.

Secondly, make effective use of information technology to conduct various student evaluations through multiple channels. Employ methods such as questionnaires, student discussions, and learning achievement sharing events to obtain students' feelings and opinions about teachers' course instruction both online and offline.

Lastly, strengthen the publicity and education about student evaluations, ensuring that students have a correct understanding of the role and significance of student evaluations. Help students recognize that student evaluations are closely related to their academic development and learning interests. Make them realize that student evaluations can change teachers' classroom teaching methods, thereby improving students' learning outcomes.

4.4 Feedback and Improvement (Act)

The ultimate goal of student evaluations is to improve the quality of teaching, which requires continuous identification and resolution of issues in teaching. Therefore, the timeliness of student evaluation is a key criterion for assessing its effectiveness in continually improving teaching quality [10].

Firstly, analyze the process-oriented and results-oriented evaluations in student evaluations to obtain information and suggestions for improving the quality of teacher course instruction. Provide timely, accurate, and efficient feedback to departments and teachers based on this information. Relevant departments should establish a linked mechanism based on problem analysis and resolution, formulate rectification plans, and ensure that continuous improvement efforts are implemented. Feedback on student evaluations emphasizes efficiency, while improvement in teaching focuses on the effectiveness of problem resolution.

Secondly, establish a system of student evaluation information officers to collect opinions and suggestions from students about the entire process of course instruction. Provide timely and effective feedback to teachers regarding problems identified by students during the evaluation process. Teachers can adjust teaching content and methods in a short period to improve teaching quality.

5   Key Issues Addressed by the Student Experience-Centric Student Evaluation System

5.1   Construction of a Student-Centric Evaluation System

The proposed system adheres to the "student-centric" approach, scientifically formulating evaluation criteria that balance quantitative and qualitative aspects. By incorporating open-ended questions, the system provides students with a more extensive and freer space to express opinions, promoting a comprehensive and adaptive evaluation approach that genuinely reflects students' expectations of quality teaching.

5.2   Optimization of Evaluation Methods Covering the Full Learning Process

The new system introduces a combined formative and summative evaluation approach, utilizing both online and offline channels to gather diverse student opinions on teachers' instructional methods. This comprehensive coverage ensures a holistic view of the learning experience and outcomes, contributing to a more effective evaluation process.

5.3   Establishment of Data Collection and Processing Mechanism

Institutions are encouraged to create a robust data management system, leveraging data mining techniques for comprehensive analysis. This approach enhances the utilization of student evaluation data for quality monitoring, tracking, and continuous improvement, providing a solid foundation for the enhancement of teaching quality.

5.4   Implementation of a Scientific and Effective Feedback and Continuous Improvement Mechanism

The establishment of a feedback and improvement mechanism ensures that the information obtained from student evaluations is promptly and efficiently relayed to relevant departments and teachers. The system's efficiency lies in its ability to address issues swiftly, promoting continuous improvement in teaching quality by holding teachers accountable or incentivizing positive changes.

6   Conclusion

The primary mission of higher education is to cultivate valuable talents that meet societal needs. Given that students are the central figures in this educational process, all teaching and management activities should naturally revolve around a "student-centered" approach [11]. The current student evaluation system has become a foundational element in the higher education quality assurance system. Constructing a student evaluation system based on the student experience perspective not only emphasizes the students' central role but also establishes a scientific and effective feedback and continuous improvement mechanism. This approach ensures that the student evaluation system contributes significantly to the ongoing enhancement of teaching quality, ultimately elevating the quality of talent cultivation in higher education.

This optimized version aims to enhance clarity, logical structure, and language precision. If you have specific areas you would like further improvement or any additional preferences, please let me know.

Acknowledgements. This research was funded by Department of Education of Guangdong Province, grant number j2jw-C9223037.

References

1. Dunrong, B., Fan, M.: On student evaluation of teaching and improvement of the teaching quality assurance system in HEIs. J. High. Educ. **28**(12), 77–83 (2007)
2. Jianzhong, W., Chang, L., Ruilin, W.: Where does the student evaluation of teaching go in china—an analysis based on the research of four cases from the united states, Europe and Australia. China High. Educ. Res. **2018**(10), 87–92 (2018)
3. Tingting, Z.: Analysis of student evaluation index system in some foreign universities. China Univ. Teach. **2012**(02), 89–94 (2012)
4. Dongsheng, Y.: Excellent undergraduate education evaluation: approach and value. Res.High. Educ. Eng. **2012**(03), 126–131 (2012)
5. Yimin, H.: Building a student-centered undergraduate teaching quality standard. China Univ. Teach. **2017**(10), 88–91 (2012)
6. Yuehong, G.: A study on the adjustment of university student evaluation index system based on student perspective. Acta Univ. Medicinalis Nanjing (Soc. Sci.) **56**(3), 268–272 (2013)
7. Li, W., Na, G.: Construction of Undergraduate Course Teaching Quality Evaluation Index. Res. High. Educ. Eng. **2012**(03), 126–131 (2012)
8. Jie, L., Yuanyuan, D.: A research on the application of humane administration of students' assessment on the teachers. Tsinghua J. Educ. **26**(6), 54–58 (2005)
9. Lingli, L., Jianhui, Y.: Increasing multi-party communication to construct a people-oriented system of student-evaluation of teaching. J. Qiongzhou Univ. **19**(1), 36–37 (2012)
10. Chuantun, X.: The establishment of the students' teaching evaluation system based on the principle of continuous improvement-taking Jimei university as an example. J. Jimei Univ. **18**(3), 70–75 (2017)
11. Jianfang, Z.: Research and practice of "student-centered" internal teaching quality assurance system in colleges and universities. Heilongjiang Res. High. Educ. **37**(05), 138–141 (2019)

User Experience in Tangible
and Intangible Cultural Heritage

Research on the Value Development and Spatial Experience of Rural Ecological Landscape in Lingnan

Yali Chen[1](✉), Mingyu Sun[1], and Yao Wei[2](✉)

[1] School of Design South China University of Technology, Guangzhou, China
chenyali@scut.edu.cn
[2] Beijing General Municipal Engineering Design and Research Institute Co., Ltd., Beijing, China
191986769@qq.com

Abstract. Natural ecology is the unique resource advantage of rural settlements, which has gradually become a symbol of beauty and characteristics different from modern cities. The essence of China's five thousand years of farming ecological culture and the value pursuit of ecological civilization in the new era have natural compatibility. With the development of rural revitalization, the value of ecological landscape has been excavated and developed, which has also changed the spatial pattern between production, life and ecology. The scope of ecological space is expanded, the spatial distribution boundary is gradually blurred and the degree of dilution is increased, and new composite functional spaces appears. By sorting out the logical relationship between Lingnan rural complex ecosystem and multi-functional space, this paper analyzes the relationship between settlement ecology and business type, form and culture based on the current situation, summarizes the distribution characteristics of its spatial functions, and studies the realization path of ecological landscape value and the improvement of rural spatial experience. In the process of ecological landscape value development research, according to the regional characteristics of Lingnan water cultural landscape, focus on the "five senses" experience value of water ecological landscape, evaluate the distribution of water ecological sensitive areas in Lingnan rural, so as to grasp the degree of value development of natural resources, and summarize the impact of water ecology in the process of spatial development of traditional settlements in Lingnan. Finally, from a multi-dimensional perspective, targeted development strategies for the ecological landscape value of settlements were proposed. Based on ecological industry, economic development, spatial aesthetics, regional culture and surrounding resources, planning design and future prospects were proposed for the development of ecological landscape value of Lingnan rural areas, and sustainable and high-quality development paths for the water ecological landscape value of Lingnan settlements were summarized.

Keywords: Lingnan countryside · water ecology · landscape experience · value development · sustainable development

© The Author(s), under exclusive license to Springer Nature Switzerland AG 2024
A. Marcus et al. (Eds.): HCII 2024, LNCS 14715, pp. 249–266, 2024.
https://doi.org/10.1007/978-3-031-61359-3_18

1 Introduction

In recent years, rapid socio-economic development has brought great changes to China's rural settlements, especially in the Lingnan region. As an important area of economic development zone in southern China, the settlement changes in Lingnan region reflect the collision and integration of traditional culture and modern development to a certain extent. Historically, Lingnan villages have rich cultural heritage and unique ecological environment, but with urban expansion and socio-economic development, the pattern of the spatial functions has undergone great changes, resulting in the loss and neglect of the traditional cultural and environmental values of the settlements.

The spatial reconstruction of rural areas in China is an important dimension of rural transformation, which involves the land resource utilization of rural settlements, the change of human settlement environment and the transformation of economic development [1, 2]. For the traditional rural settlements in Lingnan area, the growth process is closely related to the surrounding environment, especially the wide distribution of water system, which makes the proportion and radiation range of water ecological space in Lingnan villages different from that of general rural settlement space. According to the existing research, scholars mainly start from the level of land use for the spatial reconstruction of rural settlements [3], pay attention to the social problems of the "hollowing" of traditional rural settlements [4, 5], and study the spatial morphology [6], spatial differentiation [7], influencing factors and dynamic mechanisms [8, 9], tourism development [10], evaluation system [11, 12]. There is a lack of attention to the spatial distribution and change process of "ecology-format-form-culture" of rural settlements from a comprehensive perspective. The interweaving of water in Lingnan rual areas leads to the spatial layout of villages forming a comb layout with water as the vein and road as the network, and its water ecology and other spaces show a superimposed and inclusive distribution state. With the development of modernization and industrialization, land use and landscape patterns evolve frequently [13], and general rural construction often focuses on the development of business formats, broadens the space and intensity of industrial development, showing the situation that business space gradually occupy ecological space, resulting in an imbalance of rural production, life and ecology [14].

In addition, the value development of Lingnan villages is relatively inefficient, the potential is not fully realized, and lacks reasonable resource management. The rich historical and cultural resources and unique ecological environment of the settlements in Lingnan are of high value, but due to the lack of scientific and systematic planning and management, these resources have not been reasonably developed and utilized. Some settlements only stay at the level of traditional cultural heritage protection, but the bottom number of cultural heritage has not been figured out, and many cultural resources are at risk of extinction [15]. Located in a special intertwined water network and as part of the natural and cultural heritage, the water ecological landscape plays an important ecological function and cultural significance in the Lingnan countryside. However, the traditional landscape planning model of settlements water system has not yet been formed, and the research directions are mostly the research and inheritance of the water management wisdom in famous towns and villages with major historical functions [16] and the ecological planning of water landscape [17]. But the mountain-water resources near the common villages have not been properly protected and managed, resulting in water pollution and the deterioration of water ecological environment. With the modernization of traditional settlements, the space and function of water ecology have gradually changed, and the functions of fire prevention, defense and irrigation have gradually declined, while the functions of landscape construction and public space shaping have improved [18], so the value of water ecological landscape needs to be viewed at from a new perspective.

In summary, the development and spatial experience of Lingnan rural ecological landscape face many problems and challenges. In order to effectively solve these problems, we carry out research on the value development and experience degree of relevant water ecological landscapes, put forward effective development and design strategies to expand the sustainable development direction of Lingnan countryside.

2   Literature Review

2.1   Complex Ecosystem of Traditional Settlements

The ecosystem of traditional settlements refers to the general term of living and non-living common organisms that are linked and interact with each other in a certain form of material and energy exchange within the territorial scope of the settlement. Its ecosystem is a "natural-social-economic" composite system [19], which is a complex of life forms. Liu Binyi, Wang Yuncai and other scholars proposed that the rural landscape should be based on five index factors of habitability, accessibility, compatibility, sensitivity and beauty, the evaluation index system of rural landscape should be guided by human settlements [20]. In the ecological landscape planning of Lingnan countryside, the organic combination of four elements of ecology, business format, form and culture which called "four states" should be considered [21].

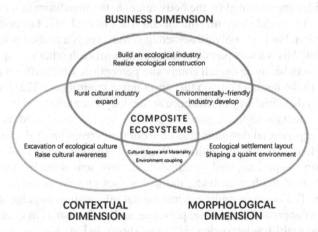

Fig. 1. Traditional settlements conform to the ecosystem structure map.

As shown in Fig. 1, for traditional rural settlements, the ecosystem is both the advantage and the bottom line, and all production and life are carried out on the ecosystem.

The close integration of traditional settlements and ecology forms a unique ecological landscape. At the same time, there is no substitute for this ecological resource, once it is destroyed, both life and production of the settlement will not develop sustainably. Therefore, ecology is the primary consideration. The format of business means the industrial productivity, and the industrial development of the countryside should develop in the direction of modernization, ecology, science and technology. The economic base determines the superstructure, one of the key goals in rural revitalization is to make farmers rich. The development of business forms is the key element second only to ecology, and can also be integrated with ecology. Maximizing the value of ecological resources and transforming them into ecological industries can promote the industrial transformation of traditional settlements and optimize the industrial structure. While realizing ecological construction, it also promotes production development and improves economic level, so as to give back to ecological construction, which can form a multi-level circulation body of ecological resources with multi-industry integration. Form and culture represent the social system, form refers to the three-dimensional form of physical space, showing the social form of the whole settlement, while culture is the connotation, which refers to the historical culture and spiritual symbolism and is the key element that distinguishes it from other settlements. These "four states" are interrelated and complementary, and together constitute a harmonious and coordinated composite ecosystem. The disorder of some elements will cause the imbalance of other elements, affecting or destroying the entire system.

2.2   The Phenomenological Experience of the Body

Judging the experience of feeling in the environment can be studied from the theory of the body phenomenology. Body phenomenology, proposed by Merleau-Ponty, mainly emphasizes that the human body is the basis of all perceptual and cognitive activities. The experience and feeling obtained by the body refers to the transformation of the original objective abstract material space into the mental space of the body. The body is the main body of perception, but it not only possessed of senses, but is a unified perceptual body, which is connected by various parts who cooperate with each other in a special way, so that the experiencer forms an overall composite perception, which affects the judgment and evaluation of the human body on the surrounding environment [22].

Perception is the initial way of existence of the body. People first get in touch with the external environment through intuition, and all the senses are connected with each other. Therefore, the experiential design is studied from the perception of the five senses and the four-layer phenomenal body intuitively feels and experiences the landscape. Among them, perception has primacy and synesthesia, the five senses are the most direct and fastest perception of the human body, the five senses include vision, hearing, touch, smell and taste, The organs capture environmental information to judge the landscape characteristics of appreciable, audible, playable, and tasting, so as to establish a multi-dimensional and multi-level experience [23], as shown in Fig. 2.

The landscape space experience design should connect the surrounding environment elements through each senses of the human being to meet the all-round sensory experience. Landscape provides people with various types of perceptual information. Various perceptual systems cooperate and transform to form a rich and multi-layered sense of

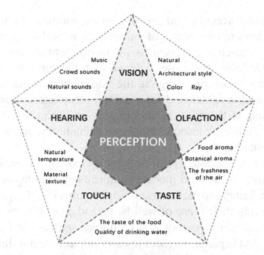

Fig. 2. Sensory experience map of traditional settlement landscape.

landscape experience when people are in the environment [24]. Space refers to the field environment where the human body is located, and only when people are affected by the environment in the space and produce corresponding emotions or associations can they produce the experience of "sense of place", which is the process of spatial cognition and positioning. For the space, it should not only stay in the perceptual state of viewing, but also enhance the connection and communication between people and the site through more interactive design.

Therefore, the improvement of the experience of landscape space should first pay attention to the use of multi-sensory perception, the difference of hard and soft quality, morphological changes, etc. can bring different psychological feelings. Starting from the human body's vision, hearing, smell and taste, we should divide enough rich functional partitions and mobile viewing routes to create a full range of high-quality sensory experience and orderly space.

3 Research Method

3.1 Ecological Value Extraction and Cognition

The reconstruction of rural space under the value development of rural ecological landscape in Lingnan is the comprehensive manifestation of its transformation, and the main factors affecting the development of landscape value include market docking and transformation of production mode, villagers' value cognition, planning and management. Market demand is the fundamental way to promote industrial development and the path of economic upgrading. The urbanization of the Pearl River Delta has generated huge trade flows and market demand, which has accelerated the transformation and development of Lingnan's industries. In the face of the advantages of rural ecological resources, the industrial development is oriented to ecology, and the ecological industrialization of Lingnan countryside is mainly in the two directions of tourism industry and agricultural and commercial industry. Regular and irregular leisure tourism activities are carried out to attract urban residents to experience life in settlements and sell agricultural products at the same time, so as to achieve the positive interaction between ecology and economy. It is necessary to strengthen the close dialogue with the surrounding areas, establish an information sharing platform, integrate the information of the surrounding scenic spots, obtain comprehensive demand information, formulate corresponding products and services according to the needs of different groups, meet diverse needs, integrate and link agriculture, landscape resources and tourism industry, and achieve coordinated development and sustainability.

Through the value development of of ecological landscape, the traditional cognition is changed, the sharing of the high income from ecological industry and the publicity and education guide farmers to realize more value returns of ecological landscape. For rural farmers, improving their sense of well-being and economic strength is the fundamental guarantee to keep farmers rooted in traditional settlements for a long time. The responsible team should organize farmers to carry out technical training, teach modern agricultural technology, and improve agricultural technology and knowledge. Guiding farmers to participate in the management and construction of ecological resources in rural areas, encouraging farmers to operate themselves under the development of eco-cultural tourism industry can improve income stability and full employment to achieve a sufficient material life. It reshapes the local villagers' perception of ecological value from the perspective of actual benefits by improving infrastructure construction and the quality of life, and can consolidate the mass foundation for the further development of the ecological landscape. Hrough the coordinated development of industries and the development of the cultural value of ecological resources, the competitiveness and development power of the entire Lingnan rural industry can be enhanced, and the sustainable development of ecology, business forms and culture can be promoted.

3.2 Types and Development of Ecological Resources

In view of the value development of traditional settlements landscape in Lingnan and the maximum use of its ecological value and unique regional resources, the development of rural tourism has become the most sustainable and ecological development direction. The process of value development of Lingnan rural landscape will gradually change from the traditional endogenous "population growth + self-sufficiency" driving model to the outward-looking "tourism demand + industrial output" driving model. The spatial reconstruction process of traditional settlements adapts to changes of local communities and the needs of new mobile tourism groups [25]. The different combinations of "ecological space, morphological space, cultural space, and business space" in the new rural composite space create a composite space with unique charm and function through the mutual penetration and integration of different fields.

As shown in Table 1, most of the new composite spaces are formed by the combination of ecological elements and other spatial elements in rural areas. The continuous extension of the value of ecological elements has formed the overlap of various elements and ecology in different spaces, resulting in the largest proportion of ecological elements in the overall site. The most prominent manifestation of the new composite space is the change of rural land types [2, 26]. In the traditional rural space utilization type, it not

Table 1. Spatial typology and representation of Lingnan villages.

The type of space		Characterization of land use type
Traditional village space	Ecological space	It refers to the land used for the ecological environment outside the village, including rivers, mountains, woodlands, wastelands, etc
	Format space	It includes cultivated land for traditional agricultural production, fish ponds, and land for tourism industry (tourism facilities, parking lots, etc.) and other industrial land (such as industrial land)
	Literary space	Historical and cultural inheritance sites generally refer to traditional architectural spaces and public service lands with cultural inheritance value
	Morphological space	The form of a building community formed by ordinary residential land and public places
A new type of composite space	Ecology and morphology are compounded	The combination of natural environment and modern buildings or facilities, such as the integration of ecological agricultural parks and agricultural facilities, forms a rural form with ecological and traditional atmosphere
	Ecology and business forms are compounded	The integration of the natural environment and the agricultural industry, such as the combination of picking gardens, happy markets and rural tourism, realizes the dual benefits of ecology and economy
	Complex form and business format	The integration of traditional architectural features with cultural tourism, agriculture and other industries, such as the combination of farmhouses and experience areas, shows the history, culture and style characteristics of the countryside, and promotes rural economic development and industrial upgrading

only meets the living needs of local residents, but also meets the space consumption needs of outsiders. In addition, a large number of spatial agglomeration and industrial clusters generated by it promote the formation of a complete supporting infrastructure system and public service system in the space, resulting in a fundamental change from the original traditional space type. Due to the important position of water system in the rural layout of Lingnan, the value of water ecology has been valued and reflected from various aspects such as architectural layout, decorative symbolism, and spiritual beliefs. At present, the combination of rural ecology and business forms in Lingnan is one of the important considerations in the work of rural revitalization, which is no longer limited to the form and non-material level, but can also have the value of actual economic returns.

4   Data Collection and Analysis

4.1   Lingnan Rural Space Experience Research

From the perspective of regional synergy, this paper establishes a model of Lingnan rural tourist experience by selecting samples and conducting field investigation, questionnaire survey and tourist interviews according to the spatial changes of the "four states" of Lingnan countryside. The model selects factors such as tourism environment, tourism facilities, tourism services, cultural display and tourists' willingness to construct an evaluation index system of Lingnan rural ecological landscape experience. In the research process, SPSS software was used to quantify the survey data, the accuracy of the survey results was analyzed by data statistics and factor analysis, and the influence of variables on the experience degree is tested according to the contribution rate of factor variance, and finally the evaluation and impact factor analysis of Lingnan rural tourism experience degree are completed, so as to obtain the relationship and influence between tourists' experience perception and post-tour behavior, establishing a comprehensive evaluation system of tourist experience degree [27].

According to the construction of the evaluation system, the questionnaire is designed to investigate the degree of tourism experience. Tourism experience degree is designed based on the comprehensive evaluation system of tourist experience, including four experience elements: environment, facilities, culture and services. Among them, the sub-items of each element are 5 in environmental experience (regional climate, mountain and forest style, water landscape quality, and environmental sanitation), the facility experience is divided into 7 (accommodation, catering, tour facilities, Booking System, transportation, and network coverage), 5 in cultural experience (festival activities, folk customs experience, picking experience, depth of connotation, and sense of cultural scene), and 4 in service experience (tour guide service, science and technology service, shopping service, and after-sales service). 2 travelers' wishes include whether they are willing to revisit and whether they are willing to recommend to friends and family. In terms of index assignment, the most commonly used Likert scale in the field of social survey was used to evaluate the sense of experience, evaluation and post-intention. In the design of specific questions, a 5-level scale was adopted, that is, the experience degree of each evaluation index system was divided into five levels: "high, relatively high, average, relatively low, and low", and through continuous processing, the values were assigned 5 points, 4 points, 3 points, 2 points, and 1 points. Whether you are willing to revisit and whether you are willing to recommend to relatives and friends are divided into 5 levels: very willing, willing, unsure, unwilling, and very unwilling, which are also represented by 5–1 points [28].

4.2 Data Results Analysis

Based on the overall analysis of the content of the questionnaire survey, it can be concluded that the importance of the influencing factors of rural ecological landscape experience are "in the order of environmental experience > cultural experience > facility experience > service experience", indicating that rural ecological landscape experience is the primary factor of rural tourism development, and people's pursuit of rural tourism experience focuses on environment and culture. This is in line with the definition and analysis of tourism motivation in tourism psychology. The expectation of the two is the highest. In the actual score, the facility experience and cultural experience score are the lowest, respectively 3. 709 and 3. 741. The results show that there is a large gap between the tourists' expectations of cultural experience and the actual feelings of rural tourism. It also further indicates that the cultural connotation of different villages in the same region has little difference, and the current form of expression cannot meet the novelty needs of tourists.

As shown in Table 2, in terms of environmental experience, the feedback from the survey questionnaire data shows that tourists had the lowest quality of water landscape, with only 3.664 points, indicating that tourists do not have a strong sense of the interaction between people and water in Lingnan countryside, and that most of the interaction with water in the interview was limited to visual appreciation. The scores of regional climate and mountain scenery are at the forefront, especially tourists' expectations of mountain scenery before visiting are not very high, but in the actual tourism process, tourists feel strongly about it, indicating that the overall experience of ecological landscape is excellent. However, according to the survey, most of the agricultural space in Lingnan countryside is subordinated to construction activities, and the increase of the population of villagers leads to the evolution of some cultivated land into scattered residential places, which lacks reasonable planning.

In terms of facility experience, through the experience of tourists after traveling, it is found that tourists have the lowest evaluation of tour facilities, with an average of only 3.513 points, indicating that there are many criticisms in the construction of rural tourism service facilities in Lingnan. Combined with the actual survey, it is found that in addition to the large scenic spots, the construction and standardization of rural tourism service system such as tourist distribution (service) center, parking lot, and streamline design system still need to be further improved. The scores in characteristic accommodation, special catering, tourism and transportation are also low, and the open space of the villages has a scheme that copies urban design, and the space utilization is too simple. In the Lingnan countryside, where the tourism industry is relatively underdeveloped, the new construction of buildings still lacks the inheritance of traditional culture. Many three or four floors of all-cement buildings are incompatible with the whole, and they copy the public's rural building architectural style, which is seriously homogeneous. As for the existing historical buildings, there is a lack of renovation and maintenance, and their architectural structures and skin styles are damaged to varying degrees.

In terms of cultural experience, the factor load of folk customs experience and picking experience was 0.821 points and 0.728 points, indicating that tourists value both the most. However, in the actual score, the score of picking experience activity is relatively low, indicating that the actual display and performance level of agricultural picking

Table 2. 4 Factor analysis of tourists' experience degree.

Observe variables	Indicator variables	Factor load	Index average	Experience averages	Eigenvalue	Cumulative variance contribution rate
Environmental experience	Regional climate	0.736	4.112	3.886	2.806	65.36%
	Mountains and forests	0.585	4.321			
	Water landscape quality	0.694	3.664			
	Environmental Hygiene	0.686	3.942			
Facility experience	Lodging	0.603	3.756	3.709	2.512	59.61%
	Catering	0.623	3.665			
	Tour Kit	0.490	3.513			
	Booking System	0.719	3.651			
	Traffic	0.547	3.551			
	Network coverage	0.507	3.958			
Cultural Experience	Festive events	0.583	4.037	3.741	3.005	68.32%
	Folklore experience	0.622	3.561			
	Cultural depth	0.728	3.765			
	Picking experience	0.821	4.226			
	A sense of cultural scene	0.684	3.314			
Service Experience	Guided tours	0.545	4.322	3.870	1.812	52.44%
	Technology services	0.678	3.615			
	Shopping services	0.691	3.654			
	After-sales service	0.699	3.887			
Tourist wishes	Willingness to revisit	0.531	3.824	3.997	1.654	61.32%
	Willingness to recommend	0.495	4.169			

experience in the design of Lingnan rural activities is low, and the quality of activities needs to be further improved. From the point of view of the lowest score, tourists have the lowest evaluation of the Lingnan cultural and historical sense of scene, tourists are not satisfied with the experience effect of the same simple furnish to show Lingnan culture, and the similarity of tourism products in many scenic spots is serious, which reduces the tourism experience of tourists.

From the scores of all secondary index variables, in addition to the above indicators, combined with the tourists' visits, it is found that the tourists' experience of Lingnan rural water ecological landscape, agricultural picking experience, and cultural customs activities are low, indicating that the development of Lingnan rural areas in these aspects still needs to be improved. Based on the experience degree of Lingnan countryside, the path to enhance landscape value and experience sense is formulated from the "four state" level, especially the ecological level, as shown in Fig. 3.

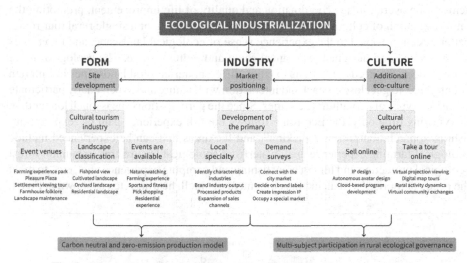

Fig. 3. Lingnan Rural Ecological Landscape Experience Improvement Path.

5 Discussion

5.1 Spatial Function Planning

Narrative experience refers to the language of the site. The landscape composed of materials has the function of cultural information transmission and narrative, which can arouse people's understanding of spiritual culture through the evolution of different scenes and the construction of the site. Therefore, for the overall spatial planning of Lingnan countryside, it is necessary to establish a set of targeted land use adjustment strategies based on the in-depth analysis of the current situation of rural land use and a comprehensive understanding of its landscape and spatial language, which are carefully divided into five adjustment zones: landscape restoration block, landscape protection area, building demolition block, building retention block and building rectification block.

Within the landscape restoration block, the layout and pruning of natural and agricultural landscapes are optimized to improve the overall quality and ornamental value of the landscape, and enhance the visual beauty of the farmland. For the site after the demolition of redundant and scattered buildings, the overall environmental landscape atmosphere and quality of the countryside can be improved through vegetation planting or construction of public facilities. Within the building retention block, buildings of historical and cultural value are evaluated and identified in detail, and corresponding conservation measures are formulated. These measures include structural reinforcement, maintenance and protect utilization, etc., can enhance the habitability and safety of traditional buildings to ensure that the historical and cultural values of these buildings are fully protected, transmitted and revitalized for re-use. In the building rectification block, the exterior of a large number of newly built cement buildings are mainly remodelled, the optimization of internal space and the improvement of energy efficiency are aimed to achieve the overall image coordination and quality of life improvement, promoting the implementation of cultural tourism projects in the planning of a single rural tour route, better attention is paid to the experience sense of ecological landscape, and two routes are renovated and designed: ecological route and cultural route. The ecological route mainly meets the needs of tourists to enjoy different agricultural landscapes in Lingnan countryside, to get close contact and interaction with nature and to personally participate in various types of agricultural activities. Since the participation time is much longer than the viewing time only, the Eco-route follows the 6-h experience path of "exploration-fishing-appreciation-presence-picking", and the areas that can be experienced include ecological farming experience area, waterfront ecological leisure area, mountain forest ecological protection and hiking area, fishing and camping experience area, etc., to meet the needs of tourists' visual, tactile, enjoyment of smell, hearing, etc., as shown in Fig. 4.

Fig. 4. Lingnan rural ecological route design idea diagram.

The cultural route mainly satisfies the tourists' appreciation of the traditional cultural buildings in Lingnan countryside and the experience of the characteristic agricultural industry. According to the sightseeing path of "enter-find-browse-visit-taste", the 4-h short-term travel experience avoids the excessive fatigue of tourists, and the areas that can be experienced include the core historical and cultural area, handicraft and intangible cultural heritage display area, traditional folk house experience area, characteristic catering and commercial areas, public activities and entertainment areas and other lively and cheerful entertainment venues full of local cultural atmosphere can satisfy tourists' visual, auditory, taste and other perceptual pleasures, as shown in Fig. 5.

Fig. 5. Lingnan rural cultural route design idea diagram.

5.2 Regional Scenery and Activity Experience

The activity nodes on each route are designed to meet the needs of different tourists and provide a richer and more diverse travel experience. At the same time, it also contributes to the protection and inheritance of Lingnan rural water culture and ecological environment, the functions and senses affected by each zone and activity node are shown in Table 3:

In the planning of residential and cultural areas, the focus is on the maintenance and renewal of the traditional Lingnan building community form, highlighting and retaining the characteristic elements of Lingnan traditional architecture, such as sloping roofs, arcades, patios, etc., restoring and protecting them to maintain their historical and cultural value and enhance the visual experience. Building materials and technologies are updated, new building materials and technologies, such as reinforced concrete, steel structures, etc., are adopted to strengthen and transform traditional buildings, to improve their seismic resistance, waterproofing and other properties, while maintaining their traditional appearance and style. On the basis of maintaining the appearance and style of traditional buildings, modern facilities and functions are added, such as elevators, air conditioning, intelligent management, etc., to improve the quality of life and comfort of residents. In the process of maintaining traditional buildings, we also pay attention to ecological environmental protection, adopting environmentally friendly materials and energy-saving technologies to reduce the impact on the environment. These improvements help to maintain the historical and cultural value of the traditional Lingnan architectural community, while improving its residential and use functions to provide a better living and tourism experience for local residents and tourists.

Table 3. 6 Node design, function and sensory experience.

Zone attributes	function	Sensory categories	Sensory experience
Core Historic and Cultural District	Preserve historic buildings and showcase their historical and cultural heritage	Sight, sound, touch	Visit historic buildings, listen to guided tours, participate in cultural activities, and more
Handicrafts and intangible cultural heritage exhibition area	Showcase handicraft skills and intangible cultural heritage	Sight, touch, taste	Watch the handicrafts being made, taste handicrafts, learn about intangible cultural heritage, and more
Ecological farming experience area	Protecting the farmland landscape and providing farming experience activities	Sight, hearing, touch, taste	Participate in farming activities, learn about the growing process of crops, taste local produce, etc
Waterfront ecological recreation area	Protect the ecological environment of the water area and provide a water-friendly leisure place	Sight, Hearing, Touch,	Enjoy water features, participate in water sports, free fishing, and more
Forest ecological protection and hiking area	Strengthen the ecological protection of mountains and forests, and provide hiking routes and facilities	Sight, hearing, touch, smell	Hike adventures, see natural scenery, learn about wildlife, and more
Traditional Folk House Experience Zone	Renovate traditional houses, provide homestay services, and experience the local way of life	Sight, hearing, touch, smell	Stay in traditional houses, taste local food, participate in local cultural activities, and more
Specialty dining and commercial areas	Local food and handicraft markets are available to meet the shopping and dining needs of tourists	Sight, hearing, taste, smell	Taste local specialties, buy handicrafts, learn about local business culture, and more
Public Activities & Entertainment Zone	It provides public activity plazas and entertainment facilities, and holds various public events such as celebrations and performances	Sight, hearing, touch, smell	Participate in various festivals, performances, entertainment, and more

In the agricultural ecological landscape area, the design focuses on the use of land and the sustainable value development of cultivated land. Through the application of organic fertilizers, biological fertilizers, etc., the content of soil organic matter is increased, soil structure and fertility are improved,, and the pollution of soil and water resources is reduce. Crop rotation, intercropping and other planting methods are adopted to alleviate soil continuous cropping obstacles and maintain soil health and sustainable use. At the same time, the construction of water ecological landscape should be strengthened, and remediation and restoration should be considered first, mainly including improving the water quality and ecological environment of water bodies through dredging, slope protection and other measures. According to the characteristics of water resources and historical and cultural background of each village in Lingnan, the node design of the water landscape is carried out to coordinate the water landscape with the overall style of the village and improve the landscape quality of the village. Waterscape facilities, such as waterscape sculptures, fountains, pools, etc., are improved to increase the ornamentation and interaction of waterscapes and provide better leisure and entertainment interaction space for villagers and tourists.

Experience is obtained through the movement of the body in space, not limited to staying in static, but constantly obtaining the unity of body and consciousness, space and time through a dynamic process. Tourism experience activities are an important part of rural economic development. By providing rural tourism, farming experience and other services, tourists are attracted to experience rural life, increasing the visibility and attractiveness of the countryside, and driving economic benefits. Cultural inheritance activities are an important way to protect and promote traditional rural culture. By holding traditional festivals, folk performances and other activities, villagers and tourists can understand and inherit the local culture and history, enhancing the sense of identity and cohesion of rural culture. These activities strengthen the communication and interaction of the site, and have a deeper experience of the surrounding environment.

In addition, the degree of experience can not only be improved in route planning, sight design and scene creation, but also in cloud design through technology applications, interactive experience design and other means to enhance tourists' in-depth participation and experience. Through the design of diversified activities and experiences, people can get close to nature, feel the agility and power of nature. Through innovative methods and tools, such as virtual reality and augmented reality, visitors can more intuitively understand and experience the charm of the traditional residential ecological landscape.

In summary, through the spatial planning and activity design of "ecology-industry-form-culture" and the online-offline development interaction, the value and experience of Lingnan's rural ecological landscape are comprehensively developed, the ecological development is fully integrated with the industry, culture and form to promote the combination of rural industries with tourism, culture and other industries, so as to realize the diversified and complementary development of industries. Through the coordinated development of the industry, the competitiveness of the entire industry can be enhanced, and the multi-level circulation of ecological resources with multi-industry integration can be built. It can transform ecological resources into ecological capital, and realize the benign interaction between ecology and economy, breaking through the boundaries of time and space and carrying out internal and external linkage, and inject new vitality into the rural development of Lingnan.

6 Conclusion

The content of this article focuses on the ecological landscape value development and spatial experience design of Lingnan settlements. Firstly, through a comprehensive analysis of the problems and advantages of the environment in the Lingnan settlements, the change of spatial pattern of ecological landscape in Lingnan settlement and its driving factors were discussed. Secondly, this paper focuses on the spatial layout, landscape characteristics and spatial experience of the ecological landscape of Lingnan settlements, analyze and evaluate the effects and problems of the existing rural ecological landscape development activities in Lingnan, and put forward strategies and measures for improvement and optimization. This paper focuses on the combination of value development and spatial experience of Lingnan settlement water ecological landscape, comprehensively considers ecological spatial planning and people's perception and experience of landscape, seeks to establish a sustainable management and protection mechanism, and emphasizes the importance of integrated management and sustainable development.

The in-depth study of the ecological landscape of traditional settlements in Lingnan reveals a complex system that interweaves nature and culture, history and modernity. These landscapes are not only natural beauty, but also carriers of history and culture, which have witnessed the development and changes of the Lingnan region. Through the in-depth research on the aquatic landscape, we can better understand the interrelationship between the natural environment and human activities in the Lingnan region. In the future, the research on the ecological landscape of traditional Lingnan settlements will continue to explore its ecological and cultural values and how to better enhance the experience of tourists. This will not only help protect and inherit these precious natural and cultural heritages, but also provide new impetus for the sustainable development of the Lingnan region. Through continuous and in-depth research and exploration, we look forward to fully excavating and displaying the value of the ecological landscape of traditional Lingnan settlements in the future, emitting a more brilliant light.

Funding. This research was funded by Humanities and Social Sciences Project Planning Fund of the Ministry of Education, grant number 23YJAZH013. This research was funded by Guangdong Provincial Philosophy and Social Sciences "14th Five-Year Plan" Fund, grant number GD22CYS23.

References

1. Zhang, X.L.: Study on rural spatial system and its revolution: A Case Study of South Jiang-su Region. Nanjing Normal University Press, Nanjing (1999)
2. Long, H.L.: Land use and rural transformation development in China. Science Press, Beijing (2012)
3. Han, F., Cai, J.M.: The evolution and reconstruction of peri-urban rural habitat in China. Geograph. Res. **30**(7), 1271–1284 (2011)
4. Wang, C.X., Yao, S.M., Chen, C.H.: Empirical study on "village-hollowing" in China. Scientia Geographica Sinica **25**(3), 257–262 (2005)
5. Xue, L.: Study on the inner decaying village and the countermeasures with Jiangsu province as the case. City Plann. Rev. **25**(6), 8–13 (2001)

6. Jia, Z.Y., Zhou, Z.X.: Morphological classification of traditional settlements in mountainous areas based on three-dimensional quantification and factor clustering methods: a case study of Miao settlements in southeast Guizhou. J. Mt. Sci. **37**(3), 424–437 (2019). https://doi.org/10.16089/j.cnki.1008-2786.000435

7. Wang, L., Zeng, J.: Spatial differentiation characteristics and types of village and town settlements in southwest Shandong: a case study of Heze city. Geogr. Res. **40**(8), 2235–2251 (2021)

8. Xi, H., Xiao, L., Liu, R.Q.: Evolution characteristics and driving mechanism of rural settlements in the marginal zone of the ancient city: a case study of Miaohou village in Han-cheng. Shaanxi. Areal Res. Dev. **37**(2), 158–162 (2018)

9. Yang, Y., Hu, J., Liu, D.J.: Research on the spatial differentiation and influencing factors of ethnic traditional villages in Guizhou province: based on six types of ethnic traditional villages. Arid Land Resour. Environ. **36**(2), 178–185 (2022). https://doi.org/10.13448/j.cnki.jalre.2022.053

10. Yan, M.M., Mei, Q., Wang, M.K.: Research on the development of rural tourism system from the perspective of complex adaptive system theory: a case study of Zhonghaoyu village, Zibo city Shandong province. Areal Res. Dev. **40**(5), 125–130 (2021)

11. Xiao, L.S., Yu, Z.W., Ye, H.: The research of coupling rural development and economy cluster in Fujian province. Acta Geogr. Sin. **70**(4), 615–624 (2015)

12. He, Y.H., Fan, S.G., Zhou, G.H.: Evaluation of rural transformation development in Hunan province based on major function oriented zoning. Prog. Geogr. **37**(5), 667–676 (2018)

13. Liu, D.Z., Du, S.S., Wang, C.X.: The change of tourism-oriented rural landscape pattern and the response of ecosystem service value: a case study of Taihu national tourism resort in Wuxi city, Jiangsu Province. Bull. Soil Water Conserv. **41**(5), 264–275,286 (2021). https://doi.org/10.13961/j.cnki.stbctb.2021.05.035

14. Yang, Y.Q.: The path selection of China's rural revitalization from the perspective of urban-rural integration. Discuss. Mod. Econ. **6**, 101–106 (2018). https://doi.org/10.13891/j.cnki.mer.2018.06.015

15. Chen, X.L., Yang, S.F.: The effectiveness, problems and countermeasures of the protection and inheritance of Lingnan traditional farming culture: From the perspective of rural industry revitalization. Agri. Archaeol. **01**, 170–176 (2023)

16. Lin, Q.: Research on the ecological wisdom of water management in traditional villages in Jinhua City, Zhejiang. Beijing Forestry University, Beijing (2020)

17. Chen, B.Y.: Research on water landscape ecological planning, design and technology of Dawei Village, Panyu District. South China University of Technology, Guangzhou (2010)

18. Yang, X.: Spatial landscape planning of the Lingnan water system. Hebei Agricultural University, Baoding (2013)

19. Fu, R., Hu, X.J.: A brief analysis of the comparison between rural ecosystem and urban ecosystem in China. Shanxi Architect. **14**, 6–7 (2007)

20. Wang, C.Y., Liu, B.Y.: On china's rural landscape and rural landscape planning. Chin. Garden **01**, 56–59 (2003)

21. Xi, J.C., Wang, S.K., Zhang, R.Y.: Spatial reconstruction and optimization of "production-life-ecology" in tourist rural settlements: a case study of Gougezhuang village in Yesanpo tourism area, Hebei province. J. Nat. Resour. **31**(03), 425–435 (2016)

22. Merleau-ponity, M.: The Primacy of Perception. Northwestern University Press, Evanston (1964)

23. Tang, X.X., Sun, X.M.: Experiential landscape design based on Meropont body phenomenology. Quest **12**, 188–192 (2015). https://doi.org/10.16059/j.cnki.cn43-1008/c.2015.12.037

24. Karson, R., Kiley, D.: Conversation with Kiley. Landscape Architect. **76**(2), 50–57 (1986)

25. Xi, J.C., Wang, X.G., Kong, Q.Q.: Micro-scale social spatial reconstruction of the tourist village in the past 25 years: A case study of Gouge Village in Yesanpo Hebei Province. Geogr. Res. **33**(10), 1928–1941 (2014)
26. Long, H.L.: Land consolidation and rural spatial restructuring. Acta Geographica Sinca **68**(8), 1019–1028 (2013)
27. ZhangSun, F.R.: Strategies for improving tourist satisfaction in red tourist attractions. Dev. Res. **06**, 154–160 (2018). https://doi.org/10.13483/j.cnki.kfyj.2018.06.023
28. Qi, L.B.: Statistical analysis and fuzzy comprehensive evaluation of Likert scale. Shandong Sci. **02**, 18–23+28 (2006)

Bibliometric Analysis on Intangible Cultural Heritage and Experience Marketing in China

Ting Chen[1], Zhiwei Zhou[1(✉)], and Zhen Liu[2]

[1] Management School, Guangzhou City University of Technology, Guangzhou 510800, China
zhouzw@gcu.edu.cn
[2] School of Design, South China University of Technology, Guangzhou 510006, China

Abstract. With the development of Chinese society and the progress of science and technology, the inheritance and development of the intangible cultural heritage are facing challenges. The topic 'how to protect and inherit the intangible cultural heritage' has become one of the most intense topics in the society. Experience marketing, as a new marketing method in the new economic era, makes the brand better leaving a deep impression in the minds of consumers. Although current Chinese studies have repeatedly conducted research on how to protect the intangible cultural heritage, few studies have further sorted out the connection between the intangible cultural heritage and experiential marketing. Therefore, this paper is to explore the intangible cultural heritage and marketing strategy, to address intangible culture with digital products and experience marketing strategy that could lead to future experience marketing strategy innovation and development with intangible culture and digital product integration in mind. A quantitative research method has been adopted, for which a **bibliometric approach via** CiteSpace software tool has been employed for analyzing the data obtained with intangible cultural heritage and marketing within China Knowledge Network (CNKI) since October 2010. The results suggest that in the digital marketing of intangible cultural heritage, intangible cultural heritage are better preservation, transformation and dissemination via digital products (games), which has a great significance to the permanent preservation and dissemination of intangible cultural heritage. In the future, with the social attention to intangible culture and through digital for intangible culture, it could provide a good platform for promoting intangible culture, with experience marketing and consumers as the center, creating a unique experience, and making the core connotation of intangible culture, which could become a new research trend in the field of marketing.

Keywords: Intangible · Cultural · Heritage · Experience · Marketing · Bibliometric · China · Digitalize

1 Introduction

Intangible cultural heritage is a brilliant result of the people across all ethnic groups in the long history of life and production, practice, accumulation, and creation, and handed down from generation to generation, which is the cultural brand and wisdom crystallization of a nation [1]. If the intangible cultural heritage is not protected and inherited in time, it will disappear [2]. Studies on the related fields of the intangible cultural heritage inheritance and marketing have been conducted, combining the intangible cultural heritage with modern elements, and strengthening the protection and inheritance of the intangible cultural heritage, such as research on multiple integration and innovation of intangible cultural heritage products marketing [3], analysis of cross-border marketing communication of intangible cultural heritage IP [4] and the impact of short video marketing promotion on the development of intangible cultural heritage "Guangdong Embroidery" [5]. In addition, in the current involved in the "intangible" and "marketing" two keywords related research, are mostly focused on building gen products and brand image [6], and for the traditional art class intangible IP refining and redesign, with emerging media technology and promotion channels for traditional art class intangible into the new era [4]. However, there is a lack of strategic research on the integration of intangible cultural heritage into digital products and experiential marketing, which leads to the problem of innovative development of intangible cultural heritage and experiential marketing strategies, and to the stagnation of the integrated development of intangible cultural heritage and digital products. Therefore, this paper is to explore the intangible cultural heritage and marketing strategy, to address intangible culture with digital products and experience marketing strategy that could lead to future experience marketing strategy innovation and development with intangible culture and digital product integration in mind.

2   Method of Data Collection and Analysis

This paper adopts the method of quantitative research to explore the key knowledge on marketing strategy for the inheritance of the intangible cultural heritage.

2.1   Data Collection

This paper employs China CNKI (CNKI) as the data source, and carries out literature search with "theme = " intangible cultural heritage" and "marketing", and the time span is to year 2023. The retrieval results of the papers (all journals) in the CNKI are selected as the research objects, and the retrieval time is October 21, 2023.

2.2   Analysis Method

This paper uses the bibliometric analysis via CiteSpace software to analyze the collected data with the author, keywords, and clustering, highlight the word of marketing strategy research knowledge map, explore hot spots and marketing strategy research development trend from the perspective of intangible cultural heritage marketing strategy, and make a clear understanding of the research hotspots and trends in recent years.

3 Results

3.1 A Bibliometric Analysis

Analysis of the Literature Quantity Distribution based on the Time Axis. The number of literature published and the publication time are the criteria to judge the research hotspots in this field. Through the CNKI journal theme for "intangible" and "marketing" search literature year distribution analysis, as shown in Fig. 1, it is found that "intangible" and "marketing" associated research started in 2010; in 2010–2015, the articles published less, no more than 5; and since 2016, the articles began to grow, at its peak in 2023 with 60 articles. In general, the research on "intangible cultural heritage" and "marketing" is still on the rise. From the changing trend of the number of publications, the field will continue to increase in the future. The reason of the number of publications reaching at a high level in 2021 could be that year 2021 is the first year of the 14th Five-Year Plan in China, of which the "prosperity and development of cultural undertakings and cultural industries" in the 14th Five-Year Plan formulated by China [7], will be continuously improved in the future to the field.

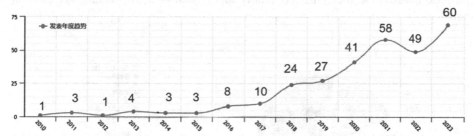

Fig. 1. Document volume distribution map of "intangible cultural heritage" and including "marketing" theme in 2010–2023.

Distribution Analysis of Literature Subject Fields. By analyzing the subject distribution of the literature, the distribution of research topics in each subject can be understood. According to the literature data provided by CNKI, it is found that the themes of "intangible cultural heritage" and "marketing" focus on intangible cultural heritage, intangible cultural heritage, strategic research, cultural and tourism integration, and intangible cultural heritage enterprises. The distribution of major disciplines is shown in Fig. 2, of which culture ranked the top of number of published articles, accounting for 18.54%, followed by enterprise economy and light industry industry, accounting for 11.39%, followed by art, calligraphy, sculpture and photography, accounting for 9.35%, and the fourth is tourism (9.01%), accounting for more than 50% in total.

Distribution Analysis of Focused Fields. By analyzing the distribution of the number of published journals, core journals in this field are concerned to intangible cultural heritage and marketing related topics. Through the visual analysis of CNKI, as shown in Fig. 3, during 2010–2023, "intangible" and "marketing" themes in the most journals

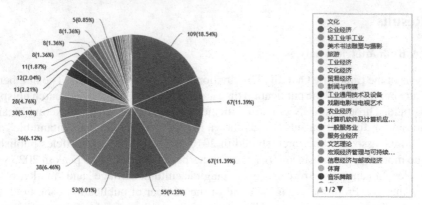

Fig. 2. Subject distribution chart of "intangible cultural heritage" and including "marketing" theme literature in 2010–2023.

is modern marketing (business) and western leather, accounted for 12.07%, followed by Guangxi quality supervision guide, marketing and cultural industry, modern marketing (business), western leather, Guangxi quality supervision guide, marketing, and cultural industry.

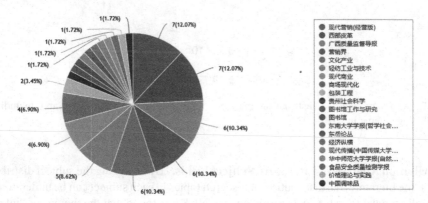

Fig. 3. Distribution chart of "intangible cultural heritage" and including "marketing" theme literature journals in 2010–2023.

3.2 Core Author Analysis

Visualization Atlas of the Core Author. The CiteSpace software has been used to analyze the authors of 228 selected papers. From 2010 to 2023, the top 10 authors to "intangible cultural heritage" and "marketing" related articles have been listed, As shown in Fig. 4, the first is Hou Ling, who has published 13 articles, and Zhou Xiating, Liu Jing, Tang Tianyi, Liu Yanran, Ren Ya, Zhang Dongyi, Liu Jiting, Wang Xinyue, and Hu Yongqian have published two articles each.

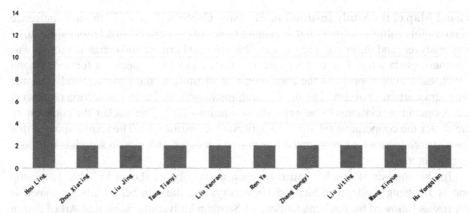

Fig. 4. Map of the publication volume of the core authors of the "intangible cultural heritage" and including the "marketing" theme in 2010–2023.

By using the CiteSpace visual analysis software, the author cooperation knowledge map in this field from 2010 to 2023 was obtained, as shown in Fig. 5, 192 nodes and 92 connections are formed, in which each node represents the corresponding author, and each connection represents the cooperation between authors. The thicker the connection, the closer the authors cooperate. According to the analysis of the knowledge graph, there is relatively little cooperation network between authors, and researchers are in a decentralized state. The cooperation team is mainly cooperation between two people, with Hou Ling as the key node. It can be seen that Hou Ling, Tang Tianyi, Liu Yanran, Zhang Dongyi, Liu Jiting and Hu Yongqian have all cooperated in two groups.

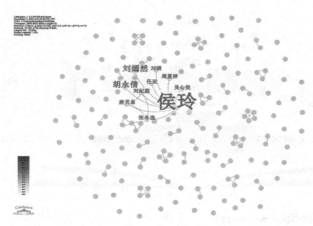

Fig. 5. Co-occurrence map of the core authors of China's "intangible cultural heritage" including the "marketing" theme research.

Visual Map of the Study Institution. By using CiteSpace software, the co-occurrence of intangible cultural heritage and marketing topics of cooperative institutions since 2010 was analyzed, and the visual map of intangible cultural heritage and marketing topics was obtained, as shown in Fig. 6. There are 164 nodes and 23 connections formed, among which each node represents the corresponding institution, the node size indicates the number of articles published by the research institution, and each connection represents the cooperative relationship between the institutions [16]. The thicker the connection, the closer the cooperative relationship between the institutions. The results showed that the research institutions cooperated less with each other, and most research institutions were scattered.

In the number of articles issued by each university, as shown in Table 1, the top one is Jincheng College of Sichuan University, and the number of articles issued is 10. It was followed by Jincheng College of Sichuan University, School of Art of Anhui University of Finance and Economics, and School of Art of Xiangtan University, all with three articles. Finally, Changzhou textile and garment vocational and technical college, Jiangsu normal university institute of media and film and television, central China normal university national cultural industry research center, Xiamen university Jiageng College, Tianjin university of technology, Beijing union university school of tourism, Zhejiang university city college of media and humanities college, and Shandong normal university business school, the number of articles are 2 respectively.

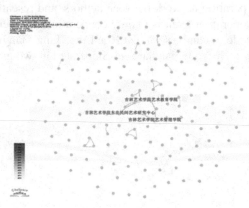

Fig. 6. Cooperation map of research institutions with Chinese "intangible cultural heritage" and "marketing" theme.

3.3 Analysis of Hot-Spot Keywords

Keyword Co-occurrence Map Analysis. By using the keyword co-occurrence map analysis in CiteSpace software, as shown in Fig. 7, the keyword co-occurrence map related to "intangible cultural heritage" and "marketing" has 210 nodes and forms 239 connections, and the overall network density is 0.0109. Keywords represent the core theme of the paper, and the keywords that often appear in the literature can be regarded

Table 1. Core research institutions of China's "intangible cultural heritage" and including the "marketing" theme.

serial number	frequency	institution	serial number	frequency	institution
1	10	Jincheng College of Sichuan University	7	2	The National Research Center for Cultural Industry, Central China Normal University
2	3	Sichuan University Jincheng College Computer and Software	8	2	Kah Kee College of Xiamen University
3	3	Art College of Anhui University of Finance and Economics	9	2	Institutes Of Technology Of Tianjin
4	3	School of Art, Xiangtan University	10	2	School of Tourism, Beijing Union University
5	2	Changzhou Textile and Garment Vocational and Technical College	11	2	School of Media and Humanities, City University of Zhejiang University
6	2	School of Media, Film and Television, Jiangsu Normal University	12	2	Business School of Shandong Normal University

as research hotspots in this field. The keywords of intangible cultural heritage, marketing strategy, network marketing, cultural and creative products, intangible cultural heritage, and other keywords appear frequently in the keyword co-occurrence map, with relatively large nodes, with the frequency of 29,15,13,12, and 11 respectively.

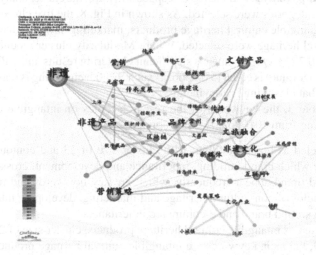

Fig. 7. Co-occurrence map of Chinese "intangible cultural heritage" with the theme of "marketing".

The centrality of keywords is mainly used to measure the importance of the keyword co-occurrence map. As shown in Table 2, the keywords with high centrality are heritage (0.19), then heritage (0.09), cultural and creative products (0.06), and Internet + (0.06). Among them, intangible cultural heritage has the highest frequency and the highest centrality in keyword co-occurrence, and is the most closely associated with other keywords, which highlight the core research themes in the field from 2010 to 2023.

Table 2. Frequency and central statistical table of China's "intangible cultural heritage" and "marketing" theme.

serial number	Keyword frequency			serial number	Keyword frequency		
	frequency	centrality	keyword		frequency	centrality	keyword
1	29	0.19	intangible cultural heritage	1	29	0.19	intangible cultural heritage
2	15	0.04	marketing strategy	2	11	0.09	Intangible cultural heritage
3	13	0	network marketing	3	12	0.06	Cultural and creative products
4	12	0.06	Cultural and creative	4	4	0.06	互联网+
5	11	0.09	Intangible cultural heritage	5	8	0.05	Intangible cultural heritage products
6	8	0.05	Intangible cultural heritage	6	7	0.05	Cultural and tourism integration
7	8	0.03	brand	7	3	0.05	innovate
8	7	0.05	Cultural and tourism	8	15	0.04	marketing strategy

Keyword Cluster Map Analysis. By using Citespace software, the cluster analysis was conducted, and five categories were selected. As shown in Fig. 8, the five cluster labels of brand building, intangible cultural heritage products, marketing strategy, marketing, and intangible cultural heritage were selected. Where Modularity cluster module value (Q value) is equal to 0.7743, Q > 0.3 means significant clustering results, and Silhouette cluster module value (S value) is equal to 0.9066, as such S > 0.5 clustering is reasonable and S > 0.7 means that clustering is convincing.

As shown in Table 3, the keywords of the research topics on intangible cultural heritage and marketing from 2010 to 2023 focus on five clusters:

(1) Cluster # 0, labeled as brand building, with cluster size of 23 and contour value of 0.881, among which brand building, inheritance and development, cross-border e-commerce, and brand appear frequently, which are key hot words and research hotspots in the fields of non-cultural heritage and marketing, developing intangible cultural heritage around brand and e-commerce inheritance.

(2) Cluster # 1, labeled as intangible cultural heritage products, cluster size of 21, contour value of 0.9, the main keywords are intangible cultural heritage products, cultural and tourism integration, and digital collection. At present, the development path of non-genetic inheritance is mainly the integration of cultural and tourism, which enables non-genetic inheritance to transform regional resource advantages into industrial advantages, to drive economic development and inherit the intangible cultural heritage.

(3) Cluster # 2, labeled as marketing strategy, cluster size 14, contour value 0.928, key words include marketing strategy, cultural and creative products, and marketing. As the driver of intangible cultural heritage, cultural and creative products fully display the cultural and artistic value and market value of cultural and creative products,

make the intangible cultural heritage return to the mass culture, and promote the inheritance and development of "intangible cultural heritage".

(4) Cluster # 3, labeled as marketing, cluster size 12, contour value 0.897, the main key hot words are marketing, communication, and public welfare marketing.

(5) Cluster # 4, labeled as intangible cultural heritage, cluster size 12, contour value 0.897, hot keywords include intangible cultural heritage, path, and Internet.

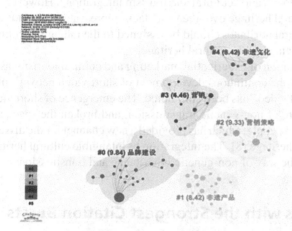

Fig. 8. Cluster map of China's "intangible cultural heritage" and "marketing" theme.

Table 3. Cluster table of Chinese "intangible cultural heritage" and "marketing" theme keywords.

Cluster number	Cluster size	Clustering tag names	Cluster profile	Clustering keywords
0	23	brand building	0.881	Brand building; inheritance and development; cross-border e commerce; brand; intangible cultural heritage
1	21	Intangible cultural heritage products	0.9	Intangible cultural heritage products; integration of culture and tourism; digital collection; brand; intangible cultural heritage
2	14	marketing strategy	0.928	Marketing strategy; cultural and creative products; marketing; intangible cultural heritage; intangible cultural heritage
3	12	marketing	0.897	Marketing; communication; public welfare marketing; Kuaishou intangible cultural heritage ip; local opera
4	12	Intangible cultural heritage products	0.897	Intangible cultural heritage; path; Internet; intangible cultural heritage; Internet +

Analysis of the Strongest Citation Burst Map of Keywords. "Burst words" refers to the key words that are more frequently cited in a certain period of time. Burst word analysis is used to find research hotspots and academic frontiers [16] Using CiteSpace software, Minimum Duration was set to 2 years, $\gamma = 0.2$, and 11 emerging the strongest citation burst words appeared from 2010 to 2023, as shown in Fig. 9.

As shown in Fig. 9, the brand research intensity emerging in 2019 is the strongest, with the emergence intensity of 2.13, followed by a short video study in 2021 with an emergent intensity of 1.3. In year 2014, study on inheritance, with an intensity of 1.2.

From the perspective of the mutation of keywords, in 2014, "inheritance" is a hot keyword in the field of intangible cultural heritage and marketing. Many intangible cultural heritage cultures are at the boundary of extinction, and how to inherit the intangible cultural heritage has become the focus of attention. From 2015 to 2018, digital development and marketing methods of intangible cultural heritage has been explored to build the cultural industry. In 2019, "brand" was a hot keyword in the related fields of intangible cultural heritage and marketing, focusing on the emerging keywords of "development strategy", "experience marketing", and "cultural and tourism integration". However, the inheritance of intangible cultural heritage over the years lacks representative brands and influence, and the brand cultural attributes should be assigned to the intangible cultural heritage products to boost the intangible cultural heritage.

The research on the integration of experiential marketing and cultural tourism lasted for a year. Since 2021, due to the continuous development of short video network platform, the emergence of "short video" has been stimulated. The emergence of short video has broken the regional nature of non-genetic transmission, and broken the space and time limit of communication in people, which has provided a new channel for the dissemination of intangible cultural heritage [8]. The integration of intangible cultural heritage with short videos innovates the way of non-genetic inheritance and transmission.

Top 11 Keywords with the Strongest Citation Bursts

Keywords	Year	Strength	Begin	End	2010 - 2023
传承	2014	1.2	2014	2017	
数字化	2015	1	2015	2020	
市场营销	2016	0.93	2016	2019	
文化产业	2018	1.06	2018	2019	
品牌	2019	2.13	2019	2021	
开发策略	2019	0.98	2019	2020	
体验营销	2019	0.98	2019	2020	
文旅融合	2019	0.64	2019	2020	
品牌建设	2020	0.7	2020	2021	
短视频	2021	1.3	2021	2023	
营销	2014	0.86	2021	2023	

Fig. 9. Burst map of China's "intangible cultural heritage" and keywords with the theme of "marketing".

Timeline Analysis of Keyword Clustering. The keyword timeline chart is used to indicate the main research content of a certain research subject changing over time, and reveal the research trend in a certain period of time. Using CiteSpace software, a timeline map of intangible cultural heritage and marketing was generated (Fig. 10).

In the intangible cultural heritage cluster, brand marketing related research first appeared in 2010, and has continued to the present.

In the cluster of intangible cultural heritage products, the relevant research on the innovation and development of intangible cultural heritage was published in 2018, and the branding research on intangible cultural heritage products began to increase in 2019, and by 2023, it has become a new trend.

In the cluster of cultural and creative products, related research on cultural and creative products appeared in 2022, developing into product development, and content marketing.

In the inheritance cluster, related research on protection, inheritance and marketing has been published since 2013, and related research on the digital marketing model began in 2017. In 2021, the relevant research on short video was published. In the era of financial media, short video platforms have received close attention in the studies, providing a new channel for the dissemination of intangible cultural heritage and focusing on new media marketing.

In the cluster of intangible cultural heritage, related research on Internet + appeared in 2018, developing towards IP and the living inheritance of intangible cultural heritage.

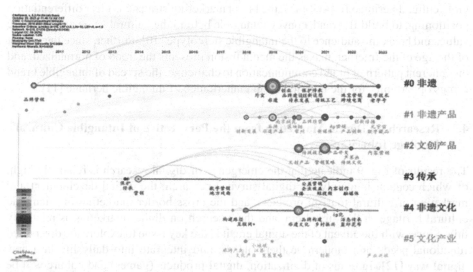

Fig. 10. Cluster timeline map of keywords containing Chinese "intangible cultural heritage" and "marketing" theme.

4 Discussion

This paper sorts out the research and academic articles on Chinese intangible cultural heritage and marketing related topics, and analyzes the keyword co-occurrence map, high frequency keywords and centrality, cluster timeline map, and keyword emergent map.

4.1 Research on Brand Marketing from the Perspective of Intangible Cultural Heritage Inheritance

The results of keyword cluster map analysis show that the cluster of brand building is large, and the frequency of keywords such as brand building and brand are high. The content is mainly the brand marketing of non-heritage brands, the integration of intangible cultural heritage products and tourism, and the creation of IP brands to inherit intangible cultural heritage. The results of Fig. 9, in 2019 to 2021, suggest that the highest brand research present strength, intangible, and a hot spot in the field of marketing keywords, from which the symbol behind the brand can project consumer self-image, when the brand associated with some meaning. This condenses, form a specific user group, to promote intangible heritage, so the brand is genetic inheritance and the development of important ways [9].

In addition, the results of Fig. 10 show that in 2018, related studies on Internet + appeared and gradually developed towards IP. IP can enable the cross-border integration between intangible cultural heritage and different brands, for which focus is on finding partners matching attributes and goals, refining the representative elements of both sides, and realizing the superposition and win-win of brand commercial value and intangible cultural heritage IP [4]. Since, the brand marketing strategy is clear differentiation positioning, to build IP brand, convey intangible behind the cultural value and aesthetic value, and break the audience to the intangible stereotype [10]. Further, since the advent of the age of the Internet, makes the media fusion presents the trend of normalized, and the inherent pattern of brand communication to challenge, the spread of intangible brand brings opportunity for the inheritance and inheritance of intangible heritage [11].

4.2 Research on Digital Marketing from the Perspective of Intangible Cultural Heritage Inheritance

The results of Fig. 9 indicate that the emergence of digital research is relatively high, of which content is mainly the digital survival research, the digital development and marketing of cultural tourism products, and the cross-border marketing of intangible cultural heritage in the digital era, and the research on digital marketing is relatively thin. Since, with the advent of the digital era, it is the key issue to explore the diversified functional needs and modern aesthetic needs, and integrate into daily life in a new digital way [12]. In terms of digitization, digital products (games) and culture will be integrated, for which it can not only in better spread traditional culture, but also in cultivate the stickiness of players, to promote the healthy development of China's game industry [13].

4.3 Research Hotspots and Trends

The research on the marketing strategy based on non-genetic inheritance mainly focuses on the brand marketing of intangible cultural heritage, the digital marketing of intangible cultural heritage, the integration of intangible cultural heritage and tourism, IP involvement in the field of intangible cultural heritage, and the combination of intangible cultural heritage and short video. It can be found that from the time map, the brand has not stopped, and the research under the theme of intangible cultural heritage, and the digitization research has only been published in recent years. The results of the emergence of key words suggest that the relevant research on experiential marketing of intangible cultural heritage has only appeared for one year; and the carriers carrying intangible cultural heritage are limited to cultural and creative products, tourist locations, and time-honored brands, which are rarely related to the dissemination of intangible cultural heritage from the digital game industry. Hence, the construction of the intangible cultural heritage brand is necessary [14]. The attention to the satisfaction of service and the spiritual satisfaction need to be paid for integrating own brand culture, innovation, and feelings. In addition, experience marketing is not only to provide customers with high-quality products, but also to provide them with specific situations to feel the intangible cultural heritage [6]. At the same time, the intangible cultural heritage can not only stay in the past, but can be enabled through digital games for innovative practices and breakthroughs [15]. However, at present, there is a lack of integration of intangible cultural heritage into game product collocation experience marketing, through the dissemination and inheritance of intangible cultural heritage, strengthen the influence of game brand, and convey the brand value, which could be a new trend.

5 Conclusion

At present, there are many ways to conduct the correlation between intangible cultural heritage and marketing, such as the brand marketing of intangible cultural heritage, the integration of intangible cultural heritage and tourism, and the combination of intangible cultural heritage, and short video. This paper analyzes the brand marketing under the inheritance of intangible cultural heritage, through the enabling brand attributes, which assist to protect and develop the intangible cultural heritage, while the brand marketing of intangible cultural heritage can gather and form a specific user group, attract users to understand, learn, and participate in the non-genetic inheritance, and promote the non-genetic inheritance and development. In the digital era, how to break the traditional marketing model, protect and develop the intangible cultural heritage is facing great challenges. This paper finds that in the digital marketing of intangible cultural heritage, intangible cultural heritage are better preservation, transformation and dissemination via digital products (games), which has a great significance to the permanent preservation and dissemination of intangible cultural heritage. In the future, with the social attention to intangible culture and through digital for intangible culture, it could provide a good platform for promoting intangible culture, with experience marketing and consumers as the center, creating a unique experience, and making the core connotation of intangible culture, which could become a new research trend in the field of marketing.

Acknowledgments. This study was funded by the 2022 Teaching Reform Project of Guangzhou City University of Technology, "Cultivation of School Level First-class Marketing Major" (No. 57/JY220132).

References

1. Zhou, Y.: Research on design and development strategy of Yangzhou tourism cultural and creative products from the perspective of intangible cultural heritage. Artist **07**, 139 (2020)
2. Wang, D.: Intangible cultural heritage cultural and creative products development and marketing model strategy exploration. Art Technol. **31**(07), 100–101 (2018)
3. Wen, C.: Discussion on the diversified integration and innovation of intangible cultural heritage product marketing. Cooperative Econ. Technol. **10**, 90–92 (2022)
4. Fan, C., Li, X.: Analysis on the cross-border marketing communication of intangible cultural heritage IP — Based on the perspective of traditional art intangible cultural heritage. Media Watch **12**, 85–90 (2022)
5. Liu, F., Li, J., Fan, W.: Impact of short video marketing and promotion on the development of intangible cultural heritage "Yue Embroidery." West. Leather **43**(08), 126–127 (2021)
6. Zhang, J., Qu, R., Liu, J., Yin, W., Wang, L.: Take Anji Bamboo as an example. West. Leather **43**(17), 130–131 (2021)
7. Xiao, M.: Recommendation algorithm + short video: Intangible cultural Heritage marketing portfolio innovation. Soc. Sci. Guizhou Province **02**, 141–147 (2021)
8. Deng, R.: Short video opens up a new path for non-genetic inheritance and transmission. China Press **08**, 20–21 (2020)
9. Wang, H.: Research on the marketing strategy of traditional art and intangible cultural heritage brands based on SICAS model. Beauty Times (top) **08**, 48–54 (2023)
10. Guo, F.: TikTok analysis of the brand marketing strategy of short video. Writing **04**, 178–179 (2021)
11. Hong, J.: Intangible cultural heritage brand marketing and communication strategy based on media convergence. Shanghai Arts Crafts **02**, 75–77 (2023)
12. Yang, J.: Research on the cross-border integration of intangible cultural heritage handicrafts in the digital era — Take Guangxi Mang bamboo weaving technology as an example. Footwear Proc. Des. **3**(01), 50–52 (2023)
13. Wang, X.: Research on the influence of the integrated development of "game + traditional culture" on players' cultural identity — Take the game skin of king of glory as an example. Int. Public Relat. **06**, 150–151 (2021)
14. Zhang, J.: Research on the marketing and promotion of intangible cultural brands in Hebei province. Mod. Mark. (Bus. Version) **03**, 112–113 (2020)
15. Huang, L., Wu, Y.: Take "king of glory" as an example. Humanistic World **04**, 43–48 (2023)
16. Dou, J., Zhang, B., Qian, X.: Review of research in the field of AI-enabled cultural heritage — visual analysis based on CiteSpace. Packag. Eng. **44**(14), 1–20 (2023)

Visitor's Museum Experience Model in Mixed Reality Environment from the Perspective of 4E Cognition

Ren Long[1], Wenyi Han[1] (ORCID), Ao Jiang[2,3]($\boxtimes$), and Xin Zeng[1]

[1] Huazhong University of Science and Technology, Wuhan 430000, Hubei, China
[2] Nanjing University of Aeronautics and Astronautics, Nanjing 210000, Jiangsu, China
aojohn928@gmail.com
[3] Imperial College London, London, UK

Abstract. With the advancement of technology, museums are evolving beyond static displays of artifacts to become more innovative and interactive cultural hubs. Embodied cognition plays a crucial role in this transformation. Cognition is the process of understanding and interacting with the world through physical means such as senses, movement, and spatial perception. In museums, it influences how we experience exhibits, remember history, and comprehend culture. Concurrently, the integration of mixed reality technology can extend existing spatial scenarios, assisting museums in integrating key information within exhibition spaces, thereby enhancing the overall user experience. This paper, grounded in the 4E cognition theory (Embodied Cognition, Extended Cognition, Embedded Cognition, and Enactive Cognition) and incorporating the Vision OS experience elements, employs a combined approach of qualitative and quantitative research methods. It explores the primary factors influencing participants' museum experiences and proposes a new model to measure the impact of mixed reality on museum visitors' experiences and cognition, providing new theoretical tools for advancing museum digitization efforts and the design practices of mixed reality experiences.

Keywords: User Experience · Museum · Mixed reality · 4E cognition

1 Introduction

With the continuous innovation of digital information technology, museums have gradually expanded their exhibition forms to include Augmented Reality (AR) and Virtual Reality (VR) [1]. However, these advancements have primarily focused on display technologies, overlooking the fact that the body serves as a means of understanding, experiencing, and perceiving the world [2]. Therefore, there is a need for further research in the cognitive perspective on Mixed Reality (MR) applications in museums and user experience [3].

Mixed Reality is a virtual technology that merges both Virtual Reality and Augmented Reality, allowing virtual and real objects to coexist in the same space and generate real-time interaction [4]. Through the intervention of cognitive theory, this research

A. Marcus et al. (Eds.): HCII 2024, LNCS 14715, pp. 281–295, 2024.
https://doi.org/10.1007/978-3-031-61359-3_20

focuses on two aspects. Firstly, it establishes the museum experience's focal point beyond the objects, specifically examining the relationship between people and the environment reflected in the coexistence of "real" and "virtual" objects [5]. Secondly, it recognizes the viewer's body as a mediator between the "environment" and "objects," where the integrity of the viewer's body and the interaction between the body and the real or virtual environment are crucial cognitive factors.

This study explores the following questions: What are the key factors influencing visitors' experiences in MR museum experiences as a novel digital experience?

How does cognitive theory overcome the surface issues arising from the intervention of digital technology? Beginning with the 4E cognition theory and its associated research, this research delves into specific method models and practical strategies applicable to the design of Mixed Reality experiences in museums. It synthesizes the four dimensions of cognitive theory – "Embodied Cognition," "Extended Cognition," "Embedded Cognition," and "Enactive Cognition." Incorporating elements from the Vision OS experience, the study aims to construct an experiential model for mixed reality museum applications based on both quantitative and qualitative research. The ultimate goal is to provide theoretical insights and practical inspirations for the design of MR museums.

The contribution of this work is twofold:

- Introducing 4E cognitive theory into the realm of museum MR experience design, through interdisciplinary theoretical research, helps uncover the interactive mechanisms between mixed reality content in museums and audience cognition.
- Proposing a museum mixed reality experience model from the perspective of 4E cognition, this study further explores the comprehensive experiential factors and levels of visitors in the museum mixed reality environment.

2   Related Work

2.1   4E Cognition

4E cognition refers to the collective term for Embodied Cognition, Embedded Cognition, Enactive Cognition, and Extended Cognition [6]. These four concepts are interrelated and mutually construct a closely connected whole [7]. The term 4E cognition first emerged during a workshop on embodied psychology at Cardiff university in July 2006 [8] and was formally introduced into the research arena at the 4E cognition conference hosted by Shaun Gallagher at the University of Central Florida the following year [9]. In 2016, Nears provided an interpretation of 4E embodiment, stating that embodied cognition relies on the cognitive agent's body (embodiment), which extends into the external world (extension), integrates into the background of the environment (embedding), thus interacting with the world, including people and objects, leading to cognition and action (enaction) [10]. This process clearly delineates how the body interacts with the surrounding spatial environment to achieve the mutual influence of cognition and action, emphasizing the interactive relationship between the individual and their surrounding spatial environment [11].

Embodied Cognition. Scholars assert that cognitive processes are composed of both brain processes and the broader structure and processes of the body [12]art. Cognitive processes depend on the body, which establishes direct connections with the environment through the perceptual system [13]. Embodied cognition emphasizes that the body is an integral part of cognition, shaping and supporting cognitive processes through bodily perception and actions [14].

Extended Cognition. Extended cognition emphasizes the physical environment of cognition [15]. Clark suggests that the physical world serves as an external information storage system related to cognitive processes such as perception, memory, reasoning, and experience [16]. Extended cognition highlights that cognition can extend to the use of external tools and technologies, expanding and extending within the environment in various ways.

Embedded Cognition. Embedded cognition posits that the body is embedded in specific spatial contexts [17]. When performing cognitive tasks, individuals can cleverly utilize the structures in the environment to alleviate the information processing burden that would otherwise occur internally. Therefore, embedded cognition emphasizes that cognition is not only a process within an individual's brain but also interacts with the surrounding environment and socio-cultural context.

Enactive Cognition. The concept of enactive cognition complements the previous three by adding a temporal dimension [18]. It emphasizes that cognition is not merely passively receiving information but actively constructing through participation and interaction.

In summary, the 4E cognitive framework provides a comprehensive understanding of cognition by acknowledging the intricate interplay between the body, environment, and external tools [19], emphasizing the active role of the individual in constructing cognition through interaction.

2.2 Vision OS

Vision OS is the first operating system developed by Apple Inc. Specifically designed for spatial computing, targeting the Vision Pro platform. It encompasses three fundamental concepts: Windows, Volumes, and Spaces [20]. This paper systematically organizes, summarizes, and synthesizes the design specifications of Vision OS based on these three concepts.

Windows. A window is a 2D interface similar to other windows, allowing operations such as resizing, free movement, and fixation. Each application includes one or more windows (Table 1).

Volumes. Volumes can be considered as an extension of windows, or as 3D manifestations of windows, allowing users to observe and interact in a more comprehensive and three-dimensional manner (Table 2).

Space. Spaces represent the domains in which users immerse themselves in the mixed reality world, serving as containers for "Windows" and "Volumes" [21]. Spaces not only

Table 1. Window experience design elements

Name	Content	Cognitive Dimension
Visual area	Users find it easy to see content in the center of their field of view, with a broader horizontal view. Windows on the sides rotate inward around the user, centered on them	Embodied Cognition
Real-time feedback	Distinct interactive states – idle, hover, selected, selected switch, and non-selectable – are reflected through subtle visual styles, directing the user's attention to the expected elements	Embodied Cognition
Basic interface principle	Design principles and specifications for icons, dimensions, materials, font layout, colors, animations, and other elements	Embodied Cognition
Logical correlation	Consistency in mapping between the virtual and real worlds is crucial. Users must perceive their surrounding environment, and the windows should adapt to varying lighting conditions	Extended Cognition
Environment switch	When users switch from one virtual window to another, the transition needs to be smooth and natural	Extended Cognition

Table 2. Volumes experience design elements

Name	Content	Cognitive Dimension
Spatial depth	Expressing a sense of hierarchy through distance, layering, lighting cues, macro details, and thickness to help viewers establish connections among objects within the space	Embedded Cognition
Spatial size	The size and proportional relationships among virtual elements contribute to the spatial structure of the virtual environment, impacting the perceptual coherence for users	Embedded Cognition
Stereo control	Elements such as bottom-hover accessories are positioned for quick, content-related operations, enhancing the user's operational space in the mixed reality environment	Extended Cognition

accommodate virtual windows but also interact with the user's surrounding environment, creating an interactive visual and perceptual experience (Table 3).

Table 3. Space experience design elements

Name	Content	Cognitive Dimension
Input mode	There are three primary input methods: indirect interaction, direct interaction, and voice interaction, allowing users to interact with the virtual environment in a more natural, intuitive, and personalized manner	Embodied Cognition
Dynamic pose	The interface's optimal position is determined based on the user's real-time or personalized posture, with dynamic adjustments of the virtual interface's position and orientation according to actual circumstances and needs	Embodied Cognition
Spatial spectrum	The shape of the spatial canvas can undergo various changes in three-dimensional space. It can be adjusted based on specific application scenarios and user needs, ranging from highly immersive experiences to the fusion of virtual and real worlds	Enactive Cognition
View sharing	By sharing windows, opportunities for collaborative experiences are created, allowing anyone in the shared space to have the same experience	Enactive Cognition

3   Research Design

3.1   Method and Framework

The research framework consists of two main components, as illustrated in Fig. 1: Qualitative Research—employing on-site observation and in-depth interviews, and Quantitative Research—utilizing questionnaire analysis. By integrating and cross analyzing the qualitative and quantitative findings, key experiential elements within the 4E cognitive framework are extracted. This process aims to provide a robust foundation for subsequent design strategies.

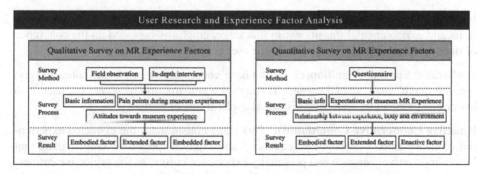

Fig. 1. User research and experience element analysis framework

Qualitative Research. Conducting on-site visits to various museums involves observing visitors' behaviors, interaction patterns, and the level of engagement within the experiential zones [22]. The focus is on understanding their physical responses and how users mutually influence their environment. A select group of users is chosen for in-depth interviews to gather subjective perceptions and expectations regarding the digital museum experience. The goal is to extract and summarize experiential elements from these insights.

Quantitative Research. The survey questionnaire comprises two parts. The first part captures basic user information, including gender, age, education, occupation, frequency of museum visits, and experience with six major categories of digitized museum projects. The second part consists of Likert scale test questions, developed based on the experiential structural factors derived from qualitative research. The questionnaire questions are also developed by incorporating relevant established scales from existing literature.

3.2 Qualitative Survey

The research focused on two types of scenarios for observation and interviews. The first type involves digitized museums, including the Hubei Provincial Museum, Hangzhou Museum, and Liangzhu Museum. This segment emphasizes the interactive behaviors and usage patterns of user groups in front of interactive exhibits. The second type involves online virtual museums, exemplified by the online Palace Museum, where user attention and interaction efficiency are observed, excluding the factor of the physical presence.

Based on the practical circumstances, a total of 6 users were selected for observation and interviews in this phase of the research. The findings from the interviews were extracted, summarized, and analyzed, with the results presented in Fig. 2.

Summarizing the research in the related work and qualitative survey stages, the experience factors are summarized into four dimensions: embodied control cognition, extended fusion cognition, embedded spatial cognition and enactive cooperative cognition.

Embodied Control Cognition(a). It comprises three experiential factors: "visual system," "audio-tactile system," and "body orientation system." In this stage, observers establish an overall understanding of the museum space.

Extended Fusion Cognition(b). It consists of two experiential factors – logical connections and environmental transitions: In this stage, emphasis is placed on the coherence of user operations, providing guidance for user actions.

Embedded Spatial Cognition(c). This phase encompasses two experiential factors: "spatial depth" and "spatial scene." Through the construction of scenarios, users can better comprehend the authentic historical applications of artifacts.

Enactive Cooperative Cognition(d). This stage consolidates the extracted experiential elements into "collaborative feedback" and "spatial spectrum," emphasizing that individuals actively engage and personally experience culture as the subjective entities.

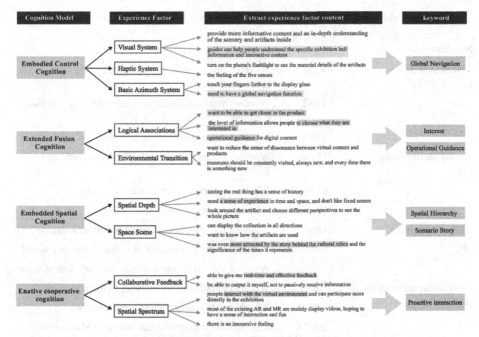

Fig. 2. Experience factor extraction

3.3 Questionnaire Design and Hypotheses

The questionnaire design is comprised of two parts: the first part gathers basic information about users, including gender, age, education, occupation, and other demographic details. The second part consists of scale test questions. The questionnaire items are primarily developed based on the experiential structure dimensions derived earlier and are aligned with relevant mature scales from existing literature. Here, (a), (b), (c), and (d) represent four main dimensions, while (f) signifies the user experience, as illustrated in Table 4.

In conclusion, this study further proposes hypotheses, specifically, hypotheses regarding the effectiveness of the independent variables within the four main dimensions of embodied control cognition, extended fusion cognition, embedded spatial cognition, and enactive cooperative cognition. These variables include "visual system (H1)," "audio-tactile system (H2)," "body orientation (H3)," "environmental transitions (H4)," "logical connections (H5)," "spatial depth (H6)," "spatial scene (H7)," "collaborative feedback (H8)," and "spatial spectrum (H9)." These nine factors are hypothesized to impact the user experience (dependent variable).

Table 4. Museum mixed reality experience indicators and sources.

Subdimension	Code	Item Description
Visual system (a)	VIS1	Whether information is displayed clearly and layout is reasonable
	VIS2	Whether virtual content provides more information than real
	VIS3	Whether color matching is pleasing
Audio-tactile system (a)	CON1	Whether sound effects and dubbing are real and vivid
	CON2	Whether interaction modes are diversified
	CON3	Whether there is tactile perception
Body orientation (a)	ORI1	Whether movement of objects is real and natural
	ORI2	Whether there is a feeling of being in another world
	ORI3	Whether virtual element moves with my line of sight
Environmental transition (b)	EXT1	Whether experience is relevant to the real world
	EXT2	Whether exhibits are related to each other
	EXT3	Whether I can perceive real world in MR experience
Logical connections (b)	LOG1	Whether virtual content is related to each other
	LOG2	Whether interaction behavior conforms to habits in real
	LOG3	Whether there is clear operational guidance
Spatial depth (c)	DEP1	Whether there is a spatial hierarchy
	DEP2	Whether there is a sense of time travel
	DEP3	Whether it match the size of the physical world
Spatial scene (c)	SCE1	Whether use scenario of cultural relic is displayed
	SCE2	Whether cultural relics are displayed in all aspects
	SCE3	Whether the historical significance and historical background of the cultural relics are displayed
	SCE4	Weather I can broaden my horizons
Collaborative feedback (d)	FEE1	Whether the level of physical involvement is high

(continued)

Table 4. (*continued*)

Subdimension	Code	Item Description
	FEE2	Can the system give me real-time and effective feedback
	FEE3	Whether I can control the situation in the scene
Spatial spectrum (d)	SPE1	Whether there is an immersive experience in history
	SPE2	Whether it can help me focus on the current content
	SPE3	Whether the existence of time is forgotten
Useful(f)	UE1	Whether digital/MR content is necessary in museum experience
Learnable(f)	UE2	Whether the operation is easy to learn
Memorable(f)	UE3	Whether the content is easy to remember
Effective(f)	UE4	Whether it is helpful to me
Efficient(f)	UE5	Whether the experience is productive
Desirable(f)	UE6	Whether the experience is satisfactory to me

4 Results

4.1 Sample Collection

This survey employed a combination of online and offline methods, targeting young users who have participated in museum MR experiences or have some awareness of digital museum experiences. A total of 222 questionnaires were collected, with 201 being deemed valid. The gender distribution was 59% male and 41% female, with the majority (74.1%) falling within the age group of 18–25 years, and 20.9% belonging to the 26–35 age group.

4.2 Reliability and Validity Analysis

Reliability is one of the crucial indicators for assessing the reliability of research data [23]. According to the results in Table 5, the overall Cronbach's alpha coefficient is 0.959, significantly exceeding the standard value of 0.7. Moreover, the Cronbach's alpha coefficients for all ten variables are also well above 0.7, indicating excellent measurement reliability for each variable in the questionnaire model. Additionally, the substantial standard factor loadings exceeding 0.5 in Table 5 demonstrate a strong correlation between all measurement indicators and their corresponding latent variables. The composite reliabilities (CR) for all measurement variables are above 0.7, and the average variances extracted (AVE) values are above 0.5 for all groups except for the CON group, which is considered acceptable. In summary, the convergent validity of the questionnaire is quite satisfactory.

As indicated by the results in Table 6, the square root of the AVE values for each variable is greater than the correlation coefficient between any two variables, demonstrating

Table 5. Reliability and convergence validity analysis.

Constructs/items	Cronbach's alphas	Item loadings	AVE	CR
Visual system (VIS)	0.708	0.756	0.506	0.754
VIS1	0.685			
VIS2	0.740			
VIS3				
Audio-tactile system (CON)	0.761	0.736	0.486	0.738
CON1	0.724			
CON2	0.596			
CON3				
Body orientation (ORI)	0.762	0.798	0.581	0.806
ORI1	0.806			
ORI2	0.716			
ORI3				
Environmental transition (EXT)	0.780	0.793	0.560	0.792
EXT1	0.756			
EXT2	0.707			
EXT3				
Logical connections (LOG)	0.745	0.766	0.531	0.771
LOG1	0.784			
LOG2	0.650			
LOG3				
Spatial depth (DEP)	0.745	0.762	0.531	0.771
DEP1	0.774			
DEP2	0.653			
DEP3				
Spatial scene (SCE)	0.746	0.864	0.631	0.872
SCE1	0.705			
SCE2	0.878			
SCE3	0.836			
SCE4				
Collaborative feedback (FEE)	0.741	0.762	0.534	0.774
FEE1	0.784			
FEE2	0.663			
FEE3				

(continued)

Table 5. (*continued*)

Constructs/items	Cronbach's alphas	Item loadings	AVE	CR
Spatial spectrum (SPE)	0.784	0.810	0.592	0.814
SPE1	0.784			
SPE2	0.741			
SPE3				
User experience (UE)	0.682	0.858	0.506	0.860
UE1	0.726			
UE2	0.670			
UE3	0.674			
UE4	0.695			
UE5	0.810			
UE6				

Table 6. Discrimination validity test results.

	VIS	CON	ORI	EXT	LOG	DEP	SCE	FEE	ENA	UE
VIS	0.506									
CON	0.095	0.486								
ORI	0.120	0.115	0.581							
EXT	0.107	0.096	0.156	0.560						
LOG	0.096	0.083	0.118	0.121	0.531					
DEP	0.098	0.094	0.130	0.121	0.107	0.531				
SCE	0.104	0.090	0.124	0.117	0.107	0.111	0.631			
FEE	0.098	0.091	0.137	0.121	0.106	0.112	0.114	0.534		
ENA	0.130	0.118	0.175	0.153	0.133	0.141	0.142	0.154	0.592	
UE	0.111	0.100	0.125	0.118	0.111	0.117	0.122	0.119	0.149	0.506

excellent discriminant validity of the scale. This indicates that the scale is suitable for subsequent linear regression analysis.

4.3 Regression Analysis

This paper conducts a linear regression analysis to examine the hypothesized relationships among variables [24]. The independent variables include the visual system, audio-tactile system, body orientation, environmental transitions, logical connections, spatial depth, spatial scene, collaborative feedback, and spatial spectrum. The dependent variable is the user experience.

Firstly, the fitting of the linear regression model in this analysis is satisfactory, with an R^2 value of 0.632, exceeding the threshold of 0.6. This indicates that the results

Table 7. Multiple regression analysis.

Variables	β	Std. Error	Sig
Constant		0.266	0.007
Visual system	0.170	0.064	0.007
Audio-tactile system	0.132	0.064	0.044
Body orientation	− 0.195	0.057	0.009
Environmental transition	0.013	0.063	0.868
Logical connections	0.147	0.064	0.041
Spatial depth	0.187	0.063	0.012
Spatial scene	0.204	0.058	0.002
Collaborative feedback	0.115	0.051	0.074
Spatial spectrum	0.111	0.056	0.012
Dependent variable: User experience			
β = Standardized regression coefficient			

of this analysis can reliably and accurately reflect the impact of the nine independent variables on the user experience. Secondly, with an F-value of 36.503 and $P < 0.001$, the regression equation is significant, indicating that at least one of the nine independent variables has a significant impact on the dependent variable.

According to the data in Table 7, the visual system ($\beta = 0.170$, $P < 0.05$), audio-tactile system ($\beta = 0.132$, $P < 0.05$), logical connections ($\beta = 0.147$, $P < 0.05$), spatial depth ($\beta = 0.187$, $P < 0.05$), spatial scene ($\beta = 0.204$, $P < 0.05$), and spatial spectrum ($\beta = 0.183$, $P < 0.05$) all have a significantly positive impact on the user experience. The remaining variables do not hold this significance.

5   Findings and Discussion

After extracting the elements of mixed reality experience, a further hybrid reality experience structure model is constructed based on the 4E cognition theory, aiming to explore how the four structural levels of mixed reality experience are interwoven (Fig. 3).

The coupling relationships among embodied control cognition, extended fusion cognition, embedded spatial cognition, and enactive cooperative cognition form a tightly interwoven network in the mixed reality experience. They interact and influence each other, collectively shaping people's cognition and experiences. Embodied control cognition focuses on the role of the body in the cognitive process, combined with embedded spatial cognition, where the user's body movements and position become part of the digital experience, influencing their perception of the virtual environment. Extended fusion cognition emphasizes the extension of cognition through digital tools and the environment, coupled with enactive cooperative cognition. Digital tools become a medium for creative expression and integration. Consequently, users extend their cognitive domains

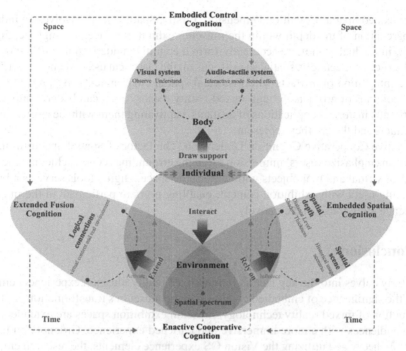

Fig. 3. Museum mixed reality experience coupling model.

through digital tools, participating in the processes of generation and creation. This intricate coupling not only immerses participants more deeply into the mixed reality experience but also expands the boundaries of cognition, providing possibilities for a more enriching and vivid museum mixed reality experience.

Specifically analyzing the four dimensions: Embodied Control Cognition Dimension. Firstly, the Visual System plays a crucial role in embodied control cognition. When observing exhibits, the individual's visual system is triggered, influencing the comprehension of cultural information. Secondly, the Audio-Tactile System, through the tactile experience of touching exhibits and the design of sound effects, stimulates the sensory system, creating a more intimate sensory connection and providing a more intuitive and profound experience.

Extended Fusion Cognition Dimension. This dimension encompasses the factor of logical connections, which refers to the rational connections between exhibits, virtual content, and the environment. Logical connections in mixed reality museums contribute to the construction of individuals' cognitive structures. When there is a well-established logical connection among exhibits, virtual content, and the environment, individuals find it easier to comprehend the inherent relationships between these elements, constructing a completer and more organic cognitive framework. Additionally, robust logical connections can reduce cognitive conflicts, minimizing confusion and bewilderment during the perception process, allowing individuals to focus more effectively on the experience itself.

Embedded Spatial Cognition Dimension. Firstly, Spatial Depth involves an individual's perception of the depth within the museum exhibition space. Through depth perception, individuals can more accurately form a cognitive understanding of the overall spatial structure. Secondly, spatial scene focus on the historical usage scenes of artifacts, i.e., the integration of artifacts with historical spatial environments. By presenting the usage scenarios of artifacts through mixed reality means, users can better comprehend the authentic historical applications of artifacts, captivating them with the stories behind the artifacts and the era they represent.

Enactive Cooperative Cognition Dimension. The factor of Spatial Spectrum in this dimension emphasizes users' immersion through surrounding scenes, achieving the integration of virtual and real objects within the same space. Digital tools serve as a bridge connecting users with exhibition content, enabling users to participate in the museum experience more freely and creatively.

6 Conclusion

This study delves into the key factors in the mixed reality museum experience, emphasizing the significance of embodied cognition in the museum's transformation. With the introduction of mixed reality technology, museum exhibition spaces are extended, providing audiences with a more immersive and enriched experience. Grounded in the 4E cognition theory and utilizing the Vision OS experience elements, the research employs a combination of qualitative methods such as on-site observations and user interviews, as well as quantitative analysis using SPSS. It systematically investigates the primary factors influencing participants' museum experiences. Based on this exploration, a new experiential model is proposed to comprehensively assess the influencing factors and mechanisms of the mixed reality museum experience. However, the study has some limitations, particularly in the depth of quantitative analysis. Future research could further explore complex relationships among experiential factors through more refined data analysis, offering specific design recommendations. Additionally, practical validation of the model's effectiveness can be pursued in subsequent studies.

References

1. Olsson, T., Ihamäki, P., Lagerstam, E., Ventä-Olkkonen, L., Väänänen-Vainio-Mattila, K.: User expectations for mobile mixed reality services: an initial user study. In: European Conference on Cognitive Ergonomics: Designing beyond the Product --- Understanding Activity and User Experience in Ubiquitous Environments. 1–9. VTT Technical Research Centre of Finland, FI-02044 VTT, FIN (2009)
2. Li, Y.-C., Liew, A.W.-C., Su, W.-P.: The digital museum: Challenges and solution. In: 2012 8th International Conference on Information Science and Digital Content Technology (ICIDT2012), pp. 646–649 (2012)
3. Galani, A.: Mixed reality museum visits: using new technologies to support co-visiting for local and remote visitors (2003)
4. He, Z., Wu, L., Li, X.: (Robert): When art meets tech: the role of augmented reality in enhancing museum experiences and purchase intentions. Tour. Manag. 68, 127–139 (2018). https://doi.org/10.1016/j.tourman.2018.03.003

5. Hovhannisyan, G., Henson, A., Sood, S.: Enacting virtual reality: the philosophy and cognitive science of optimal virtual experience. In: Schmorrow, D.D., Fidopiastis, C.M. (eds.) Augmented Cognition, vol. 11580, pp. 225–255. Springer International Publishing, Cham (2019). https://doi.org/10.1007/978-3-030-22419-6_17

6. Newen, A., Gallagher, S., De Bruin, L.: 4E cognition: historical roots, key concepts, and central issues. In: Newen, A., De Bruin, L.Gallagher, S.(eds.) The Oxford Handbook of 4E Cognition. Oxford University Press (2018)

7. Menary, R.: Introduction to the special issue on 4E cognition. Phenomenol. Cogn. Sci. **9**, 459–463 (2010). https://doi.org/10.1007/s11097-010-9187-6

8. Van Der Schyff, D., Schiavio, A., Walton, A., Velardo, V., Chemero, A.: Musical creativity and the embodied mind: exploring the possibilities of 4E cognition and dynamical systems theory. Music. Sci. **1**, 205920431879231 (2018). https://doi.org/10.1177/2059204318792319

9. Shen, Y.: Research on cognitive integration issues (2021)

10. Steiner, P.: Normativity and the methodology of 4E cognition: taking stock and going forward. In: Casper, M.-O. Artese, G.F. (eds.) Situated Cognition Research: Methodological Foundations, vol. 23, pp. 103–126. Springer International Publishing, Cham (2023). https://doi.org/10.1007/978-3-031-39744-8_7

11. Christ, O., Sambasivam, M., Roos, A., Zahn, C.: Learning in immersive virtual reality: how does the 4E cognition approach fit in virtual didactic settings? In: Ahram, T., Taiar, R. (eds.) IHIET 2021. LNNS, vol. 319, pp. 790–796. Springer, Cham (2022). https://doi.org/10.1007/978-3-030-85540-6_100

12. Danish, J.A., Enyedy, N., Saleh, A., Humburg, M.: Learning in embodied activity frame-work: a sociocultural framework for embodied cognition. Int. J. Comput.-Support. Collab. Learn. **15**, 49–87 (2020). https://doi.org/10.1007/s11412-020-09317-3

13. Jäger, N., Schnädelbach, H., Hale, J.: Embodied interactions with adaptive architecture. In: Dalton, N.S., Schnädelbach, H., Wiberg, M., Varoudis, T. (eds.) Architecture and Interaction. HIS, pp. 183–202. Springer, Cham (2016). https://doi.org/10.1007/978-3-319-30028-3_9

14. Foglia, L., Wilson, R.A.: Embodied cognition. WIREs Cogn. Sci. **4**, 319–325 (2013). https://doi.org/10.1002/wcs.1226

15. Arnau, E., Estany, A., González Del Solar, R., Sturm, T.: The extended cognition thesis: Its significance for the philosophy of (cognitive) science. Philos. Psychol. **27**, 1–18 (2014). https://doi.org/10.1080/09515089.2013.836081

16. Clark, M.S., Fiske, S.T.: Affect and Cognition: 17th Annual Carnegie Mellon Symposium on Cognition. Psychology Press (2014)

17. Heersmink, R.: Dimensions of integration in embedded and extended cognitive systems. Phenomenol. Cogn. Sci. **14**, 577–598 (2015). https://doi.org/10.1007/s11097-014-9355-1

18. Ye, H., Zeng, H., Yang, W.: Enactive cognition: Theoretical rationale and practical approach. Acta Psychol. Sin. **51**, 1270–1280 (2019). https://doi.org/10.3724/SP.J.1041.2019.01270

19. Barrett, L.: The evolution of cognition: a 4E perspective. In: Newen, A., De Bruin, L., Gallagher, S (eds.) The Oxford Handbook of 4E Cognition. Oxford University Press (2018)

20. Inc., A.: VisionOS Overview. https://developer.apple.com/visionos/

21. Inc., A.: Principles of spatial design - WWDC23 – Videos. https://developer.apple.com/videos/play/wwdc2023/10072/

22. Kisiel, J.: An examination of fieldtrip strategies and their implementation within a natural his-tory museum. Sci. Educ. **90**, 434–452 (2006). https://doi.org/10.1002/sce.20117

23. Hinton, P., McMurray, I., Brownlow, C.: SPSS Explained. Routledge (2014)

24. Chen, T., Guo, W., Gao, X., Liang, Z.: AI-based self-service technology in public service delivery: user experience and influencing factors. Gov. Inf. Q. **38**, 101520 (2021). https://doi.org/10.1016/j.giq.2020.101520

The Impact of Gamified AR Format
on Engagement for Site Museum Tours

Ren Long[1], Xin Zeng[1], Ao Jiang[2]($\boxtimes$), Wenyi Han[1,2], and Xingqiao Yang[1,2]

[1] Industrial Design Department, School of Mechanical Science and Engineering, Huazhong University of Science and Technology, 430074, Wuhan, Hubei, China
[2] Industrial Design Department, College of Mechanical and Electrical Engineering, Nanjing University of Aeronautics and Astronautics, Nanjing, China
aojohn928@gmail.com

Abstract. In the museum experience, digital technologies such as AR are constantly updating the user experience, and gamification interventions are likewise increasing the interest and effectiveness of visitors' learning. This paper investigated the effect of a gamified AR format on engagement during a simulated guided tour of the Qujialing Site Museum in Hubei Province, China. Twenty-five participants from Huazhong University of Science and Technology (HUST) simulated two tour formats of the Qujialing Site Museum before and after on an AOC monitor and an iPhone 13 mobile device(One simulating a conventional audio-visual tour and one in the form of a gamified AR format). The results showed that the gamified AR format significantly increased participants' engagement in the tour ($p = 0.029 < 0.05$), and the mean scores of the six dimensions of engagement were higher than those of the pre-test, with EN(4.42) scoring the highest on the post-test, followed by PU(4.38), FI(4.37), NO(4.31), FA(4.18), AE(4.16) scoring the lowest.These findings on engagement subscale attributes may have implications for future AR and gamification design in museums to enhance a better tour experience, although this has not been shown to maximize engagement.

Keywords: Gamification · AR · Site Museum · Engagement

1 Introduction

In the new media era, museums are facing the transformation from one-way communication to multi-dimensional experience, and digitization has profoundly changed the way of development and means of display of museums. Games and gamification are one of the future trends in the application of new technologies, and more and more researchers and educators are realizing the ability of games to stimulate effective learning and creative inquiry among learners and peers, and are beginning to observe and study the ways in which games are used in the field of education from a variety of new perspectives. Gamification designs incorporate game elements such as competition, rewards, and interaction to enhance the appeal and effectiveness of learning experiences. This trend has raised concerns about the prospects of its application in museum education.

A. Marcus et al. (Eds.): HCII 2024, LNCS 14715, pp. 296–309, 2024.
https://doi.org/10.1007/978-3-031-61359-3_21

As educational and cultural institutions, museums have unique educational resources, and the application of gamification design is expected to enrich the educational activities of museums and enhance the interest and effectiveness of visitors' learning. However, how to combine relatively traditional educational activities with fascinating games to realize the goal of "the gamer is the learner, and the learner is also the gamer" has become the goal of exploration and pursuit for the aspirants in the education sector today [1].

With the popularization and development of smart mobile devices, the improvement of sensor integration performance, the continuous emergence of software development kits and the advancement of visual technology and network technology, AR has a huge potential for application in the cultural and tourism, entertainment, manufacturing, education and other industries, and has already achieved certain results. AR-based museum applications digitize information about collections and incorporate virtual information such as text, animation, models, and audio of cultural relics in real situations to stimulate visitors' senses and make up for the information gap in a more natural and vivid display. Visitors can get richer knowledge, newer experience, and real-time interactive participation. Using the technical advantages of AR to empower museums can give exhibits more multi-dimensional display space and deeper educational significance, meet the deeper needs of users in the new era, and help promote and pass on the culture of museums.

In the application of museum gamification based on AR technology, the audience is changed from "passive acceptance" to "interesting interaction", which can break the pattern of single output, effectively reduce the cognitive load of tourists, help tourists to deeply understand the museum collections, enhance the effect of museums to disseminate culture and educate the public, and provide theoretical references for the future digitalization practice of museums. Qujialing Site is the place where the "Qujialing Culture" was discovered and named and is one of the birthplaces of Chinese farming culture. Jingmen Qujialing Site Museum, located in the South Service Area (Museum Area) of the Qujialing Archaeological Site Park in the Qujialing Management Area of Jingmen City, is a state-owned museum of the cultural relics system established on March 8, 2017. This paper presents a metrics process on user experience engagement based on the design practice of a gamified AR tour format for the Qujialing Site Museum.

2 Theoretical Background: Gamification and Engagement

2.1 Gamification on AR Technology

The term "gamification" was first coined by Nick Pelling in 2002. Different scholars in different fields have different views and expressions on the definition of gamification, but the most widely used definition is "the adoption of gamification elements in non-game contexts" [2]. In the book Reality is Broken: Why Games Make Us Better and How They Can Change the World, Jane McGonigal, a famous game designer, defines gamification as the use of game design techniques and game elements to solve non-game problems such as business, social impact, etc., with the main emphasis on the means and goals of gamification. According to McGonigal, gamification should achieve the goals of "more satisfying work", "more assured success", "stronger social connections" and "greater meaning"[3]. Hamari, a professor of gamification studies at the University of Tampere in Finland, points out that gamification is not just about game elements and console systems, points out from the perspective of user experience that gamification can help users reach their goal plans while effectively enhancing the user experience [4].

With the use of augmented reality technology in education more and more, the combination of this technology and gamified learning also brings many advantages:

(1) Enhance the learning state that is otherwise unattainable. With the help of computer software to simulate things that are hard to reach in real life, through well-designed.Through the use of computer software to simulate things that are hard to reach in real life, the teaching content can be visualized and easily understood through the well-designed teaching content expressed in a variety of media ways, such as simulating the solar system.

(2) Create an exploratory educational concept. Since AR technology generates virtual objects in a realistic scene or environment that can present parts of reality that cannot be seen, it requires players to utilize software that incorporates augmented reality technology scanning to complement the whole learning process, which is also a process of exploration.

(3) Enhance interactivity and increase player interest. Traditional educational games have a single form of expression and are even treated as disposable consumer goods. Compared with traditional static education methods, augmented reality learning forms provide more expansion space, with greater attractiveness and playability, and stimulate the audience's interest in the content.

2.2 Engagement

Pine et al. say that "in the future, the experience economy will become the mainstream of the age" in their book The Experience Economy [5]. In this context, the design field is gradually shifting to user-centered design [6]. User engagement is a quality of user experience characterized by the depth of a user's cognitive, temporal, emotional, and behavioral investment in interacting with a digital system [7]. O'Brien views engagement as a state that a user is in, and the process of a user moving between states can also be referred to as the process of engagement. The process of migrating between states can also be referred to as the process of participation.

To date, self-reports are the most widely used measure of emotional somatic test measure. The method is mainly in the form of scales or interviews that allow the users to self-assess their emotional state in the moment or during the interaction. The method is mainly in the form of scales or interviews. O'Brien proposed the User Engagement Scale (UES) based on Jacques and Webster and Ho's research findings on self-report measures based on user experience attributes [8]. The UES was constructed by O'Brien through an iterative process of developing and evaluating two online surveys in the e-commerce space, an effort that resulted in a 31-item self-reporting tool consisting of six dimensions (see Table 1) [9]. The 31-item User Engagement Scale has been used to assess engagement in a variety of environments: information searches, online news, online video, education, consumer applications, haptic technologies, social networking systems and video games [10].

Table 1. 6 Dimensions of User Engagement Scale.

Dimensions	Definition
FA- Focused Attention	Feeling absorbed in the interaction and losing
PU-Perceived Usability	Negative affect experienced as a result of the interaction and the degree of control and effort expended
EN-Endurability	The overall success of the interaction and users' willingness to recommend an application to others or engage with it in future
NO-Novelty	Curiosity and interest in the interactive task
FI-Felt Involvement	The sense of being "drawn in" and having fun
AE-Aesthetics	Aesthetic appeal, the attractiveness and visual appeal of the interface

3   Method

3.1   Participants

Demographic information of the 25 participants is shown in Table 2. They were recruited and volunteered at Huazhong University of Science and Technology (HUST) in Hubei Province, China, at the end of the process, each participant received a snack pack worth 50 RMB. All participants have relevant experience in visiting museums and have some knowledge of video games and AR technology.

Table 2. Participants' demographic information.

Total participants = 25	
Gender	Females (68%), Males (32%)
Age	0–18 (0%), 19–22 (16%), 23–26 (72%), 27- (12%)
Majors	Mechanical Engineering, product design, computer Science and Technology, business management, law, sociology, pedagogical

3.2   Instruments and Materials

The experiment was conducted in a multi-functional conference room at Huazhong University of Science and Technology in China. The simulated regular site tour video at the beginning and AR Simulated Reality Background Images were played on a 27" 240Hz AOC (model number: C27G2Z) monitor connected to a ROG Strix 5 laptop. The gamified AR simulation excursion was prototyped by Figma and then installed on a mobile device (iPhone 13, RAM 4 GB, ROM 128 GB, 6.1-inch display with a resolution of 2532x1170 pixels at 60 Hz). The questionnaires were filled out on an iPad Air 4.

The User Engagement Scale was measured by a 5-point Likert scale. The scale was adapted from O'Brien's scale to fit the museum visit situation translated into Chinese form and posted on an online platform for pre- and post-test data collection [11]. Table 3 shows the original scale, adapted English and Chinese translations. 8 items labeled with "z" (PU1z, PU2z, PU3z, PU4z, PU5z, PU6z, PU8z, EN3z) of the PU and EN dimensions were reverse-coded.

Table 3. User Engagement Scale adaptation.

Items		Factor
1	I lost myself in this shopping experience I lost myself in this visiting experience 在这次游览中,我很忘我	FA1
2	I was so involved in my shopping task that I lost track of time I was so involved in my visiting task that I lost track of time 在这次游览中,我太投入任务以至于忘记了时间	FA2
3	I blocked out things around me when I was shopping on this website I blocked out things around me when I was visiting this museum 在这次游览中,我屏蔽了周围事物	FA3
4	When I was shopping, I lost track of the world around me When I was visiting, I lost track of the world around me 在这次游览中,我忘记了真实的世界	FA4
5	The time I spent shopping just slipped away The time I spent visiting just slipped away 在这次游览中,时间就这样溜走了	FA5
6	I was absorbed in my shopping task I was absorbed in my visiting task 在这次游览中,我是全神贯注的	FA6
7	During this shopping experience I let myself go During this visiting experience I let myself go 在这次游览中,我放空了自己(放任自流)	FA7
8	I felt frustrated while visiting this shopping website I felt frustrated while visiting g this museum 在这次游览中,我感到很沮丧	PU1z
9	I found this shopping website confusing to use I found this museum confusing to visit 在这次游览中,我感到很困惑	PU2z
10	I felt annoyed while visiting this shopping website I felt annoyed while visiting this museum 在这次游览中,我感到很烦躁	PU3z

(continued)

Table 3. (*continued*)

Items		Factor
11	I felt discouraged while shopping on this website I felt discouraged while visiting this museum 在这次游览中,我感到气馁	PU4z
12	Using this shopping website was mentally taxing Visiting this museum was mentally taxing 在这次游览中,我感到耗费精力	PU5z
13	This shopping experience was demanding This visiting experience was demanding 在这次游览中,我感到要求很高	PU6z
14	I felt in control of my shopping experience I felt in control of my visiting experience 在这次游览中,我感觉能够完全掌控自己的游览体验	PU7
15	I could not do some of the things I needed to do on this shopping website I could not do some of the things I needed to do on this museum tour 在这次游览中,我无法完成我需要完成的事	PU8z
16	Shopping on this website was worthwhile Visiting this museum was worthwhile 这次游览是值得的	EN1
17	I consider my shopping experience a success I consider my visiting experience a success 这次游览是成功的	EN2
18	This shopping experience did not work out the way I had planned This visiting experience did not work out the way I had planned 这次游览与我预想的效果不符	EN3z
19	My shopping experience was rewarding My visiting experience was rewarding 这次游览是有意义的	EN4
20	I would recommend shopping on this website to my friends & family I would recommend visiting this site museum to my friends & family 我会向亲朋好友推荐在此遗址博物馆游览	EN5
21	I continued to shop on this website out of curiosity I continued to visit this site museum out of curiosity 出于好奇,我将继续在该遗址博物馆游览	NO1
22	The content of the shopping website incited my curiosity The content of the site museum incited my curiosity 该遗址博物馆的展览内容激发了我的好奇心	NO2
23	I felt interested in my shopping task I felt interested in my visiting task 这次游览任务让我很感兴趣	NO3

(*continued*)

Table 3. (*continued*)

Items		Factor
24	I was really drawn into my shopping task I was really drawn into my visiting task 这次的游览任务真的吸引住了我	FI1
25	I felt involved in this shopping task I felt involved in this visiting task 这次的游览任务让我很有参与感	FI2
26	This shopping experience was fun This visiting experience was fun 这次的游览很有趣	FI3
27	This shopping website is attractive This site museum is attractive 这个遗址博物馆整体很有吸引力	AE1
28	This shopping website was aesthetically appealing This site museum was aesthetically appealing 这个遗址博物馆展陈很有美感	AE2
29	I liked the graphics and images used on this shopping website I liked the graphics and images used in this site museum 我喜欢这个遗址博物馆使用的图像图形(等元素)	AE3
30	This shopping website appealed to my visual senses This site museum appealed to my visual senses 这个遗址博物馆对我的视觉感官很有吸引力	AE4
31	The screen layout of this shopping website was visually pleasing The design of this site museum was visually pleasing 这个遗址博物馆设计是美观大方的	AE5

3.3 Procedure

Figure 1 summarizes the test procedures of the study. After viewing the simulated first-view tour video, participants filled out a pre-test questionnaire regarding their demographic information and engagement with the simulated tour of the Qujialing Site Museum in the regular tour format.

Participants then used their mobile devices to experience a gamified AR tour of the Qujialing Site Museum in response to a picture of their location on the display. The layout of the session was consistent with the framework of the content presented in the video (cultural origins, development process, key artifacts, etc.). At the end of the session participants then filled out a post-test questionnaire measuring the gamified AR format tour of the site museum.

The collected data were analyzed in SPSS software (Figs. 2 and 3).

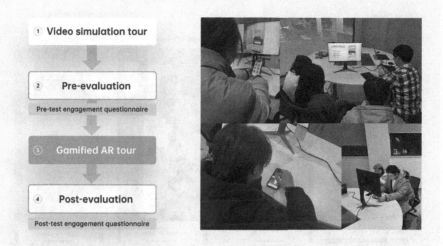

Fig. 1. Flow diagram of the testing process(left) and pictures of the participants watching the simulated tour via video and experiencing the gamified AR format tour(right).

Fig. 2. Demo Homepage

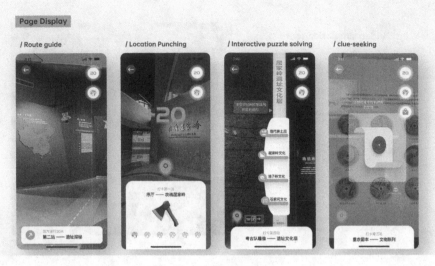

Fig. 3. Key Display Pages

4 Results

4.1 Reliability Analysis

Due to the variability in the translation of the UES scale into different languages, 4 items (post-test: FA1 CITC—-0.903, FA7 CITC—0.107, PU6 CITC—0.122, PU7 CITC—0.242) were excluded from this study. Table 4 demonstrates the Cronbach's Alpha for each item of engagement and the six dimensions of the gamified AR form tour (post-test) in the data. The Corrected Item-Total Correlation was higher than 0.50 for all of the items, ranging from 0.541 to 0.909. If items are deleted, Cronbach's Alpha ranges from 0.845 to 0.918, indicating that the items are highly reliable.

Table 5 demonstrates Cronbach's Alpha for each item of engagement and the six dimensions of the video simulation tour (pre-test) in the data. The Corrected Item-Total Correlation was higher than 0.50 for all of the items, ranging from 0.531 to 0.880. As the 4 items were deleted, Cronbach's Alpha ranges from 0.718 to 0.949, indicating that the items are highly reliable.

After excluding the 4 items, all constructs have achieved acceptable reliability.

4.2 Site Museum Tour Engagement

The mean scores of the six dimensions of this study on pre- and post-test engagement in site museum visits are shown in Tables 6 and 7, and the mean scores of the post-test are higher than the pre-test for all dimensions: Focused Attention (4.18 > 2.81), Perceived Usability (4.38 > 3.84), Endurability (4.42 > 3.42) Novelty (4.31 > 3.21), Felt Involvement (4.37 > 2.89), Aesthetics (4.16 > 2.89). Tables 8 shows that the total distribution of pre- and post-test engagement pairs t-test t = -3.96, p = 0.029 < 0.05, the mean of the total scores after the intervention of the gamified AR format was greater

Table 4. Gamified AR Tour(post-test) Engagement Items' Reliability

Elements	Item	Corrected Item-Total Correlation	Cronbach's Alpha if Item Deleted	Cronbach's Alpha
FA-Focused Attention	FA item 2	0.663	0.810	0.845
	FA item 3	0.697	0.800	
	FA item 4	0.572	0.841	
	FA item 5	0.685	0.804	
	FA item 6	0.682	0.811	
PU-Perceived Usability	PU item 1	0.541	0.851	0.869
	PU item 2	0.744	0.815	
	PU item 3	0.574	0.845	
	PU item 4	0.730	0.823	
	PU item 5	0.725	0.818	
	PU item 8	0.663	0.827	
EN-Endurability	EN item 1	0.702	0.827	0.860
	EN item 2	0.617	0.846	
	EN item 3	0.575	0.866	
	EN item 4	0.837	0.787	
	EN item 5	0.705	0.824	
NO-Novelty	NO item 1	0.840	0.874	0.914
	NO item 2	0.909	0.809	
	NO item 3	0.753	0.935	
FI-Felt Involvement	FI item 1	0.844	0.688	0.858
	FI item 2	0.650	0.800	
	FI item 3	0.742	0.801	
AE-Aesthetics	AE item 1	0.851	0.891	0.918
	AE item 2	0.791	0.900	
	AE item 3	0.835	0.892	
	AE item 4	0.819	0.898	
	AE item 5	0.711	0.915	

Table 5. Video Simulation Tour(post-test) Engagement Items' Reliability

Elements	Item	Corrected Item-Total Correlation	Cronbach's Alpha if Item Deleted	Cronbach's Alpha
FA-Focused Attention	FA item 2	0.754	0.865	0.892
	FA item 3	0.781	0.860	
	FA item 4	0.811	0.856	
	FA item 5	0.776	0.860	
	FA item 6	0.587	0.900	
PU-Perceived Usability	PU item 1	0.742	0.841	0.873
	PU item 2	0.612	0.866	
	PU item 3	0.623	0.864	
	PU item 4	0.781	0.833	
	PU item 5	0.618	0.863	
	PU item 8	0.739	0.842	
EN-Endurability	EN item 1	0.709	0.827	0.852
	EN item 2	0.770	0.791	
	EN item 3	0.531	0.853	
	EN item 4	0.776	0.791	
	EN item 5	0.563	0.852	
NO-Novelty	NO item 1	0.705	0.846	0.865
	NO item 2	0.848	0.718	
	NO item 3	0.686	0.864	
FI-Felt Involvement	FI item 1	0.743	0.907	0.900
	FI item 2	0.809	0.853	
	FI item 3	0.865	0.801	
AE-Aesthetics	AE item 1	0.870	0.932	0.947
	AE item 2	0.880	0.930	
	AE item 3	0.851	0.935	
	AE item 4	0.849	0.936	
	AE item 5	0.826	0.949	

Table 6. Mean Scores of Pre-test's Six Dimensions

Subscale	Number items	Mean	SD	Median
FA-Focused Attention	5	2.81	0.98	2.80
PU-Perceived Usability	6	3.84	0.88	4.00
EN-Endurability	5	3.42	0.86	3.40
NO-Novelty	3	3.21	0.96	3.33
FI-Felt Involvement	3	2.89	1.19	2.67
AE-Aesthetics	5	2.89	1.18	2.60

Table 7. Mean Scores of Post-test's Six Dimensions

Subscale	Number items	Mean	SD	Median
FA-Focused Attention	5	4.18	0.62	4.00
PU-Perceived Usability	6	4.38	0.71	4.67
EN-Endurability	5	4.42	0.54	4.60
NO-Novelty	3	4.31	0.73	4.67
FI-Felt Involvement	3	4.37	0.63	4.33
AE-Aesthetics	5	4.16	0.73	4.40

Table 8. Descriptive Statistics and P-values

After video simulation tour (pre)		After gamified AR tour (post)			
Mean(SD)	Median	Mean(SD)	Median	t	p
86.96(14.55)	119.00	116.08(23.81)	88.00	-3.96	0.029*

Significance: * $p < 0.05$

than before the intervention, and the format significantly increased the engagement of the site museum visit (Fig. 4).

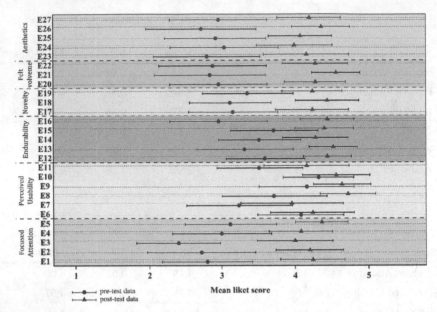

Fig. 4. Mean Likert scores per item from the engagement questionnaire (circles) after the video simulation tour and (triangles) after the gamified AR tour.

5 Conclusion

The engagement scores of the pre- and post-tests indicated that the format of the site museum tour through gamified AR significantly increased participant engagement, with the mean scores of all post-test dimensions being higher than those of the pre-test. It was also found that compared to the six dimensions of engagement, the highest score in the posttest was EN (4.42), followed by PU (4.38), FI (4.37), NO (4.31), FA (4.18), and the lowest score in AE (4.16). That is to say, in the practice of gamified AR design with Qujialing Site Museum as an example, the social boards such as leaderboards effectively enhance endurability, the mechanism of gamified rewards as an example can effectively enhance the user perception, the immersive experience of AR and the gamified interaction make the users feel novel and focused, and the interface can be further improved in terms of aesthetics.

In this study, we did not adopt the combination of subjective and objective measurements at present, and we will introduce physiological signal-based measurements for further research in the future.

References

1. Tiejun, W.: Educational Games Shanghai Breakout. China Distance Education (2004)
2. Deterding, S., Dixon, D., Khaled, R., et al.: From game design elements to gamefulness: defining "Gamification". In: International Academic Mindtrek Conference: Envisioning Future Media Environments. ACM (2011).https://doi.org/10.1145/2181037.2181040

3. McGonigal, J.: Reality is Broken: Why Games Make Us Better and How They Can Change the World. Zhejiang People's Publishing House (2012)
4. Huotari, K., Hamari, J.: Defining gamification - a service marketing perspective. In: The 16th International Academic Mindtrek Conference. NewYork, ACM, pp.17–22 (2012)
5. Pine, B.J., Pine J., Gilmore, J.H.: The Experience Economy: Work is Theatre & Every Business a Stage. Harvard Business Press, Boston (1999)
6. Norman, D.A., Draper, S.W.: User Centered System Design: New Perspectives on Human Computer Interaction (1986)
7. O'Brien, H.: Theoretical perspectives on user engagement. In: O'Brien, H., Cairns, P. (eds.) Why Engagement Matters, pp. 1–26. Springer, Cham (2016). https://doi.org/10.1007/978-3-319-27446-1_1
8. O'Brien, H.L.: Defining and measuring engagement in user experiences with technology. Dalhousie University Ph.D. thesis (2008)
9. O'Brien, H.L., Cairns, P., Hall, M.: A practical approach to measuring user engagement with the refined user engagement scale (UES) and new UES short form. Int. J. Hum.-Comput. Stud. **112**, 28–39 (2018). https://doi.org/10.1016/j.ijhcs.2018.01.004
10. O'Brien, H.: Translating theory into methodological practice. In: O'Brien, H., Cairns, P. (eds.) Why Engagement Matters, pp. 27–52. Springer, Cham (2016). https://doi.org/10.1007/978-3-319-27446-1_2
11. O'Brien, H.L., Toms, E.G.: The development and evaluation of a survey to measure user engagement. J. Am. Soc. Inf. Sci. **61**(1), 50–69 (2014). https://doi.org/10.1002/asi.21229

User Experience Evaluation of an Immersive Virtual Reality Experience: The Case of the Palmela Dukes' Mausoleum in Lisbon's Prazeres Cemetery

Paulo Noriega[1,2] , Mariana Sousa[1,2], Francisco Rebelo[1,2] ,
and Elisângela Vilar[1,2(✉)]

[1] CIAUD, Research Centre for Architecture, Urbanism and Design, Lisbon School of
Architecture, Universidade de Lisboa, Rua Sá Nogueira, Polo Universitário do Alto da Ajuda,
1349-063 Lisboa, Portugal
{pnoriega,epbvilar}@edu.ulisboa.pt, frebelo@fa.ulisboa.pt
[2] ITI- LARSyS, Universidade de Lisboa, Rua Sá Nogueira, 1349-063 Lisboa, Portugal

Abstract. All over the world, there is a lot of our history that is still inaccessible to everyone. From historical facts, cultural patterns, and music, to paintings, sculptures, and buildings, many of these cultural and architectural heritages have restricted access or are hidden behind private patrimony. In this context, this applied research is focused on developing technology-based resources to engage users with cultural heritage, mainly those related to cemetery heritage. Thus, it investigates the prospective role of VR as a vehicle for unveiling one of the prominent heritage sites within the Prazeres Cemetery, namely the Mausoleum of the Dukes of Palmela. In this way, this paper aims to present part of larger project that has as main goal the development of an Immersive Virtual Reality (IVR) experiences for cemeterial tourism. The project was developed considering three main phases, the exploratory phase, the generative phase, and the evaluative phase, but for this paper purpose, only the last one will be detailed. The main objective is to present the pilot tests made with the prototype developed for the Dukes of Palmela Mausoleum VR experience. The tests were made mainly to evaluate Use experience (UX) while interacting with an IVR experience. The primary findings indicate that the three emotions most experienced by the participants after the interaction were: Interest, Astonishment, and Fear. Additionally, the performance test showed effective memory retention among participants, indicating the potential of VR experiences to evoke meaningful engagement and learning.

Keywords: Virtual Reality · Interaction Design · Cemeterial Tourism ·
Patrimony · User Experience

1 Introduction

One of the fundamental drivers of tourism lies in the combination of curiosity and the quest for personal satisfaction, prompting the movement of millions of individuals annually to diverse destinations offering leisure pursuits. This phenomenon renders tourism

© The Author(s), under exclusive license to Springer Nature Switzerland AG 2024
A. Marcus et al. (Eds.): HCII 2024, LNCS 14715, pp. 310–327, 2024.
https://doi.org/10.1007/978-3-031-61359-3_22

one of the most lucrative and significant activities of the 20th century [1]. One of the important types of tourism is Heritage, that encompasses both natural and cultural sites. It involves traveling to experience places, artifacts, or activities that are believed to be authentic representations of people and stories from the past [2]. Thus, the preservation and development of cultural heritage objects, including monuments, traditions, and crafts, are essential for the effective development of international tourism and sustainable regional development [3].

Cemetery tourism reflects a growing interest in heritage tourism and the exploration of cultural landscapes. Cemeterial tourism refers to the practice of visiting cemeteries as tourist attractions. It has gained popularity in recent years, with historic cemeteries being classified as national heritage and receiving infrastructure improvements and guided tours [4]. It is seen as a way to explore non-traditional spaces with great potential for tourist attraction. The combined memorial, recreational, and touristic use of cemeteries can help preserve their economic management and long-term value [5].

The concept of cemeteries transcends mere repositories of mortal remains, encompassing profound historical, cultural, and artistic significance that shapes societal perceptions and identity. Originating from the establishment of iconic models like the Parisian Père-Lachaise in 1804, the evolution of public cemeteries in 19th-century Lisbon, exemplified by Prazeres Cemetery (1834) and Alto de São João Cemetery (1834), mirrors societal attitudes towards death in Portugal [6]. According to André (2006), these spaces, described as scenographic, serve as tangible representations of collective memory and historical narrative, with individual graves reflecting personal histories and societal values. The author posits that the cemetery space ultimately showcased an emerging bourgeoisie that identified with and projected onto the space through the architectural constructions of burial plots, serving as an ode to the family, with a progressive increase in construction dimensions. This observation underscores the societal dynamics at play within cemetery spaces, reflecting evolving cultural values and socio-economic trends. This is an example of the importance of cemeteries as part of the Heritage tourism.

The advent of digital transformation has precipitated a notable shift in the landscape of tourism, wherein technology is commonly perceived as a facilitator of enhanced user experiences during travels [7]. Cemetery tourism can promote and disseminate cultural heritage, and the use of virtual reality experiences can enhance the user's cultural experience [8].

In this context, this paper aims to present a study about User experience (UX) while interacting with an Immersive Virtual Reality (IVR) experience to the Duke of Palmela´s mausoleum, one of the largest private mausoleums in Europe situated at the Prazeres Cemetery, Lisbon, Portugal.

The paper is structured as follows: Sect. 2 discusses the theoretical framework, focusing on the Dukes of Palmela Mausoleum as the subject of this IVR experience. It then describes the application of VR in tourism, specifically Heritage tourism, and examines the role of User Experience (UX) in interactive tourism interfaces. Section 3 outlines the methodology employed for developing the prototype and conducting user testing, while Sect. 4 presents the primary findings and discussion. Finally, Sect. 5 concludes the paper.

2 Theoretical Reference

2.1 The Dukes of Palmela Mausoleum

The Prazeres Cemetery, in Lisbon, is the home to the grand Mausoleum of the Palmela's Dukes, which stands as a testament to Portugal's rich heritage and cultural legacy [8]. A primary objective behind a mausoleum construction is to create a familial pantheon for the deceased, evolving into a resting space for the family akin to a new home. This "home" facilitates familial reunification beyond earthly life, serving as a beacon of collective redemption to be realized on the day of the "Final Judgment" [9].

The moment that someone observes this mausoleum, it initiates a journey through the Masonic symbolism, architecture, art, and, above all, the history embodied and transmitted by the family within their sepulcher.

The mausoleum was commissioned by D. Pedro de Sousa Holstein (1781–1850), the 1st Duke of Palmela, and was designed by the architect Giuseppe Cinatti. Nowadays is considered one of the biggest private mausoleums in Europe. According to Queiroz and Alves [10], the mausoleum of the Dukes of Palmela, constructed between 1848–1849, is unparalleled within the landscape of 19th-century Portuguese funerary architecture, both in its architectural design and the artistic treasures it encompasses.

The mausoleum, with a clear Masonic influence, draws inspiration from two distinct sources: Egyptian and Greek. The Egyptian inspiration is evident in the pyramid-shaped structure of the building, symbolizing the perpetuation of the memory of significant historical events and illustrious figures within Masonic tradition. Conversely, the Greek influence is manifested in the Doric portico at the entrance, adorned with thematic motifs such as vegetal elements, simplicity, and ambiguity. The tympanum of the portico initially featured the coat of arms of the Palmela family, surmounted by a Celtic cross, alongside an entablature decorated with vegetal themes and inscribed with the text "*Jazigo da Família do Duque de Palmella / Anno de MDCCCXLIX (1849)*", see Fig. 1.

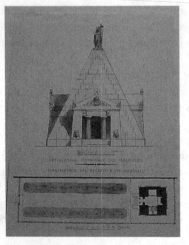

Fig. 1. First sketch and the actual entrance of the mausoleum (retrieved from [11])

Within the sepulcher lie works of remarkable value, such as the cenotaph, a low-relief piece crafted by the Italian sculptor Antonio Canova (1757–1822) and dedicated to the father of the 1st Duke of Palmela, Alexandre de Sousa Holstein (1751–1803). The first floor, initially designated for an altar, now houses the tombs of Palmela family members. The lower floor is purportedly dedicated to a familial pantheon, featuring a ceiling adorned with poppy decorations symbolizing eternal rest for those interred, including the 1st Duke of Palmela, his successors, and other family-related individuals. Embarking on a journey within the mausoleum of the Dukes of Palmela transports visitors into another domain, akin to stepping into a time capsule or museum (see Fig. 2). From encountering art, emotion, architecture, and family history to paying respects to the deceased, visitors are immersed in a wealth of information and knowledge about the family, which played a significant role in the country's history. The experience of visiting this site is profoundly enriching, particularly when accompanied by insights into the art, history, Masonic symbolism, and intricate details present throughout the mausoleum and its surroundings.

Fig. 2. Photos of the Altar on the ground floor and the family pantheon on the lower floor retrieved from [11].

2.2 Virtual Reality (VR) and Heritage Tourism

Virtual Reality is perceived as a technology with significant potential to positively impact tourism, as its utilization within this sector has progressed alongside advancements in the technology itself [12]. Immersive virtual reality (IVR) technologies have revolutionized tourism by offering new experiences and opportunities for engagement in various destinations, utilized to captivate tourists and enhance their overall experience. Indeed, there are many tourist destinations that are not easily accessible, undergoing some form of degradation, or temporarily closed to the public, for instance. According to Baker [13], tourism can harness these technologies for various purposes: previewing real-world experiences, enhancing on-site experiences, reliving memories post-travel, and sometimes substituting for travel altogether.

Heritage Tourism is an area that can benefit from new technologies. Via VR, tourists gain access to areas that are otherwise inaccessible or restricted, necessitating preservation from the potential impacts of mass tourism, for example. Additionally, they can receive culturally enriching information communicated in an engaging manner. Some examples of applications using VR in the field of heritage tourism are: *The Salla World War II*, a Virtual visit, in VR, to an inaccessible historical cemetery located between Finland and Russia, and *Anne Frank house VR,* a virtual visit to Anne Frank´s house, in Amsterdam.

2.3 Virtual Reality (VR) and User Experience (UX)

In recent years, VR technology has emerged as a transformative force across various industries, including tourism, by offering immersive experiences that transcend traditional boundaries. At the core of the success of VR applications lies the concept of user experience (UX), which assumes a pivotal role in shaping the overall effectiveness and enjoyment of these virtual environments.

UX stands as a fundamental aspect of design, revolving around the crafting of optimal interactions with services or products. This entails enhancing usability and fostering positive emotional responses throughout the user's journey, alongside considerations for factors such as usefulness and post-interaction memory [15]. The emphasis on creating designs that are not only aesthetically pleasing but also of high quality and effectively functional underscores the indispensability of user experience design [14].

A primary objective of VR is to transport users into immersive virtual worlds. Effective UX design enhances immersion by optimizing sensory inputs, including visual, auditory, and tactile stimuli, thereby crafting compelling and believable virtual environments [15]. These immersive experiences have been empirically shown to evoke strong emotional responses and enhance user engagement [16].

When designing for VR, the user's experience, including interactions, narratives, and game design elements, emerges as central to achieving high engagement and increased presence. UX encompasses the holistic interaction between users and VR environments, incorporating factors such as usability, engagement, and emotional impact, which crucially influence user satisfaction, retention, and the overall effectiveness of VR applications, thereby ensuring a positive experience [17, 18].

Emotional engagement stands as a key component of user experience, significantly influencing user enjoyment and retention in VR experiences. Immersive virtual environments possess the potential to elicit powerful emotional responses, ranging from awe and excitement to fear and empathy [19]. Designing VR experiences that evoke positive emotions and foster meaningful connections can consequently enhance user satisfaction and foster long-term engagement [20].

Usability represents a cornerstone of user experience, particularly within VR environments where intuitive interaction holds paramount importance. Well-designed VR interfaces and navigation systems contribute significantly to user comfort and ease of use, thereby reducing cognitive load and enhancing overall satisfaction [21]. Notably, improvements in usability have been correlated with increased user adoption and retention rates in VR applications.

VR technologies provide immersive and interactive experiences that can enhance user engagement, enjoyment, and flow, leading to higher levels of satisfaction [22]. Additionally, the realism and atmosphere created by VR reconstructions contribute to emotional engagement and interest in exploring the virtual environment [23].

3   Methodology

This paper aims to present part of larger project that has as main goal the development of a IVR experiences for cemeterial tourism. The project was developed considering three main phases, the exploratory phase, the generative phase, and the evaluative phase, but for this paper purpose, only the last one will be detailed. Thus, the main objective is to present the pilot test made with the prototype developed for the Dukes of Palmela Mausoleum VR experience. The tests were made mainly to evaluate Use experience (UX) while interacting with an IVR experience.

In the exploratory phase, three methods were employed: literature review, case studies, and exploratory interviews. This phase entails research, data collection, selection, and analysis of information relevant to the investigation, such as topics on heritage and cemetery tourism, and cemetery heritage, VR, and other investigative topics related to the project's exploratory idea. A critical collection of articles, authors working within the addressed areas, books, and theses was conducted, leading to the subsequent selection, analysis, and synthesis of the acquired information. Concerning the case studies, once selected, each case underwent analysis followed by conclusions drawn on both positive and negative aspects. Exploratory interviews were conducted with a guide and historian from the Prazeres Cemetery, as well as a semi-structured interview with a member of the Palmela family, aimed at uncovering stories related to the mausoleum and the family. Additionally, discussions were held with members of the cemetery department of the Lisbon City Council to understand the needs of visitors/tourists to the site.

In the subsequent phase, the generative phase, a qualitative interventionist methodology was contemplated for active research, with two stages, incorporating the principles and strategies of interaction design. Initially, the target audience was delineated through direct observation and semi-structured interviews conducted with cemetery visitors, alongside tourist guides and historians affiliated with the Prazeres Cemetery. Data acquired in the exploratory phase, in addition to insights garnered from direct observation and interviews with various stakeholders, were instrumental in formulating main requirements for the development of the immersive and interactive VR experience during the generative phase.

Within this generative phase, both the narrative structure and the storyboards detailing the interactive virtual experience were meticulously crafted (more information about this process can be seen in Sousa [8]). These storyboards were subsequently transposed into three-dimensional (3D) models, thus culminating in the creation of a prototype. The prototype served as the foundational for the subsequent evaluative phase, which will be delineated with further detail in the subsequent discourse.

3.1   The Prototype of the Dukes of Palmela Virtual Experience

The VR experience prototype was developed based on the storyboards. 360° images were collected from the Dukes of Palmela mausoleum and used as bases for the development on Unity software together with the VR Easy, and proprietary scripts developed by the ergoUX Lab – FAULisboa. A mixed approach based on merging 360° images with 3D modelling was used to insert elements into the scene, such as the virtual characters of the 3rd Duchess and the 1st Duke of Palmela (see Fig. 3).

Fig. 3. 3D models of the 3rd Duchess and the 1st Duke of Palmela and a scene from the VR experience using mixed 360°images and 3D modelling (retrieved from [11]).

The VR experience consisted in a journey guided by these two members of the Palmela's family through the mausoleum, considering its art pieces, architecture, historical events, and family events. Game elements, such as quiz and interactive elements, such as buttons, were also inserted to increase user´s engagement.

All interactions and navigation were made considering a gaze-based approach. This decision was based in improving accessibility levels and considering that it requires a smaller learning effort, compared to hand controllers. So, to navigate between scenes, users need to look to a pre-defined point (a target). Along the journey, users were also able to watch some videos and receive more information. For this, the camera and the information icons were inserted into the virtual environment. They can be seen, together with the target, on Fig. 4. The experience was designed to 15 min of duration, considering to be used as part of an exhibition at the Prazeres cemetery.

Fig. 4. A scene with the information icon, the target to move for the next scene, and the camera icon (retrieved from [11]).

3.2 The Evaluative Phase

The evaluative phase was made considering a pilot test with the prototype of the Dukes of Palmela Virtual Experience. For this, UX and Usability were assessed.

The pilot test was made with eleven students (8 female) and aged between 20 and 30 years old (mean = 24 years old).

For interacting with the VR system, a Quest 2 head-mounted display (HMD) was used. The HMD was linked via wire to the experimenter's computer reproducing the participants view. It allows the experimenter to monitor the whole experience, observing the participants behavior into the virtual environment while interacting with the prototype. As mentioned, all interactions were made considering a gaze-based approach.

The Pilot Test Application Protocol. The pilot test was divided into 5 phases: phase 1 - a brief explanation of the experience, signing of the Informed Consent Form, and demonstration of equipment interaction; phase 2 - the VR experience (interaction with the prototype); phase 3 - application of evaluation tools (after interaction with the prototype); phase 4 - space for participant feedback; phase 5 - end of participation. The tests were conducted at ergoUX Lab, the Ergonomics, Usability, and User Experience laboratory of FAULisboa. Upon arrival at the laboratory, phase 1 started. Participants were welcomed by the researcher, who introduced themselves, thanked them for their participation, and provided a brief overview of the experience. Subsequently, the Informed Consent Form was provided, containing information on the study's objectives, data security, confidentiality, and its use solely for academic purposes, and safety, along with authorizations for image and voice usage, for participants to read and sign (in duplicate, with one copy retained by the participant) if they agreed to participate in the study. Following this, the equipment was presented, and a brief VR usage session was conducted to familiarize participants with the defined interaction method (gaze-based).

In phase 2, participants were invited to put on the HMD and experience the prototype of the Virtual Experience at the Mausoleum of the Dukes of Palmela. This interactive session spanned approximately 15 min. Upon concluding the interaction, marked by the participant reaching the final scene of the prototype, the researcher proceeded to remove the HMD and transition to phase 3.

In phase 3, the usability and UX tests to be conducted individually were explained and demonstrated. The first method employed was the Geneva Emotions Wheel [24]. Prior to its application, the test was elucidated, and a brief simulation illustrating its functioning was conducted to ensure participants understood how to utilize it. Following its implementation, the Performance Test ensued, focusing on the memorization and recall of 8 significant moments in the narrative. In parallel, the SAM [25] was administered for the same 8 moments. Following the SAM application, participants completed the Presence Questionnaire [26], and finally, the System Usability Scale (SUS) [27] was administered to gauge the level of ease of use of the experience. Upon completion of the SUS questionnaire, phase 4 commenced, during which participants were asked to provide feedback on the experience and/or mention any details they deemed relevant.

Phase 5 marks the conclusion of participation. During this phase, the contacts of participants who expressed interest in learning about the study's results were collected. The researcher reiterated their gratitude for participation.

The Instruments.

GEW - Geneva Emotions Wheel [24]. This instrument is a "theoretically derived and empirically tested instrument to measure emotional reactions to objects, events, and situations." [28].

It consists in *"of discrete emotion terms corresponding to emotion families that are systematically aligned in a circle"* [29].

In the GEW (Fig. 5), there are 20 families of emotions, and for each of them, it is possible to choose different intensity values represented by circles (with increasing size variation). There are also response options where the participant can choose a different emotion from those listed in the tool and the option to report that no emotion was felt. The response options in the GEW are represented as "peaks," corresponding to different intensity levels for each family of emotion, from low intensity closer to the center of the wheel to the highest intensity further away from the wheel [29]. This is a comprehensive method for measuring the emotions felt by individuals, although the range of words within each emotion family is broad. This method was employed to understand the three main emotions elicited by the VR experience and their respective intensities.

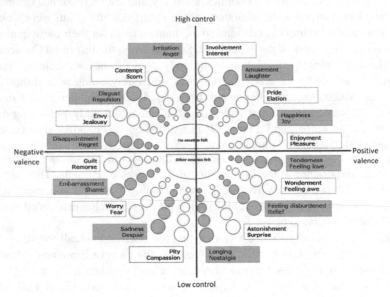

Fig. 5. The Geneva Emotions Wheel (retrieved from [29])

Performance Test. The performance test was conducted by recalling eight key moments of the narrative. The aim of this test is to assess the retention of information provided during the interaction. Eight moments of the VR experience, considered significant in the narrative due to the information they contain, were evaluated. To assess these eight moments, images of each one were shown, and two questions were asked: "Do you remember this moment?" and "What do you remember?" Participants responded freely to each question, without there being correct or incorrect answers. The responses were recorded and subsequently analyzed.

SAM - Self-Assessment Manikin. The SAM [25] method is a non-verbal, pictorial eval-uation method that allows measuring valence, arousal, and dominance associated with both the affective response of a person and a variety of stimuli [25]. At SAM the three dimensions (i.e., valence, arousal, and dominance) are displayed in three axes. The level of each dimension is represented by five images in each axe, varying according to its intensity level. According to Bradley and Lang [25], *"SAM ranges from a smiling happy figure, to a frowning, unhappy figure when representing the pleasure dimension, and ranges from an excited, wide-eyed figure to a relaxed, sleepy figure for the arousal dimension. The dominance dimension represents changes in control with changes in the size of SAM: a large figure indicates maximum control in the situation"*. As participants can choose the exactly point of the image, or the point between images, the scale has 9 points. For this study, only valence and arousal axes were used (Fig. 6). The purpose of SAM was to understand the levels of valence and arousal elicited by recalling each of the 8 moments.

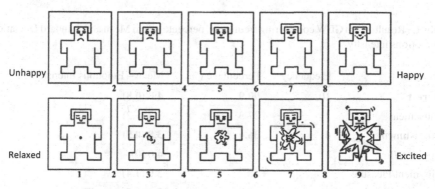

Fig. 6. SAM scale used for the test (adapted from [25])

Presence Questionnaire. Presence is a core factor for an immersive VR experience. Witmer and Singer [30] defined presence as a mean with which a person feels in a place even when he/she is physically in another. To measure presence for this study, the Portuguese version of the Presence Questionnaire was used [26].

The Presence Questionnaire consists of seven independent dimensions and one global measure: Involvement, Naturalness, Interface Quality, Resolution, Auditory, Haptic, Immersion, and Overall. It comprises twenty-one questions, of which eighteen were used for this study (questions related to the haptic dimension were excluded as they did not fit the scope of the study). Participants' answers are collected through a seven points Likert-type scale.

SUS – System Usability Scale questionnaire. The System Usability Scale (SUS) is a reliable and cost-effective usability scale that can be used for global evaluations of system usability [27]. Moreover, this tool can measure the perceived ease of use of a wide range of digital products and services, aiding UX professionals in determining the presence or absence of a systemic issue to devise a design solution accordingly [31].

In this project, the SUS method was employed to understand users' assessment of the usability of the virtual reality experience in which they participated.

For SUS recording, the Usability DataLogger v5.1.1 was utilized, which is an Excel-based tool designed to assist in collecting usability test data.

4   Results and Discussion

To facilitate understanding, results for each instrument will be presented next.

Geneva Emotions Wheel Results. The frequency of responses for each emotion was evaluated, along with the percentage of each emotion felt and the mean with the standard deviation their intensity. The results of the GEW application showed that, overall, the three emotions most felt by the participants were: Interest, Astonishment, and Fear. Main results can be seen on Table 1.

Table 1. Results from GEW considering frequency, percentage and Mean and Standard Deviation for emotions intensity.

Emotions	Frequency	Percentage (%)	Mean – Emotions Intensity (SD)
Interest	**10**	**90.9**	**4.0 (0.8)**
Amusement	3	27.3	3.3 (1.2)
Astonishment	**4**	**36.4**	**3.8 (0.5)**
Happiness/Joy	1	9.1	4.0 (0)
Enjoyment/Pleasure	2	18.2	3.0 (1.4)
Wonderment	2	18.2	2.5 (0.7)
Compassion	3	27.3	3.7 (0.6)
Sadness/Despair	2	18.2	3.0(1.4)
Worry/Fear	**5**	**45.5**	**3.0 (1.2)**
Embarrassment	1	9.1	2 (0)

Among the most felt emotions, Interest and Astonishment were the ones with the highest intensity. It is worth noting that, even though fear was more frequent than admiration, the intensity reported by participants was lower. Regarding the remaining seven mentioned emotions, it is important to highlight the average intensity of the "compassion" emotion, which was 3.7, although mentioned by only three participants. This mentioned emotion may be related to the narrative of the life of the 3rd Duchess of Palmela, "by herself," which ultimately generates compassion from the participant. As "astonishment," chosen by four participants, is attributed to the fact that, as stated by the participants after selecting this emotion, they feel admiration for the Palmela family and the mausoleum they managed to construct.

Performance Test. To analyze data from participants verbalized answers considering the eight selected scenes, a table was created containing important details to be recalled by the participants, and if they remembered. It is worth noting that there were no right or wrong answers; the aim was solely to understand which moments the participants remembered and what they recalled within those moments to determine if most of the information conveyed in the VR experience remained in the participants' memory. Thus, when analyzing participants verbalizations, if they mentioned the and important detail previously listed by research team, this detail was marked into the table, and at the and their frequency of recall was accounted. The most recalled scenes were 1, 5 and 7 (Fig. 7), however all of them had percentages above 50% (Fig. 8).

Fig. 7. The most recalled scenes (Scene 1, Scene 5 and Scene 7, respectively), retrieved from [11]

It was expected that Scene 1 would be one of the most recalled due to the interaction features it presents; it was the beginning of the experience. In it, a question appeared that participants had to answer, and they acquired a key to continue in the experience.

Participants recalled Scene 5 as the location with paintings depicting the life of the Duchess of Palmela. The sound effect, present in Scene 7, representing the voice of the Duke coming from downstairs, was a remarkable aspect, with the information conveyed by the voice being recalled by most of the participants (8 out of 11).

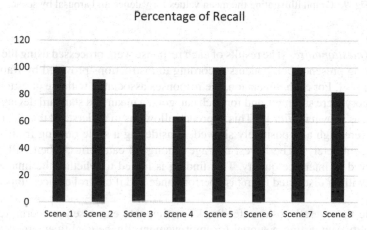

Fig. 8. Graph illustrating the overall percentage of recall for each of the eight scenes presented.

SAM - Self-Assessment Manikin. The outcomes of each response encompassing both affective valence and arousal for each of the 8 scenes presented, were analyzed considering the mean value in a 9 points scale (Fig. 9). Scene 5 (mean 6.7 out of 9) depicted a corridor with abundant information, making it the scene with the highest affective valence, followed by Scene 1(6.5 out 9) and Scene 8 (6.4 out 9). These two scenes involved significant interaction between the participant and the environment, hence the elevated valence. Additionally, they were the second and third moments with the highest activation after Scene 2 (7.1 out 9), confirming the high level of valence (pleasure and excitement) experienced during interaction with the environment and the desire to progress to the next scene. The Scene 2 was the one with an explosion, thus it was expected the high arousal attained. And the results indicated that, in general, Scene 7 showed the lowest valence, whereas Scene 5 had the highest valence. Scene 2 demonstrated the highest level of arousal, while Scene 6 displayed the lowest.

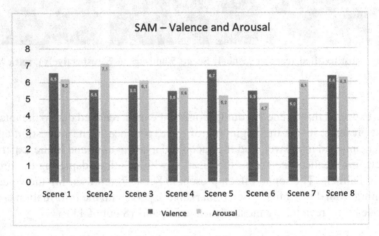

Fig. 9. Graph illustrating the mean values for valence and arousal by scene.

Presence Questionnaire. The results of each response were processed using the method of calculating presence components according to instructions provided by Raposo and colleagues [26]. For each dimension, the responses associated with the questions in the same category were summed, and for each category, a mean and standard deviation were calculated, as shown in Fig. 10. This approach allows us to understand that the response averages were high and positively skewed, considering a scale ranging from 1 (not at all) to 7 (completely). The lowest average among all categories, albeit still positive, was observed in interface quality. This finding is linked to whether the image quality interfered with or distracted from task performance and if control devices impeded task execution.

Despite the overall positive feedback, participants expressed concerns regarding image quality, suggesting potential for improvement. Image quality emerged as a critical aspect of the experience, particularly given the acquisition and utilization of 360° photos depicting locations rich in detail, which necessitate high-quality visuals for an

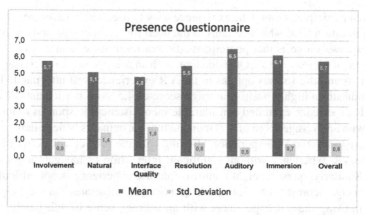

Fig. 10. Graph illustrating the mean and standard deviation values for each dimension of the presence questionnaire.

immersive effect. Even with the efforts to enhance image quality through editing, the camera used, namely the Insta360 Evo, with its respectable 18MP resolution, failed to achieve the desired maximum quality standards. The immersion category achieved a notably high average score of 6.1 out of 7, indicating participants' heightened sense of immersion during the virtual experience. Auditory stimuli and feedback also received high ratings, averaging 6.5 out of 7, suggesting that ambient sounds and narration positively contributed to participants' overall experience. Additionally, the involvement category received positive feedback, with an average rating of 5.7 out of 7, reflecting participants' engagement with the visual aspects of the environment, adaptation speed, and comfort with interaction within the virtual space. Despite not achieving complete involvement, participants demonstrated a positive engagement level with the virtual narrative. The "natural" category assesses the authenticity of interactions, the usability of gaze-based navigation, and the coherence between virtual and real-world experiences. Despite a generally positive rating averaging 5.1 out of 7, it ranked second lowest among all categories. Initial concerns regarding gaze-based navigation were largely alleviated by positive participant responses. Importantly, gaze-based navigation holds promise for enhancing inclusivity by facilitating interaction for individuals with mobility limitations or technology adaptation challenges.

SUS – System Usability Scale questionnaire. Answers were collected considering a Likert-type five points scale, varying from 1 (totally disagree) to 5 (totally agree). Each question was assessed for its mean with standard deviation, and minimum and maximum scores. Furthermore, the overall SUS percentage was 83.4. Results can be seen on Table 2.

Regarding the initial query, participants displayed a neutral stance with a mean score of 3.3, suggesting no strong inclination towards frequent use of the VR experience tested. Verbal feedback from some participants indicated that while they enjoyed the experience, they expressed reluctance to use it frequently if it remained the same. However, they expressed a willingness to engage more frequently if there were continuous alterations to the experience. The second question yielded a mean score of 4.6, indicating that participants did not perceive the experience as unnecessarily complex. Question three suggests that participants found the experience easy to use, with an average score of 4.5. Regarding question four, which pertains to the need for technical assistance, the overall average response suggests that participants did not require assistance overall, with an average score of 4.1 (SD = 1.2). Question five, with an average score of 4.5, suggests that participants found the various options in the VR experience well integrated. The sixth question indicates a highly positive average score of 4.5, with participants disagreeing that the VR experience exhibited considerable inconsistency. Responses to the seventh question, with an average score of 4.7, indicate that participants believe individuals will quickly learn to use the VR experience, aligning with the project's objective of creating an intuitive VR experience without significant interaction or navigation complexities for users. Similarly, question eight confirms that the experience is not difficult to use, with an average score of 4.8. The ninth question demonstrates that participants felt confident in using the VR experience, with an average score of 4.2. Lastly, the tenth question reaffirms that extensive learning about the VR experience is not necessary before use, with an average score of 4.6. Overall, the responses to the 10 questions were overwhelmingly positive and aligned with the objectives of the VR experience, despite the first question being the only one with neutral or lower responses. With a score of 83.4, according to the SUS scale, the overall rating confirms acceptability and positivity, with the scale ranging from 0 to 100, where 0 represents unacceptable and highly negative, and 100 represents better than imaginable and highly positive.

Table 2. Results for the SUS Questionnaire

Questions	Mean (SD)	Min	Max:
1	3,3 (1,0)	2	5
2	4,6(0,5)	4	5
3	4,5(0,5)	4	5
4	4,1 (1,2)	1	5
5	4,5 (0,7)	3	5
6	4,5 (0,7)	3	5
7	4,7 (0,6)	3	5
8	4,8 (0,4)	4	5
9	4,2 (0,9)	3	5
10	4,6 (0,9)	2	5
Mean			

5 Conclusion

The study investigated the utilization of virtual reality (VR) as an instrument for heritage promotion, especially within the tourism domain. Despite its limited application in heritage promotion within Portugal, the increasing global adoption of VR technology has significantly broadened access to previously inaccessible or overlooked heritage sites. In addition to enhancing traditional tourism offerings, VR serves as an educational tool, enriching visitor experiences by providing immersive and interactive encounters with cultural heritage.

Through the integration of immersive VR technology and user experience (UX) design principles, users are presented with intuitive interfaces and sensory-rich experiences, fostering deeper connections, and understanding of virtual heritage sites. This integration has democratized access to heritage tourism, allowing individuals from diverse backgrounds and geographical locations to embark on virtual journeys of discovery and preservation. Moreover, the synergistic combination of immersive VR technology and UX design contributes to the preservation and promotion of cultural heritage by ensuring its accessibility and relevance for future generations.

The evaluation of pilot tests conducted on the Dukes of Palmela Mausoleum VR prototype revealed that participants predominantly experienced feelings of interest, admiration, and fear, aligning with project desired emotional responses. Since the experience takes place in a mausoleum, it was intended for some fear to be felt, creating a positive tension to increase engagement. In one of the project iterations, not described in this paper, this emotion was not present, but it was achieved through the inclusion of a background sound effect.

Additionally, the performance test showed effective memory retention among participants, indicating the potential of VR experiences to evoke meaningful engagement and learning.

Despite limitations in testing with the intended audience, participants positively received the VR experience, underscoring its potential for educational and immersive tourism experiences. This underscores the transformative impact of VR in reshaping perceptions of heritage sites and enhancing visitor engagement, ultimately enriching cultural understanding and appreciation on a global scale.

Acknowledgments. This study was partially supported by CIAUD Project UID/EAT/4008/2020, ITI-LARSyS-FCT Pluriannual funding 2020–2023 (https://doi.org/10.54499/UIDB/50009/2020) and the Fundação para a Ciência e Tecnologia - FCT (https://doi.org/10.54499/DL57/2016/CP1365/CT0003).

Disclosure of Interests. The authors have no competing interests to declare that are relevant to the content of this article.

References

1. Gómez-Vega, M., Picazo-Tadeo, A.J.: Ranking world tourist destinations with a composite indicator of competitiveness: to weigh or not to weigh? Tour. Manag. 72, 281–291 (2019). https://doi.org/10.1016/j.tourman.2018.11.006
2. Kan, M.H.M., Ashfaq, M., Humayon, A.A., Kan, M.: Tourists' attitudes toward cultural heritage: pre- and post-visit evaluation. In: Tourist Behavior. Apple Academic Press (2022)
3. Muštra, V., Perić, B.Š, Pivčević, S.: Cultural heritage sites, tourism and regional economic resilience. Pap. Reg. Sci. 102, 465–482 (2023). https://doi.org/10.1111/pirs.12731

4. Del Puerto, C.B., Baptista, M.L.C.: Espaço cemiterial e Turismo: campo de ambivalência da vida e morte. Rev. Iberoam. Tur. **5**, 42–53 (2015)
5. Sallay, Á., Mikházi, Z., Gecséné Tar, I., Takács, K.: Cemeteries as a Part of Green Infrastructure and Tourism. Sustainability **14**, 2918 (2022). https://doi.org/10.3390/su1405 2918
6. André, P.: Modos de Pensar e Construir os Cemitérios Públicos Oitocentistas em Lisboa: o caso do Cemitério dos Prazeres. Rev. Inst. História Arte., 67–105 (2006)
7. Gutierriz, I.E., Lopes, I.M., Rodriguez, V., Fernandes, P.O., Jatoba, M.N.: O QR Code e as formas de perceção criativa no turismo cemiterial. RISTI Rev. Ibérica Sist. E Tecnol. Informação., 423–433 (2019)
8. Sousa, M., Rebelo, F., Noriega, P., Vilar, E.: Creating cultural experiences in a cemetery: a storyboard for a VR user interaction. In: Martins, N., Brandão, D. (eds.) Advances in Design and Digital Communication II: Proceedings of the 5th International Conference on Design and Digital Communication, Digicom 2021, November 4–6, 2021, Barcelos, Portugal, pp. 195–208. Springer International Publishing, Cham (2022). https://doi.org/10.1007/978-3-030-89735-2_17
9. Flores, F.M.: Jazigo dos Duques de Palmela - Uma simbólica Maçónica - Maçonaria e Maçon(s). https://www.freemason.pt/jazigo-duques-palmela-uma-simbolica-maconica/. Accessed 14 Feb 2024
10. Ferreira Queiroz, J.F., Alves, R.: Evocações da casa nobre na tumulária romântica. In: Actas do 4° Congresso Internacional Casa Nobre: Um património para o futuro, 2017, ISBN 978–972–9136–83–2, pp. 734–745. Município de Arcos de Valdevez (2017)
11. Sousa, M.: A Realidade Virtual como forma de promover o património cemiterial: o caso do Jazigo dos Duques de Palmela (2022)
12. Guttentag, D.A.: Virtual reality: applications and implications for tourism. Tour. Manag. **31**, 637–651 (2010). https://doi.org/10.1016/j.tourman.2009.07.003
13. Baker, J., Nam, K., Dutt, C.S.: A user experience perspective on heritage tourism in the meta verse: empirical evidence and design dilemmas for VR. Inf. Technol. Tour. **25**, 265–306 (2023). https://doi.org/10.1007/s40558-023-00256-x
14. Orlova, M.: User Experience Design (UX Design) in a Website Development: Website redesign (2016). http://www.theseus.fi/handle/10024/120948
15. Slater, M., Sanchez-Vives, M.V.: Enhancing our lives with immersive virtual reality. Front. Robot. AI **3**,(2016). https://doi.org/10.3389/frobt.2016.00074
16. Bailenson, J.: Experience on Demand: What Virtual Reality is, How it Works, and What it Can Do. W. W. Norton, New York, NY (2019)
17. Falcão, C.S., Soares, M.M.: Application of virtual reality technologies in consumer product usability. In: Marcus, A. (ed.) Design, User Experience, and Usability. Web, Mobile, and Product Design: Second International Conference, DUXU 2013, Held as Part of HCI International 2013, Las Vegas, NV, USA, July 21-26, 2013, Proceedings, Part IV, pp. 342–351. Springer Berlin Heidelberg, Berlin, Heidelberg (2013). https://doi.org/10.1007/978-3-642-39253-5_37
18. Pagano, A., Palombini, A., Bozzelli, G., De Nino, M., Cerato, I., Ricciardi, S.: ArkaeVision VR game: user experience research between real and virtual paestum. Appl. Sci. **10**, 3182 (2020). https://doi.org/10.3390/app10093182
19. Riva, G., Wiederhold, B.K., Mantovani, F.: Neuroscience of virtual reality: from virtual exposure to embodied medicine. Cyberpsychology Behav. Soc. Netw. **22**, 82–96 (2019). https://doi.org/10.1089/cyber.2017.29099.gri
20. Sutcliffe, A.G., Poullis, C., Gregoriades, A., Katsouri, I., Tzanavari, A., Herakleous, K.: Reflecting on the design process for virtual reality applications. Int. J. Hum.-Comput. Interact. **35**, 168–179 (2019). https://doi.org/10.1080/10447318.2018.1443898

21. Bowman, D.A., Gabbard, J.L., Hix, D.: A survey of usability evaluation in virtual environments: classification and comparison of methods. Presence Teleoperators Virtual Environ. **11**, 404–424 (2002). https://doi.org/10.1162/105474602760204309

22. Schott, C., Marshall, S.: Virtual reality for experiential education: a user experience exploration. Australas. J. Educ. Technol. **37**, 96–110 (2021). https://doi.org/10.14742/ajet. 5166

23. Irshad, S., Rambli, D.R.A.: User experience satisfaction of mobile-based AR advertising applications. In: Zaman, H.B., Robinson, P., Smeaton, A.F., Shih, T.K., Velastin, S., Jaafar, A., Ali, N.M. (eds.) Advances in Visual Informatics, pp. 432–442. Springer International Publishing, Cham (2015). https://doi.org/10.1007/978-3-319-25939-0_38

24. Scherer, K.R.: What are emotions? And how can they be measured? Soc. Sci. Inf. **44**, 695–729 (2005). https://doi.org/10.1177/0539018405058216

25. Bradley, M.M., Lang, P.J.: Measuring emotion: the self-assessment manikin and the semantic differential. J. Behav. Ther. Exp. Psychiatry **25**, 49–59 (1994). https://doi.org/10.1016/0005-7916(94)90063-9

26. Vasconcelos-Raposo, J., Melo, M., Barbosa, L., Teixeira, C., Cabral, L., Bessa, M.: Assessing presence in virtual environments: adaptation of the psychometric properties of the presence questionnaire to the Portuguese populations. Behav. Inf. Technol. **40**, 1417–1427 (2021). https://doi.org/10.1080/0144929X.2020.1754911

27. Brooke, J.: SUS: a quick and dirty usability scale. Usability Eval. Ind. 189 (1995)

28. The Geneva Emotion Wheel - Swiss Center for Affective Sciences – UNIGE. https://www.unige.ch/cisa/gew/. Accessed 16 Feb 2024

29. Sacharin, V., Schlegel, K., Scherer, K.R.: Geneva Emotion Wheel Rating Study. University of Geneva, Swiss Center for Affective Sciences, Geneva, Switzerland (2012)

30. Witmer, B.G., Singer, M.J.: Measuring presence in virtual environments: a presence questionnaire. Presence Teleoperators Virtual Environ. **7**, 225–240 (1998). https://doi.org/10.1162/105 474698565686

31. Bangor, A., Kortum, P., Miller, J.: Determining what individual SUS scores mean: adding an adjective rating scale. J. Usability Stud. **4**, 114–123 (2009)

Research on the Application of Digital Technology in Museum-Based Aesthetic Education of Children

Shangqi Sun[✉]

Beijing Normal University, No.19, Xinjiekouwai Street, Haidian District, Beijing 100875, People's Republic of China
sshangq@163.com

Abstract. The rapid development of digital technology has gradually expanded its application in the field of children's education, providing new perspectives for the deep integration of technology and aesthetic education. This research aims to explore the application of digital technology in museum-based aesthetic education for children, intending to leverage advanced technology to offer children a more enriching, interactive, and inspirational learning experience. Firstly, the paper delineates the current application status of digital technology in the Chinese educational landscape and analyzes the challenges faced by museum-based aesthetic education for children. Secondly, through empirical case studies, it summarizes the evolution of children's aesthetic education exhibitions from traditional multimedia installations dominated by images and sound towards more innovative applications of digital technology. This includes cutting-edge technologies such as artificial intelligence and augmented reality, creating a more immersive, interactive, and educationally meaningful learning environment for children. This approach effectively stimulates children's interest in art and culture, promoting in-depth learning. In conclusion, this paper summarizes the instructional effects of digital technology in museum-based aesthetic education for children, discussing its feasibility as a beneficial supplement to traditional aesthetic education methods. The application of digital technology not only encompasses artistic creation, technological experiences, and scientific knowledge, but also integrates the essence of Chinese culture and world civilization. This holds profound significance and guiding influence in enhancing children's understanding of concepts such as sustainable development, environmental protection, cultural transmission, and the shared destiny of humanity.

Keywords: Digital Technology · Children Aesthetic Education · Museum · Immersive Exhibition · Global Literacy

1 Research Background

1.1 Background of the Rapid Development of Digital Technology

With continuous innovation in big data, cloud computing, artificial intelligence, virtual reality and other technologies, network ecology, intelligent life and school education have undergone profound changes. We are now living in an era of information explosion where digitalization has become a trend that is profoundly changing the way we live and work.

Digitization is not just about converting information into a digital format, it also changes the way we process and use information more efficiently by allowing us to extract valuable insights from large amounts of data. With improved computing power and the accumulation of big data, artificial intelligence (AI) and machine learning will play an increasingly important role in driving digitization forward. They will help us better understand and utilize data to improve decision-making accuracy and efficiency.

In October 2022, CPC's 20th National Congress report clearly pointed out that promoting digitization in education is an essential measure for building a learning society with lifelong learning opportunities for all. In this new era background, promoting aesthetic education teaching through digital methods at primary and secondary schools becomes not only a key measure but also a goal that should be pursued to strengthen aesthetic education.

The World Digital Education Conference held in January 2024 highlighted how the new round of scientific technological revolution deepens as industrial revolution progresses further, thus making digital technology increasingly becoming a leading force driving fundamental changes in human society's thinking patterns organizational structures operation modes while providing significant opportunities for innovation reshaping development despite bringing forth new challenges.

1.2   Museums Play a Crucial Role in Public Aesthetic Education

The internationally recognized definition of a museum states that it is a non-profit permanent institution open to the public, serving society and social development purposes. Its mission is to collect, preserve, research, disseminate, and display tangible or intangible heritage for educational, research, and entertainment purposes. Similarly, China defines museums as non-profit organizations that collect, protect, and exhibit evidence of human activities and the natural environment for education, research, appreciation. These institutions are registered by the appropriate authorities according to law. The functions and institutional nature of museums have been defined and summarized accordingly. Museums are not merely spaces for displaying artworks; they also serve as lifelong learning environments. Public art education aims to provide everyone with opportunities and abilities to appreciate artistry and beauty. Art museums must fulfill their educational function by employing various strategies while breaking through inherent barriers, in order to establish a "learning ecosystem" for planning public art education.

Chinese museums can be broadly categorized into four types: history museums, art museums science, technology museums and comprehensive museums. Wu Hongliang, President of Beijing Academy Painting once remarked, "As means characteristics effectiveness information communication continue change museum public education needs adapt development Times cognitive habits transform more research results accessible resources". Professor Zheng Qinyan, Director Children's Art Education Research Center Central Academy Fine Arts also stated, "Museums possess vast collections precious cultural relics artistic resources which can not only stimulate children's".

The Recommendation on the Protection and Promotion of Museums and Collections, their Diversity, and their role in Society, drafted by the International Council of Museums and UNESCO in 2015, provides a comprehensive overview of the educational function of museums, pointing out that museums participate in formal and non-formal education and lifelong learning through educational and teaching activities.

With the development of society, the material living standard of the people has been fully guaranteed, and the spiritual and cultural needs have been further highlighted, and the public's desire to learn cultural knowledge through museums has become more and more strong. The power of museums is beyond imagination, "to the museum to punch" has become a new trend, and the number of museum visitors has become an important barometer reflecting the degree of participation in social learning. Since the 18th National Congress of the Communist Party of China, the museum research education of primary and secondary school students in China has been rich in practice and considerable development. Since February 2023, museums around the country have opened close ties and cooperation with schools and social institutions, and launched public education activities with rich themes and diverse forms. Museums have become an important part of primary and secondary education and an indispensable "second classroom" for young people, which plays an important role in cultivating and enhancing their spiritual quality and cultural self-confidence.

1.3 Disciplinary Trend Background of Increasing Proportion of Children's Aesthetic Education

On December 22, 2023, the Ministry of Education issued a Notice on the Comprehensive Implementation of Aesthetic Education in Schools, which emphasizes the need to strengthen aesthetic education in schools and promote art education and teaching reform. This reform should align with scientific and technological progress, educational trends, and the physical and mental characteristics of teenagers. In addition to art classes, other subjects can also integrate digital aesthetic education extensively. Digital aesthetic education offers vast opportunities not only within school but also beyond its boundaries. As society progresses and the economy develops, there is a growing demand for improving quality of life. Enhancing public appreciation for art through utilizing museum resources has become a top priority for museum education.

Currently, art exhibitions have entered the digital era by providing an imaginative space that offers a learning experience distinct from traditional aesthetic education methods. Many galleries and museums have creatively employed digital images, 360-degree panoramic collections, and 3D displays of artworks. By scanning codes or following voice guides, visitors can gain comprehensive understanding of works or interact with them using mobile phones. Through mobile clients, stationary works come alive in virtual spaces bridging physical-virtual connections while facilitating online-offline interactions between audiences and artists.

Primary and secondary schools should fully utilize societal resources for aesthetic education by adopting synchronous classrooms and sharing high-quality online resources among others means so that students at these levels can effectively engage in artistic exploration.

2   Progress in the Application of Digital Technology for Children's Aesthetic Education in Museum Exhibitions

In museum exhibition design, the evolution of media has experienced many stages. Originally, the direct presentation of paper media such as newspapers, periodicals and magazines made text messages no longer rely on oral communication. Then the phonograph and radio technology began to develop, the rise of broadcast media, information no longer exists in the form of a single text, but through the way of sound to touch people's hearing, bringing a new dimension to media communication. The progress of the application [5] of digital technology has made the display of pictures and images no longer limited to paper media, but through digital presentation, making the exhibits more vivid and three-dimensional. Sound technology provides a richer perceptual experience for the audience through audio Tours or exhibition narration. Video technology is widely used in exhibitions to show history, culture and other content through videos, films and other forms. The rise of virtual reality (VR) technology has brought museum displays to a more immersive stage, where visitors can enter a virtual scene through VR glasses as if they were there. Augmented reality (AR) technology superimposes virtual elements onto real scenes, adding interest and interactivity to the exhibition. The outbreak of artificial intelligence at the beginning of 2023 makes the introduction of artificial intelligence bring more intelligent possibilities for museum display design. Through AI technology, museums can achieve more personalized and intelligent tour services, making recommendations based on the interests and needs of visitors. This personalized digital experience will further enhance the attraction and engagement of museum exhibitions, break the limitations of traditional displays, and create a richer and more interactive cultural experience for visitors.

In this study, the exhibition "1 Tree ·1 World - ANOBO World Children's Science and Technology Art Tour", which was held at the China Millennium Monument Art Museum and Today Art Museum in Beijing in July 2023, was analyzed as a case study. The exhibition is not only rich in artistic creation, scientific and technological experience and scientific knowledge, but also integrates the essence of Chinese culture and world civilization, and significantly improves the project curriculum design, exhibition teaching AIDS research and development, scenario-based teaching experience creation and other aspects. It not only provides interactive guides for children, enhance children's understanding of sustainable development, environmental protection, civilization transmission, community of human destiny and other concepts, but also provide parents with educational concept guidance, while providing parent-child interaction problems for each family, to build a warm parent-child interaction experience and full of interesting immersive scene teaching experience.

The "1 Tree 1 World" exhibition is very different from the traditional curatorial exhibition, belonging to the "educational curatorial exhibition", which was first proposed by the American curatorial Committee. It takes "children" as the core element, allowing children to create large-scale installation art works together with artists at home and abroad, "learning by doing, reflecting by playing". Secondly, we get rid of the traditional single mode of designers and artists as the main body of exhibition creation, and take children's works as the design prototype, turning the exhibition site into a PBL co-creation course. Children are not only feelers and participants, but also builders.

2.1 Digital Audio Technology

In the exhibition "1 Tree 1 World", Scenocosme, an emerging French art group, interprets the invisible connection between the human body and the environment in a poetic way through the project "Mysterious Forest". Through the audience's participation and intervention in the work, the exhibition space is changed and shaped, providing a unique sensory experience for the audience.

With the five-sense experience as the core of the exhibition goal, the work visualizes children's curiosity about plants, interprets questions such as whether trees can make sounds and the sound differences of different leaves into music, weakens visual perception and strengthens hearing through the dark exhibition space, so as to achieve the "non-everyday" state of senses, and allocates the overall mechanism of children's perception. In the dark space, only the plants radiate a faint light. Viewers can explore using flashlights or cell phone light to illuminate the fluorescent flowers scattered on the branches. Each flower is fitted with optical sensors that transcribe pulses and light variants into a computer program that interprets plant language through sound. The gestures and movements of the audience can generate or overlay streams of sound, as well as modify their tones and fluctuations. Each flower has a different sound, and the sound universe evolves and diversifies according to the ever-changing intensity of light and public intervention. The accidental interaction of the audience brings unpredictability to the works, so that children can interact with the works, understand that plants have five senses like people, and think about the sensory life and expression of plants, so as to cultivate empathy and care for plants in life.

2.2 Digital Imaging Technology

Immersive Audio-Visual Interaction. The installation of "Building Dreams" takes trees as the image, and constructs a forest where present and future, children's growth and education ideals intersect through three levels of guiding, guarding and building dreams. The digital multimedia image begins with the image of the trees with history and meaning in the China Children's Center Park, and then evolves into the ecological and natural trees with well-known objects, the trees with different styles of artistic expression, and the trees with whimsical design creativity. Among them, the trees in the China Children's Center Park change synchronously with the exhibition period from summer to autumn. Nature, children, artists, educators, those unique "trees" and "people" in reality and imagination grow each other through the interactive interpretation of audio-visual multimedia, creating immersive and artistic experience, feeling the beauty of natural trees and the power of growth, and seeing the diversified and unique ways of children and trees living together from children's creative expression of trees.

Situational Drama Performance. Trees grow in the process of nature and human civilization with their silent and firm attitude, and civilization continues to inherit and develop in the form of trees. Whether mythological fantasy or historical story, tree culture always follows human beings. Learn classic stories about trees in different cultural backgrounds, appreciate and tolerate different cultures, and then re-create them in improvisational performances, and innovate on the basis of cultural inheritance; Acting allows children to experience the emotions of the characters, thereby developing empathy, creativity, communication and collaboration skills, and self-confidence.

With the theme of trees in world culture, the little theater of "Knowledge of Wood · Answer Wood · Play with Wood" leads the children to learn about 10 historical or mythical stories spanning the East and West, such as Fusao God Bird, building wood as a nest, tying peaches to offer longevity, folding willow trees to send love, Hongdong pagoda tree, poplars to praise, millennia-old pines, green mountains, Athens olives, and Christmas trees. Through props and slides, children can enter the story of the tree, participate in the improvisation and re-creation, direct and perform a light and shadow puppet play about the tree, experience the emotions of the characters, feel the close relationship between humanity and nature, understand the connotation of diversified tree culture and historical changes, and explore the root of culture, the source of the nation, and the road to development. Respect, understand and tolerate cultural differences to enhance cultural identity and national self-confidence.

2.3 XR Technology

Augmented Reality (AR) Technology. "Earth Speakr" is an art project launched by artist Olafur Eliasson in 2020 during the German presidency of the Council of the European Union. The work uses augmented reality (AR) technology to allow children to record videos through an app of the same name. The artist encourages children to pay attention to their surroundings, pay attention to real-world ecological issues by putting themselves in the shoes of everything, and speak out boldly for the Earth. The children's creative and sincere comments show that as a new force for the next generation, they are able to express their views clearly and confidently, and actively participate in the discussion of social issues.

The educational goal is to stimulate children's desire and curiosity to explore their surroundings, and to practice sustainable living in small everyday things by putting themselves in the shoes of everything. The program encourages children to take the podium, exercise their public expression skills, and deepen their responsibility and passion for protecting the environment.

In the "Earth Speakr" pavilion, several screens loop images of children from around the world participating in co-creation projects initiated by artist Eliasson. Through AR augmented reality technology, children "incarnated" into paper cups, tables and other objects, representing everything in the world to speak for the earth, causing the audience to resonate. Everyone's attitude has an impact on the world. The exhibition shows the potential power of youth as the next generation by showing the views of children from different countries and languages on the world and the future, as well as their brave voices.

Virtual Reality (VR) Technology. For the viewing experience of the audience, the traditional way is to put the exhibits in the exhibition hall, and the audience can feel the works based on knowledge or experience. However, viewing of the intuitive plane is relatively weak. With the help of modern technology such as VR, more intuitive expression can be achieved and the distance between the audience and the work can be shortened. The work "Eye Tree" is the VR work of Yang Shuai, the founder of Baby Project. It tells the growth story of an eye tree, starting from a seed and gradually maturing process, so that children can experience the virtual tree of intention.

In the face of the great change of AIGC technology today, the founder explores the path of digital art creation. The study used more than 600 paintings created over 20 years as the basis for a collaborative research project to enable digital art creation with more advanced technology. Yang Shuai's works cover all the elements expressed in VR and show the shock to the audience's psychology through elements such as black and white composition and deep dreams. The digital art space offers more freedom than traditional painting can achieve and expect new works to emerge.

2.4 AI Digital Technology

In the past, artificial intelligence technology was rarely applied in art and education scenes, but it has gradually made great breakthroughs in recent years, showing the charm and unlimited potential of modern technology, and paving the way for the combination of science and technology and art. The French writer Flaubert said: "Art and science always part at the foot of the mountain, and finally meet at the top." The fusion of art and technology in this exhibition has reached its extreme, and people are amazed and will not leave. In this exhibition, Microsoft Research Asia and ANOBO collaborated to present the "AI Nuwa Tree of the Future" and the MUZIC exhibition generated by family exclusive music, the new form of "AI co-creation" will stimulate children's greater interest in cutting-edge technology and inspire them to work together to build a better world.

NUWA Infinite Vision Generation Model. As the consumption-based attention economy has gradually shifted to a production-based creative economy, more and more people have become everyday creators, using various photo and video editing tools to innovate or recreate works of art. However, high-quality visual art creation is never an easy task, often requires professional skills and equipment, and takes a lot of time. At the same time, daily visual art creation has an increasing demand for higher resolution images or longer duration videos. NUWA is a cutting-edge exploration of the automatic generation of visual art works at the scientific level, aiming to provide visual art creators with more intelligent tools to support them to better develop their creativity.

NUWA (Neural visUal World reAtion) is a multi-modal model developed by Microsoft Research Asia. Through natural language instructions, NUWA can generate, transform and edit between text, images and videos, and can generate high-resolution images of any size or long-term videos. The creativity and vitality represented by the name "Nuwa" are fully reflected in the joint creation of the young artist and AI, presenting the future tree watered by technology and art to the audience. The AI Nuwa Tree of the Future exhibition offers children the opportunity to experience cutting-edge science and technology. In the middle of the splendid field, where trees of different shapes grow, Hug Bear calls for young artists to light up this "tree of the future" with creative magic. The participating young artists will create the "One world" in their hearts into leaves. Through the secondary creation of NUWA's artificial intelligence model, it will be expanded into an immersive projection picture, creating an immersive new media interactive space, and the leaf pattern drawn by children on paper in the form of immersive new media will be extended into a giant picture, injecting power into the "Tree of the future". Transforming children's paintings into dynamic light and shadow Spaces is intended to encourage young artists to exert their imagination and creativity, believing that they have great energy to influence the world. Enhance the influence and appeal of children's paintings, and convey that "your ideas can affect others and affect the world". By watching the extension of AI to the picture, children have an intuitive understanding of AI technology and help children develop scientific and technological literacy.

Muzic Artificial Intelligence Music Research Project. Muzic is Microsoft Research Asia's research project around AI music understanding and generation, with the aim of better helping music understanding and generation through machine learning and artificial intelligence technologies. Muzic covers a variety of topics in music understanding (including music retrieval/classification/transcription/separation/recognition) and music generation (including song writing, accompaniment and arrangement, singing synthesis, music timbre synthesis, and sound mixing). Each family that comes to visit and interact can answer a series of questions to generate their own music.

3 Inspiration of Digital Technology in Collaboration with Innovative Development of Children's Aesthetic Education

3.1 Integration of Artistic Creation, Technological Experience and Scientific Knowledge

Digital technology provides a new learning platform for children, integrating artistic creation, scientific and technological experience and scientific knowledge. Through virtual reality (VR) [3], augmented reality (AR) and other technologies, children can immerse themselves in artistic activities such as creative painting and music creation, and understand scientific knowledge more vividly with the help of technological experiences. This diversified learning style not only expands children's creative thinking, but also promotes their comprehensive understanding of different subjects.

3.2 Guide Emotional Education and Value Construction

The application of digital technology in children's aesthetic education is not only related to technology itself, but also pays more attention to emotional education and value construction. Develop children's emotional expression and understanding through stories, music, interactive experiences and other forms presented by digital media. At the same time, creative digital content can help guide children to construct positive values, cultivate their positive attitude towards life, and make aesthetic education an important way to build character.

3.3 Integrate the Essence of Chinese Culture and World Civilization

The application of digital technology enables children to experience the essence of Chinese culture and world civilization more intuitively. Through virtual visits to museums and immersive historical experiences, children are able to gain insight into traditional culture and incorporate it into their creations. This integration not only helps to inherit Chinese culture, but also expands children's cognition of the world and provides a solid foundation for their future cross-cultural communication.

Despite the continuous iteration of media communication forms, the core values of traditional media have been preserved in this process of constant change. The inheritance and continuation of media texts will continue. Looking back at the entire history of media development, the continuous progress of science and technology promotes the innovation of media forms, but the information and text conveyed by the media maintain their importance in the inheritance and continuation. This constant core has been present throughout the history of media evolution.

The application of digital technology in aesthetic education has long-term signifi- cance and guiding role in cultivating children's understanding of sustainable develop- ment, environmental protection, civilization transmission, community of human destiny and other concepts. The diversity of information presented by digital media encourages children to think more deeply about social and environmental issues, thereby develop- ing their sense of social responsibility. Through digital technology, children are able to understand these abstract and important concepts more vividly, laying the foundation for the future construction of society and the inheritance of civilization.

Under the impact of the digital age, museum public education needs to keep pace with The Times and better transform research results into amiable and perceptible public education resources. In addition, museums should pay attention to the needs of children of different ages and create distinctive and personalized museum courses to enrich their aesthetic experience. Educators also need to improve their professional quality, in-depth understanding and development of various aesthetic education methods, continuous accumulation of educational experience, improve the level of public service.

References

1. Hongyan, L.: From the perspective of art education to explore the school aesthetic education and interdisciplinary integration path. Heilongjiang J. (006) (2023)
2. Ting, X.: An example of the application of information technology in art extracurricular activities. Educ. Res. Rev. (Elementary Educ. Teach.) (07), 60–63 (2023)
3. Xiwen, L., Jianfu, Z., Junhua, Z.: Research on innovative development of children's aesthetic education integrated with digital technology. Packag. Eng. **44**(10), 444–450 (2023)
4. Jingjing, P.: Thinking on the educational dimension of art museums. Educ. Vis. (06), 62– 65(2022)
5. Ziyu, A.: Transformation and development of public education in art museum of new media era. Tianjin Academy of Fine Arts (2021)
6. Hao, Z.: Research on the development policy of internet sharing of basic educational resources. Yunnan Normal University (2021)

User Experience Research in China's Tourism Industry Based on Knowledge Map

Wenfeng Xia[1], Genqiao Wang[1], and Zhen Liu[2(✉)]

[1] Guangzhou City University of Technology, Guangzhou 510800, People's Republic of China
xiawf@gcu.edu.cn
[2] South China University of Technology, Guangzhou 510006, People's Republic of China
liuzjames@scut.edu.cn

Abstract. With the further development of China's economy, the demand for tourism has increased dramatically, and the importance of User Experience (UX) as a key factor in the tourism industry has become increasingly important. Therefore, Understanding the current situation of UX in China's tourism industry, finding the key factors affecting UX, identifying and solving the main problems, and researching the development history are of great significance in guiding the future development of UX research. However, no scholars have yet to conduct a comprehensive combing of core Chinese journals for this field and analyse the research through knowledge map. Hence, this paper adopts scientific bibliometric method to select all the journal articles collected by China National Knowledge Infrastructure (CNKI) and uses CiteSpace and SATI as the research tools to carry out a comprehensive analysis. The results show that: 1) China's research on the themes of "User Experience" and "Tourism" started in 2011, and the research disciplines are mainly distributed in the fields of Tourism, Computer Software and Computer Application, Trade and Economy; 2) Based on the analysis of the co-occurrence diagram of the knowledge map, the research mainly focuses on "User Experience", "Service Design" and "Tourism". And 3) From the knowledge map of authors and major research institutions, it can be seen that the research on User Experience in China's tourism industry is more concentrated, with a high degree of cooperation, but currently there is still no relatively fixed large-scale research team.

Keywords: User Experience · Tourism · Knowledge Map · China

1 Introduction

Joseph Pine, the father of the experience economy, pointed out in his book "The Experience Economy" that the experience economy is the fourth economic growth point following agriculture, industry, and services. [1] Nowadays, according to a report from the Chinese government's website, by the end of 2022, the total output value of China's agriculture, industry, and service sectors exceeded 120 trillion yuan. This indicates that with the further development of China's economy, considerable objective economic growth has already been achieved in the three sectors of agriculture, industry, and services. Therefore, the development of the experience economy will have a profound impact on

A. Marcus et al. (Eds.): HCII 2024, LNCS 14715, pp. 340–356, 2024.
https://doi.org/10.1007/978-3-031-61359-3_24

China's future economic development. Tian Yun and Wang Zhen proposed that in the era of the experience economy, while users' demands focus on product quality, there is an increasing emphasis on psychological and experiential feelings [1]. As a result, User Experience, which is at the core of the experience economy, is playing an increasingly important role in China's national consumption, becoming a hot topic of research and attention in many industries.

User Experience (UX) is a purely subjective feeling established during the process of using a product. However, for a well-defined user group, the commonalities of User Experience can be recognized through well-designed experiments [2]. The tourism industry primarily aims to satisfy customers' inner needs, allowing tourists to feel happy during their travels, which requires focusing on tourists' inner experiences and providing experiential activities and services [3]. Therefore, User Experience is directly related to the experience of tourism and affects various enterprises as well as related economic income. Studying the development history of User Experience in China's tourism industry and grasping the research trends in this academic field will benefit subsequent scholars in conducting continuous, innovative, and economically valuable research in this area.

2 Material and Method

2.1 Data Source

This paper uses the China National Knowledge Infrastructure (CNKI) academic journal database as the data source, searching for literature with "Subject = User Experience and Tourism" covering all years. To ensure the scientific nature of the literature sample research results, this paper selects all search results from the academic journal database as the research subject, with the search date being November 10, 2023. Using CiteSpace for data preprocessing, a total of 295 valid documents were obtained as research samples.

2.2 Research Method

The application of information visualization technology is one of the important ways to study literature, which can quickly grasp the current development and future trends of the field. CiteSpace is frequently used among literature rsearch tools, capable of drawing various maps, with good visualization effects, suitable for multiple database formats, and can measure specific field literature to explore the key paths of discipline evolution and detect the frontier of discipline development [4]. Therefore, this paper uses CiteSpace software to analyze annual publication volume, authors and institutions, keyword co-occurrence, clustering, and burst terms, drawing a research knowledge map of User Experience in the tourism industry. Additionally, to prevent the influence of a single software, SATI software is also used for assistance. From the perspective of User Experience, this paper discusses the hotspots and development trends of research experience in the tourism industry, providing a clearer direction for scholars in this field.

3 Research Results and Analysis

3.1 Bibliometric Analysis

Analysis of Literature Quantity Distribution Based on Timeline. The number of publications and the timing of publications are one of the standards for judging the research heat of a field. The annual volume of publications related to User Experience and tourism reflects the theoretical level and development speed of User Experience research in China's tourism industry. This paper analyzes the annual distribution of 295 papers obtained by searching CNKI journals with the subject words "User Experience" and "Tourism" and finds that research on "User Experience" and "Tourism" in China began in 2011 (see Fig. 1). Although the number of publications increased each year from 2011 to 2014, the annual publication volume did not exceed 10 papers. Starting from 2014, the publication volume began to show a significant increasing trend, with a substantial increase in the number of publications in 2014–2015 and 2017–2018, reaching more than 20 papers, and peaking in 2018 with 42 papers. However, with the outbreak of the COVID-19 pandemic in 2020, there was a certain decline in research in this field from 2020 to 2022. After the opening of China's epidemic prevention and control policies in 2023, research in this field showed a surge trend, with the current publication volume reaching 38 papers. Overall, the research related to "User Experience" and "Tourism" shows an overall upward trend in academia. Based on the current trend of literature quantity, it is predicted that the publication volume in this field will continue to increase in the future. The fundamental reason lies in the continuous development stage of China's economy. After the pandemic, with the recovery and development of the domestic economy and tourism industry, consumer tourism will also become an important source of economic growth in many places.

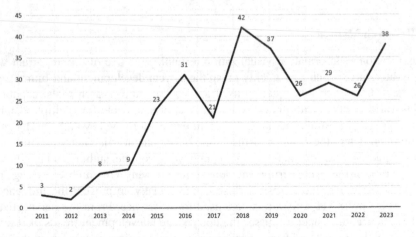

Fig. 1. Yearly comparison of the number of articles issued, 2011–2023.

Preliminary Overview of Literature Discipline Distribution. Analyzing the distribution of literature fields can reveal the research distribution of the study topic across various disciplines. Since CNKI can only perform statistical analysis on unedited literature data, this paper takes a preliminary look at the 303 documents retrieved and, through visualization, finds that the research discipline distribution mainly focused on the theme "User Experience" and "Tourism" is primarily concentrated in the field of economics, involving tourism, computer software, trade, information, post, and other areas (see Fig. 2). The main discipline distribution is shown in Fig. 2. It can be observed that the highest proportion of publications is in tourism literature, accounting for 37.24%, followed by computer software and computer applications at 15.02%, and trade economics at 11.73%, with just these three accounting for over 60% of the total. Ranked fourth is information economics and postal economics at 6.38%. Ranked fifth is general industrial technology and equipment at 5.56%.

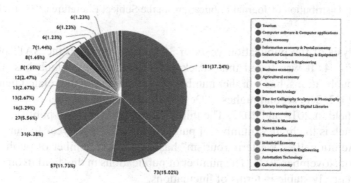

Fig. 2. Distribution of Literature in Subject Areas (303 articles).

Statistical Analysis of Literature Journals. Analyzing the distribution of the number of journals in which the literature is published can provide an understanding of the attention given by core journals in the field to the theme of User Experience and its association with brands. Through CNKI's visualization analysis, it can be seen that from 2011 to 2023, the top 10 journals publishing literature on "User Experience" with a focus on "Tourism" are, in order: "Packaging Engineering" "Design" "Tourism Overview" "Industrial Design" "Popular Literature and Art" "Modern Business" "Art and Design (Theory)" "Shopping Mall Modernization" "Western Leather" and "Hunan Packaging" as shown in Fig. 3. The journal with the most publications in this field is "Packaging Engineering" with a total of 22 articles, accounting for 24.44%, indicating that "Packaging Engineering" has the most focused research on this theme in the field. Following with a high number of publications are "Design" with 17 articles, accounting for 18.89%, and "Tourism Overview" with 10 articles, accounting for 11.11%. The combined proportion of just these top three exceeds 50%, with "Industrial Design" ranking fourth with 9 articles, accounting for 10%. Ranked fifth is "Popular Literature and Art" with 8 articles, accounting for 8.89%. Overall, the literature distribution for the research theme of "User Experience" that includes "Tourism" is mainly in the fields of packaging, design, tourism, industry, and literature and art.

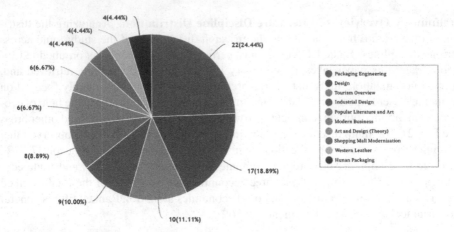

Fig. 3. Distribution of Journal Publications in the Subject Literature (303 articles).

An analysis of the publication years of 303 articles through the SATI platform is shown in Fig. 4. It was found that "Packaging Engineering" which has the highest number of publications, had a higher number of publications in the related field in 2013, 2019, and 2022. The second highest, "Design" had a higher number of publications in the related field in 2018 and 2022. The third, "Tourism Overview" published 6 articles in 2016, which is the highest number of publications in a single year for any journal in this field. Additionally, "Western Tourism" has the highest number of publications for the year as of November 2023. The number of publications in this field in other journals has been relatively stable in terms of fluctuations.

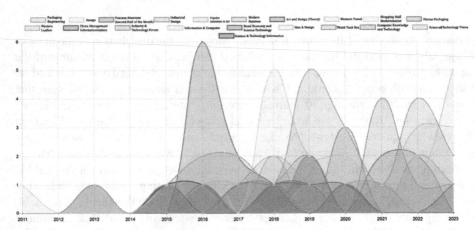

Fig. 4. Trends in the number of publications.

3.2 Analysis of Core Authors and Institutions

Visualization Map of Core Authors. This paper conducts an author analysis on 295 sample literature pieces using CiteSpace software, identifying the top twelve authors in terms of publication volume related to the theme of User Experience and tourism from 2011 to November 2023. As shown in the Fig. 5, Rui Zhou has published 6 academic articles, Yanzhang Xu has published 3 academic articles, Yali Cao and Zi Ye, Rui Sun, Yanmei Zhao, Yue Yuan, Yue Shu, Yuchan Du, Fanghan Jiang, Nan Huang, Yankai Liu, and Yang Geng have each published two articles.

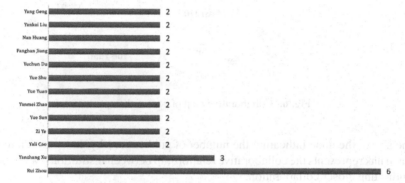

Fig. 5. Core author publication map.

Using CiteSpace visualization analysis software, the author collaboration knowledge map in this field from 2011 to 2023 was obtained (see Fig. 6). There are a total of 273 nodes and 133 links, with each node representing an author and each link representing the collaboration relationship and the year of collaboration between authors. The thicker the link, the closer the collaboration [5].

From the analysis of the collaborative map of core authors (see Fig. 6), it can be seen that most of the research in this field is carried out in the form of teams, with collaborations mostly involving three or more people. Among them, Rui Zhou is the main researcher in this field, participating in the most collaborative teams and having the highest number of published collaborative articles, totaling six. At the same time, the collaboration relationships shown in the Fig. 6 indicate that most research teams do not collaborate frequently, with the number of collaborations around once. Only Rui Zhou and Fanghan Jiang have participated in collaborations two or more times. Overall, the current research in this field is mainly conducted by small, dispersed teams, lacking in close collaboration, and large-scale academic research teams have not yet formed.

Visualization Map of Research Institutions. Using CiteSpace software, a co-occurrence analysis of collaborative institutions was conducted on 295 journal articles on the theme of User Experience and Tourism from 2011 to November 2023(see Fig. 7). The resulting visualization map of User Experience and tourism, as shown in Fig. 7, comprises 222 nodes and 37 links. Each node represents a corresponding institution,

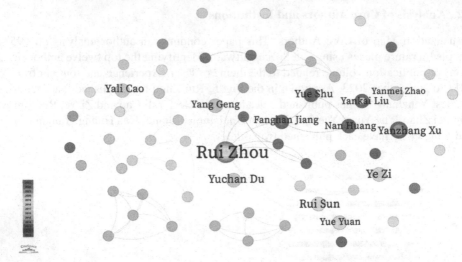

Fig. 6. Collaborative map of core authors.

with the size of the node indicating the number of publications by that research institution. Each link represents the collaborative relationship between institutions, with thicker links indicating closer collaboration.

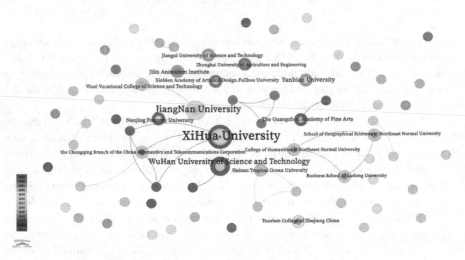

Fig. 7. Collaborative map of research institutions.

The map reveals that there is a close cooperation among research institutions, with few scattered distributions. This study has ranked the institutions that have published two or more articles by the number of publications as shown in Table 1. From this, it can be seen that the research in this field is mainly divided into three echelons. The first echelon is Xihua University, with a publication count of seven articles. The second echelon includes

Jiangnan University and the School of Art and Design at Wuhan University of Science and Technology, each with four publications. The third echelon consists of College of Humanities at Northeast Normal University, the School of Geographical Sciences at Northeast Normal University, the Chongqing Branch of the China Aeronautics and Telecommunications Corporation, Zhongkai University of Agriculture and Engineering, Nanjing Forestry University, Jilin Animation Institute, The Guangzhou Academy of Fine Arts, Yanbian University, Wuxi Vocational College of Science and Technology, Jiangxi University of Science and Technology, Tourism College of Zhejiang China, Hainan Tropical Ocean University, XiaMen Academy of Arts and Design. FuZhou University and Business School of Ludong University, each with two publications.

Table 1. Core research institutions.

Serial Number	Frequency	Institution
1	7	XiHua University
2	4	WuHan University of Science and Technology
3	4	JiangNan University
4	2	College of Humanities at Northeast Normal University
5	2	The School of Geographical Sciences at Northeast Normal University
6	2	The Chongqing Branch of the China Aeronautics and Telecommunications Corporation
7	2	Zhongkai University of Agriculture and Engineering
8	2	Nanjing Forestry University
9	2	Jilin Animation Institute
10	2	The Guangzhou Academy of Fine Arts
11	2	Yanbian University
12	2	Wuxi Vocational College of Science and Technology
13	2	Jiangxi University of Science and Technology
14	2	Tourism College of Zhejiang China
15	2	Hainan Tropical Ocean University
16	2	XiaMen Academy of Arts and Design,FuZhou University
17	2	Business School of Ludong University

3.3 Bibliometric Analysis

Keyword Co-occurrence Map Analysis. A keyword co-occurrence map analysis was conducted using CiteSpace, as shown in Fig. 8. It was found that the keyword co-occurrence map for research related to "User Experience" and "Tourism" consists of 276 nodes and

453 links, with an overall network density of 0.0115. Keywords represent the core topics and research areas of the literature, and high-frequency keywords in the literature can be considered as research hotspots in the field. [5] The map reveals that terms such as User Experience, Service Design, Tourism, Interaction Design, Smart Tourism, Cultural and Tourism Integration, Rural Tourism, and Interface Design appear frequently in research, indicating their high relevance. Additionally, keywords like tourist attractions, Large Data, Development Strategies, Museums, Tourism Websites, Product Design, and Design Strategies also have significant research presence. The research themes in this field also include topics closely related to the recent developments in Chinese tourism, such as Customized Services, Digital Culture and Tourism, 3D Modeling, Cultural and Creative Products, and the Toilet Revolution.

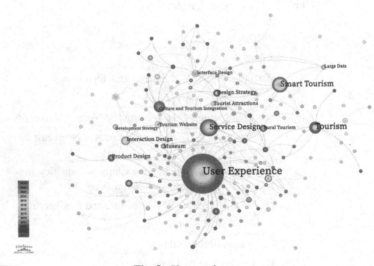

Fig. 8. Keyword co-occurrence map.

The centrality of keywords is primarily used to measure the importance of nodes within the keyword co-occurrence network map. Additionally, if the centrality coefficient of a keyword is greater than 0.1, it indicates that the keyword has high centrality and plays a significant influential role in the keyword co-occurrence network map. [6] According to Table 2, the keywords with a centrality greater than 0.1 are "User Experience" "Service design" "Tourism" and "Smart Tourism."

By combining the frequency of keyword emergence and centrality statistics in Table 2, it is evident that "User Experience" appears most frequently among the keywords and has the highest centrality, indicating the closest connection with other keywords and being a research focus in the field. Following that, "Service Design" and "Tourism" also have high frequencies and centralities, suggesting that much of the research is exploring service design optimization in tourism. In addition, "Smart Tourism" also has a relatively high frequency and centrality compared to other keywords, indicating that smart tourism has also become a key focus area in the research of user experience in China's tourism industry.

Table 2. High-frequency Keywords and Statistics of Word Frequency and Centrality.

Serial Number	Time of appearance	Keyword	Frequency	Centrality
1	2011	User Experience	117	0.90
2	2016	Service Design	27	0.11
3	2015	Tourism	18	0.21
4	2011	Interaction Design	18	0.06
5	2014	Smart Tourism	16	0.16
6	2018	Culture and Tourism Integration	13	0.10
7	2011	Rural Tourism	8	0.05
8	2013	Interface Design	6	0.10
9	2014	Tourist Attractions	6	0.05
10	2017	Large Data	5	0.05
11	2011	Development Strategy	5	0.03
12	2013	Museum	5	0.00
13	2011	Tourism Website	4	0.02
14	2017	Product Design	4	0.01
15	2018	Design Strategy	4	0.01

Keyword Clustering Map Analysis. CiteSpace offers four methods for extracting cluster labels. Upon comprehensive consideration, the labels extracted using the LLR (Log-likelihood Ratio) algorithm are more in line with the actual situation and exhibit less repetition. Therefore, this paper employs the LLR algorithm to perform cluster analysis on the sample literature, selecting the top 10 clusters, resulting in a keyword map as shown in Fig. 8. The Modularity cluster module value (Q value) is 0.6588, which is generally considered significant with a Q > 0.3 indicating a pronounced structural significance. The Silhouette average silhouette value (S value) is 0.9322, which is generally considered convincing with an S > 0.7 indicating that the clustering is persuasive [6].

From Fig. 9, it is evident that the research hotspots in China's tourism industry User Experience from 2011 to 2023 focus on the top 10 issues related to User Experience, Smart Tourism, Tourism, Interaction Design, Cultural and Tourism Integration, Service Design, Interface Design, Rural Tourism, Applet, and Augmented Reality.

Keyword Burst Analysis. Burst words are primarily based on keywords and represent the sudden emergence of specialized terms in the literature published over a certain time span, reflecting the research hotspots within that period. They are mainly characterized by two aspects: the distribution of the burst words over the years and the intensity of the burst. [7] In this paper, for the analysis of burst words in the research sample literature, the Minimum Duration is set to 1 year, with r = 0.7, and a visual analysis is conducted to produce the keyword burst map as shown in the Fig. 10.

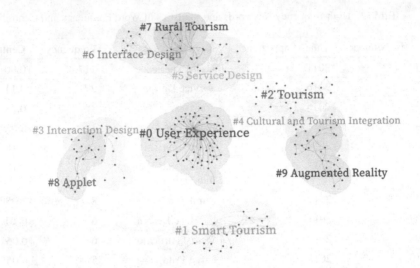

Fig. 9. Keyword Clustering Map.

The analysis reveals that from 2011 to 2023, there were 14 burst words in the field of user experience research in China's tourism industry. The burst word with the highest intensity in 2021 was "cultural-tourism integration" reaching 3.4. Following that, the burst word "Interface Design" appeared in 2013 with an intensity of 2.73. The third-ranked burst word "Interface Design" appeared in 2011 with an intensity of 2.56.

Looking at the overall appearance of burst words by year, from 2011 to 2017, "Interface Design" "Smart Tourism" "Tourism Industry" "Online Tourism" and "3D Modeling" were the main burst words in the research of User Experience in China's tourism industry. In particular, the study of User Experience in interface design in 2013 was very prominent, with the highest burst intensity. During this period, the internet economy developed rapidly, along with fast domestic economic growth and high-speed development of the tourism industry. With the development of the internet economy and the tourism industry, coupled with the increasing popularity of mobile phones, various tourism apps emerged, and the demand for app interfaces that enhance User Experience quickly increased. Starting in 2018, research on interaction design became a new research hotspot. According to the "2018 China Tourism Industry Development Report" the penetration rate of mobile tourism continued to increase, with mobile devices becoming an important channel for tourism consumption. On one hand, with the increased popularity of smartphones and the continuous boom of the internet economy, the public's demand for mobile interaction products kept rising. On the other hand, the development of mobile interaction products is having a profound impact on various domestic industries, and its role in promoting socio-economic development is becoming increasingly evident. In 2019, driven by economic development, the increasing demand for enhanced tourism experiences led to service design and the "Toilet Revolution" becoming research hotspots, continuing into 2020. In the same year, Guangdong Province and user research became the research hotspots of that year. From 2021 to 2022, "Cultural and Tourism Integration" "Applet" and "Product Design" successively became hotspots in the research of User Experience in China's tourism industry and continue to this day. At the same time, between 2021 and 2022, China faced the COVID-19 pandemic, which posed a great challenge to the tourism industry. With the continuous development of the internet economy, the online tourism and interactive service sectors may welcome more development opportunities.

Top 14 Keywords with the Strongest Citation Bursts

Keywords	Year	Strength	Begin	End	2011 - 2023
Interface Design	2013	2.73	2013	2016	
Smart Tourism	2014	1.8	2014	2018	
Tourism Industry	2015	1.36	2015	2017	
Online Tourism	2015	1.31	2015	2018	
3D modeling	2015	1.23	2015	2015	
Festival Tourism	2016	1.19	2016	2016	
Interaction Design	2011	2.56	2018	2019	
Service Design	2016	1.96	2019	2020	
Toilet Revolutionary	2019	1.45	2019	2020	
User Study	2020	1.21	2020	2020	
Guangdong Province	2020	1.21	2020	2020	
Cultural and Tourism Integration	2018	3.4	2021	2023	
Applet	2022	1.43	2022	2023	
Product Design	2017	1.21	2022	2023	

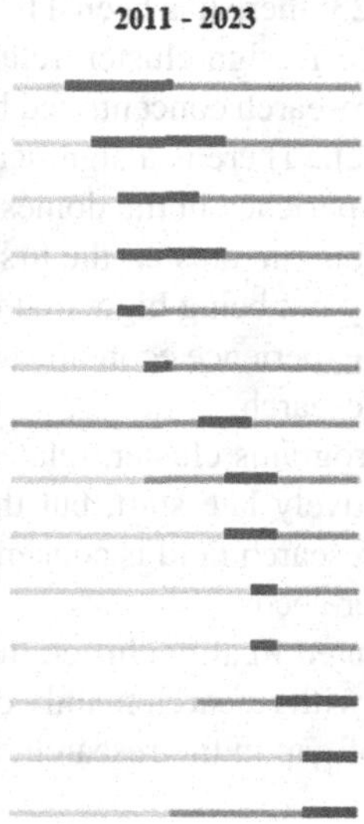

Fig. 10. Keyword Emergence Map.

Keyword Clustering Timeline Analysis. Using the CiteSpace visualization analysis software, a timeline map of User Experience research in China's tourism industry is generated based on cluster analysis, as shown in Fig. 11. There are a total of 10 clusters on the map, with each cluster label being a keyword from the co-occurrence network. The keywords are arranged according to the year of their appearance within their respective clusters, displaying the development of keywords in each cluster.

In the User Experience cluster, research related to User Experience and Tourism first appeared in 2011 and has since developed rapidly, evolving from virtual reality, tourism products, and gamification to multi-dimensional development in tourism design.

In the Smart Tourism cluster, research began in 2014, mainly focusing on big data, while also extending to multiple dimensions such as innovation development, transportation, and urban tourism.

In the Tourism cluster, the first related literature study originated in 2015, with the cluster research focusing on keywords such as tourism, cultural creativity, and industry development.

In the Interaction Design cluster, related literature was published as early as 2011, with the main volume of publications concentrated between 2018–2020, focusing on keywords such as tourism websites and development strategies.

In the Cultural-tourism Integration cluster, the earliest research focused on museums and experience design, with the first related study published in 2011. Subsequent research mainly focused on smart scenic spots, the metaverse, and other smart fields, showing a continuous trend of integration with the internet economy.

In the Service Design cluster, related research has been published since 2015, and subsequent studies have shown a development direction from tourism commodities and the tourism industry to User Experience and the overall tourism experience. In the recent years of 2022–2023, there has been a trend of gradual integration with local cultures.

In the Interface Design cluster, related research was first published in 2011, with the main body of research concentrated between 2015–2018. After 2018, there has been less related research. There is a significant gap in the field of interface design research related to User Experience in the domestic tourism industry.

In the Rural Tourism cluster, the first literature was published in 2011, with overall publication density not being high, mainly concentrated in 2014 and 2018, focusing on keywords such as experience economy and tourism attractions. There is a certain degree of gap in related research.

In the Mini-programs cluster, related research literature was initially published in 2015, with a relatively late start, but the research heat significantly increased during 2022–2023. The research field is concentrated on cultural and creative products, design strategies, and user needs.

In the Augmented Reality cluster, domestic scholars began to focus on related field research in 2015, with research mainly concentrated in 2018 and 2022. Overall, there is a certain degree of gap in the research, and there may be a trend of increased research in the future.

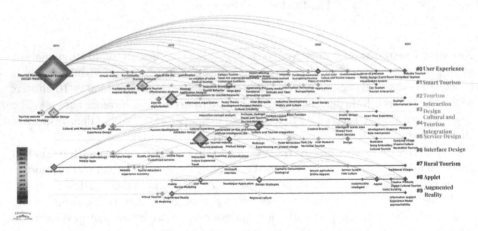

Fig. 11. Keyword timeline map.

4 Discussion

4.1 Research on User Experience in China's Tourism Industry from the Perspective of APP Experience

Through a comprehensive analysis of the literature and selection of documents related to the keyword "APP" a total of 69 papers were obtained. These mainly include aspects such as APP design, APP User Experience research, and APP operations, with content primarily involving APP interface design and APP interaction experience. The content mainly involves studies on User Experience in tourism APP user interface design [8], APP design research based on User Experience [9], tourism APP analysis and interaction design [10], interaction design of tourism APPs under the UGC model [11], and User Experience design research for Internet + tourism APPs [12]. Zeliu Tong suggests that due to the popularity and portability of smartphones, online tourism APPs bring new opportunities and challenges to the development of online tourism providers. Consumer demand determines the basic scope of User Experience, as people are no longer purchasing products or services, but rather the expectation of a certain experience [2]. Yuexue Kong, Yang hang, Yanan Wang, Yunpei Lu, and Hejiang Shen propose that with the rapid growth of mobile phone users, users are paying more attention to applications and experiences that provide online services, and tourism APPs are becoming an important business platform for various tourism providers to meet user needs [13].

4.2 Research on User Experience in China's Tourism Industry from the Perspective of Service Experience

Through a comprehensive analysis of the literature and selection of documents related to the keyword "Service" a total of 46 papers were obtained. The content mainly involves key areas such as smart tourism service systems, service design, and smart and digital services. The main content involves research on ecological tourism service system design [14], research on service innovation performance in cultural-tourism integration [15], tourism service drone design [16], ancient village tourism service design [17], special tourism service system design [18], and system development research for tourism services [19]. Yanmei Zhao mentions that service design focuses on User Experience and service quality, which is essentially user-centered, creating products and services that are functional, easy to use, accessible, and can generate a good experience. [20] Miao Wang, Dongming Ma, and Hao Qian believe that service design in the tourism industry, centered on User Experience, should include multiple perspectives. They propose a user-centered experiential service design for tourism, combining geographical and historical elements with user behavior, emotions, pain points, and opportunities to analyze more intuitively and objectively understand users. [21]

4.3 Research on User Experience in China's Tourism Industry from the Perspective of Product Experience

Through a comprehensive analysis of the literature and selection of documents related to the keyword "product" a total of 29 papers were obtained. These mainly cover tourism product design, product innovation, and product experience, including research on rural tourism cultural and creative product design [22], design research on red cultural and creative products [23], product packaging experience design strategies [24], interface interaction design of online tourism products [25], museum product design strategies [26], innovation strategies for tourism cultural and creative products [27], research on innovation trends in aviation tourism products [28], and research on redesigning cultural tourism products [29]. Peng Wang suggests that User Experience has special significance for tourism management and also mentions that designers of tourism products should empathize with consumers' psychology at the beginning of product design and development, considering what kind of products can move consumers and the market, which all require the integration of User Experience design. Yuqi Liang proposes that the frequently appearing scenario marketing in recent years is about letting users fully experience products and find resonance with the brand's core concept and their own level [30].

5   Conclusion

This paper uses CiteSpace visualization analysis software to analyze all the literature journals on China National Knowledge Infrastructure (CNKI) with the themes of "User Experience" and "Brand" up to the cutoff date of November 10, 2023, and draws the following conclusions:

1. Looking at the number of publications and the timeline, the field of User Experience research in China's tourism industry began to emerge in 2011 with three related publications and has since gradually developed. In terms of the growth rate of the number of publications, the field entered a rapid growth phase in 2014, with the most significant increase occurring in 2018, reaching 21 publications. Afterward, the number of publications began to stabilize. However, in the past two years, there has been an increasing trend and a larger growth rate in publications. Overall, research with the themes of "User Experience" and "Tourism" shows a clear upward trend, and the number of studies in this field is expected to continue to grow in the future.
2. From the perspective of academic fields and publication journals, journals with the themes of User Experience and tourism involve multiple disciplines such as Tourism, Computer Software, Trade Economics, Information Economy and Postal Economy, Industrial Technology, etc. However, there is a clear concentration in disciplines, with the top three—Tourism, Computer Software and Applications, and Trade Economics—accounting for more than 60% of the total. The published journals are concentrated in fields such as packaging, design, and tourism, with the top three being "Packaging Engineering" at 24.44%, "Design" at 18.89%, and "Tourism Overview" at 11.11%. In summary, this indicates that the fields of packaging and design have conducted more in-depth research on this theme.
3. Looking at the distribution of core authors and institutions, most researchers in this theme conduct collaborative research, often in teams of around three people, with fewer researchers conducting independent studies. In terms of research institutions, universities are the main research bodies, supplemented by social enterprises. There is a dense network of cooperation between various universities and enterprises,

with frequent cross-institutional collaborations, showing a partially clustered trend in scientific research.

In terms of research hotspots, research on User Experience in China's tourism industry mainly focuses on themes based on the APP experience perspective, service experience perspective, and product experience perspective. According to the keyword burst analysis, themes such as User Experience in China's tourism industry based on interface design, smart tourism, online tourism, etc., are continuously emerging and developing and may become the main focus and development trend of research in this field in the future.

References

1. Yun, T., Zhen, W.: Research on the application of interaction design of tourism products under experience economy. Design **2019**(32), 123–125 (2019)
2. Zeliu, T.: Analysis of tourism APP based on user experience. Tourism Manage. Res. **2017**(05), 45–46 (2017)
3. Kongxin, L., Baosong, W.: Implications of experience economy development for China's tourism development. Taxation **2017**(03), 94 (2017)
4. Na, X., Lanling, H.: Visualization and analysis of tourism service design research based on CiteSpace. Packag. Eng. **43**(24), 204–214+196 (2022)
5. Xinyuan, L., Heng, Z., Xinyue, W., Zejia, Q.: Analysis of hotspots and frontiers of domestic enterprise knowledge transfer research based on scientometrics. Intell. Sci. **37**(03), 169–176 (2019)
6. Dan, W., Xiaoxi, X., Chenhui, J.: Visualization analysis of research hotspots and evolution of China's economic development. Sci. Ind. **22**(05), 15–22 (2022)
7. Shaohui, C., Yan, W.: Scientific knowledge map analysis of Chinese social thought research - a comprehensive application based on Citespace and Vosviewer. J. Shanghai Jiao Tong Univ. (Philosophy and Social Science Edition) 26(06), 22–30 (2018)
8. Weihua, Y.: Analysis of tourism APP interface design based on user experience. Humanit. Sci. Technol. **2022**(65), 95 (2022)
9. Sun, Y., Lv, X.: Travel APP design based on user experience - Tou + Travel APP as an example. Sci. Technol. Innov. **2021**(03), 94–95 (2021)
10. Jing, Y.: Discussion on the analysis and interaction design points of tourism app. Sci. Technol. Perspect. **2021**(30), 68–70 (2021)
11. Qian, Y., Yongxiang, L.: Exploration of interaction design of tourism APP under UGC mode. Design **2015**(13), 155–157 (2015)
12. Xiaoyin, W.: Research on user experience design of tourism APP based on "Internet +." Sci. Technol. Inf. **2016**(31), 1–3 (2016)
13. Yuexue, K., Yang, Z., Yannan, W., Yunpei, L., Hejiang, S.: Functional evaluation of comprehensive tourism APP based on user experience. **45**(01), 87–92 (2021)
14. Xiaolei, D., Dai, L., Yaxu, L.: Design of rural tourism ecological service system under the background of smart tourism. Packag. Eng. **39**(04), 199–202 (2018)
15. Yanzhang, X.: Innovative performance strategy of urban culture and tourism integration service under the view of meta-cosmos. City Watch 2023(02), 136–145+169 (2023)
16. Qian, X., Qian, Z., Jinsan, H., Crystal, X., Wenjin, W., Chen, H.: Design of tourism service drone based on user experience optimization. Packag. Eng. **41**(10), 83–89 (2020)
17. Ruibo, S., Xiaotong, S.: Laiwu "one line five villages" ancient village tourism service design based on user experience. Art and Design(Theory) (04), 108–112 (2019)

18. Fenghu, C., Lingling, L.: Design of Chengyang Bazhai specialized tourism service system based on user experience. Hunan Packaging 2021(05), 10–14+23 (2021)

19. Minghui, Z., Keyun, L., Hao, X.: Development and realization of Guangxi tourism service system based on JAVA technology. Shandong Ind. Technol. **2019**(09), 160–162 (2019)

20. Yanmei, Z.: Research on cultural experience and service design of China Cao Yun Museum. Design **2018**(24), 99–101 (2018)

21. Miao, W., Dongming, M., Hao, Q.: Research on the design of "Tongdao" personalized tourism APP based on service design. Packag. Eng. **40**(16), 232–238 (2019)

22. Jie W.: Research on rural tourism cultural and creative product design in modern context. Packaging Engineering 2023, 44(14), 419–428 (2023)

23. Xujia, K.: Strategy research on the design of Hunan red cultural and creative products under the background of cultural and tourism integration. Vis. Design **03**(16), 57–59 (2023)

24. Nan, H., Yue, S.: Research on the design strategy of red tourism product packaging experience. Packag. Design **43**(06), 65–67 (2023)

25. Wei, W., Peng, H., Linhao, H., Yiran, L.: Interactive interface design of online tourism products under SOLOMO mode. Creative Design Source **2018**(03), 60–65 (2018)

26. Yishu, F., Jiang, C.: Research on product design of movie museum with psychological empathy. Packag. Eng. **44**(20), 282–289 (2023)

27. Belt, L., Yayan, C., Sanyin, Z., Dazhen, W., Lin, S.: Research on innovation design of Shaoguan tourism cultural creative products. Innov. Entrepreneurship Theory Res. Pract. **3**(13), 184–186 (2020)

28. Lan, L.: Innovation trend of air. Air Transp. Bus. **2018**(03), 46–49 (2018)

29. Ling, L.: Innovation trend of air travel products under big data. Air Transp. Bus. **2018**(03), 46–49 (2018)

30. Yanmei, Z.: Research on the redesign of Huaian cultural tourism products under the concept of service design. Popular Lit Art **2018**(12), 75–77 (2018)

31. Peng, W.: Research on user experience in tourism product design and development. Technol. Entrepreneur **2014**(01), 21 (2014)

Author Index

A. Marcus et al. (Eds.): HCII 2024, LNCS 14715, pp. 357–358, 2024.
https://doi.org/10.1007/978-3-031-61359-3

Printed in the United States
by Baker & Taylor Publisher Services